# *HOW TO CITE*

# *LEGAL AUTHORITIES*

# HOW TO CITE
# LEGAL AUTHORITIES

*Derek French, BSc*

BLACKSTONE
PRESS LIMITED

First published in Great Britain 1996 by Blackstone Press Limited,
9–15 Aldine Street, London W12 8AW. Telephone 0181-740 2277

© Derek French, 1996

ISBN: 185431 317 0

British Library Cataloguing in Publication Data
A CIP catalogue record for this book is available from the British
Library.

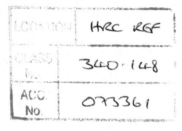

Typeset by Montage Studios Limited, Tonbridge, Kent
Printed by Livesey Ltd, Shrewsbury, Shropshire

# CONTENTS

# *PREFACE*

The purpose of this book is to help anyone who has to cite a legal authority to do so in accordance with conventions which are familiar to lawyers in the United Kingdom. These conventions are also used throughout the British Commonwealth and in the Republic of Ireland. The book is intended for all who cite legal authorities, whether as students, practitioners or academics, and also for editors and proof-readers.

The book began as a list of standard abbreviations for law reports, which I compiled for use in editing and writing books. To this list I have added a description of the rules of legal citation, not only in relation to cases, but also for statutes, Parliamentary materials, delegated legislation, and books and articles. The book recommends a particular style of presentation of citations which I have found effective, but also describes alternatives.

I thank Geoffry Allen, Debbie Butler, Heather Saward and Jennifer Strachan for reading the book before publication and giving valuable help, and I thank Moira Greenhalgh for the index.

*Derek French*
*16 October 1996*

# 1 PRINCIPLES OF LEGAL CITATION

## 1.1 PURPOSE OF CITATION

Lawyers establish what the law is on any particular subject by applying relevant principles from the acknowledged sources of law, which are legislation, decided cases, and the writings of other lawyers. They may also refer to non-legal materials to support or illustrate aspects of their arguments.

A lawyer who makes a statement about the law for other lawyers must identify the sources of all the principles of law being used: this is done so that anyone can go to the sources to check that they support what is being argued or to find out more information.

The statement identifying the source of a legal principle is known as the citation of the authority for the principle.

Lawyers have to cite and follow up an enormous number of authorities in their work, and they have customary ways of writing citations in an abbreviated form. Not everyone follows exactly the same rules on writing citations.

A citation must show precisely and unambiguously what it is that is being cited, but it must also be convenient for both writer and reader. For convenience, writers like to use abbreviated citations, and readers probably prefer citations which do not take too long to read, but they also want the abbreviations to be readily intelligible.

## 1.2 HOUSE STYLE

When preparing a document for a particular use, for example, for presentation as a dissertation, use within a law firm or publication in a journal, it may be found that there are rules about some aspects of the way in which citations must be presented. These rules may cover, for example:

(a)  where the citation should be placed;
(b)  how the citation should be punctuated;
(c)  whether there should be spaces between certain characters;
(d)  which letters should be capitalised.

Usually, these rules are concerned only with presentation and do not affect the information to be conveyed by the citation. Often their main justification is aesthetic: they ensure a consistent style of presentation of associated documents (a 'house style'). People processing text within an organisation may do so more efficiently if working to a consistent style. People familiar with one house style often find it very difficult to adapt to another, and may even refuse to do so. Whether you conform to a house style specified by others for your writing will, of course, depend on your relationship with the people who want the house style to be followed.

This book is mainly concerned with the information to be given in citations. It uses a preferred style set out in numbered recommendations. Many of the recommendations are followed by 'alternatives' describing other popular styles. A personal house style can be made up by specifying which of these recommendations and alternatives are to apply.

## 1.3  PLACING

The citation of the authority for a statement may follow the statement in the text of the document (example 1.1) or may be in a note placed elsewhere in the document which is referred to by a reference placed after the statement (example 1.2).

*Example 1.1*
Every private company must have at least one director (Companies Act 1985, s. 282).

*Example 1.2*
Every private company must have at least one director.[1]

[1]Companies Act 1985, s. 282.

The choice between citations in the text and citations in notes is fundamental and will be explored in section 1.4.

Often a text statement is in the form of a discussion of an authority and so the citation of the authority appears in the statement (example 1.3).

*Example 1.3*
The Companies Act 1985, s. 282, requires every private company to have at least one director.

In a document in which citations are normally given in notes, part of a citation which is in a statement may be put in a note (example 1.4).

*Example 1.4*
The Companies Act 1985[1] requires every private company to have at least one director.

[1]Section 282.

In examples 1.1 and 1.2, the citation is grammatically separate from the statement which it supports but its connection is shown by the layout of the document. In examples 1.3 and 1.4 the citation is grammatically part of the statement (though in example 1.4 part of it is treated as separate).

## 1.4 CITATIONS IN TEXT OR NOTES

The style of presentation of citations depends to some extent on whether they are placed within the text of a document or in separate notes.

Placing citations in notes is regarded by many people as a mark of learning. For most readers, repeatedly moving from text to notes is profoundly irritating, and notes make the process of preparing documents much more complex, especially when they are amended. In many documents, notes are used not only for citations but also for other information.

If it is decided to place citations within the text of a document then recommendation 1.1 applies. If it is decided to use notes then recommendation 1.2 applies.

### 1.4.1 Citations in text

*Recommendation 1.1*
Place a citation in parentheses after the statement for which the authority is being cited. Commonly this will put it at the end of a sentence (before the final full point), as in example 1.1, but it may be in the middle of a sentence (example 1.5). If the statement for which the authority is being cited is itself in parentheses then punctuate with a colon instead of a second pair of parentheses, as in example 1.6. If there is more than one authority then mark the change from one to another with a semicolon (example 1.7).

*Example 1.5*
Every private company must have at least one director (Companies Act 1985, s. 282) but a company with Table A as its articles of association must have at least two directors unless the members determine otherwise (Table A, reg. 64).

*Example 1.6*
Section 317 requires every director of a company (including a shadow director: s. 317(8)) to declare interests in company contracts to the board of directors.

*Example 1.7*
A director's interest in his or her own service contract is an interest which must be disclosed (*Toms v Cinema Trust Co. Ltd* [1915] WN 29; *Runciman v Walter Runciman plc* [1992] BCLC 1084).

*Alternative to recommendation 1.1*

(a)   The commonest alternative to the style of punctuation in recommendation 1.1 is to use a colon as in example 1.8. This has the disadvantage that it is virtually impossible to use in the middle of a sentence because there is nothing to mark the end of the citation.

(b)   A less common alternative is a dash, as in example 1.9; in the middle of a sentence, a second dash can mark the end of the citation.

*Example 1.8*
Every private company must have at least one director: Companies Act 1985, s. 282.

*Example 1.9*
Every private company must have at least one director — Companies Act 1985, s. 282 — but a company with Table A as its articles of association must have at least two directors unless the members determine otherwise — Table A, reg. 64.

## 1.4.2   Citations in notes

A note may be placed at the foot of the page on which it is referred to (a 'footnote') or in the margin of that page (a 'marginal note') or at the end of the paragraph, chapter or other division of the document in which it is referred to, or at the end of the document (an 'endnote'). References to footnotes may be by numbers, letters or symbols. Different types of note may have different types of reference.

Number and letter references are usually superior: [1], [2], [3] etc.; [a], [b], [c] etc. They may also be in normal size in parentheses: (1), (2), (3) etc.; (a), (b), (c) etc. However, as numbers and letters may appear in parentheses in text for other purposes (for example, in references to subdivisions of statutes or to identify items in a list), this form of reference may be confusing. One way of avoiding confusion is to distinguish the reference typographically, for example, by putting it in bold (this is done in statutory instruments).

The traditional sequence of symbols is * † ‡ ¶ ||, and then in duplicate ** and so on. As typewriters usually had only * it has long been common to use *, **, *** etc.

A number sequence can continue to the end of the document, or start afresh at divisions of the document such as new chapters, or start afresh after a fixed number, such as 99. Letter or symbol sequences are often started afresh on each new page and so are most appropriate for footnotes or marginal notes.

Notes to a text are commonly made less legible than the rest of the text by using a smaller type size or less interlinear spacing.

*Recommendation 1.2*
Place the reference mark for a note containing a citation after the statement for which the authority is cited and after any punctuation. But where the statement is itself in parentheses put the reference before the closing parenthesis. Put the reference mark before the note in the same typography (superior, bold etc.) as in the text. Begin the note with a capital letter and end with a full point.

*Example 1.10*
Every director of a company (including a shadow director[1]) must declare interests in company contracts to the board of directors.[2]

[1]Companies Act 1985, s. 317(8).
[2]Companies Act 1985, s. 317.

## 1.5 DESCRIBING THE RELEVANCE OF A CITED AUTHORITY

Most often, the relevance of a cited authority to the statement in the text is that the statement simply sets out the principle enunciated in the source, or is a direct quotation from the source. As grammatically separate citations (see section 1.3) are most often of this type it is unnecessary to introduce such a citation with a phrase such as 'as stated in' or 'as decided in'. But phrases like these can be used where the citation is grammatically part of a text statement.

*Example 1.11*
Citation grammatically separate from the text statement:

A registered company is a legal person separate from its members (*Salomon* v *A. Salomon and Co. Ltd* [1897] AC 22).

Citation grammatically part of the text statement:

It was decided in *Salomon* v *A. Salomon and Co. Ltd* [1897] AC 22 that a registered company is a legal person separate from its members.

Sometimes a cited authority merely illustrates a statement in the text or is even contrary to the statement. Then the citation must be accompanied by an explanation of the relevance of the authority (such as 'see, for example,' or 'but ——— is to the contrary'). This explanation may make the citation grammatically part of the text statement. Alternatively the citation and explanation may be put into a separate sentence, either in the text or in a note.

The term 'cf.' (an abbreviation of the Latin *confer* meaning 'compare') should be used only when some indication is given of what insight might be gained by making the comparison. The misuse of 'cf.' to mean 'see' should be avoided. When short conventional signals are italicised (which is not recommended here, see section 1.7) then 'cf.' is italicised.

## 1.6   IBID., LOC. CIT.

In citations, 'ibid.' (from the Latin *ibidem*, meaning 'in the same place') is used to mean that the same authority is being cited as in the immediately preceding citation. Accordingly it can be used only when the same authority is repeatedly cited with no intervening citations of other authorities. It should be used only in a citation which is a grammatically separate statement in parentheses or in a note. Sometimes, 'ib.' is used instead of 'ibid.' and sometimes the punctuation is omitted. Americans, perhaps more logically, prefer 'id.' (from the Latin *idem*, meaning 'the same'). When any of these terms is the first word of a footnote it should be given a capital 'I' but it is unnecessary to spell out in full the word from which it is derived.

When a specific point in an authority, such as a page in a law report, book or article, is to be referred to in successive citations, the term 'loc. cit.' (from the Latin *loco citato*, meaning 'in the place cited') may be used in citations after the first.

The combination 'ibid., loc. cit.' means 'the same authority at the same point'.

When short conventional signals are italicised (which is not recommended here, see section 1.7) then all these terms are italicised.

## 1.7   TYPOGRAPHY

In the traditional presentation of printed English, text is set in an upright typeface like the one these words are set in but with some words in a *contrasting sloping typeface* called 'italic'. Italics are widely used in citations, for example, in case names and book titles. The traditional way of indicating to a typesetter that words in a manuscript are to be set in italics is to underline them with a single straight line. Where the typographical style for citations would require italicisation but they are to appear in a document for which italics are not available then underlining can be used instead.

The purpose of italicising certain characters in a text is to contrast them with the rest of the text. Accordingly if the typographical design of a document requires a passage to be in italics anyway then the contrast has to be achieved in reverse by not using italics. However, especially in headings, it may be preferred to ignore the citation conventions so as not to harm the effect of the typographical design of the document.

Sometimes a rule is adopted that short conventional signals such as 'cf.'. 'ibid.' and 'see' should be italicised but that is not recommended here.

## 1.8 FURTHER READING

For the history of legal citation see:
Byron D. Cooper, 'Anglo-American legal citation: historical development and library implications' (1982) 75 Law Libr J 3.

Several articles in vol. 23 of the *International Journal of Legal Information* survey legal citation practice in various countries in the light of a proposal for international harmonisation. The general view of these articles seems to be that harmonisation is impracticable. See in particular:
Pierre Legrand, 'Sigla law' (1995) 23 Int'l J Legal Info 123 (describing British practice).
Walter Rodinò, 'For a uniform international citation system' (1995) 23 Int'l J Legal Info 102.

# 2  CASES

## 2.1  CASES AS SOURCES OF LAW

When lawyers speak of 'cases' as a source of law they mean primarily the judgments delivered by courts and tribunals in legal proceedings. Occasionally they also refer to the evidence and legal arguments in proceedings. There is a long history of making records of legal proceedings in a form that will be useful to lawyers as a source of law and circulating them, at first in manuscript, then in printed form and now electronically. This activity is known as 'law reporting' and its products are 'law reports'. The dominant form of publication of law reports for the past four centuries has been in printed volumes each containing reports of many cases (each proceeding culminating in a judgment being regarded as a separate case). In the seventeenth and eighteenth centuries, the characteristic form of publication was a single volume, or sometimes a few volumes, of reports prepared by an individual reporter, often reporting cases over a long period. In the nineteenth and twentieth centuries, the characteristic form of publication has been as a serial in numerous volumes published over many years with each volume reporting cases decided recently. Law reports are also published along with other items in periodicals and newspapers and in textbooks.

## 2.2  PUBLICATION OF REPORTS OF CASES

### 2.2.1  Yearbooks (13th to 16th centuries)

Manuscript notes of proceedings in courts are known from at least as early as the 1270s. In some of the earliest manuscripts, cases are arranged by subject matter but it soon became common to set out the cases in approximately chronological order, grouping them according to the law term in which they were heard, and then putting the terms for a particular regnal year together. Accordingly the reports were known as 'terms',

'terms and years' or simply 'the years' or 'the books of years' or, later, as 'the yearbooks'. (Regnal years are explained in the List of Regnal Years. For the dates of law terms see section 2.5.)

Printed yearbooks seem to have first appeared in the early 1480s and there were hundreds of editions over the next two centuries. Yearbooks from as far back as the first year of Edward II were published in this period but many years were not printed, and there are no printed yearbooks for any time after the 27th year of Henry VIII (1535–6). There seems to have been no custom of publishing yearbooks immediately after the year reported — for the period 1480–1535, the gap between end of year and publication seems to have been never less than 10 years. Presumably this reflected a lack of a strong doctrine of precedent at that time.

The printed texts were published in a collected edition in 11 volumes in 1678–80 by George Sawbridge, William Rawlins and Samuel Roycroft. This is known as the 'standard' or 'vulgate' edition. A reprint of this edition was published by Professional Books in 1981. In the standard edition, the cases, known then as 'placita', are numbered with arabic figures, with a new sequence of numbers for each term.

The yearbooks are in law French, though all court records at this time, including writs, written pleadings and judgments, were in Latin, and it is unclear how much law French was actually spoken in court. The manuscripts are full of contractions and abbreviations which are reproduced in the printed versions, presumably because they were familiar enough to lawyers of the time. It is, however, difficult for modern readers to become accustomed to them.

The standard edition of the yearbooks includes additional reports for two periods. For the fifth year (*anno quinto* in Latin) of Edward IV there is an alternative report which is significantly longer than is usual for yearbooks and is therefore known as 'long quinto'. For the years 1 to 50 of Edward III there is the 'Liber Assisarum et Placitorum Corone' (book of assizes and pleas of the Crown).

Whether there was any organisation of law reporting in the yearbook period is unknown and, remarkably, none of the manuscripts or published yearbooks names its reporter, though some names have been discovered in other sources or deduced by scholars (see J.H. Baker, 'John Bryt's reports (1410–1411) and the year books of Henry IV' [1989] CLJ 98).

Since the early nineteenth century, historians have expressed regret that more of the reports from the yearbook period have not been published. They have also regretted that because the reports concentrate on what the reporters considered the legally significant points of each case, historically important details have been omitted, and they have found that the printed editions do not accurately reproduce the manuscript sources. Accordingly, scholarly editions have appeared from time to time. Some volumes appeared between 1863 and 1911 in what was known as the 'Rolls Series', which was a series of historic documents published initially under the general direction of the Master of the Rolls, Sir John Romilly. From 1903 onwards editions of yearbooks have slowly appeared in the series of Publications of the Selden Society. Both the Rolls Series and the Selden Society volumes give an English translation as well as the original text.

### 2.2.1.1  Further reading

J.H. Baker, *Manual of Law French*, 2nd ed. (Aldershot: Scolar Press, 1990).

W.C. Bolland, 'The Book of Assizes' (1925) 2 CLJ 192.

Sir William Holdsworth, *A History of English Law*, vol. 2 (London: Methuen, 1936), pp. 525–56.

E.W. Ives, 'The purpose and making of the later year books' (1973) 89 LQR 64.

Charles C. Soule, 'Year-book bibliography' (1901) 14 Harv L Rev 73.

### 2.2.2  Named reporters (sixteenth to nineteenth centuries)

From the last quarter of the sixteenth century, although publishers were still issuing the anonymous yearbooks reporting cases up to 1536, they also began to issue volumes of reports bearing the names of individuals as 'reporters'. These have become known as 'nominate' reports and became the predominant form of published reports up to the middle of the nineteenth century.

At first, these books were single-volume collections of a lawyer's notes of cases, often ones he had participated in as counsel or judge (there are no women reporting cases in this period) and they vary widely in the amount of information they give. At first, as with the yearbooks, it does not seem to have been considered necessary to publish reports of cases soon after they were decided.

From about the mid eighteenth century, law reporting became more regularised and some barristers made a career of reporting. There seems to have been a system under which each court had one or more 'authorised reporters' whose reports were required to be cited in court proceedings and who were assisted by the provision of pleadings and other documents. An authorised reporter often reported over many years, publishing a series of reports in several volumes. Publication of authorised reports was often notoriously slow but some reporters recognised a growing need for speedy publication. For example, Durnford and East's reports of King's Bench cases 1785–1800 became known as the 'Term Reports' because the report of each law term's cases was published soon after the end of the term.

Each reporter in this period normally concentrated on a single court.

Although the reports from this period are usually known as 'nominate' reports, in fact a few important series are known by their title rather than by the name of the reporter. These include the *Common Bench Reports*, *House of Lords Cases*, *Modern Reports*, *Term Reports* and *Queen's Bench Reports*.

### 2.2.2.1 Further reading

John William Wallace, *The Reporters Arranged and Characterized*, 4th ed. (Boston Mass, 1882; reprinted Buffalo NY: Dennis & Co., 1959).

### 2.2.3 General reports

In the nineteenth century, a new form of law report publishing was developed in which a publisher assembled a team of reporters covering all the superior courts so as to produce a general law report which could be expected to have a large market. These reports were published in weekly or monthly parts so that reports of cases could appear soon after the cases were decided. The *Law Journal Reports* (the first volume of which was completed in 1822), the *Jurist* (1838) and the *Law Times* (1843) are important examples. The *Weekly Reporter* and the *Times Law Reports* followed in the second half of the nineteenth century.

In the mid 1860s the Bar and the Law Society established the Incorporated Council of Law Reporting for England and Wales to publish, under the general title of *Law Reports*, reports of cases in all the superior courts prepared by the Council's own reporters, many of whom had previously been authorised reporters. A similar body was established in Ireland shortly after. In 1936 publication began of the *All England Law Reports*. Since the cessation of the *Times Law Reports* in 1952, the *Law Reports* and the *All England Law Reports* have been the only general series of law reports in England. However, there has been a great diversification of law reporting during the twentieth century by the establishment of numerous series of reports specialising in particular areas of law rather than particular courts.

### 2.2.3.1 Further reading

W.T.S. Daniel, *History and Origin of the Law Reports* (London, 1884; reprinted London, Wildy & Sons, [1968]).
Three articles in the *Law Librarian* include descriptions by the managers of the modern series of general law reports of how reports are produced:
C.J. Ellis, 'Law reporting today' (1975) 6 Law Libr 5 (on the *Law Reports*).
Paul Brown, 'Law reporting: the inside story' (1989) 20 Law Libr 15 (on the *All England Law Reports*).
Peter Nicholson, 'The production of law reports and the dissemination of legal information' (1991) 22 Law Libr 122 (on the *Scots Law Times*).

For an earlier description of editing the *Law Reports* see:
Sir Frederick Pollock, 'English law reporting', in *Essays in the Law*
(London: Macmillan, 1922), pp. 241–57. This is a revised version of an
article first published in (1903) 19 LQR 451.

### 2.2.4   Qualifications of reporters

In the days when all judgments were delivered orally so that a report could
be compiled only by someone who noted what was said, courts adopted a
rule that a report would only be considered authoritative if vouched for by
'an impartial person, [who] gives the authority of his name to the matter'
(per Lord Brougham LC during argument in *Re Richards, ex parte Hawley*
(1834) 2 Mont & A 426 at p. 435). Lord Brougham indicated that a
barrister's declaration of the correctness of a report would be acceptable,
and this was confirmed when Lord Esher MR said that the *Times Law
Reports* were acceptable 'because they are reports by barristers who put
their names to their reports' (*West Derby Poor Law Guardians* v *Atcham
Poor Law Guardians* (1889) 6 TLR 5 during argument at p. 6). This was
interpreted as meaning that only a barrister can report a case (*Birtwistle*
v *Tweedale* [1954] 1 WLR 190). It is now provided by the Courts and Legal
Services Act 1990, s. 115, that a report of a case made by a person who is
a solicitor or who has a right of audience in relation to all proceedings in
the Supreme Court shall have the same authority as if it had been made
by a barrister. According to an article in the *Justice of the Peace* ('*JP
Reports*' (1987) 151 JPN 795), it had already been accepted by courts in the
early 1980s that reports prepared by solicitors could be cited.

### 2.3   CASE NAMES

### 2.3.1   Citation by name

When citing a case in legal writing it is necessary to state the name of the
case and where a report of it can be found. In England and other common
law jurisdictions, cases are generally known by their names, rather than
by a court file number or by the volume and page number of an official
report. In England, most cases are reported in several series of law reports
and so the name of a case must be given so that someone who does not have
access to the report cited can locate the case in another report or refer to
comment on it in books or articles which cite other reports. The main
exception is reported cases of the Social Security Commissioner which are
cited by report number.

   The name of a case in a citation should be taken from the heading of the
case in the report being cited, but various elements of a heading may be

omitted as detailed in recommendation 2.2. If cases are cited from more than one report it is necessary to standardise some parts of the names as stated in recommendation 2.3.

## 2.3.2 Types of case name

The form of the name of a case depends on the nature of the proceedings reported. Examples of many common forms are given in recommendation 2.1, which gives recommended punctuation and typography for each type of case name.

*Recommendation 2.1*
This recommendation lists a number of common types of case name and gives recommended punctuation and typography for each type. Although this recommendation is concerned only with the case name, the law report reference for each case has also been given. Law report references are discussed in detail later in this chapter.

In general it is recommended that a case name should be in italic apart from the symbols 'd' and 'v' and, in a case in the Court of Justice or Court of First Instance of the European Communities, the case number. (Names are usually not italicised in a table of cases.)

Types of case name:

(a)  Two parties' names separated by 'v' for 'versus'.

*Example 2.1*
*Foss* v *Harbottle* (1843) 2 Hare 461

Use 'v' even if the heading of the report uses 'against' or 'and'.

One or more of the parties may be identified only by initials. If both parties are identified by initials only and the heading gives a paren-thesised description of the subject matter of the case then this description is part of the case name.

*Example 2.2*
*X Ltd* v *Morgan-Grampian (Publishers) Ltd* [1991] 1 AC 1
*Z Ltd* v *A-Z* [1982] QB 558
*F* v *F (Minors) (Custody: Foreign Order)* [1989] Fam 1

*Alternative to recommendation 2.1(a)*
Italicise the symbol 'v' and/or follow it with a full point.

(b)  As in (a), but followed by ', *ex parte*' and a third party's name.

*Example 2.3*
*R* v *Secretary of State for Employment, ex parte Equal Opportunities Commission* [1995] 1 AC 1

*Alternative to recommendation 2.1(b)*

(i)     Omit the comma.
(ii)    Abbreviate '*ex parte*' to '*ex p.*'.
(iii)   Use a capital '*E*'.
(iv)    Do not italicise '*ex parte*' or '*ex p.*'.

(c)   As in (a) but preceded by a fictitious party's name (usually 'Doe') and the symbol 'd' (for 'on the demise of').

*Example 2.4*
*Doe* d *Mudd* v *Suckermore* (1836) 5 Ad & El 703

Use 'd' even if the heading of the report uses 'dem' or 'on the demise of'.

*Alternative to recommendation 2.1(c)*
Italicise the symbol 'd' and/or follow it with a full point.

(d)   The name of a company or individual or of a matter before the court preceded by '*Re*' (meaning 'in the matter of').

*Example 2.5*
*Re Bank of Credit and Commerce International SA* [1992] BCLC 570
*Re an Inquiry under the Company Securities (Insider Dealing) Act 1985* [1988] AC 660

Instead of beginning the heading of a case with '*Re*' the house style of some reports may be to use '*In re*' or 'In the matter of'. If it is appropriate to make citations consistent (see recommendation 2.3) then a single form should be chosen. '*Re*' is the recommended form.

(e)   As in (d), but followed by ', *ex parte*' and the name of the person making the application.

*Example 2.6*
*Re Tucker, ex parte Tucker* [1990] Ch 148

*Alternative to recommendation 2.1(e)*
As alternative to recommendation 2.1(b).

(f)   As in (d), but followed by ', X's Case' where X is the name of a person.

*Example 2.7*
*Re Caribbean Co., Crickmer's Case* (1875) LR 10 Ch App 614

There are variations on this form such as 'X's Claim', 'X's Policy'. Occasionally two parties' names separated by 'v' are followed by ', X's Case'.

*Example 2.8*
*Devaynes* v *Noble, Clayton's Case* (1816) 1 Mer 572

*Alternative to recommendation 2.1(f)*
Put 'X's Case' in parentheses and omit the comma.

(g)   As in (d) followed by a comma and two parties' names separated by 'v' for 'versus'.

*Example 2.9*
*Re Greene, Greene* v *Greene* [1949] Ch 333

(h)   The phrase '*Re* a Company' or '*Re* a Debtor' followed by a court file number.

*Example 2.10*
*Re a Company (No. 007923 of 1994)* [1995] 1 WLR 953
*Re a Debtor (No. 415-SD-1993)* [1994] 1 WLR 917

*Alternative to recommendation 2.1(h)*
Omit parentheses.

(i)   The name of a ship.

*Example 2.11*
*The Zafiro* [1960] P 1

If a ship's name is preceded by the definite article in a case heading then the definite article is treated as part of the case name.

(j)   The name of a person preceded by '*Ex parte*'.

*Example 2.12*
*Ex parte Coventry Newspapers Ltd* [1993] QB 278

(k)   The phrase 'Attorney-General's Reference' followed by a number.

*Example 2.13*
*Attorney-General's Reference (No. 1 of 1994)* [1995] 1 WLR 599

(l)   Either '*R*' or the title of a public official followed by the name of a relator.

*Example 2.14*
*Attorney-General (McWhirter)* v *Independent Broadcasting Authority* [1973] QB 629

In the heading of a report, the relator's name may be preceded by the phrase 'on the relation of' (as in the report of this case at [1973] 1 All ER 689) or its Latin equivalent, '*ex relatione*' (or '*ex rel.*' as in the heading at [1973] QB 629).

(m)   If two or more different cases have the same name because they involve the same parties then the second, third etc. to be reported may have (No. 2), (No. 3) etc. added to the name.

*Example 2.15*
*Re Bank of Credit and Commerce International SA (No. 10)* [1995] 1 BCLC 362

These numbers are added by the editor of the law report, not the court, and different reports may give the same proceedings different numbers.

*Example 2.16*
*Re Maxwell Communications Corporation plc* [1993] 1 WLR 1402 is *Re Maxwell Communications Corporation plc (No. 2)* in the *All England Law Reports* ([1994] 1 All ER 737) and *Re Maxwell Communications Corporation plc (No. 3)* in *British Company Cases* ([1993] BCC 369).

(n)   A case name in any of the preceding forms followed by its court file number in the Court of Justice or Court of First Instance of the European Communities (see section 2.15).

### 2.3.3    Omission of elements of a heading

*Recommendation 2.2*
For citation purposes, take the name of a case from the heading of the report being cited but simplify as follows:

(a)   If there is more than one party on one or both sides of an action, or an application is *ex parte* more than one applicant, omit the names of all parties after the first. Similarly, omit the phrases 'and another', 'and others' and 'et al.' in lists of parties.

*Example 2.17*
The heading of the case reported at [1962] 1 WLR 832 is:

Jones and Another v. Lipman and Another

It is cited as:

*Jones* v *Lipman* [1962] 1 WLR 832

(b)   If a report is of joined cases which the heading lists separately then the citation uses only the first case to be named.

*Example 2.18*
The case reported at [1995] 1 WLR 953 is headed:

*In re* a Company (No. 007923 of 1994)
*In re* a Company (No. 007924 of 1994)

It is cited as:

*Re a Company (No. 007923 of 1994)* [1995] 1 WLR 953

('*In re*' is changed to '*Re*' as in recommendation 2.1(d).) However, if the heading does not list the cases separately then it is not altered in that respect.

*Example 2.19*
The case reported at [1995] Ch 46 is headed:

*In re* a Debtor (Nos. 49 and 50 of 1992)

It is cited as:

*Re a Debtor (Nos. 49 and 50 of 1992)* [1995] Ch 46

(*'In re'* is changed to *'Re'* as in recommendation 2.1(d).)

(c)   In the name of a company, omit 'The' at the beginning of the name; omit commas unless necessary to avoid ambiguity; abbreviate 'Company' to 'Co.', 'Limited' to 'Ltd' and 'public limited company' to 'plc'.

*Example 2.20*
The heading of the case reported at [1893] AC 396 gives the appellants' name as:

The Balkis Consolidated Company, Limited

The case is cited as:

*Balkis Consolidated Co. Ltd* v *Tomkinson* [1893] AC 396

(d)   Omit the forenames of parties who are individuals.

*Example 2.21*
The heading of the case reported at [1996] 1 WLR 51 gives the appellant's name as:

David Eves

It is cited as:

*Eves* v *Hambros Bank (Jersey) Ltd* [1996] 1 WLR 251

But a corporate or firm name which includes one or more forenames (or initials of forenames) of an individual must be given in full.

*Example 2.22*
*James Lazenby and Co.* v *McNicholas Construction Co. Ltd* [1995] 1 WLR 615
*Hindcastle Ltd* v *Barbara Attenborough Associates Ltd* [1996] 2 WLR 262

Formerly, when citing a corporate or firm name which included one or more forenames (or initials of forenames) of an individual, it was common to put the forename or initials in parentheses after the surname but this is not recommended (see also section 2.19).

(e) If a party is identified by its own name and a trading name (introduced by the phrase 'trading as' or 't/a') then omit the reference to the trading name.

(f) Omit descriptions of parties who are named. Descriptions such as 'an alien', 'a bankrupt', 'deceased' (or 'decd'), 'a firm', 'in administration', 'in liquidation', 'in receivership', 'inspector of taxes', 'valuation officer' (or 'v/o'), or 'pauper' (or 'poor' or *in forma pauperis*') may be omitted if the party is named. But if only the initial of a party is given then the description (most often it is 'A Minor') should be given in the citation.

(g) Omit a statement of a party's role in the proceedings, such as 'appellant', 'petitioner', 'respondent'.

(h) If a woman's married and maiden names are given in the heading of a Scottish case, use only the last name given (which is the married name).

*Example 2.23*
The heading of the case reported at [1932] AC 562 gives the appellant's name as:

M'Alister (or Donoghue) (Pauper)

The heading of the same case reported at 1932 SC (HL) 31 gives the name as:

(Poor) Mrs Mary M'Alister or Donoghue

It is cited as:

*Donoghue* v *Stevenson* [1932] AC 562, 1932 SC (HL) 31

(i) Omit a heading in the form 'Re the ———— Act' unless there is nothing else in the title.

*Example 2.24*
The heading of the case reported at 4 De G J & S 63 is:

In the Matter of the Companies Act, 1862; and In the Matter of The Great Ship Company, Limited. Parry's Case.

It is cited as:

*Re Great Ship Co. Ltd, Parry's Case* (1863) 4 De G J & S 63

('In the Matter of' is changed to *'Re'* in accordance with recommendation 2.1(d). The company's name is simplified in accordance with recommendation 2.2(c).)

(j)    Omit descriptions of the report itself such as 'Note' or 'Practice note' unless nothing else would be left in the heading.

*Example 2.25*
The heading of the case reported at [1987] AC 45 is:

Note
Bank of Tokyo Ltd. v. Karoon and Another

It is cited as:

*Bank of Tokyo Ltd* v *Karoon* [1987] AC 45

*Alternative to recommendation 2.2(j)*
The description '(Note)' may be put after the case name.

(k)    It is common in writing on criminal law to omit the phrase '*R* v' from a case name but the phrase is usually not omitted when a comparatively small number of criminal cases are cited in a work primarily devoted to civil law. The phrase 'v *R*', used mostly in Privy Council appeals in criminal matters, is not omitted even in works devoted to criminal law. (In the names of cases to which the Crown is a party *R* stands for *Rex* (the King) or *Regina* (the Queen) as appropriate.)

## 2.3.4    Standardisation of names

Different publishers of law reports have different house styles for case names, and some commonly occurring parties, such as the Commissioners of Inland Revenue and the Commissioner of Police for the Metropolis have their names given in different forms (Inland Revenue Commissioners, Metropolitan Police Commissioner) in different reports of the same case. Some series of reports devoted to criminal law, such as the *Criminal Appeal Reports* and the *Criminal Appeal Reports (Sentencing)*, omit '*R* v' from case names.

*Recommendation 2.3*
The names of cases from different sources using different house styles may be standardised. This is especially desirable if a table of cases is to be provided.

*Example 2.26*
It may be decided that in all cases involving the Commissioners of Inland Revenue their name is to be 'Inland Revenue Commissioners' regardless of how they are named in the headings of cited case reports. It may be decided that '*R* v' is to be omitted from all case names regardless of whether it is omitted in the headings of cited case reports.

## 2.3.5 Abbreviation

Headings in law reports rarely abbreviate words in case names, apart, nowadays, from the indications of corporate status noted in recommendation 2.2(c). However, abbreviation was once popular in law books.

*Recommendation 2.4*
Do not abbreviate any words in a case name, except for the indications of corporate status noted in recommendation 2.2(c). Where a significant number of cases are cited involving one particular party, that party's name may be abbreviated, if the abbreviation is widely known or a list of abbreviations is provided.

*Example 2.27*
It may be decided to abbreviate 'Director of Public Prosecutions' to 'DPP'. Depending on which version of the name is chosen as standard (see example 2.26), it may be decided to abbreviate 'Commissioners of Inland Revenue' to 'CIR' or 'Inland Revenue Commissioners' to 'IRC'.

Case names often seem clumsily long, and giving them in full is often felt to impede the flow of a sentence. There is therefore a great temptation to abbreviate case names. The considerable problem is that a case which the writer knows by heart is usually unknown to many readers, who may waste much time trying to work out what the abbreviated name might refer to, so that the object of creating a text that is easy to read is not achieved. Abbreviation of case names may cause difficulties with automatic generation of a table of cases by a computer program. It should also be said that fear of long case names is often unwarranted.

*Recommendation 2.5*
Do not abbreviate the name of a case when it is first mentioned in a document. If the document is long enough to be divided into chapters and/or by section headings, and a case is mentioned in more than one chapter or section then its name should be given in full when it first appears in each chapter or section. Even if there are no headings, the name should be given in full when it is first mentioned after an extended interruption in the discussion of it.

After the first mention of a case in a document or section of a document, its name may be abbreviated, but this is not compulsory. In general the larger the number of cases discussed the more inappropriate it is to abbreviate their names, though where a name is repeated close by (in the same sentence, for example) some form of abbreviation (e.g., by using 'ibid.') is normally expected.

An abbreviation of a case name should give the reader some chance of guessing what the full name might be. It should preferably start with the same word as the full name. A common device is to take the name (or part of the name) of one party, X, in a case and refer to the case as '*X's* case'.

If the same case is cited repeatedly with no intervening citations of other authorities then 'ibid.' may be used (see section 1.6).

When a point within a report is being cited it may not be necessary to refer to the case name at all, see recommendation 2.19(c).

*Example 2.28*
*Salomon* v *A. Salomon and Co. Ltd* [1897] AC 22 might be referred to as '*Salomon's* case'.

## 2.3.6   Indications of corporate form

In the nineteenth century it was common to omit the word 'Limited' from a company name. It is often important to know whether parties to cases are individuals or companies, but omitting the word 'Limited' can make it difficult to discover the status of a party. Some series of reports, including the *Law Times Reports* and the *Times Law Reports*, used to put the word 'Limited' in parentheses. Although the practice of omitting 'Limited' was rightly abandoned long ago by editors of law reports, it was revived, and is still followed, by the editors of *Current Law*.

*Recommendation 2.6*
If a term indicating corporate status, such as 'Limited', 'Ltd', 'plc', 'GmbH' or 'SA', is included in the heading of a report being cited then do not omit it from the citation. If such a term is in parentheses then omit the parentheses.

*Example 2.29*
The heading of a case reported at 11 WR 84 is:

Re The Rockall Fishing, Fish Oil, and Fish Manure Company (Limited)

It is cited as:

*Re Rockall Fishing, Fish Oil and Fish Manure Co. Ltd* (1862) 11 WR 84

The name has been simplified as described in recommendation 2.2(c).

### 2.3.7 Constituents of a corporate body

It is common to omit descriptions of the constituents of a corporate body if doing so will not leave an ambiguous name.

The name of a municipal corporation in an old form such as 'Mayor, Aldermen and Burgesses of X' may be changed to 'X Corporation'.

*Example 2.30*
The heading of the case reported at [1891] AC 106 names the appellants as:

The Governor and Company of the Bank of England

It is cited as:

*Bank of England* v *Vagliano Brothers* [1891] AC 107.

The heading of the case reported at [1905] AC 392 names the appellants as:

Lord Mayor, etc., of Sheffield

It is cited as:

*Sheffield Corporation* v *Barclay* [1905] AC 392.

### 2.3.8 Variation of name at different stages

A case may be reported in separate reports at first instance and on appeal, and again on further appeal, and the reports of the case at different stages may have different headings.

*Recommendation 2.7*
In accordance with recommendation 2.2, the name to be used in the citation of a case which is reported under different names at different stages is the name in the heading of the report being cited, which will depend on which stage of the case is being discussed.

*Example 2.31*
The case reported at [1974] AC 370 is an appeal to the House of Lords from a decision of the Divisional Court of the Queen's Bench Division. The Divisional Court's decision was reported at [1973] 1 WLR 317 under the name *Ray* v *Sempers* but in [1974] AC the case is headed:

Director of Public Prosecutions
and
Ray

The case in the House of Lords is cited:

*Director of Public Prosecutions* v *Ray* [1974] AC 370

*Alternative to recommendation 2.7*
Some people prefer to cite such a case under the name it had at the previous stage.

For parallel citations of reports at different stages, see section 2.8.

### 2.3.9  Popular names

Some cases, especially in public law, have popular titles which bear no resemblance to the heading of any law report.

*Example 2.32*
*Council of Civil Service Unions* v *Minister for the Civil Service* [1985] AC 374 is popularly known as:

the GCHQ case

*Recommendation 2.8*
Do not use a popular title for a case without explaining it when it is first used or in a table of abbreviations.

## 2.3.10 *Ex parte*

*Recommendation 2.9*
If a case heading is in the form *Ex parte* A, *re* B (which was usual in the nineteenth century) then cite it in the form *Re B, ex parte A*.

*Example 2.33*
The heading of the case reported at 2 Mont & A 426 is:

*Ex parte* Hawley. In the matter of Richards

It is cited as:

*Re Richards, ex parte Hawley* (1834) 2 Mont & A 426

('In the matter of' is changed to '*Re*' in accordance with recommendation 2.1(d).)

## 2.3.11 Practice directions

A reported practice direction is treated as a case. The title is in the form *Practice Direction, Practice Statement* or *Practice Note* followed by a summary (in parentheses) of the subject matter; but different series of reports have different house styles for titling.

*Example 2.34*
*Practice Direction (Contempt: Reporting Restrictions)* [1982] 1 WLR 1475

## 2.3.12 Anonymous cases

Cases in early reports do not have titles and, often, the parties are not named at all. Such a case may be cited as '*Anonymous*' or cited without a name at all, the law report reference being sufficient citation. The cases in the *Reported Decisions of the Social Security Commissioner* and its predecessors are also anonymous and are cited by report number only.

## 2.4 CITATION OF LAW REPORTS

## 2.4.1 Introduction

Following the name of a case in a citation is a statement of where a report of it may be found, or a statement that it is unreported.

English law reports are very diverse, perhaps more so than in any other jurisdiction.

## 2.4.2   Citing printed law reports other than in daily newspapers

A citation of a law report must identify:

(a)   The publication in which the report appeared: this is usually done by using an abbreviation.
(b)   If the publication is in more than one volume, the volume in which the report appears.
(c)   The page on which the report starts.

### 2.4.2.1   *Abbreviated titles*

In a citation of a case, the publication containing the cited report is usually identified by an abbreviation of the publication's title or of the name of its author. Present-day serials devoted to law reporting usually have the abbreviated title by which they are to be cited printed prominently on the title-page or verso of bound volumes, and often as a running headline on every opening. This practice seems to have originated with the *Law Reports* in 1876 (when the recommended citation was put at the beginning of the index). Before then, abbreviations were widely used but were not standardised. No doubt a writer, if aware of an abbreviation used previously, would adopt it, but even important collections of case law, such as the early digests, did not include tables of abbreviations.

One of the objectives of this book is to recommend abbreviations for publications cited by lawyers. This is done in the List of Recommended Forms of Citation for Law Reports and Other Publications.

*Recommendation 2.10*

(a)   Cite a publication listed in the List of Recommended Forms of Citation for Law Reports and Other Publications in this book by the abbreviation recommended in that list.
(b)   Cite a publication which is not in that list but which itself states how it is to be cited by the abbreviation recommended in the publication itself.
(c)   Cite a publication which is not in that list, and which does not state how it is to be cited, by an abbreviation used by others if one can be found. Such a publication may be cited by its full title and this is recommended if the publication is not primarily legal. If such a publication is to be cited many times in a document then an abbreviation may be devised for the

purpose and should be explained in the document in, for example, a list of abbreviations.

*Alternative to recommendation 2.10*
Many alternative abbreviations are listed in the List of Abbreviations for Law Reports and Other Publications in this book. Where an abbreviation in that list is not the recommended abbreviation it is followed by an = sign and then the recommended abbreviation.

*2.4.2.2   Capitalisation, spacing, punctuation and typography of abbreviations*

*Recommendation 2.11*
Follow the capitalisation and spacing of abbreviations used in the List of Recommended Forms of Citation for Law Reports and Other Publications in this book. Do not punctuate abbreviations except for the parentheses used in some recommended abbreviations. Do not set abbreviations in italics or underline them (except in a heading or other portion of text which the typographical design of the document requires to be italic or underlined).

*Alternative to recommendation 2.11*
Some people prefer to put a full point after each letter or group of letters forming an abbreviation of a word. This may be qualified by a further rule that no full point is necessary for an abbreviation of a word which includes the last letter of the word, and/or a rule that no full points are necessary between and after adjacent capital letters.

*2.4.2.3   Volumes*
An important feature which complicates the citation of multi-volume law reports is that two different systems of volume numbering are in use:

(a)   using volume numbers;
(b)   using volume years.

*2.4.2.4   Volume numbers*
The publishers of many law reports and legal periodicals simply number successive volumes 1, 2, 3, and so on. This is done, for example, with the *Property, Planning and Compensation Reports* and the *Reports of Tax Cases*. In a citation, the volume number is put before the abbreviated title.

*Example 2.35*
Volume 62 of the *Reports of Tax Cases* is cited:

62 TC

This form of volume numbering is also used for citing nominate reports published in more than one volume.

*Example 2.36*
Volume 2 of the 11 volumes of Thomas Hare's *Reports of Cases Adjudged in the High Court of Chancery* is cited:

2 Hare

For the early reports of the Council of Law Reporting for England and Wales, it is necessary to put the letters 'LR' before the volume number.

*Example 2.37*
Volume 2 of the 10 volumes of *Law Reports. Chancery Appeal Cases* is cited:

LR 2 Ch App

*2.4.2.5   Volume years*
For many law reports and legal periodicals, a volume is identified by the year for which it was published — the volume year. Most English and Irish publications using this system put the volume year in square brackets.

*Example 2.38*
The volume of *Law Reports. Queen's Bench Division* published for 1995 is cited:

[1995] QB

Occasionally one volume is published for more than one year.

*Example 2.39*
A volume of the *Reports of Bankruptcy and Companies Winding-up Cases* was published for 1934 and 1935. It is cited:

[1934-5] B & CR

For some other publications (including most published in Scotland) the volume year is given without brackets.

*Example 2.40*
The volume of the *Scottish Civil Law Reports* published for 1995 is cited:

1995 SCLR

If there is more than one volume for a year then the volumes are numbered in succession through the year (starting at 1 at the beginning of each year) and that volume number is placed between the volume year and the abbreviated title. There is a space before and after the volume number.

*Example 2.41*
The second volume of the *All England Law Reports* for 1995 is cited:

[1995] 2 All ER

Some publications using volume-year numbering have only one volume for some years but more than one volume in other years. For the years in which there is only one volume, the number 1 is not put after the volume year.

*Example 2.42*
There were two volumes for 1991 of the *Law Reports. Queen's Bench Division*, but only one volume for 1992. The first volume for 1991 is cited:

[1991] 1 QB

but the volume for 1992 is cited:

. [1992] QB

When volume-year numbering is used, the year on a volume usually indicates only the position of the volume in the sequence — usually it does not mean that the volume reports only cases decided in that year or that the volume was published in that year.

*Example 2.43*
[1995] QB contains reports of cases decided in 1993, 1994 and 1995.
[1991] NI was published in 1993.

In a few reports, notably the *Reports* of the Court of Justice of the European Communities and the *All England Law Reports Reprint*, the year used to number a volume is the year in which all the cases reported in that volume were decided.

*2.4.2.6 Choosing whether to use volume numbers or volume years*
Only the publisher of a law report can decide that it is to be cited by volume year.

The style of volume numbering to be used when citing a law report will normally be shown on the title-page or verso and on the spine of a bound volume, and often in running headlines on every opening.

Because only lawyers put square brackets round years it is sometimes thought that all law reports should be cited in that way and reference is made, for example, to a report in [1996] *The Times*. However, the only occasion when it is appropriate to put the year in square brackets is when it is being used as a volume identifier: square brackets are not put round a year just because it forms part of a legal citation. Unfortunately even some law-report publishers who adopt successive numbering of volumes recommend that a volume be cited not only by its volume number but also by the year of publication in square brackets: this is recommended, for example, by the publishers of *Medical Law Reports*. This confusion of the two systems of volume numbering means that, for example, [1996] 7 Med LR is not, as would be expected, the seventh of the 1996 volumes but the seventh volume of the whole series, which happened to be published in 1996.

Although the bound volume is the basic unit of a serial publication, most law reports and legal periodicals now being published appear initially in paper-covered 'parts' with the intention that a certain number of successive parts will be bound together to form a volume, the numbering of the pages continuing throughout the volume rather than beginning anew with each part. (In practice, a library may decide that what the publisher regards as one volume is actually too thick to be bound as a single book and may have it bound as two or more. On the other hand, some libraries save on binding costs by binding together in one volume what the publisher regards as two or more volumes.) Publishers of law reports usually sell complete volumes in their own bindings.

*Recommendation 2.12*

(a)   When citing a publication listed in the List of Recommended Forms of Citation for Law Reports and Other Publications in this book, identify the volume being cited in the way recommended for that publication in the list. The recommended form of citation for a publication shows whether to use a volume number, [volume year] (i.e., the volume year in square brackets), or volume year without brackets. If the volume year is to be used and a further number must be given because there is more than one volume a year then this is shown in the recommended form of citation and the notes state how many volumes there have been for each year so far.

(b)   When citing a publication which is not in that list, do not use a year to identify a volume unless that is the form of citation recommended in the publication itself.

(c)   No volume identifier is used in a citation of a publication (and none is shown for the publication in the List of Recommended Forms of Citation for Law Reports and Other Publications) if there has only ever been one volume of the publication.

### 2.4.2.7   *Continuously paginated works*

Sometimes, publishers who have issued law reports in more than one volume have numbered the pages continuously through all the volumes (that is, the pagination does not start again at 1 at the beginning of each volume). This was done, for example, when some of the early nominate reports were published in the seventeenth century. Strictly, if a page number is given in a citation of such a publication then the volume number is superfluous. Nevertheless it has traditionally been seen as a kindness to give the volume number when citing early reports published in this way, especially as binders did not state the pagination of volumes on their spines. The continued use of volume numbers when such reports are now only consulted in the *English Reports* where there is no physical separation of the volumes is defensible because the volume numbers appear in the running heads in the *English Reports* and because citations are traditionally edition-neutral (see section 2.11.1).

### 2.4.2.8   *Continuously paginated volumes*

Even though a volume is issued in parts, if the pagination is continuous (that is, it does not start again at 1 at the beginning of each part) then, when giving a page number, it is unnecessary to state which part the page is in. As it is usual for the parts to be bound together it is unnecessary to assist readers to choose which part to consult. Nevertheless the publishers of some periodicals which use volume-year numbering recommend that citations should give the issue number after the volume year as well as the page number of an item being cited, even though the issues are paginated continuously through the volume. Issue numbers seem to be superfluous in citations of such periodicals and this is indicated in the List of Recommended Forms of Citation for Law Reports and Other Publications.

### 2.4.2.9   *Giving a date when the year for which the volume is published is not the volume identifier*

### Recommendation 2.13

When citing a report in a volume of law reports which is not numbered by volume year, give the year in which judgment was delivered in the case, in parentheses, after the name of the case and before the law report citation.

*Example 2.44*
The case of *Craven* v *White* was decided by the House of Lords in 1988 and is reported in vol. 62 of *Reports of Tax Cases* and so may be cited as:

*Craven* v *White* (1988) 62 TC 1

The same case is reported in the volume of *Law Reports. House of Lords* for 1989, and if that report is cited, the citation is:

*Craven* v *White* [1989] AC 398

Volume 62 of *Reports of Tax Cases* was published in 1993 but the year of publication is not used to identify the volume, which is sufficiently identified by the number 62. But [1989] is the only way of identifying the volume of *Law Reports. House of Lords* in which the report appears: the volume is not numbered in any other way.

*Alternative to recommendation 2.13*

(a) Up to the end of the nineteenth century the date of decision of a case was rarely, if ever, given and could be omitted now.

(b) The publisher's bound volumes of reports which are intended to be cited by volume number may also give the date of publication on the spine. The date of publication of a volume is also commonly put on the spine of a library binding. Some people accordingly give that date rather than the date of decision of the case. However, it is not convenient to quote the date of publication of many older reports, especially if they are available only in modern editions such as the *English Reports,* and so the convention of quoting publication dates is undoubtedly not followed consistently. Recommendation 2.13 is intended to give consistent treatment of all cases in reports not numbered by volume year and is the convention followed in such reference books as the *Law Reports Index.*

*2.4.2.10* English Reports
All the nominate reports prior to the mid eighteenth century and all the authorised reports up to 1865 (apart from reports of cases in the Bail Court) were reprinted in the 176 volumes of the *English Reports* published from 1900 to 1930. The text of the original reports is printed without any rearrangement and the original pagination of each report is shown precisely. As most law libraries have few if any of the original editions of the nominate reports, most readers usually consult them in the *English Reports.* If one has a citation to a report which is reprinted in the *English Reports* then, as long as one knows which volume of the *English Reports* includes the cited volume of the original report (that information is given

in the List of Recommended Forms of Citation for Law Reports and Other Publications in this book), it is easy to find the relevant page from the running headlines at the top of the pages of the *English Reports*.

*Example 2.45*
*Waters* v *Taylor* (1808) is reported at 15 Ves Jr 10. Volumes 12–16 of Francis Vesey Junior's *Reports of Cases Argued and Determined in the High Court of Chancery* are reprinted in vol. 33 of the *English Reports*. *Waters* v *Taylor* (1808) 15 Ves Jr 10 will be found on p. 658 of 33 ER. So *Waters* v *Taylor* can be cited as *Waters* v *Taylor* (1808) 33 ER 658.

Where a report of a case is reprinted in the *English Reports*, the reference to the volume and page number in the *English Reports* is commonly given as a second, parallel citation (often only in a table of cases), but, in England at least, it is still customary to cite primarily the volume and page number of the original edition.

### 2.4.3   Citing law reports in newspapers

In England, law reports signed by barristers appear in the *Daily Telegraph*, *Financial Times*, *Guardian* and *Independent* newspapers. Law reports in *The Times* are not signed but occasionally a note is published that they are 'supplied by barristers of the Incorporated Council of Law Reporting for England and Wales'.

*Recommendation 2.14*
Cite a law report in a newspaper by the title of the newspaper followed by the date of the issue in which the report appeared (not the date of the judgment). Put the year in which judgment was given in the case in parentheses after the name of the case.

*Example 2.46*
*Secretary of State for Trade and Industry* v *Arif* (1995) *The Times*, 25 March 1996

*Alternative to recommendation 2.14*
The recommendation to give the year of decision is so that citations of newspaper reports are in a form that is consistent with citations of other reports (see recommendation 2.13). However, the year of decision is often not given.

A news report of a case is not an authoritative law report and may have been prepared without appreciation of the legal significance of what is being reported. A news report may be cited by giving the title of the newspaper and the date of the issue with a phrase such as '(news item)'.

### 2.4.4   Citing cases in yearbooks

*Recommendation 2.15*

(a)   Cite a yearbook case in the form:

(calendar year of hearing) YB regnal year (edition if not the standard edition), folio number (preceded by f.) or page number (preceded by p.) depending on edition, term, placitum number (preceded by pl.) if there is one

(b)   The principal series of modern editions may be indicated by the following abbreviations:

(AF) Ames Foundation
(RS) Rolls Series
(SS) Publications of the Selden Society

(c)   Names of terms may be abbreviated as follows:

| | |
|---|---|
| Easter | Pasc. |
| Hilary | Hil. |
| Michaelmas | Mich. |
| Trinity | Trin. |

*Example 2.47*
(1491) YB 21 Edw IV, f. 12, Mich., pl. 4

*Alternative to recommendation 2.15*
The recommendation to include the calendar year of a case makes citations of cases from yearbooks consistent with citations from other reports (see recommendation 2.13). However, it was not customary in the past and would probably not be done now in specialist studies. (It is clear that some of the old printed editions have been arbitrarily divided into terms or include cases which have been assigned to the wrong term and/or year.) Other abbreviations for terms are in use.

### 2.5   LAW TERMS

Reports of cases up to the reorganisation of the superior courts in 1875 often date cases by law term and regnal year, and early reports do not give

(d) In some reports each case has an item number which is cited instead of a page number.

(e) The number of the page (or folio etc.) is not preceded by any description such as 'page' or 'p.'.

The List of Recommended Forms of Citation for Law Reports and Other Publications in this book states for each report whether citation is by page, folio, column, item etc.

*Example 2.50*
In the report of *R* v *Boal* in [1992] QB, the judgment of the Court of Appeal starts at p. 594. It is preceded by the indexing keywords, headnote etc. and the heading for the case is on p. 591. So it is cited as:

*R* v *Boal* [1992] QB 591

The report of *Re City Equitable Fire Insurance Co. Ltd* in [1925] Ch reports proceedings both at first instance in the Chancery Division of the High Court and on appeal in the Court of Appeal. The heading of the case is on p. 407 so the report is cited as:

*Re City Equitable Fire Insurance Co. Ltd* [1925] Ch 407

The report of proceedings in the Court of Appeal starts (with a report of the arguments) at p. 500 and may be cited as:

*Re City Equitable Fire Insurance Co. Ltd* [1925] Ch 407 at 500

The additional information about the starting point of the Court of Appeal proceedings is not essential and those proceedings could alternatively be cited as:

*Re City Equitable Fire Insurance Co. Ltd* [1925] Ch 407

The report of *Niger Merchants Co.* v *Capper* in 18 ChD is printed as a footnote to the report of *Cercle Restaurant Castiglione Co.* v *Lavery* (which starts at p. 555). The footnote is at the foot of pp. 557–9 and is cited as:

*Niger Merchants Co.* v *Capper* (1877) 18 ChD 557 n

## 2.7 IDENTIFICATION OF COURT

In Britain, unlike the USA, when citing a case it is not considered essential to identify the court in which it was decided. However, this is often done, if only for appellate decisions.

*Recommendation 2.17*
If the identity of the court in which a cited case was decided is to be added to the case citation then do so by putting the name of the court, or the relevant abbreviation from table 2.1, after the law report reference.

*Table 2.1    Recommended abbreviations for names of courts*

| Abbreviation | Court |
|---|---|
| CA | Court of Appeal |
| CCA | Court of Criminal Appeal |
| CCR | Court for Crown Cases Reserved |
| ChD | Chancery Division |
| ChDC | Divisional Court of the Chancery Division |
| CFI | Court of First Instance of the European Communities |
| C-MAC | Courts-Martial Appeal Court |
| CP | Common Pleas |
| CPD | Common Pleas Division |
| CPDC | Divisional Court of the Common Pleas Division |
| CSess 1st Div | Court of Session First Division |
| CSess 2nd Div | Court of Session Second Division |
| CSess Ex Div | Court of Session Extra Division |
| CSess IH | Court of Session Inner House |
| CSess OH | Court of Session Outer House |
| DC | Divisional Court |
| EAT | Employment Appeal Tribunal |
| ECJ | Court of Justice of the European Communities |
| Ex | Exchequer |
| ExCh | Exchequer Chamber |
| ExD | Exchequer Division |
| ExDC | Divisional Court of the Exchequer Division |
| FamD | Family Division |
| FC | Full Court |
| HC | High Court |
| HL | House of Lords |
| KB | King's Bench |
| KBD | King's Bench Division |
| KBDC | Divisional Court of the King's Bench Division |
| LC | Lord Chancellor |
| LJJ | Lords Justices and/or Lord Chancellor forming Court of Appeal in Chancery |
| MR | Master of the Rolls |
| NP | Nisi Prius |

| Abbreviation | Court |
|---|---|
| PC | Privy Council |
| PDAD | Probate Divorce and Admiralty Division |
| QB | Queen's Bench |
| QBD | Queen's Bench Division |
| QBDC | Divisional Court of the Queen's Bench Division |
| RPCt | Restrictive Practices Court |
| SC | Supreme Court |
| ShCt | Sheriff Court |
| V-C | Vice-Chancellor |

*Example 2.51*
*Salomon v A. Salomon and Co. Ltd* [1897] AC 22, HL

*Alternative to recommendation 2.17*
Instead of using a comma, put the name or abbreviation in parentheses.
Many other abbreviations of court names are in use.

## 2.8   PARALLEL CITATIONS

Sometimes more than one law report of a case is cited. If the cited reports
have significantly different headings it may be helpful to indicate this,
either because the reader may be more familiar with an alternative name
for the case or to confirm that the report, though differently headed, is the
one intended. An alternative name is usually preceded by 'sub nom.', an
abbreviation of the Latin *'sub nomine'* (meaning 'under the name').

*Recommendation 2.18*

(a)   Set out parallel citations as in example 2.52.

*Example 2.52*
*Re Steel Wing Co. Ltd* [1921] 1 Ch 349, 90 LJ Ch 116 (sub nom. *Re Steel
Ring Co.*)

(b)   Where different stages of a case are cited use a semicolon to
separate them, as in example 2.53.

*Example 2.53*
*Salomon v A. Salomon and Co. Ltd* [1897] AC 22, 66 LJ Ch 35, HL; [1895]
2 Ch 323 (sub nom. *Broderip v Salomon*), ChD and CA

*Alternative to recommendation 2.18(a)*
A semicolon may be used instead of a comma, but it is recommended that
the semicolon be reserved for separating different stages.

## 2.9  CONSOLIDATED CASES

When several different cases are heard together, especially on appeal, the
court may divide its judgment into sections dealing with each case separately.
Although the whole case is cited by the name of the case given first in the
heading, one of the other cases may be cited in the form given in example 2.54.

> *Example 2.54*
> Six joined appeals are reported together at [1994] Ch 205. The first
> named is *Ridehalgh* v *Horsefield* and so the report is cited by that case
> name. But if attention is to be drawn to another of the appeals then the
> citation may be in the form:
>
> *Philex plc* v *Golban* reported with *Ridehalgh* v *Horsefield* [1994] Ch 205

## 2.10  CITING A POINT IN A REPORT

A point in a report is cited by giving its page number after the number of
the page where the report starts. Many reports are printed with letters at
the side of each page which can be used to identify a position on the page,
but in practice the letters usually have an annoyingly imprecise relationship with the passage sought to be identified.

*Recommendation 2.19*

   (a)   To cite a particular page within a report of a case give the citation
of the case followed by 'at p.' and the page number. Marginal letters may
be added to define a place on a page.
   (b)   To cite a passage extending over two or more pages use 'pp.' instead
of 'p.' and give the first and last pages of the passage. It is not adequate to
state just the first page plus 'ff.' (meaning 'following pages') or 'et seq.',
either of which invite reading the rest of the volume.
   (c)   If a citation of a point in a case immediately follows a citation of the
case itself, or a citation of another point in the same case, the case citation
can be omitted on the second occasion.
   (d)   If the report has numbered columns or folios instead of pages, use
'col.' (plural 'coll.') or 'f.' (plural 'ff.') as appropriate instead of 'p.'.

   The List of Recommended Forms of Citation for Law Reports and Other
Publications in this book states for each report whether citation is by page,
folio, column, item etc.

*Example 2.55*
*Daimler Co. Ltd* v *Continental Tyre and Rubber Co. (Great Britain) Ltd*
[1916] 2 AC 307 at p. 338
*J.H. Rayner (Mincing Lane) Ltd* v *Department of Trade and Industry*
[1990] 2 AC 418 at pp. 479–80
*R* v *Birmingham Justices, ex parte Hodgson* [1985] QB 1131 at p. 1140A–C
This point was considered in *Daimler Co. Ltd* v *Continental Tyre and
Rubber Co. (Great Britain) Ltd* [1916] 2 AC 307 in which it was said (at
p. 338) . . .

*Alternative to recommendation 2.19*

(a)   Omit the space after 'p.' or 'pp.'
(b)   Use a comma instead of 'at p.' or 'at pp.'.

## 2.11   EDITION AND MEDIUM-NEUTRAL CITATIONS

### 2.11.1 Edition-neutral citations

Throughout the history of printed law reports it has been usual to show in
each new edition of a report the pagination of the first edition and it is that
pagination which is used for citation. Accordingly, it is unnecessary to
state which edition of a law report is being cited. For the few older reports
where a second or later edition was substantially altered and does not show
the pagination of the first edition, there is usually a particular edition
which is regarded as the standard and it is the pagination of that edition
which is cited. For a report included in the *English Reports*, the pagination
shown there can be taken to be standard and can be used for citation. If it
is necessary to specify which edition of a report is being cited, this can be
done by adding the edition number or date (in parentheses) after the
abbreviation of the report.

### 2.11.2 Medium-neutral citations

When reports which have appeared as printed books also appear in other
media, such as microfilm or CD-ROM, the pagination of the printed book
is usually shown and is used for citation. Accordingly, it is unnecessary to
specify a medium in a citation of a particular report of a case.

   In the USA it has been proposed that citations of cases should not refer
to particular reports (see section 2.17.2). Such citations are described as
'vendor-neutral'. They are also 'medium-neutral' in the sense that it is
unnecessary to specify a medium in a citation of a particular case, rather
than a particular report of a case.

## 2.12  JUDGES

### 2.12.1  Per

The traditional way of identifying the judge or judges whose decision or opinion is being cited is by using the word 'per' followed by the name of the judge or judges. If short conventional signals are italicised (which is not recommended here, see section 1.7) then 'per' is italicised. Some people prefer to use 'by'.

If the judge was giving the judgment of a multi-judge court then that fact may be stated (though it often is not). If the opinion was given during argument rather than in a judgment then that fact should be stated because it affects the authority of the remark. The headnote to a report is the work of the reporter not the court and should not be quoted or cited as representing the judgment or opinion of the court.

*Example 2.56*
*J.H. Rayner (Mincing Lane) Ltd* v *Department of Trade and Industry* [1990] 2 AC 418 per Lord Templeman at pp. 479–80
*Daimler Co. Ltd* v *Continental Tyre and Rubber Co. (Great Britain) Ltd* [1916] 2 AC 307 at p. 338 per Lord Parker of Waddington
per Lord Oliver of Aylmerton in *J.H. Rayner (Mincing Lane) Ltd* v *Department of Trade and Industry* [1990] 2 AC 418 at p. 511
*North-West Transportation Co. Ltd* v *Beatty* (1887) 12 App Cas 589 at pp. 593–4 per Sir Richard Baggallay giving the judgment of the Privy Council
per Maugham J during argument in *Re Beni-Felkai Mining Co. Ltd* [1934] Ch 406 at p. 414

The Latin word *'arguendo'* is sometimes used meaning 'during argument'.

### 2.12.2  Judges' names

The correct name of a judge delivering a judgment and his or her judicial office are usually to be found at the beginning of the judgment. The following notes explain the conventions involved.

In legal writing, a judge is normally referred to by surname (or title if the judge is a peer) with an indication of the judicial post held or exercised. Most of the judicial offices are indicated by an abbreviation placed after the judge's name. When referring to a judge in connection with a case which the judge heard, the office to be given is the one held at the time of the hearing.

*Recommendation 2.20*
The recommended abbreviations for judicial offices in England and Wales (including some now abolished) are shown in table 2.2.

*Table 2.2   Judicial offices*

| Office | Abbreviation used in legal writing and placed after the surname | Description used in other contexts and placed before the surname |
| --- | --- | --- |
| baron of the Exchequer | B | Mr Baron |
| Chief Baron | CB | |
| Lord Chief Justice | CJ | |
| Chief Justice of the Common Pleas | CJCP | |
| Chief Justice of the King's Bench | CJKB | |
| Chief Justice of the Queen's Bench | CJQB | |
| circuit judge | | Judge |
| justice of the High Court | J | Mr/Mrs Justice |
| Lord Chancellor | LC | |
| Lord Justice of Appeal | LJ | Lord Justice |
| Lord Keeper of the Great Seal | LK | Lord Keeper |
| master | | Master |
| Master of the Rolls | MR | |
| President of the Family Division (since 1971) | P | |
| President of the Probate, Divorce and Admiralty Division (1875 to 1971) | P | |
| registrar | | Mr/Mrs Registrar |
| Vice-Chancellor | V-C | |

*Example 2.57*
A judge who is not a peer: French J
A judge who is a peer: Lord Taylor of Gosforth CJ

In a reference to two judges holding the same office the abbreviation is usually put only after the second name but with the last letter doubled.

*Example 2.57*
French and Judge JJ (Mr Justice French and Mr Justice Judge)
Goff and Bridge LJJ (Lord Justice Goff and Lord Justice Bridge)

*Alternative to recommendation 2.20*
When referring to a Vice-Chancellor or a Master of the Rolls who is not a peer, many people use the abbreviation after the name but put the name in full:

> Sir Raymond Evershed MR
> Sir Robert Megarry V-C

Some judges have preferred to be known by a combination of a forename and surname, for example, Vaughan Williams LJ, Swinfen Eady MR and Edmund Davies LJ (who changed his surname by deed poll to Edmund-Davies when made a lord of appeal). Sometimes it is necessary to use forenames to distinguish two judges with the same surname, for example, Peter Gibson J and Ralph Gibson J.

Where no abbreviation is given in the second column of table 2.2, the form of address given in the third column is used in legal writing.

*Example 2.59*
Judge Eric Stockdale (a circuit judge)
Mr Registrar Buckley (Companies Court registrar)
Master Cholmondeley Clarke (a Supreme Court master)

*2.12.2.1   Extra-curial reference*
The form of address given in the third column of table 2.2 may be used when referring to a statement made by a judge extra-curially (when not sitting in court).

*Example 2.60*
In an article in the *Law Quarterly Review*, Mr Justice Millett said . . .

Where no form of address is shown in the third column the title must be given in apposition before or after the judge's full name.

*Example 2.61*
At a press conference, the Lord Chancellor, Lord Mackay of Clashfern, said . . .

Sir Thomas Bingham, the Master of the Rolls

A justice of the High Court is automatically made a knight or dame on appointment (supposedly to avoid suspicion that the honour could be a reward for favouring the government when on the bench) but is nevertheless referred to as 'Mr Justice ———' or 'Mrs Justice ———'.

### 2.12.2.2 Lord of appeal (Law Lord)
A lord of appeal (Law Lord) is a peer who is referred to by peerage title.

*Example 2.62*
Lord Goff of Chieveley

### 2.12.2.3 Members of the Judicial Committee of the Privy Council
Members of the Judicial Committee of the Privy Council are referred to by full name or peerage title.

*Example 2.63*
The judgment of the Privy Council in *North-West Transportation Co. Ltd* v *Beatty* (1887) 12 App Cas 589 was delivered by:

Sir Richard Baggallay

Sir Richard had formerly been a Lord Justice of Appeal.
    The appeal from Hong Kong in *Luc Thiet Tuan* v *The Queen* [1996] 3 WLR 45 was heard by:

Lord Goff of Chieveley, Lord Steyn, Sir Brian Hutton and Sir Michael Hardie Boys

Lords Goff and Steyn are Law Lords; Sir Brian Hutton is Lord Chief Justice of Northern Ireland; Sir Michael Hardie Boys is a retired judge of the New Zealand Court of Appeal.

There were also, from 1871 to 1890, four salaried members of the Privy Council who are referred to by full name.

*Example 2.64*
Sir Barnes Peacock

### 2.12.2.4 Other judicial officers
Other judicial officers, such as district judges or magistrates may be referred to by office and name.

*Example 2.65*
the stipendiary magistrate, Sir Bryan Roberts QC

### 2.12.2.5 Deputy High Court judge
A barrister sitting as a deputy High Court judge is referred to by full name followed by 'sitting as a deputy High Court judge'.

*Example 2.66*
*Re Biddencare Ltd* [1993] BCC 757 was heard by:

Mary Arden QC sitting as a deputy High Court judge

*2.12.2.6   Circuit judge sitting in the High Court*
A circuit judge sitting in the High Court sits as a High Court judge, not a deputy, and should be described as such.

*Example 2.67*
*Elliott* v *Safeway Stores plc* [1995] 1 WLR 1396 was heard by:

Judge Paul Baker QC sitting as a High Court judge

*2.12.2.7   Retired judge*
A former High Court or Court of Appeal judge who sits in any court after retirement is referred to by full name (or title if a peer). This may be followed by an indication of the judicial office exercised.

*Example 2.68*
*A Ltd* v *B Ltd* [1996] 1 WLR 665 was heard by:

Sir John Vinelott sitting as a High Court judge

Sir John was a High Court judge from 1978 until his retirement in 1994.

### 2.12.3   Abbreviated reference after first mention

After the first mention of his or her name, a judge of the High Court, Court of Appeal or House of Lords may be referred to as 'his lordship' or 'her ladyship', a circuit judge may be referred to as 'his/her honour'. Other judicial officers may be referred to by the name of the office, prefixed (except for lay magistrates) with 'learned'.

*Example 2.69*
the learned stipendiary magistrate
the learned deputy judge

The phrase 'the learned judge' can also be used for a High Court judge sitting at first instance.

## 2.12.4 Titles of peers

Peers who hold judicial office are usually barons, which is indicated by putting 'Lord' before the baronial title.

*Example 2.70*
Lord Bingham of Cornhill CJ

A judicial peer of higher rank is usually referred to by the full title of the peerage but without numeration.

*Example 2.71*
Earl of Selborne LC
Viscount Dilhorne (a Law Lord 1969–80)
Viscount Colville of Culross QC (a circuit judge)

The title of a peer is usually a single surname but where there are two or more titles with the same surname, all those created after the first have a territorial designation added to distinguish them. For example, the title of Sir Peter Taylor (who was Lord Chief Justice from 1992 to 1996) is Lord Taylor of Gosforth to distinguish it from the titles of Lord Taylor, Lord Taylor of Mansfield, Lord Taylor of Gryfe, Lord Taylor of Blackburn and Lord Taylor of Hadfield.

## 2.12.5 Subsequent promotion

When discussing a pronouncement made by a judge at a particular time, the judicial office and, where relevant, peerage title *at that time* must be used.

*Example 2.72*
Lord Denning was:

Denning J (1944–8)
Denning LJ (1948–57)
Lord Denning (1957–62)
Lord Denning MR (1962–82)

So in a discussion of his lordship's views on the standard of proof expressed in *Miller* v *Minister of Pensions* [1947] 2 All ER 372 he is referred to as Denning J.

If necessary the phrase '(as he then was)' can be used, but this can easily become irritating if used too often, and, to avoid giving offence, requires examining the career of every judge mentioned to see if he or she was subsequently promoted.

### 2.12.6 Scotland

In Scotland, judicial office is not indicated by abbreviations. A judge of the Court of Session is given the courtesy title 'Lord ———' or 'Lady ———' using the judge's surname or the name of the judge's landed estate. The judge continues to use this title after retirement. A judge of the Court of Session is not automatically made a knight or dame on appointment.

### 2.12.7 Employment Appeal Tribunal and Restrictive Practices Court

Judges who sit in the Employment Appeal Tribunal or Restrictive Practices Court are referred to by their usual judicial titles; lay members are referred to by their full names.

### 2.13 CHOOSING WHICH REPORT TO CITE

The courts have repeatedly made clear that they favour the use of the *Law Reports* published by the Incorporated Council of Law Reporting for England and Wales. The most recent statement was in *Practice Direction (Court of Appeal: Citation of Authority)* [1995] 1 WLR 1096:

> When authority is cited, whether in written or oral submissions, the following practice should in general be followed.
>
> If a case is reported in the official *Law Reports* published by the Incorporated Council of Law Reporting for England and Wales, that report should be cited. These are the most authoritative reports; they contain a summary of argument; and they are the most readily available [that is, to the court].
>
> If a case is not (or not yet) reported in the official *Law Reports*, but is reported in the *Weekly Law Reports* or the *All England Law Reports*, that report should be cited.
>
> If a case is not reported in any of these series of reports, a report in any of the authoritative specialist series of reports may be cited. . . .
>
> It is recognised that occasions arise when one report is fuller than another, or when there are discrepancies between reports. On such occasions, the practice outlined above need not be followed. It is always helpful if alternative references are given.

In other contexts the choice of report to be cited may be dictated by the person for whom the document is being prepared, for example, a publisher of law reports may like to have its reports cited in other works it publishes. Otherwise a full report is usually to be preferred to an abbreviated one. In many areas of law virtually all the cases to be cited in a document will be found in a few specialist series specialising in that area and it will be convenient to cite them. For the period back to 1865, if a case is not reported in the *Law Reports*, then the alternative series of general reports are usually ranked in the order *All England Law Reports*, *Law Journal Reports*, *Law Times Reports*, *Times Law Reports*, but a report in one of the long-established specialist series such as the *Criminal Appeal Reports* would probably be preferred to a report in one of the general series. Before 1865, going back to the mid eighteenth century, the reports printed in the *English Reports* are preferred both because they are generally accessible and because they were considered authoritative at the time. For earlier periods some awareness of the variable quality of law reports is required. Wallace's book, cited in 2.2.2.1, is full of valuable information on the reporters of that period.

## 2.14 UNREPORTED CASES

If no report of a case has been published, its name is followed by '(unreported)' instead of a law report reference. The name of the court or tribunal and the date of the decision should be provided. If a transcript is available then information sufficient to identify the transcript, such as a Court of Appeal transcript number, should be given. If the case is known only because it has been cited elsewhere, such as in a judgment or an article, then that source should be cited.

### 2.14.1 Further reading

Victor Tunkel, 'Available at last: the Court of Appeal transcripts' (1986) 136 NLJ 1045.

## 2.15 EUROPEAN CASES

Cases before the Court of Justice and the Court of First Instance of the European Communities are given case numbers by the court registrar. The number of a case in the Court of First Instance is prefixed by 'T-'. The number of any case heard in the Court of Justice since the Court of First Instance was established (November 1989) is prefixed by 'C-'. The 'C-' prefix is not used for cases in which judgment was delivered before 16 November 1989. An interim application in a case has the number of the case followed by 'R'. Some case numbers have other suffixes, including DEP, Imm, P, REV and S-A.

*Example 2.73*
*Centrafarm BV* v *Winthrop BV* (case 16/74) [1974] ECR 1183
*Industrie des poudres sphériques* v *Council of the European Union* (case T-2/95 R) [1995] ECR II-485
*Powell Duffryn plc* v *Petereit* (case C-214/89) [1992] ECR I-1745
*Viho Europe BV* v *Commission* (case T-102/92) [1995] ECR II-17

A report of joined cases is cited by the name of only the first case listed but with the numbers of all the cases.

*Example 2.74*
The heading of the case reported at [1996] All ER (EC) 301 is:

Brasserie du Pêcheur SA v Germany
R and others v Secretary of State for Transport, ex p Factortame Ltd
(Joined cases C-46/93 and C-48/93)

It is cited as:

*Brasserie du Pêcheur SA* v *Germany* (cases C-46 and 48/93) [1996] All ER (EC) 301

The Court of Justice may also be asked to give an opinion on a proposed agreement between the European Community and one or more States or international organisations.

*Example 2.75*
*Opinion 1 / 94* [1994] ECR I-5267

What are called 'offset copies' of the typescript texts of judgments, orders and opinions of the Court of Justice are made available by the court registrar, soon after being delivered by the court. Judgments and orders of the Court of First Instance are made available in the same way.

*Recommendation 2.21*
If a report of a judgment, order or opinion of the Court of Justice or First Instance of the European Communities is available only in offset copies, cite the case by name and case number followed by a comma and the phrase 'judgment of' (or 'opinion of' or 'order of' as appropriate) and the date.

*Example 2.76*
*Blackspur DIY Ltd* v *Council* (case T-168/94) judgment of 18 September
1995

## 2.16  COMMONWEALTH CASES

Law reporting in the Commonwealth has followed the same course as in
England. There were nominate reports in the eighteenth and early
nineteenth centuries devoted to particular courts. From the mid nineteenth century onwards these were replaced by general reports such as the
*Dominion Law Reports* in Canada and the *New Zealand Law Reports*. In
the twentieth century, many series have been established devoted to
particular subjects, such as the *Australian Corporations and Securities
Reports*. Citation follows English practice. Many Commonwealth reports
have used volume-year numbering, usually with the year in square
brackets, but only a few do so at present. One Canadian innovation, which
might be welcomed elsewhere, is to give in the heading to a report a note
of the name under which it is to be cited, following rules agreed by all
Canadian law report publishers.

### 2.16.1  Further reading

McGill Law Journal, *Canadian Guide to Uniform Legal Citation*, 3rd ed.
(Scarborough, Ontario: Carswell, 1992).
University of London Institute of Advanced Legal Studies, *Manual of
Legal Citations. Part II: The British Commonwealth* (London: the Insti-
tute, 1960).

## 2.17  UNITED STATES CASES

### 2.17.1  Current US citation practice

More attention has been given to devising rules for legal citation in the
USA than anywhere else in the world. One result is *The Bluebook. A
Uniform System of Citation*, 15th ed. (Cambridge Mass: Harvard Law
Review Association, 1991). This is an elaborate legal style manual, which
requires careful consultation. One immediately noticeable difference
between current English and US practice is that in the USA it is customary
to state the date of a decision after the law report citation, not before it,
and to state the court giving the decision (unless the reporter cited reports
only one court).

*Example 2.77*
*West Publishing Co.* v. *Mead Data Central Inc.*, 799 F.2d 1219 (8th Cir. 1986)

The case was decided by the United States Court of Appeals, Eighth Circuit. The punctuation and typography of this example follow the rules of *The Bluebook*.

When citing United States cases in a document in which mostly non-US cases are cited there is inevitably a conflict between a desire for consistency (which would favour putting the date before the law-report citation) and an awareness of how odd case citations look when they are not in an expected style (an awareness that is enhanced by seeing English cases cited in the American fashion).

*2.17.1.1   Further reading*
The detail and complexity of *The Bluebook* cause much exasperation. See, for example:
James D. Gordon III, 'Oh no! A new *Bluebook*' (1992) 90 Mich L Rev 1698.
*The Bluebook* is by far the most widely used US legal style manual, but there are alternatives, including:
*University of Chicago Manual of Legal Citation* (Rochester, NY: Lawyers Co-operative Publishing Co., 1989). Also known as the 'Maroon Book'.

**2.17.2 Vendor-neutral citations**

A significant problem with a requirement that a particular series of reports must be cited is that it is not possible to cite a point within an alternative report, using the pagination of that alternative report: the pagination of the required report must be known. Some publishers in the USA, whose reports are not the ones required for citation, have indicated in their reports the pagination of the required reports. Traditionally these page numbers are marked with asterisks and so the system is known as 'star pagination'. In the late 1980s, West Publishing Co., which publishes most of the reports to which citation is required, asserted copyright in the pagination of its publications and demanded fees for licensing other publishers to star-paginate to West reports. In reaction against this it has been proposed that courts should provide their written judgments with paragraph numbers and that the standard form of citation of a US case should be:

case name, year of decision, court, opinion number, paragraph number

(The paragraph number is required only for a reference to a point within the judgment.) This form of citation is described as 'vendor-neutral'. This proposal gives primacy to the written judgment of the court, whereas the current system of citation gives primacy to the report of a judgment and originates from a time when judgments were delivered orally.

*2.17.2.1 Further reading*
L. Ray Patterson and Craig Joyce, 'Monopolizing the law: the scope of copyright protection for law reports and statutory compilations' (1989) 36 UCLA L Rev 719.
'The Final Report of the Task Force on Citation Formats' (1995) 87 Law Libr J 577.

### 2.18 CITING MORE THAN ONE CASE

*Recommendation 2.22*

(a)   If more than one case is cited then cite them in order of decision with a semicolon between each.
(b)   Any cases covered by a comment on relevance which does not apply to others may be listed after the others.
(c)   A brief description of a case may be added in parentheses after its citation.

*Example 2.78*

(a)   The question whether the winding up of a solvent company should be voluntary or compulsory is essentially one for the members to decide (*Re Beaujolais Wine Co.* (1867) LR 3 Ch App 15 at pp. 19–20; *Re London Flour Co. Ltd* (1868) 19 LT 136; *Re Madras Coffee Co. Ltd* (1869) 17 WR 643; *Re British Asahan Plantations Co. Ltd* (1892) 36 SJ 363).
(b)   In determining whether there is a majority opposing, the court may discount the views of persons connected with the company, for example, as directors, shareholders or associated companies (*Re R. and H. Grossmark Ltd* (1968) 112 SJ 416; *Re Falcon RJ Developments Ltd* (1987) 3 BCC 146; and see *Re Lowerstoft Traffic Services Ltd* [1986] BCLC 81 per Hoffmann J at p. 84 and *Re MCH Services Ltd* (1987) 3 BCC 179).
(c)   A distress put in before the commencement of a winding up (whether voluntary or compulsory) will be allowed to proceed unless there are special circumstances rendering it inequitable for the creditor to have the benefit of the proceedings (*Re Roundwood Colliery Co.* [1897] 1 Ch 373 (voluntary winding up); *Venner's Electrical Cooking and*

*Heating Appliances Ltd* v *Thorpe* [1915] 2 Ch 404 (voluntary winding up but petition for compulsory winding up also presented); *Re Bellaglade Ltd* [1977] 1 All ER 319 (petition pending); *Herbert Berry Associates Ltd* v *Commissioners of Inland Revenue* [1977] 1 WLR 1437 (voluntary winding up); *Re Memco Engineering Ltd* [1986] Ch 86 (winding-up order made).

## 2.19  TABLE OF CASES

A table of cases for a document lists every case cited in the document. Against each case there is a list of all the places in the document where the case is cited. The table does not go into detail about which points within each case have been cited.

Cases are listed in alphabetical order of name. The case names as they appear in the document are altered slightly for the table of cases so as to conform with established rules for alphabetically ordering names. Also, in a table of cases, the case names are not italicised.

(a)   The word '*Re*' together with any following definite or indefinite article are transposed to the end of the part of the name to which it refers.

*Example 2.79*
*Re an Inquiry under the Company Securities (Insider Dealing) Act 1985* [1988] AC 660 is listed as:

Inquiry under the Company Securities (Insider Dealing) Act 1985, re an [1988] AC 660

*Re Tucker, ex parte Tucker* [1990] Ch 148 is listed as:

Tucker, re, ex parte Tucker [1990] Ch 148

*Re a Company (No. 007923 of 1994)* [1995] 1 WLR 953 is listed as:

Company, re a (No. 007923 of 1994) [1995] 1 WLR 953

*Re Bank of Credit and Commerce International SA (No. 10)* [1995] 1 BCLC 362 is listed as:

Bank of Credit and Commerce International SA, re (No. 10) [1995] 1 BCLC 362

(b)   The definite article at the beginning of a ship's name is transposed to the end of that name.

*Example 2.80*
*The Zafiro* [1960] P 1 is listed as:

Zafiro, the [1960] P 1

(c)   *'Ex parte'* at the beginning of a name is transposed to the end of the name of the party it introduces.

*Example 2.81*
*Ex parte Coventry Newspapers Ltd* [1993] QB 278 is listed as:

Coventry Newspapers Ltd, ex parte [1993] QB 278

(d)   If a party is a firm or company with a name which includes an individual's surname and initials then the initials are put in parentheses after the surname.

*Example 2.82*
*Re J. Burrows (Leeds) Ltd*[1982] 1 WLR 1177 is listed as:

Burrows (J.) (Leeds) Ltd, re [1982] 1 WLR 1177

It used to be the practice to treat an unabbreviated forename in the same way but this is not now recommended.

It may be necessary to list separately cases which are not cited by name, such as decisions of the Social Security Commissioner. Cases in the Court of Justice and Court of First Instance of the European Communities may be listed both in the alphabetical table and in a separate table in numerical order of case number (within year). Otherwise, cases from different jurisdictions are usually listed together.

A table of cases may give parallel citations which are not given in the text of the document.

# 3  ACTS OF PARLIAMENT

## 3.1  INTRODUCTION

The legislation presently in force in England was enacted by Parliament over a period of more than 700 years. During that time there have been great changes in the format of legislation and in the way it is cited. This chapter covers various forms of citation but in practice the most important is citation by short title, which is used for nearly all Acts currently in force. The other important method of citation is by chapter number, which was used before short titles were invented. Citation by chapter number may be needed for Acts no longer in force, is useful for tracing the text of Acts and in principle can be used for citing almost any Act.

## 3.2  PUBLICATION OF ACTS

### 3.2.1  Text as enacted

From at least the thirteenth century, laws were promulgated by sending copies to sheriffs and justices for public proclamation. The secretariat responsible for writing these copies was the royal chancery, which kept its own copies of statutes. Surviving chancery records in the form of parchment rolls seem to date from at least 1299 and are now kept at the Public Record Office in Chancery Lane, London WC2A 1LR. Copies of statutes are also made by Parliamentary officials and kept in the Record Office in the Victoria Tower of the Palace of Westminster. The practice of depositing archival copies of Acts in the Parliamentary and Public Record Offices continues to the present day, though, since 1845, they have been copies of the printed editions rather than manuscript copies on parchment rolls.

Statutes began to be printed soon after the introduction of printing into England in 1476. A collection of statutes from Magna Carta to 1455 was printed about 1481, probably by John Lettou and William Machlinia, and, about 1486, Machlinia (probably) published the statutes of Richard III.

The Crown began to claim control over printing soon after it was introduced into England and, in particular, claimed control over the printing of Acts of Parliament, granting a monopoly on printing them to a Queen's (or King's) Printer of Acts of Parliament, though initially at least this monopoly was thought to cover only the statutes enacted in the current sovereign's reign and not collections of older Acts. Despite the declaration in the Bill of Rights (1688) that the Crown could not grant monopolies (except for patents for inventions), the appointment of a King's Printer was continued and the Crown's right to grant a monopoly for statute printing was upheld in *Miller* v *Taylor* (1769) 4 Burr 2303 and *Manners* v *Blair* (1828) 3 Bli NS 391.

Since 1889, the office of Queen's Printer has been held by the Controller of Her Majesty's Stationery Office (HMSO). Copies of Acts printed by the Queen's Printer (and known accordingly as 'Queen's Printer's copies') have always been regarded as providing authentic texts, though there is no statutory authority for this (except with regard to some private Acts), and ultimately the only authentic texts are in the Parliamentary archives, which the courts have consulted occasionally when there has been doubt about the accuracy of the Queen's Printer's copy (see, for example, *R* v *Overseers of Haslingfield* (1874) LR 9 QB 203 at p. 209).

The present system of publication of Queen's Printer's copies is that HMSO publishes the text of each Act individually as enacted, shortly after royal assent. HMSO will continue to sell and reprint an Act in this individual format as originally enacted as long as there is a demand for it. All the Acts passed in a calendar year are published together after the end of the year, either in *Public General Acts and Church Assembly Measures* or in *Local and Personal Acts* (which was titled *Local and Private Acts* before 1948). Before 1940 regular collections contained not the Acts for a calendar year but the Acts for a session of Parliament. Sessions were numbered by regnal year as explained in section 4.1. Church Assembly Measures were first included in the volume for the session 16 & 17 Geo 5. Before then, *Public General Acts and Church Assembly Measures* was titled *Public General Acts*.

The practice of publishing a collection of Acts enacted by each session of Parliament started at least as early as the beginning of Henry VIII's reign.

In 1800 a royal commission was appointed to investigate public records and it resolved to prepare a complete edition of legislation of England and Great Britain, which was published as *The Statutes of the Realm* (11 vols, 1810–28), usually known as the Record Commission edition. It includes complete texts of all Acts which the commissioners could find, enacted up to the end of 1713, including expired and repealed Acts. Volumes 10 and 11 are indexes. The Record Commission also published a collection of Scottish legislation up to 1707 called *The Acts of the Parliaments of Scotland*.

### 3.2.2  Text as amended

The great practical problem in referring to legislation is in finding out how the text as originally enacted has been amended by subsequent Acts and subordinate legislation.

HMSO publishes *Statutes in Force*. This project began in 1972. Each Act of Parliament still in force is published in a form which incorporates all amendments made up to the date it is prepared for publication (the date is shown on the title-page of the Act). The Acts published as part of *Statutes in Force* are designed to be kept in loose-leaf binders and in most libraries they are arranged under a classification of subject matter drawn up by the Statutory Publications Office. The subject classification of an Act in *Statutes in Force* is printed at the top right-hand corner of its title-page. For each subject, cumulative supplements are published from time to time listing amendments made to the Acts in that classification since they were last prepared for printing. Each Act in *Statutes in Force* is described on its title-page as being published 'by authority'. This is significant for the operation of the Interpretation Act 1978, s. 19(1) — see section 3.3.1.1.

*Statutes in Force* is a successor to three editions of *Statutes Revised*, published in 1870–85, 1888–1929 and 1950. The editions of *Statutes Revised* were in bound volumes in which the statutes were arranged chronologically. There were no facilities for updating the first two editions, and the system of updating the third edition by sticking gummed slips on to the pages soon became impractical.

*Halsbury's Statutes of England and Wales* is published by Butterworths and is now in its 4th edition. Like *Statutes in Force*, it is arranged in subjects, but the classification is different. Unlike *Statutes in Force*, the bulk of *Halsbury's Statutes* is not loose-leaf and amendments for all volumes are published annually in a single cumulative supplement which is further supplemented by a loose-leaf noter-up. When an individual volume has accumulated a large quantity of amendments it is reissued in updated form. Acts enacted since bound volumes were last issued are published for filing in loose-leaf binders. In *Halsbury's Statutes*, each section and schedule of every Act is accompanied by commentary.

Despite not being published by the Queen's Printer, *Halsbury's Statutes* is usually the most convenient source of the text of an Act. Updating is better organised than in *Statutes in Force*; there are very few typographical errors and the commentary is helpful.

### 3.3  CITATION OF ACTS

The following section describes the methods of citation available and recommends a style for each method. Recommendation 3.7 can be used to determine which method of citation is appropriate for a particular Act.

## 3.3.1 Citation by chapter number

### *3.3.1.1 Numbering by session or statute*

In the earliest years of Parliamentary legislation, Parliament was described as enacting one 'statute' each session, containing laws on different topics (a session may have lasted about a fortnight). All the legislation of a session was regarded as having been enacted at the beginning of the session and was deemed to have come into force at the beginning of the first day of the session. Later, statutes were divided into 'chapters', each chapter (or in Latin, *capitulum*, abbreviated as 'c.' or 'cap.') being devoted to a particular subject. Subsequently, each chapter was treated as a separate piece of legislation and was itself called a 'statute' or 'Act of Parliament', and that is the present practice.

Up to and including 1962, a new sequence of chapter numbers was started at the beginning of each new session of Parliament, and sessions are dated by regnal year as explained in section 4.1.

*Example 3.1*
The first Act passed in the session 10 & 11 Eliz 2, the Tanganyika Independence Act 1961, has the chapter number:

10 & 11 Eliz 2, c. 1

For the earliest legislation, before chapters were treated as separate Acts, there is a new sequence of chapter numbers for each statute in a regnal year.

*Example 3.2*
The Treason Act 1351 has the chapter number:

25 Edw 3, st. 5, c. 2

There are also some regnal years in the seventeenth and eighteenth centuries in which the legislation for a year is divided into statutes divided into chapters with a new sequence of chapter numbers for each statute.

Unfortunately, different editions of early statutes have assigned chapter numbers in different ways, and there is uncertainty about when some early statutes were enacted. There is even some uncertainty about exactly when some sessions of Parliament began and ended. When a session commenced it was not certain that it would continue into the next regnal year, and so, until after the start of the next regnal year, the session was referred to only by the number of the regnal year in which it commenced. Acts published during that period were printed with a reference to the first regnal year alone, and might even have that single regnal year as a running head in the collected edition published at the end of the session. Nevertheless such an Act should be cited by the full range of regnal years for the session in which it was passed.

Citation should normally use the numbering in the *Chronological Table of the Statutes*, which is published annually by HMSO. This numbering conforms to the rules set out in the Interpretation Act 1978, s. 19(1):

Where an Act cites another Act by year, statute, session or chapter, or a section or other portion of another Act by number or letter, the reference shall, unless the contrary intention appears, be read as referring—

(a)   in the case of Acts included in any revised edition of the statutes printed by authority, to that edition;
(b)   in the case of Acts not so included but included in the edition prepared under the direction of the Record Commission, to that edition;
(c)   in any other case, to the Acts printed by the Queen's Printer, or under the superintendence or authority of Her Majesty's Stationery Office.

The current 'revised edition of the statutes printed by authority' is *Statutes in Force* (see section 3.2.2). The Record Commission edition of Acts of England and Great Britain up to 1713 is *The Statutes of the Realm*, and the Commission's edition of Scottish legislation to 1707 is *The Acts of the Parliaments of Scotland* (see section 3.2.1).

For early statutes no longer in force, it may be helpful to give an additional reference in parentheses to the numbering in one or more other editions, in particular, to Owen Ruffhead, *Statutes at Large*, new ed. by Charles Runnington (London: Eyre and Strahan, 1786), which was for long regarded as a standard edition. (The description 'at large' means that the work gives the complete text of most of the statutes rather than a summary as in the many collections of 'statutes abridged'.) The *Chronological Table of the Statutes* includes a table of equivalent chapter numbers in Ruffhead.

### 3.3.1.2   *Numbering by calendar year*

From 1963 on, the numbering system was changed. Acts are still numbered in chronological order of enactment but now the numbering begins at 1 at the beginning of each calendar year, as provided by the Acts of Parliament Numbering and Citation Act 1962.

*Example 3.3*
The first Act passed in 1988 was the Income and Corporation Taxes Act 1988, which has the chapter number:

1988, c. 1

### 3.3.1.3   Public Acts and other Acts
There are three sequences of chapter numbers:

(a)   Public general Acts are numbered in a sequence using arabic figures. Up to and including the session 31 & 32 Vict (1867–8), the numbering was in capital roman numerals, but references to those earlier Acts are now converted to arabic figures.

(b)   Local Acts are numbered in a sequence using lower-case roman numerals. Up to 54 Geo 3 some editions use arabic figures. As will be explained below this sequence did not exist before 38 Geo 3 (1797–8).

(c)   Personal Acts are numbered in a sequence using italic arabic figures. Before 1948, personal Acts were described as 'private Acts'. Up to and including 31 & 32 Vict (1867–8), chapter numbers of private Acts were not italic.

*Example 3.4*
1982, c. 1 is the Civil Aviation (Amendment) Act 1982 (a public general Act)
1982, c. i is the Greater London Council (General Powers) Act 1982 (a local Act)
1982, c. *1* is the John Francis Dare and Gillian Loder Dare (Marriage Enabling) Act 1982 (a private Act)

Separate lists of chapter numbers of public and private Acts have been made since the statutes of 1 Ric 3 and the general rule was that Acts classed as private were not printed by the Queen's Printer. The Act 13 & 14 Vict, c. 21 (1850), s. 7, first made the provision which is now in the Interpretation Act 1978, s. 3, that every Act passed in and after the session 14 & 15 Vict is to be judicially noticed as a public Act, which means that in any court proceedings it is assumed that the Act is known to the court and does not have to be proved in evidence. Before this provision came into force, a distinction was made between Acts which were judicially noticed and those which had to be proved. An Act which had been introduced as a private Bill was not judicially noticed unless it contained a provision declaring it to be a public Act and requiring it to be judicially noticed as such. Up to and including the Acts of 37 Geo 3 (1796–7), private Acts declared to be public were numbered with the other public Acts in capital roman numerals (nowadays converted to arabic figures).

From 38 Geo 3 (1797–8) private Acts declared to be public were put in a separate list of 'public local and personal Acts'. In the session 43 Geo 3 (1802–3), the practice began of inserting in some Acts introduced as private Bills a provision that the Act was to be printed by the King's Printer and that a copy so printed was to be admitted in evidence, and such Acts were sometimes called 'quasi-public'. From 43 Geo 3 to 54 Geo 3 inclusive, quasi-public Acts were numbered among the public local and personal Acts. Up to and including 54 Geo 3 the numbers of public local and personal Acts were arabic figures in the sessional volumes published by the King's printer (though they were lower-case roman numerals in other editions).

From 55 Geo 3 (1815), quasi-public Acts were put back into the list of private Acts and numbered with arabic figures (though listed before the private Acts not printed). Also from 55 Geo 3 the King's Printer's sessional volumes began to use lower-case roman numerals for the public local and personal Acts.

*Recommendation 3.1*
When citing an Act by chapter number:

(a)   Use the numbering in the *Chronological Table of the Statutes* or, for recent Acts not in that list, on a Queen's Printer's copy of the Act.

(b)   Use the abbreviation 'c.' before a chapter number.

(c)   Use the abbreviation 'st.' before a statute number. (Statute numbers are required for early legislation before chapters were treated as separate Acts. Also there are some regnal years in the seventeenth and eighteenth centuries in which legislation is divided into statutes divided into chapters. Statute numbers are given where necessary in the *Chronological Table of the Statutes*.)

(d)   Use the abbreviation 'sess.' before a session number. (Session numbers are required for a regnal year in which there was more than one session of Parliament.)

(e)   Put a comma between a regnal year and 'st.', 'sess.' or 'c.', between a statute or session number and 'c.' and between a calendar year and 'c.'.

(f)   Give the chapter number of a public general Act in arabic figures, even if capital roman numerals were used originally.

(g)   Give the chapter number of a local Act in lower-case roman numerals; give the chapter number of an Act included in the public local and personal list from 38 Geo 3 to 54 Geo 3 in lower-case roman numerals followed by '(public local and personal)'.

(h)   Give the chapter number of a personal or private Act passed in or after 32 & 33 Vict in italic arabic figures; give the chapter number of a private Act prior to 32 & 33 Vict in arabic figures (not italic) followed by '(private)'.

(i)   If a private Act was not printed then that fact should be stated and information should be given about where a copy may be found.

(j)   If citing an Act in a document by regnal year and chapter number without giving the calendar year of enactment then provide this information somewhere in the document, for example, when the Act is first mentioned or in a table of statutes. The year may be stated in parentheses after the chapter number.

*Example 3.5*
An early statute not divided into chapters:

25 Edw 3, st. 1 (1350)

A chapter of an early statute:

25 Edw 3, st. 5, c. 4 (1351)

An Act passed in a regnal year in which there was more than one session of Parliament:

24 Geo 3, sess. 2, c. 20 (1784)

A public general Act of 1844:

7 & 8 Vict, c. 110 (1844)

An Act of 1801 in the list of local and personal Acts:

41 Geo 3, c. lxvi (1801 local and personal)

A public general Act of 1995:

1995, c. 25

*Alternative to recommendation 3.1*

(a)   Use 'ch.' or 'cap.' instead of 'c.'.
(b)   Use 'stat.' instead of 'st.'.
(c)   Omit punctuation.

### 3.3.1.4   *Statutes of uncertain date*
The editors of *Statutes of the Realm* felt unable to date some of the legislation, which they described as statutes of uncertain date (in Latin,

*temporis incerti,* often abbreviated to *temp. incert.*). These must be cited by the title given in *Statutes of the Realm,* which is also used in the *Chronological Table of the Statutes.* These titles are in Latin or law French, often abbreviated to the point of unintelligibility, and were taken from the parchment rolls. Almost all of these statutes are assigned a regnal year in Ruffhead's edition (though several are not printed at all by Ruffhead).

*Example 3.6*
Mod. calump. Esson' (uncertain date; 12 Edw 2, st. 2 in Ruffhead)

### 3.3.2 Citation by short title

*3.3.2.1 Short titles*
The standard way of citing an Act is by its short title. Authority to cite an Act by its short title is normally given by the Act itself.

*Example 3.7*
The Interpretation Act 1978, s. 27, provides:

This Act may be cited as the Interpretation Act 1978.

It has been the practice for an Act to provide for its citation by short title since the mid nineteenth century. The first such provision seems to have been in the Companies Clauses Consolidation Act 1845, s. 4. Even so, Acts did not routinely provide their own short titles until the end of the nineteenth century but now they always do. Nowadays provision for an Act's short title is made in a section at the end of the Act with the marginal note, 'Short title' or 'Citation'. In the nineteenth century the usual practice was to put the section giving the short title at the beginning of an Act. When the usefulness of short titles was recognised at the end of the nineteenth century, the Short Titles Act 1892 was passed assigning short titles retrospectively to many earlier Acts which had been enacted without short titles. The 1892 Act was repealed and replaced by the more extensive Short Titles Act 1896. Short titles for earlier Acts not covered by the Short Titles Act 1896 were provided in the Statute Law Revision Act 1948, sch. 2, and for Acts applying to Scotland in the Statute Law Revision (Scotland) Act 1964. A small number of Acts were given short titles retrospectively by the Statute Law (Repeals) Act 1977, sch. 3, and the Statute Law (Repeals) Act 1978, sch. 3.

Sometimes one Act will provide a new short title for a previous Act which already has a short title. For example, by the Finance Act 1986, s. 100(1), the Capital Transfer Tax Act 1984 may now be cited as the Inheritance Tax Act 1984. (Either short title may be used.)

The Interpretation Act 1978, s. 19(2), provides:

An Act may continue to be cited by the short title authorised by any enactment notwithstanding the repeal of that enactment.

*Example 3.8*
The fact that the whole of the Companies Act 1948 has been repealed, including its short-title provision (s. 462(1)), does not prevent continued citation of it as the Companies Act 1948.

The Law Commissions took advantage of this rule to recommend that all the provisions conferring short titles retrospectively should be repealed so as to meet their target of reducing the volume of statutes in force (Law Commission and Scottish Law Commission, *Statute Law Revision: Fifteenth Report* (Law Com. No. 233, Scot. Law Com. No. 150, Cm 2785) (London: HMSO, 1995), part 4). This recommendation was carried out by the Statute Law (Repeals) Act 1995, sch. 1, part IV.

### 3.3.2.2 Year of enactment
For almost every Act of Parliament the year in which it was passed is part of its short title and is an essential part. It is ambiguous to talk of 'the Companies Act' without specifying the year: at present both the Companies Act 1985 and the Companies Act 1989 are in force, and there have been at least 19 other Companies Acts in the past. 'Finance Act' is even more ambiguous: there is at least one Finance Act every year.
The year is always at the end of a short title.

*Example 3.9*
1985 Companies Act

is not a short title. The correct short title is:

Companies Act 1985

A small number of Acts have short titles without a year. They include:

Act of Settlement (12 & 13 Will 3, c. 2 (1700))
Act of Supremacy (1 Eliz, c. 1 (1558))
Bill of Rights (1 Will & Mar, sess. 2, c. 2 (1688))
Petition of Right (3 Cha 1, c. 1 (1627))
Riot Act (1 Geo 1, stat. 2, c. 5 (1714)) (entirely repealed)
Statute of Distribution (22 & 23 Cha 2, c. 10 (1670)) (entirely repealed)
Statute of Frauds (29 Cha 2, c. 3 (1677))

Statute of Monopolies (21 Ja 1, c. 3 (1623))
Statute of Praemunire (16 Ric 2 , c. 5 (1392)) (entirely repealed)
Statute of Uses (27 Hen 8, c. 10 (1535)) (entirely repealed)

*Recommendation 3.2*
If citing an Act in a document by a short title which does not include the
calendar year of enactment then provide this information somewhere in
the document, for example, when the Act is first mentioned or in a table of
statutes. The year may be stated in parentheses after the short title.

*Example 3.10*
Bill of Rights (1688)

*3.3.2.3   Omissions from short titles*
The short titles given by the Short Titles Act 1896 and the Statute Law
Revision Act 1948 all begin with the definite article but it is usual to regard
this as not being part of the short title.
   Up to and including the Road Traffic Act 1962 (which is the last Act in
the session 10 & 11 Eliz 2), there was always a comma before the year in a
short title (Road Traffic Act, 1962) but that use of the comma was then
abandoned and the comma may now be omitted from pre-1963 short titles.

*Recommendation 3.3*

(a)   An initial definite article is not part of a short title.
(b)   Ignore the comma before the year in a pre-1963 short title.

*Example 3.11*
Habeas Corpus Act 1679
Law of Property Act 1925

*3.3.2.4   Possessives*
When writing a short title there is a temptation to put the noun before the
word 'Act' into the genitive case. The Act itself, or a reliable reference
source should be checked before doing this, as the short title of an Act is
not normally in that form. An Act is not usually regarded as the possession
of its subject matter.

*Example 3.12*
Children's Act 1989

is not a short title. The correct short title is:

Children Act 1989

The genitive case does occur in phrases within some short titles.

*Example 3.13*
Employer's Liability (Defective Equipment) Act 1969
Employers' Liability (Compulsory Insurance) Act 1969

### 3.3.3 Abbreviated short titles

When an Act is repeatedly mentioned in a document, its short title may be abbreviated. Commonly the main words are replaced by their initials.

*Example 3.14*
The Companies Act 1985 may be referred to as:

CA 1985

Abbreviations of short titles using initial letters are very common in legal writing but they are not compulsory. The fact that abbreviations are used for some Acts that are cited many times in a document does not mean that every Act cited in the document has to be given an abbreviation.

*Recommendation 3.4*
When making up an abbreviated short title for an Act, always include the date. Explain every abbreviated short title when it is first used or in a table of abbreviations.

### 3.3.4 Long titles

An Act begins with a long title which sets out the purposes of the Act.

*Example 3.15*
The long title of the Minors' Contracts Act 1987 is:

An Act to amend the law relating to minors' contracts.

Long titles have no value for citation because there is no way of finding an Act from its long title alone. However, if an Act does not have a short title and is cited by chapter number then it is common to give its long title (or at least the first part) as well, so as to confirm the identity of the Act.

*Example 3.16*
41 Geo 3, c. lxvi (1801 local and personal) (an Act for enlarging and improving the market place within the town of Rotherham)

In the example, only the first purpose given in the long title of the Act has been quoted.

### 3.3.5 Popular titles

The earliest statutes have long been known by unofficial titles.
Some have been known by the place where they were enacted.

*Example 3.17*
The statute enacted by the Parliament held at York in October 1318 (12 Edw 2) is known as:

the Statute of York

Other early statutes are known by their opening words.

*Example 3.18*
The Latin text of the first statute of 18 Edw 1 (1290) begins *'Quia emptores terrarum & tenementorum'* (Whereas purchasers of lands and tenements), and the statute is known as:

*Quia Emptores*

Many eighteenth and nineteenth-century Acts became known by the names of people associated with them as drafters or promoters in Parliament.

*Example 3.19*
The Act 8 & 9 Vict, c. 113 (1845), which was given the short title Evidence Act 1845 by the Short Titles Act 1896, has been known as:

Lord Brougham's Act

Law reformers often did not give up after one Act: for example, at least 35 statutes have been known as 'Lord Brougham's Act'.

Although described as 'popular' titles, few of them have any currency today. Many popular titles, such as 'the Corn Laws' or 'the statute of Elizabeth' or 'Lord Brougham's Act' are too vague to be useful. More seriously, no comprehensive list of popular titles of statutes has yet been published. The lists that have been published, for example, the one in app. A to *Craies on Statute Law*, 7th ed., by S.G.G. Edgar (London: Sweet & Maxwell, 1971), are limited.

*Recommendation 3.5*
Do not use a popular title of an Act without also identifying the Act by chapter number or short title in accordance with recommendation 3.7.

> *Example 3.20*
> Lord Brougham's Act (Evidence Act 1845)

### 3.3.6 Collective titles

Sometimes an Act of Parliament provides not only a short title for itself but also a 'collective title' by which it and a number of other Acts may be cited together.

> *Example 3.21*
> The Official Secrets Act 1989, s. 16(2), provides that:
>
> This Act and the Official Secrets Acts 1911 to 1939 may be cited together as the Official Secrets Acts 1911 to 1989.

One has to work out for oneself (though perhaps it is not too difficult) that the phrase 'the Official Secrets Acts 1911 to 1939' is defined in the Official Secrets Act 1939, but the definition there involves yet another collective title. Eventually, one can work out that the phrase 'the Official Secrets Acts 1911 to 1989' means the Official Secrets Act 1911, the Official Secrets Act 1920, the Official Secrets Act 1939 and the Official Secrets Act 1989.

The legislation which conferred short titles retrospectively has also given some Acts retrospective collective titles.

Collective titles have little value as a means of citing Acts of Parliament because it is so difficult to find out what they mean. It is necessary to find and examine all but the first of the Acts involved in order to find out which Acts are covered by a collective title. Collective titles for Acts still in force are noted in the annual *Index to the Statutes* but only under the subject heading where the Acts are classified, so it is necessary to discover what that heading is before the collective title can be found from that source.

*Recommendation 3.6*
Do not use a collective title without explaining what it means, on its first occurrence in a document or in a list of abbreviations.

### 3.3.7 Choosing the form of citation

Any Act, even if wholly repealed, passed in or after 1940 (since when volumes of statutes have been published by HMSO by calendar year) can be cited by short title alone, with no reference to its chapter number. The text of such an Act can easily be located from its short title. If any part of it is still in force then it can be found in the alphabetical index to either *Statutes in Force* or *Halsbury's Statutes*. If it has all been repealed then its place in the annual collections of statutes can be found in the alphabetical list at the beginning of the collection for the year in which it was enacted (that year being part of the Act's short title).

It is suggested that it is helpful to give the session and chapter number in addition to the short title for any Act passed before 1940 which is now wholly repealed. This is because the text will probably have to be found in a collection in which Acts are arranged by session and chapter.

Citation by chapter number must be used for an old Act which never had a short title.

If an Act which was given a short title retrospectively has not been wholly repealed then the short title can be discovered easily because it will be printed as a running head on every page of the Act's text in *Statutes in Force* and as the running head of right-hand pages in *Halsbury's Statutes*. Similarly, it will be easy to find the text of such an Act from its short title by consulting the alphabetical lists of Acts in either of those works.

If an Act which was given a short title retrospectively has been wholly repealed then finding its short title, or finding the Act from a citation of its short title, may be very laborious as the original texts of the now-repealed title-conferring Acts will have to be consulted. Accordingly, if such an Act is cited by short title, it would be helpful to cite by chapter number as well (if there is a table of statutes, the citation by chapter number need only be given there) or the Act can be cited by chapter number alone.

*Recommendation 3.7*

(a)   If an Act has a short title and has not been entirely repealed then cite it by its short title (see section 3.3.2).

(b)   Cite an Act passed in 1940 or later by its short title (all Acts of this period have short titles) even if the Act has been wholly repealed.

(c)   If an Act passed before 1940 has a short title but has been wholly repealed then cite it by short title but also give the citation by chapter number (see section 3.3.1). It is sufficient to give the chapter number citation in a table of statutes.

(d)   If an Act does not have a short title then cite it by chapter number (see section 3.3.1).

(e)   For statutes of uncertain date see section 3.3.1.4.

(f)   In a table of statutes arranged by short title it is helpful to give citations by chapter number (see section 3.3.1) as well.

### 3.3.8 Abbreviated citation

If an Act is to be cited more than once in a document it may be feared that giving the full citation in accordance with recommendation 3.7 every time will be distracting to the reader (though this fear is easily exaggerated).

*Recommendation 3.8*
After an Act has been cited fully in a document in accordance with recommendation 3.7, the following methods can be used to shorten subsequent citations of the same Act:

(a)  Use an abbreviated short title (described in section 3.3.3).
(b)  An Act passed in, for example, 1995 can be referred to as the '1995 Act'. This method is available only if there is no ambiguity about which Act of a particular year is being cited.
(c)  Use 'ibid.' (see section 1.6).
(d)  When a section, schedule or other subdivision of an Act is being cited, it may not be necessary to refer to the Act at all: see recommendations 3.10, 3.11, 3.12 and 3.14.

### 3.3.9  Acts of the Parliament of Ireland

Sessions of the Parliament of Ireland up to 1800 are dated by regnal year. Acts of that Parliament have chapter numbers with the numbering beginning at 1 again each session. Acts of that Parliament still in force in Northern Ireland were given short titles by the Short Titles Act (Northern Ireland) 1951 and Acts still in force in the Republic of Ireland were given short titles by the Short Titles Act 1962 (Republic of Ireland).

*Example 3.22*
There are the following three different ways of citing the same Act:

21 & 22 Geo 3, c. 16
Bank of Ireland Act (Ireland) 1781 (short title given by the Short Titles Act (Northern Ireland) 1951)
Bank of Ireland Act 1781 (short title given by the Short Titles Act 1962 (Republic of Ireland))

There is a complete listing of Acts of the Parliament of Ireland up to 1800 in the *Chronological Table of the Statutes. Northern Ireland* published periodically by HMSO in Belfast. The text of Acts still in force in Northern Ireland is published in *The Statutes Revised. Northern Ireland*, 2nd ed. (Belfast: HMSO, 1982), which is updated by annual cumulative supplements. Some Acts are also in *Statutes in Force* (see section 3.2.2).

### 3.3.10   Northern Ireland legislation

Acts of the Parliament of Northern Ireland up to 30 March 1972 may be
cited by chapter number or short title.

Up to and including the session 6 & 7 Geo 6 (1942), chapter numbers
start at 1 again with each session of the Northern Ireland Parliament, and
sessions are dated by regnal year. From 1943 chapter numbering is by
calendar year. There are two sequences of chapter numbers: one for public
general Acts in arabic figures and one for local and private Acts in
lower-case roman numerals.

As all Northern Ireland Parliament Acts have short titles, citation by
chapter number is unnecessary except that location of the text of a wholly
repealed Act passed before 1943 is helped if session and chapter number
are given.

The short title of an Act of the Northern Ireland Parliament has
'(Northern Ireland)' between the word 'Act' and the year. If a large number
of Northern Ireland Acts are cited in a document it may be decided to
abbreviate '(Northern Ireland)' to '(NI)'. There was a comma before the
year in Acts up to the Appropriation (No. 3) Act (Northern Ireland) 1962
but that use of the comma was then abandoned and the comma may now
be omitted from pre-1963 short titles.

*Example 3.23*
Companies Act (Northern Ireland) 1932 (22 & 23 Geo 5, c. 7) (a wholly
repealed pre-1943 Act)
Companies Act (Northern Ireland) 1960
Clean Air Act (Northern Ireland) 1964

The four Measures of the Northern Ireland Assembly are cited in the
same way as Northern Ireland Acts (but their short titles have the word
'Measure' in place of 'Act').

Orders in Council making laws for Northern Ireland under the Northern
Ireland (Temporary Provisions) Act 1972 or the Northern Ireland Act 1974
are issued as United Kingdom statutory instruments and are numbered as
such (see section 5.3.1). They are also given a number prefixed by 'NI', with
a new sequence of numbers each calendar year. An Order may be cited by
year and NI number or by the title authorised by the Order itself or by its
United Kingdom statutory instrument number.

*Example 3.24*
There are the following three different ways of citing the same Order:

1995 NI 20
Polygamous Marriages (Northern Ireland) Order 1995
SI 1995/3211

These Orders are published in Belfast by HMSO. They are published with punched holes for filing in ring binders which are designed to take the Orders for a calendar year and have the spine title *Northern Ireland Statutes*. These Orders are not included in the annual collection of United Kingdom statutory instruments published by HMSO in London.

The amended text of legislation in force in Northern Ireland on 31 March 1981 (other than Acts of the Westminster Parliament) was published in *The Statutes Revised. Northern Ireland*, 2nd ed. (Belfast: HMSO, 1982) and this is updated by annual cumulative supplements.

*3.3.10.1 Further reading*
George Woodman, 'Legislation in Northern Ireland' (1987) 18 Law Libr 46.

### 3.3.11 Acts of the Parliaments of Scotland

Acts of the Parliaments of Scotland up to 1707 may be cited by chapter number or by short title.

Chapter numbering in the *Chronological Table of the Statutes* published annually by HMSO starts at 1 again with each session of Parliament and a session is identified by the calendar year in which it was held or, if there were two sessions in a year, the date of the session. (Up to 1599 the calendar years start on 25 March.)

*Example 3.25*
Act 3 December 1540, c. 10
Act 14 March 1540, c. 10

(Using years beginning on 1 January, 14 March 1540 would be called 14 March 1541.)

As in England, various editions of Scottish Acts assign chapter numbers in different ways.

Acts then still in force were given short titles by the Statute Law Revision (Scotland) Act 1964, s. 2 and sch. 2. These short titles all begin with the definite article but this may be treated as not being part of the short title.

*Example 3.26*
The short title of the Act 3 December 1540, c. 10 is:

Citation Act 1540

Acts of the Parliaments of Scotland still in force are published by HMSO in *Statutes in Force* (see section 3.2.2).

### 3.3.12 Distinguishing legislatures

If Acts from several legislatures are cited it may be helpful to add after the citation of an Act an indication of which legislature enacted it. This may be omitted for Acts of the jurisdiction with which the document is primarily concerned.

*Example 3.27*
21 & 22 Geo 3, c. 46 (Ireland)
Short Titles Act 1962 (Republic of Ireland)
Statute Law Revision (Northern Ireland) Act 1976 (United Kingdom)

### 3.4   CITING A POINT IN AN ACT

### 3.4.1   Edition-neutral references

Although printed editions of Acts of Parliament are paginated, a point within an Act is never identified by page number but by number of section or schedule and, if necessary, further subdivision. The authentic numbering of sections, schedules and other subdivisions of an Act is that of the official edition of the Act specified in the Interpretation Act 1978, s. 19(1), which is set out in section 3.3.1.1. Normally this edition will be *Statutes in Force* (see section 3.3.2). As all other modern editions of Acts, whether published by HMSO or other publishers, adopt the same numbering, references to points within Acts by section or schedule and other subdivision are the same whatever edition of the Act is consulted (but see section 3.6 on amendments).

### 3.4.2   Sections

The main text of an Act is divided into numbered 'sections'. Nowadays the section numbers are printed in bold arabic numerals: **1, 2** etc., though until the mid nineteenth century they were in capital roman numerals: II, III etc. (the first section was not usually numbered at that time).

*Recommendation 3.9*
When referring to a section of an Act give the section number in arabic figures, whatever the original typography. The figures need not be bold unless that is required by the typographical design of the document.

*Recommendation 3.10*

(a) To cite a section of an Act, give a citation of the Act in accordance with recommendation 3.7 or 3.8 followed by a comma, the abbreviation 's.' and the section number. If two or more sections are cited, use 'ss.' instead of 's.'.

(b) The citation of the Act may be omitted if it has already been cited in the text (not just in a heading) and it is clear which Act is being referred to. Usually, the name of the Act should not be omitted if the last time it was mentioned was in a different chapter or other division of the document or if other legislation has been mentioned since.

(c) If omitting the citation of the Act means that the citation of the section begins a sentence then use 'Section' or 'Sections' instead of an abbreviation.

*Example 3.28*

(a) Companies Act 1985, s. 6
Companies Act 1985, ss. 4 and 5

(b) Under the Companies Act 1985, fraudulent trading is a criminal offence (s. 458).

(c) At the beginning of a sentence, when it is appropriate to omit the name of the Act:
Section 11
Sections 39 and 40

*Alternative to recommendation 3.10*

(a) Omit the punctuation.
(b) Omit the space before the section number.
(c) Use a capital 'S' (plural 'Ss').
(d) Do not abbreviate 'section' at all.
(e) Put the section reference before the short title.
(f) Instead of 's.' use 'sec.' or 'sect.' or 'Sec.' or 'Sect.' or §.

*3.4.2.1 Citation grammatically part of text statement*
When a citation of a section of an Act is grammatically part of the text, the form in recommendation 3.10 may be used, followed by a comma, or a less

abbreviated form with the section reference first followed by 'of the' and then the Act ('of' may be preferred to 'of the' if an abbreviated short title is used). At the beginning of a sentence, 'Section' or 'Sections' should be used instead of an abbreviation.

*Example 3.29*
In s. 6 of the Companies Act 1985 there are provisions supplementing ss. 4 and 5.
In s. 6 of CA 1985 there are provisions supplementing ss. 4 and 5.
Section 6 of the Companies Act 1985 supplements ss. 4 and 5.

### 3.4.3   Subsections, paragraphs, lists and subparagraphs

A section may be divided into 'subsections' numbered in arabic figures in parentheses: (1), (2) etc. The parentheses are an essential part of the reference.

A subsection may be divided into 'paragraphs' distinguished by lower-case letters in parentheses: (a), (b) etc. The parentheses are an essential part of the reference. Until recently, the letters were set in italic in Queen's Printer's copies, but this need not be done in citations.

A section that is not divided into subsections may nevertheless include a list of items, each beginning with a lower-case letter in parentheses.

Paragraphs may be divided into 'subparagraphs', which are identified by lower-case roman numerals in parentheses: (i), (ii) etc. The parentheses are an essential part of the reference.

*Recommendation 3.11*
To cite a subdivision of a section put the subsection reference after the section number without a space, then, as necessary, the paragraph reference, then the subparagraph reference. The citation of the Act may be omitted (see recommendation 3.10(b)) but omitting the section number, or anything else before the final subdivision reference is not recommended. The section number is still preceded by 's.' (or 'Section' at the beginning of a sentence), not 'subs.', 'para.' or 'subpara.'. It is not necessary for paragraph letters to be italicised.

*Example 3.30*
Companies Act 1985, s. 6(1)
Companies Act 1985, s. 6(1)(b)
Companies Act 1985, s. 6(1)(b)(i)

*Alternative to recommendation 3.11*
Put a space between section reference and subsection reference and so on.

If it is thought that the section number can be omitted without causing confusion then the subsection number is preceded by 'subs.' (plural 'subss.'). If both section number and subsection reference are omitted then the paragraph reference is preceded by 'para.' (plural 'paras'). A subparagraph reference on its own is preceded by 'subpara.' (plural 'subparas'). At the beginning of a sentence use a complete word rather than an abbreviation.

### 3.4.4   Intervening division references cannot be omitted

A description in the form 'subsection (1) of the Companies Act 1985' is ambiguous. The intervening section number must be stated.

### 3.4.5   Two or more divisions of the same section

When referring to two or more divisions of the same section, the section number need not be repeated.

*Example 3.31*
Environment Act 1995, s. 45(1)(a) and (3)

not 's. 45(1)(a) and s. 45(3)'.

It is wrong to use 'ss.' in this situation. Instead of 'and' a comma may be used (for example, s. 45(1)(a), (3)) but leaving no space (for example, s. 45(1)(a)(3)) is not recommended.
Similarly:

It is provided in subs. (1)(a) and (d) that ...

When a citation is grammatically part of the text, this is an awkward way of expressing the subject of a sentence because it is not obvious whether the verb should be singular or plural.

*Example 3.32*
Subsections (2), (4)(a) and (5) of s. 175 provide a definition of 'commercial publication' of a literary work.

is preferable to 'Section 175(2), (4)(a) and (5) provide (? provides) a definition ...'.

### 3.4.6  Parts and chapters

As well as being divided into sections, the main text of an Act may be divided into 'parts' numbered with capital roman numerals: I, II etc. The numbering of sections continues regardless of division into parts.

*Example 3.33*
In the Copyright, Designs and Patents Act 1988, ss. 1 to 179 are in part I and then ss. 180 to 212 are in part II, and so on.

Because the numbering of sections is continuous, when referring to a section it is unnecessary to specify both section and part. There is no need to say 'Copyright, Designs and Patents Act 1988, part I, s. 145' because there is only one s. 145 and it is in part I: it does not have to be distinguished from another s. 145 in another part.

Parts may be divided into 'chapters' which are numbered with capital roman numerals.

*Recommendation 3.12*

(a)  To cite a part of an Act, give a citation of the Act in accordance with recommendation 3.7 or 3.8 followed by a comma, the word 'part' and the part number.

(b)  The citation of the Act may be omitted if it has already been cited in the text (not just in a heading) and it is clear which Act is being referred to. Usually, the name of the Act should not be omitted if the last time it was mentioned was in a different chapter or other division of the document or if other legislation has been mentioned since.

(c)  Use a capital 'P' if 'part' or 'parts' begins a sentence.

(d)  A chapter is dealt with similarly but with 'ch.' in place of 'part'. When citing a chapter of a part, omission of the part number is not recommended.

*Example 3.34*
Companies Act 1985, part V
Companies Act 1985, part V, ch. VI

*Alternative to recommendation 3.12*

(a)  Abbreviate 'part' to 'pt'.

(b)  Use a capital 'P' for 'part' or 'pt' and a capital 'C' for 'chapter' or 'ch.' regardless of the position in the sentence.

(c)  Use arabic figures instead of roman numerals.

### 3.4.6.1 *Citation grammatically part of text statement*
When a citation of a part of an Act is grammatically part of the text, the form in recommendation 3.12 may be used, followed by a comma, or a less abbreviated form with the part reference first followed by 'of the' and then the Act ('of' may be preferred to 'of the' if an abbreviated short title is used). This is like the alternative treatment of sections in example 3.29.

## 3.4.7 Schedules

The main text of an Act may be supplemented by 'schedules', which are nowadays numbered with arabic figures: schedule 1, schedule 2 etc. Up to and including the Road Traffic Act 1962 (which is the last Act in the session 10 & 11 Eliz 2), schedules were identified by ordinal numbers: first schedule, second schedule etc.

*Recommendation 3.13*
Use the numbering 1, 2 etc. for schedules regardless of how they were originally presented.

A schedule is described as being 'to' rather than 'of' an Act and is 'introduced' by a provision in the main text of the Act.

*Example 3.35*
Section 295 of the Copyright, Designs and Patents Act 1988 introduces sch. 5 to the Act by saying:

The Patents Act 1949 and the Patents Act 1977 are amended in accordance with schedule 5.

In the Queen's Printer's copy of an Act a marginal note at the beginning of each schedule gives a reference to the section or sections which introduced it.

Some people think that a schedule should not be cited without also citing the provision which introduces it.

*Recommendation 3.14*

(a) To cite a schedule to an Act, give a citation of the Act in accordance with recommendation 3.7 or 3.8 followed by a comma, the abbreviation 'sch.' and the schedule number.

(b) The citation of the Act may be omitted if it has already been cited in the text (not just in a heading) and it is clear which Act is being referred to. Usually, the citation of the Act should not be omitted if the last time it

was mentioned was in a different chapter or other division of the document
or if other legislation has been mentioned since.

(c)    If omitting the citation of the Act means that the citation of the
schedule begins a sentence then use 'Schedule' instead of 'sch.'.

*Example 3.36*

(a)    Friendly Societies Act 1992, sch. 10
(b)    sch. 10
(c)    Schedule 10

*Alternative to recommendation 3.14*

(a)    Omit the punctuation.
(b)    Omit the space before the schedule number.
(c)    Use a capital 'S'.
(d)    Do not abbreviate 'schedule' at all.
(e)    Put the schedule number before the short title.
(f)    Instead of 'sch.' use 'sched.' or 'Sched.'.

*3.4.7.1    Citation grammatically part of text statement*
When a citation of a schedule to an Act is grammatically part of the text,
the form in recommendation 3.14 may be used, followed by a comma, or a
less abbreviated form with the schedule reference first followed by 'to the'
and then the Act ('to' may be preferred to 'to the' if an abbreviated short
title is used). At the beginning of a sentence, 'Schedule' should be used
instead of an abbreviation. This is like the alternative treatment of
sections in example 3.29.

**3.4.8    Paragraphs of schedules**

A schedule may be divided into 'paragraphs'. These are given arabic
numbers, which, unlike section numbers, are not printed in bold in
Queen's Printer's copies. Sometimes a schedule may additionally be
divided into 'parts' given roman numerals. Usually, the numbering of
paragraphs in a schedule is unaffected by division of the schedule into
parts so that when referring to a paragraph it is unnecessary to give both
part and paragraph number.

*Example 3.37*
In sch. 12 to the Companies Act 1989, paras 1 to 3 form part I and paras
4 to 9 form part II.

Unfortunately, in some schedules, the numbering of paragraphs starts again at 1 at the beginning of each new part, and then it is necessary to specify both part and paragraph when referring to a paragraph.

*Example 3.38*
Schedule 1 to the Bail Act 1976 is divided into part I, which has paras 1–9B, part II, which has paras 1–5, part IIA (paras 1–3) and part III (paras 1–4).

A schedule may be in tabular form and so without paragraphs but may nevertheless be divided into parts.

Paragraph numbering always starts again at 1 for each new schedule.

A paragraph in a schedule may be divided into subparagraphs with arabic numbers in parentheses: (1), (2) etc.

A subparagraph in a schedule may be divided into subsubparagraphs with lower-case letters in parentheses: (a), (b) etc.

A subsubparagraph may be divided into subsubsubparagraphs with lower-case roman numerals in parentheses: (i), (ii) etc.

In all the subdivisions of paragraphs, the parentheses are an essential part of the reference.

*Recommendation 3.15*

(a)   To cite a paragraph of a schedule to an Act, give a citation of the Act and schedule in accordance with recommendation 3.14(a) followed by a comma, the abbreviation 'para.' and the paragraph number. If two or more paragraphs are cited, use 'paras' instead of 'para.'.

(b)   The citation of the Act and schedule may be omitted if they have already been cited in the text (not just in a heading) and it is clear which Act and schedule are being referred to. Usually, they should not be omitted if the last time they were mentioned was in a different chapter or other division of the document or if another schedule to the Act or another piece of legislation has been mentioned since.

(c)   If omitting the citation of the Act and schedule means that the citation of the paragraph begins a sentence then use 'Paragraph' or 'Paragraphs' instead of an abbreviation.

(d)   If the schedule is divided into parts and the paragraph numbering is not continuous then the number of the part (preceded by a comma and the word 'part') must be inserted before the paragraph reference.

(e)   To cite a subdivision of a paragraph, put the subparagraph reference after the paragraph number without a space, then, if necessary, the subsubparagraph reference. The paragraph number is still preceded by 'para.', not 'subpara.' or 'subsubpara.'.

*Example 3.39*

    (a)  Building Societies Act 1986, sch. 15, para. 20
           Building Societies Act 1986, sch. 15, paras 20 and 21
    (b)  para. 21
    (c)  Paragraphs 20 and 21
    (d)  Bail Act 1976, sch. 1, part II, para. 3
    (e)  Bail Act 1976, sch. 1, part I, para. 8(1)

*Alternative to recommendation 3.15*

    (a)  Omit the punctuation.
    (b)  Omit the space before the paragraph number.
    (c)  Use a capital 'P'.
    (d)  Do not abbreviate 'paragraph' at all.
    (e)  Put the schedule and paragraph references before the short title.
    (f)  Put a space between paragraph number and subparagraph reference and between subparagraph and subsubparagraph references.

### 3.4.9  Numbering of inserted sections and so on

A new section inserted into an Act by amendment is given the number of the preceding section plus a capital letter.

*Example 3.40*
Two sections inserted after s. 390 of an Act will be numbered 390A and 390B.

New subsections, parts, chapters, schedules, and paragraphs and subparagraphs of schedules are treated in the same way.

*Example 3.41*
If two subsections are inserted after subsection (1) then they are numbered (1A) and (1B). The Companies Act 1985 now has a schedule 9A, paragraph 28A.

Care must be taken to position parentheses correctly and to distinguish lower-case and capital letters.

*Example 3.42*
Section 442(3)(c) is not the same as s. 442(3C). The first is paragraph (c) of subsection (3), the second is subsection (3C).

## 3.5  CITING MORE THAN ONE ACT OR POINT IN AN ACT

*Recommendation 3.16*

(a)  If more than one section, schedule or other subdivision of an Act is cited, cite them in numerical order with sections before schedules.

(b)  If more than one Act is cited, cite them in order of enactment with a semicolon marking the change from citation of one Act to another.

*Example 3.43*
Financial Services Act 1986, ss. 179(3)(d), (e) and (f), and 180(1)(e)
Companies Act 1985, s. 275(2) and sch. 4, para. 32(3)
Companies Act 1985, s. 449(1)(h); Financial Services Act 1986, ss. 179(3)(a) and 180(1)(e)

## 3.6  AMENDMENTS

*Recommendation 3.17*

(a)  If a provision being cited has been amended, follow its citation with a citation of the amending provision and a description such as 'as amended by', 'as substituted by' or 'inserted by' as appropriate.

(b)  Merely putting 'as amended' without identifying which amendments have actually been taken into consideration is not recommended.

(c)  Information about amendments may be unnecessary if there is a general note to the document that, unless otherwise stated, all legislation is cited as amended up to a certain date and indicating where the text so amended can be consulted.

*Example 3.44*
Insolvency Act 1986, s. 124(4) as amended by the Companies Act 1989, s. 60
Patents Act 1977, s. 51 as substituted by the Copyright, Designs and Patents Act 1988, sch. 5, para. 14
Magistrates' Courts Act 1980, s. 87A inserted by the Criminal Justice Act 1988, s. 62(1)

## 3.7  TABLE OF STATUTES

A table of statutes for a document lists every Act cited in the document. Under each Act there is a list of all the points in the Act cited in the document stating where in the document each point is cited.

It used to be common for the Acts in a table of statutes to be listed in chronological order by Parliamentary session or (for Acts from 1963 on) calendar year and chapter number, but now listing in alphabetical order of short title is usual, though occasionally lists in both orders may be provided.

When listing is by short title, Acts without short titles may be put in a separate list arranged chronologically.

When listing is by short title, chapter numbers may be provided, even if they are not given in the main text of the document, to assist in locating the text of each Act.

If Acts from more than one jurisdiction are cited there may be separate lists for each jurisdiction.

## 3.8   FURTHER READING

F.A.R. Bennion, *Statutory Interpretation*, 2nd ed. (London: Butterworths, 1992). Pages 124–41 contain a description of the procedure for enacting and publishing public general Acts with a particularly detailed account of the procedure for royal assent.

C.T. Carr, 'Calendar-year statutes' (1940) 56 LQR 459. Explains the change from publication of a collection for each Parliamentary session to a collection for each calendar year and gives examples of citation under the sessional system.

M.L. Dunlap, 'The arrangement of *Statutes in Force*' (1982) 13 Law Libr 3.

Law Commission and Scottish Law Commission, *Interpretation Bill* (Law Com. No. 90, Scot. Law Com. No. 53, Cmnd 7235) (London: HMSO, 1978). Paragraph 7 explains the background to the Interpretation Act 1978, s. 19(1).

Alex Noel-Tod, 'What's in a name? The statute book and popular titles' (1989) 20 Law Libr 29.

## 3.9   SUMMARY OF RECOMMENDED FORMS OF CITATION OF ACTS

To cite an Act of Parliament that has a short title:

Interpretation Act 1978

To cite an Act of Parliament that does not have a short title:

7 & 8 Vict, c. 111 (1844)

To cite a section:

Companies Act 1985, s. 6

To cite a subsection:

Companies Act 1985, s. 6(1)

To cite a paragraph in a subsection:

Companies Act 1985, s. 6(1)(b)

To cite a subparagraph in a subsection:

Companies Act 1985, s. 6(1)(b)(i)

To cite a part:

Companies Act 1985, part V

To cite a chapter:

Companies Act 1985, part V, ch. VI

To cite a schedule:

Companies Act 1985, sch. 1

To cite a paragraph in a schedule where it is not necessary to identify the part of the schedule:

Companies Act 1985, sch. 1, para. 2

To cite a paragraph in a schedule where it is necessary to identify the part of the schedule:

Bail Act 1976, sch. 1, part III, para. 1

To cite a subparagraph in a schedule:

Companies Act 1985, sch. 1, para. 2(1)

To cite a subsubparagraph in a schedule

Companies Act 1985, sch. 1, para. 2(1)(a)

To cite a subsubsubparagraph in a schedule

Companies Act 1985, sch. 1, para. 2(1)(b)(i)

# 4 PARLIAMENT

## 4.1 DATING OF SESSIONS

A session of Parliament is the period from the time Parliament first meets in accordance with the sovereign's command after a prorogation or dissolution to the time when the sovereign again either prorogues or dissolves it. After a prorogation, the same Parliament will meet to begin a new session, but after dissolution a new Parliament must be elected.

Nowadays a session normally runs from mid November in one year to early November the next year. A public Bill introduced during a session must pass through all its stages and receive royal assent before the end of the session or it is lost, but consideration of private Bills may continue from one session to the next.

A session is normally dated by the years in which it was held.

*Example 4.1*
The session which began 16 November 1994 and ended 8 November 1995 is:

session 1994–95

For the purpose of numbering Acts of Parliament up to and including 1962, a session is identified by the regnal year or years in which it was held. Regnal years are explained in the introduction to the List of Regnal Years. Almost all sessions in the nineteenth and twentieth centuries started in one regnal year and ended in the next.

*Example 4.2*
The session which started 31 October 1961 and ended 25 October 1962 took place in the 10th and 11th years of the reign of Elizabeth II and is:

10 & 11 Eliz 2

A session which extended over three regnal years is described by using all the regnal year numbers.

*Example 4.3*
The session which began 26 October 1948 and ended 16 December 1949
is:

12, 13 & 14 Geo 6

For a session which started in one reign and finished in another, the
regnal years of both sovereigns are used.

*Example 4.4*
The session which began 31 October 1951 and ended 30 October 1952 is:

15 & 16 Geo 6 & 1 Eliz 2

If there were two or more sessions in a regnal year then they are
numbered session 1, session 2 etc., abbreviated as sess. 1, sess. 2 etc.

*Example 4.5*
24 Geo 3, sess. 2

## 4.2  HANSARD

### 4.2.1  Publication

Publication of verbatim reports of proceedings in Parliament developed
during the nineteenth century and has been associated with the Hansard
family of printers and publishers. Regular reports of Parliamentary
proceedings were made by William Cobbett from 1803, and Thomas
Curson Hansard acquired the right to publish these, producing the
*Parliamentary Debates from the Year 1803 to the Present Time* in 41 vols
(1812–20), then *Parliamentary Debates. New Series* in 25 vols (1820–30).
Hansard also published the retrospective *Parliamentary History of England from the Earliest Period to the Year 1803*, begun by Cobbett and
completed by John Wright, in 36 vols (1806–20). Proceedings from 1830 to
1891 were reported in *Hansard's Parliamentary Debates*, 3rd series, in 356
vols (1831–91), but the Hansard business became insolvent and the next
series was published without Hansard's name as *Parliamentary Debates.
Authorised Edition*, 4th series, in 199 vols (1892–1908). Each volume of
reports up to the end of the 4th series contains reports of debates in both
Houses of Parliament.

From 1909 reporting has been, and still is, by staff employed by
Parliament, and the House of Commons and the House of Lords have been
reported in separate volumes. At first the title of the 5th series was

*Parliamentary Debates (Official Report)* but *(Hansard)* was added after *Parliamentary Debates* as from vol. 394 (reporting 11 November 1942–23 November 1943) of the House of Commons division and vol. 130 (reporting 24 November 1943–8 March 1944) of the House of Lords.

The *Official Report* is now published daily when Parliament is sitting, and the daily parts for each week are also issued together in paper covers as *Weekly Hansard* (for the House of Commons) and *House of Lords Weekly Hansard*. Later the report is issued in bound volumes, each of which covers a fortnight's proceedings.

From the beginning, the text of Hansard has been laid out in two columns to a page and it is the columns that are numbered not the pages. (Cobbett referred to the columns as 'pages' as he did in his *Complete Collection of State Trials*.)

Written answers to questions to Ministers have been printed in Hansard since the beginning of the 5th series and have had separate column numbers since vol. 418 (reporting 22 January–8 February 1946) of the House of Commons division and vol. 523 (reporting 7–29 November 1990) of the House of Lords.

Separate reports are issued of proceedings in standing committees (including the committees which consider Bills, though proceedings in a committee of the whole House are in the regular series of the *Official Report*).

The Hansard reports are the only reports of proceedings in Parliament which may be cited in court (*Practice Direction (Hansard: Citation)* [1995] 1 WLR 192).

### 4.2.2 Citation

Reports of Parliamentary proceedings are often cited by giving an abbreviation of the title of the series cited (which means there are different abbreviations for different series), the series number, volume number and column number.

However, it is suggested that it is simpler to refer to all the series as 'Hansard' and cite the date of the proceedings and the column number. The relevant volume can be found readily from this because the spine of each volume states the dates it covers. For proceedings from 1909 onwards it is necessary to specify whether the proceedings are in the House of Commons (HC), House of Lords (HL) or a committee.

*Recommendation 4.1*

(a)   Cite a report of proceedings in the House of Commons from 1909 on in the form:

Hansard HC, date of proceedings, col. xx
Hansard HC, date of proceedings, written answers, col. xx
Hansard HC Standing Committee A [or appropriate name of committee],
date of proceedings, col. xx

(b)   Cite reports of proceedings in the House of Lords similarly but with
HL instead of HC:

Hansard HL, date of proceedings, col. xx

and so on.
(c)   Cite reports of proceedings before 1909 in the form:

Hansard, date of proceedings, col. xx

(d)   The plural of 'col.' is 'coll.'.

*Example 4.6*
Hansard HC, 12 June 1995, coll. 493–4
Hansard HC, 7 November 1995, written answers, col. 662
Hansard HC Standing Committee D, 27 June 1989, col. 548
Hansard HL, 6 April 1989, col. 1246
Hansard HL, 28 February 1994, written answers, col. 66
Hansard, 5 May 1887, col. 931

*Alternative to recommendation 4.1*

(a)   Use 'c.' and 'cc.' instead of 'col.' and 'coll.'.
(b)   Use an alternative form of citation depending on which series is
being cited. For the 1st to 4th series:

volume number Parl Deb, 1st/2nd/3rd/4th ser., col. xx

For the 5th and 6th series:

volume number HC Deb, 5th/6th ser., col. xx
volume number HC Deb, 5th/6th ser., written answers, col. xx
volume number HL Deb, 5th ser., col. xx
volume number HL Deb, 5th ser., written answers, col. xx

### 4.2.3   Dates of the series

The series cover the following periods:

1st series: 22 November 1803–28 February 1820
2nd series: 21 April 1820–23 July 1830
3rd series: 26 October 1830–5 August 1891
4th series: 9 February 1892–21 December 1908
5th series HC: 16 February 1909–13 March 1981
5th series HL: 16 February 1909–
6th series HC: 16 March 1981–

## 4.3 BILLS

### 4.3.1 Types of Bill

An Act of Parliament is enacted when the royal assent to it is notified to Parliament, but before this can occur, a draft of the Act (called a Bill) must be introduced into Parliament and considered in accordance with Parliament's procedures. A Bill may be:

(a)   a public Bill, first introduced, during public business, into the House of Commons by a member or members, or by order of the House, or into the House of Lords by a Lord, or
(b)   a private Bill, first introduced by a petition deposited in the Private Bill Office of the House of Commons, or, if it is a 'personal Bill' (dealing with the personal affairs of an individual), by a petition deposited in the Office of the Clerk of the Parliaments for consideration by the House of Lords.

A public Bill may be:

(a)   a government Bill, introduced and taken through its Parliamentary stages by a government Minister (and so normally assured of being passed),
(b)   an unofficial member's Bill (commonly known as a 'private member's Bill' — not to be confused with a private Bill) introduced without government support.

A public Bill, whether government or private member's, may be a 'hybrid Bill' subject to a special procedure (similar to the procedure for private Bills) for consideration of private interests which it affects.

### 4.3.2 Summary of procedure on a public Bill introduced into the Commons

*First reading.*   Provided the member or members introducing the Bill are entitled under the House's Standing Orders to introduce it, first reading is a formality and the House will order the Bill to be printed and to be read a second time on a date nominated by the member in charge of the Bill. There is no debate or vote, though first reading of a private member's Bill may be preceded by a debate under the so-called '10-minute rule' (Standing Order 19) in which the member asks for the House's leave to bring in the Bill. There is in fact no reading aloud of the contents of a Bill on its first reading. The draft Bill is examined by clerks in the Public Bill Office, who give it a House of Commons Bill number and send it for printing and publication by HMSO.

*Second reading.* This is a debate by the House on the principle of the Bill. There is a vote on whether the Bill should be read a second time. The Bill cannot be amended at this stage. If the House votes not to read a second time then the Bill proceeds no further. If the Bill is read a second time then it proceeds to committee stage. (Exceptionally, Consolidated Fund and Appropriation Bills do not have a committee stage.)

*Committee.* The House of Commons has a number of standing committees, each having from 16 to 50 members appointed by the Committee of Selection, and a chair appointed by the Speaker. They are called Standing Committee A, B, C etc. After the House has resolved to read a Bill a second time, the Speaker allocates it to a standing committee unless (which is rare) the House has resolved that the committee stage be taken in some other way, such as by a committee of the whole House. At the start of its committee stage the text of a Bill will be as it was first printed after first reading. The committee stage is a consideration of the Bill clause by clause during which amendments may be approved. Committee members notify their amendments in advance and they are printed and published by HMSO. On the day of a committee stage, a 'marshalled list of amendments' is produced stating all the amendments in the order in which they are to be considered. (Sometimes preliminary marshalled lists are produced before that day.) However, the chair can permit a member to move an amendment of which no notice has been given. Accordingly, examination of the report of proceedings in committee is the only sure way of discovering what amendments were considered there. After the committee stage of a Bill is completed, the Bill is reprinted as amended (unless there have been no amendments) and the reprint is given a fresh House of Commons Bill number. Then the Bill is reported to the House for consideration (report stage).

*Report.* A Bill is considered by the House on report in much the same way as it is examined in committee except that there are stricter rules of debate and speeches are limited. Amendments may be made. On completion of the report stage the member in charge normally moves that the Bill be read a third time. In theory the Bill could be sent back to committee (recommitted), though this is very rare, or the member in charge could ask for the third reading to take place on a future date. If the third reading is not immediately after report stage and the Bill was significantly amended on report then it may be printed as amended on report, which print will have a new Bill number.

*Third reading.*   Third reading is a debate in the House on the contents of the Bill. Amendments to the Bill may be made provided they are only verbal and not substantive. When a Bill has been read a third time it has passed the Commons.

*Consideration by the House of Lords.*   When a public Bill introduced in the House of Commons has passed its third reading there, it is transmitted to the House of Lords, where it goes through the same stages — first reading, second reading, committee, report, third reading — as in the Commons. On the first reading the Bill is ordered to be printed and a date is set for second reading. It is given a House of Lords Bill number. Second reading in the Lords is, as in the Commons, a debate on general principles without any opportunity for amendment and is followed by a committee stage, though this is usually omitted for Finance and Consolidated Fund Bills. The committee stage of a Bill in the House of Lords is commonly taken by a committee of the whole House and is reported in Hansard HL, but some Bills are considered by public Bill committees whose proceedings are reported separately. After the committee stage is completed, the Bill is reprinted as amended (unless there have been no amendments) and the reprint is given a fresh House of Lords Bill number. Then it is considered on report (when there may be further amendments) and read a third time. In the House of Lords, substantive amendments are permitted on third reading.

*Resolution of differences between the two Houses.*   The House of Commons considers whether the amendments made by the Lords are acceptable. If there is any disagreement messages are passed between the Houses until the difference is resolved.

*Royal assent.*   When a Bill has passed both Houses of Parliament its title is included in one of the lists of Bills which are periodically presented to the sovereign for signature (only the list of titles is sent, not the texts of the Bills). The signature signifies royal assent to the Bill and this must be announced to both Houses (normally by the Speaker in the Commons and the Lord Chancellor in the Lords). The date of this announcement is the date of royal assent (Royal Assent Act 1967, s. 1) and is endorsed by the Clerk of the Parliaments on the copy of the Bill in his custody, immediately after the long title (Acts of Parliament (Commencement) Act 1793). The date so endorsed becomes part of the text of the Act (ibid.). An Act becomes law at the beginning of the day of royal assent unless there is provision for it to come into force on some other day, in which case it comes into force at the beginning of that day (Interpretation Act 1978, s. 4, re-enacting a provision first made by the Acts of Parliament (Commencement) Act 1793). Nowadays it is usual for an Act to provide that it is to be brought into force by Ministerial order, and in some cases this occurs many years after enactment. Before the 1793 Act, an Act was deemed to have come into force at the beginning of the Parliamentary session in which it was passed.

### 4.3.3   Public Bill introduced into the Lords

The procedure on a public Bill introduced in the Lords is the same as described in section 4.3.2 except that the House of Lords stages are taken first. Occasionally, Bills are introduced in both Houses simultaneously so that they can be dealt with in a single day.

### 4.3.4   Citation of a Bill

*Recommendation 4.2*

(a)   Cite a Bill by its title, the session of Parliament in which it was considered and the Bill number. It is helpful to state the stage of proceedings at which the Bill was printed.

(b)   If the discussion is of the Bill generally, rather than a particular point in it or stage of proceedings, then the Bill number may be omitted or the Bill may be described by reference to the Act which it eventually became.

*Example 4.7*
Detailed citation:

Companies Bill (Session 1988–89) as introduced into the House of Lords (House of Lords Bill 7)

General citation:

Companies Bill (Session 1988–89)
Bill which was enacted as the Companies Act 1989

*Recommendation 4.3*
A point within a Bill is cited in the same way as a point within an Act (see section 3.4) except that the subdivisions of the main text of a Bill (which will become sections when it is enacted) are called 'clauses' which are cited using the abbreviation 'cl.' (plural 'cll.'). If a Bill is amended by adding a new clause then all subsequent clauses are renumbered when the Bill is next printed. The same applies to new schedules, subclauses, paragraphs etc. Accordingly a citation of a point within a Bill must identify which print of the Bill is referred to.

*Example 4.8*
Companies Bill (Session 1988–89) as amended by Standing Committee D (House of Commons Bill 174), cl. 101(1)

## 4.4  COMMAND PAPERS

Command papers are documents printed for and presented to Parliament by command of the Sovereign. The command is in fact given by one of the Sovereign's Ministers, and command papers are essentially government documents. They are published by HMSO, traditionally without covers or with plainly printed paper covers, which were white for statements of government policy ('white papers'), green for discussion documents ('green papers') and blue for the Treaty Series of treaties signed and/or ratified by the government. Nowadays white and green papers usually have glossy pictorial covers.

As from 1833 command papers have been numbered in six series, all but the first being prefixed by varying abbreviations of the word 'command', as follows:

    1–4222: 1833–69
    C 1–C 9550: 1870–99
    Cd 1–Cd 9239: 1900–18
    Cmd 1–Cmd 9889: 1919–56
    ~~Cmnd 1–Cmnd 9927: 1956–86~~
    Cm 1– : 1986–

Although the command paper number is useful for identifying a document, finding a document from its command paper number alone is not easy.

*Recommendation 4.4*

(a)   Cite a command paper other than a treaty as if it were a book (see chapter 6). Treat a government department or other body such as a committee which is named at the head of the title-page as being responsible for the paper as the author; otherwise cite the paper by title. State the command paper number in parentheses after the title.

(b)   Cite a treaty by its title and command paper number: the place where it was made and the year in which it was made may also be given.

*Example 4.9*
A white paper with a government department named on the title-page:

Department of Trade and Industry, *Financial Services in the United Kingdom* (Cmnd 9432) (London: HMSO, 1985)

A report with no authorial body named separately on the title-page:

*Report of the Committee on Defamation* (Chairman, Mr Justice Faulks) (Cmnd 5909) (London: HMSO, 1975)

A treaty:

Universal Copyright Convention as revised (Paris, 24 July 1971) (Cmnd 5844)

## 4.5   PARLIAMENTARY PAPERS

Papers ordered to be printed by either House of Parliament (including reports by select committees) are numbered by session with a separate sequence of numbers for each House. They are often known as 'sessional papers'.

*Recommendation 4.5*
Cite a Parliamentary paper as if it were a book. Treat a committee or other body which is named at the head of the title-page as being responsible for the paper as the author; otherwise cite the paper by title. State the House, session and paper number in parentheses after the title.

*Example 4.10*
House of Commons Select Committee on Standards and Privileges, *2nd Report. Complaint against Mr Jonathan Aitken* (House of Commons Papers, Session 1995–96, 243) (London: HMSO, 1996)

Committee reports are numbered 1st, 2nd etc. for each session.

## 4.6 LAW COMMISSIONS

Reports of the Law Commission and Scottish Law Commission may be published either as command papers or as House of Commons papers, but most law libraries keep a complete set of the reports filed by report number so it is useful to give that number.

*Recommendation 4.6*
Cite a Law Commission or Scottish Law Commission report as a command paper (recommendation 4.4) or Parliamentary paper (recommendation 4.5) as appropriate, and give its report number.

*Example 4.11*

Law Commission, *Administrative Law: Judicial Review and Statutory Appeals* (Law Com. No. 226, House of Commons Papers, Session 1993–94, 669) (London: HMSO, 1994).
Law Commission, *Restitution: Mistakes of Law and* Ultra Vires *Public Authority Receipts and Payments* (Law Com. No. 227, Cm 2731) (London: HMSO, 1994).

# 5 SUBORDINATE LEGISLATION

## 5.1 INTRODUCTION

Subordinate legislation, otherwise known as delegated legislation, is legislation made by a person or persons other than the Queen in Parliament but by authority conferred by the Queen in Parliament.

*Example 5.1*
The Insolvency Act 1986, s. 411(1)(a), empowers the Lord Chancellor with the concurrence of the Secretary of State to make rules for the purpose of giving effect to parts I to VIII of the Act in relation to England and Wales. The Insolvency Rules 1986 have been made in exercise of this power and are an example of subordinate legislation.

## 5.2 PUBLICATION

### 5.2.1 Beginnings of publication

Before 1890 there was no systematic publishing of subordinate legislation. On the initiative of Alexander Pulling Jr, HMSO began to publish annual volumes of subordinate legislation commencing with the volume for 1890 called *Statutory Rules and Orders . . . Issued in the Year 1890*. HMSO also produced a collected edition of the rules and orders in force in 1890 (8 vols).

### 5.2.2 Statutory requirement

The Rules Publication Act 1893 provided (s. 3(1)) that all 'statutory rules' (a term defined in s. 4 of the Act) were to be sent to the Queen's Printer after they were made, to be numbered, printed and put on sale. Numbering of statutory rules under the Rules Publication Act 1893 began in 1894.

The Rules Publication Act 1893 was repealed and replaced by the Statutory Instruments Act 1946. This redefined the category of legislative documents which have to be sent to the Queen's Printer for numbering and publication, and renamed them 'statutory instruments'.

Numbering under the 1946 Act began in 1948. Every statutory instrument is separately printed and put on sale by HMSO as required by s. 2(1) of the 1946 Act.

### 5.2.3 Annual editions

HMSO publishes (as required by the Statutory Instruments Regulations 1947 (SI 1948/1), reg. 10) an annual edition called *Statutory Instruments* containing all statutory instruments issued during a calendar year, apart from instruments which had ceased to be in force at the end of the year and most instruments classified as 'local'. The first annual edition of *Statutory Instruments* was for 1948 and continued the annual volumes of *Statutory Rules and Orders* for 1890–1947. Instruments in the annual volumes were arranged under subject headings up to 1960. From 1961 on they have been in numerical order.

### 5.2.4 Revised editions

The most recent edition to be published by HMSO containing amended texts of subordinate legislation in force is *Statutory Rules and Orders and Statutory Instruments Revised to 31st December 1948*, 25 vols (London: HMSO, 1949–52) (vol. 25 is an index). Curiously the texts in vols 1–3 do not incorporate amendments. The previous edition was in 13 vols in 1904.

*Halsbury's Statutory Instruments* is on the same lines as *Halsbury's Statutes of England and Wales* (see section 3.2.2) except that complete texts are given only for the more important items. Despite its title it includes pre-1948 statutory rules and orders and pre-1890 instruments still in force.

### 5.3 CITATION

### 5.3.1 Citation by number

Citation of subordinate legislation by the number given under the Rules Publication Act 1893 is authorised by s. 3(2) of that Act and citation by the number given under the Statutory Instruments Act 1946 is authorised by s. 2(2) of that Act. In the copies of statutory instruments published individually, the number is printed at the top of the first page (under the heading 'Statutory instruments') and on the cover of any instrument published with a paper cover. The number is printed at the beginning of the instrument in the annual collected edition. Numbering is in arabic figures and starts again at 1 at the beginning of each calendar year.

*Recommendation 5.1*

(a)   Set out a number given under the Rules Publication Act 1893 (from 1894 to 1947) in the form:

SR&O year/number

(b)   Set out a number given under the Statutory Instruments Act 1946 (from 1948 on) in the form:

SI year/number

*Example 5.2*
SR&O 1912/348
SI 1992/3233

*Alternative to recommendation 5.1*

(a)   Punctuate S.R. & O. and S.I.
(b)   Use year No. instead of year/.

In addition to its main number, the heading to an instrument may give, in parentheses, a subsidiary number preceded by a letter. The series of subsidiary numbers are:

C     commencement orders bringing Acts or parts of Acts into force
L     instruments relating to fees or procedure in courts in England and Wales
S     instruments made by Scottish authorities and relating to Scotland only
NI    Orders in Council making laws for Northern Ireland

*Example 5.3*
SI 1992/902 (which brought into force a subsection of an Act) has the subsidiary number C. 32.

Except for the NI series (see section 3.3.10) these subsidiary numbers are not used in citation.

### 5.3.2   Citation by title

It is thought that every statutory instrument includes a provision for its citation by a title.

*Example 5.4*
Regulation 1(1) of SI 1992/3233 provides:

These Regulations may be cited as the Copyright (Computer Programs) Regulations 1992.

The title of a statutory instrument is printed at the head of the instrument in copies published by HMSO (whether separately or in the annual edition) after the number of the instrument and after a heading giving the instrument's subject classification. The subject headings show where the instrument will be classified in the subject indexes in the *List of Statutory Instruments* which HMSO publishes monthly and annually. They are not used in citing instruments.

In the heading to an instrument a title is always preceded by the definite article, but this is not an essential part of the title for citation purposes.

The title of an instrument always ends with the year and this is an essential part of the title.

*Recommendation 5.2*
Treat an initial definite article as not being part of the title of an item of subordinate legislation.

## 5.3.3   Abbreviated titles

When an item of delegated legislation is repeatedly mentioned in a document, its title may be abbreviated. Commonly the main words are replaced by their initials.

*Recommendation 5.3*
When making up an abbreviated title for a piece of delegated legislation, always include the date. Explain every abbreviated title when it is first used or in a table of abbreviations.

*Example 5.5*
A suitable abbreviated title for the Public Offers of Securities Regulations 1995 (SI 1995/1537) is:

POSR 1995

Abbreviations for titles of legislation using initial letters are very common in legal writing but they are not compulsory. The fact that abbreviations are used for some pieces of legislation which are cited many times in a document does not mean that every piece of legislation cited in the document has to be given an abbreviation.

### 5.3.4 Choice of method of citation

The text of an item of subordinate legislation may easily be found from its number. Since 1961 the items in the annual editions of statutory instruments have been in numerical order. Previous annual editions have numerical indexes and there is a numerical table in vol. 25 of *Statutory Rules and Orders and Statutory Instruments Revised to 31st December 1948*. There is also a numerical list in the *Table of Government Orders* published annually by HMSO and there is a Chronological List of Instruments in *Halsbury's Statutory Instruments*. An instrument can be located from its title alone by using the alphabetical list in *Halsbury's Statutory Instruments*. Despite the convenience of the numbers they are not memorable and most people prefer verbal titles. However, the titles of most present-day statutory instruments are very cumbersome.

*Recommendation 5.4*

(a)  Cite a piece of subordinate legislation by title (see section 5.3.2) but give its number as well (see section 5.3.1), when first mentioning the item in a document and/or in a table of subordinate legislation.

(b)  If many pieces of subordinate legislation with cumbersome titles are to be cited it may be preferable to cite them all by number only.

*Example 5.6*
Palace of Westminster (Appointed Day) Order 1992 (SI 1992/902)

### 5.3.5 Abbreviated citations

*Recommendation 5.5*
After a piece of delegated legislation has been cited fully in a document in accordance with recommendation 5.4, the following methods can be used to shorten subsequent citations of the same item of legislation:

(a)  Use an abbreviated title (described in section 5.3.3).

(b)  Legislation passed in, for example, 1995 can be referred to as the '1995 Order/Regulations/Rules'. This method is available only if there is no ambiguity about which legislation of a particular year is being cited.

(c)  If the first citation gave both title and number then use the number alone in subsequent citations.

(d)  Use 'ibid.' (see section 1.6).

(e)  When an article, regulation, rule, schedule or other subdivision of legislation is being cited, it may not be necessary to cite the legislation at all, see recommendations 5.7, 5.8 and 5.9.

### 5.3.6   Northern Ireland

Until 1973, subordinate legislation in Northern Ireland was issued as
'statutory rules and orders', numbered in annual sequences like United
Kingdom statutory rules and orders. From 1974 the name has been
changed to 'statutory rules'. Northern Ireland subordinate legislation may
be cited either by number or by title in the same way as United Kingdom
legislation.

*Recommendation 5.6*

(a)   Cite the number of a piece of Northern Ireland subordinate
legislation in the form:

SR&O NI year/number

(for 1922–73), or

SR year/number

(for 1974 on).
(b)   Treat an initial definite article as not being part of the title of an
item of subordinate legislation.
(c)   Cite a piece of subordinate legislation by title but give its number
as well, when first mentioning the item in a document and/or in a table of
subordinate legislation.

*Example 5.7*
Partnerships and Unlimited Companies (Accounts) Regulations (Northern Ireland) 1994 (SR 1994/133)

*Alternative to recommendation 5.6*

(a)   Punctuate S.R. & O. (N.I.) and S.R.
(b)   Use year No. instead of year/.

### 5.4   CITING A POINT IN AN ITEM OF SUBORDINATE
### LEGISLATION

### 5.4.1   Nomenclature of subdivisions

The nomenclature of the subdivisions of the main text of a statutory
instrument depends on the title of the instrument.

A statutory instrument may describe itself as an 'Order', 'Regulations' or 'Rules'. Orders include Orders in Council and Orders of Council. Very occasionally, other terms such as 'Directions' and 'Warrant' are used.

*Example 5.8*
Copyright (Recordings of Folksongs for Archives) (Designated Bodies) Order 1989 (SI 1989/1012)
Copyright (Librarians and Archivists) (Copying of Copyright Material) Regulations 1989 (SI 1989/1212)
Copyright Tribunal Rules 1989 (SI 1989/1129)
Federation of Rhodesia and Nyasaland (Dissolution) Order in Council 1963 (SI 1963/2085)
Professions Supplementary to Medicine (Registration Rules) Order of Council 1962 (SI 1962/1765)

(a)   The main text of an Order, Order in Council or Order of Council is divided into 'articles' numbered with arabic figures (1, 2 etc.) and cited by number preceded by 'art.' (plural 'arts').

(b)   The main text of Regulations is divided into 'regulations' numbered with arabic figures and cited by number preceded by 'reg.' (plural 'regs').

(c)   The main text of Rules is divided into 'rules' numbered with arabic figures and cited by number preceded by 'r.' (plural 'rr.').

*Recommendation 5.7*

(a)   To cite an article, regulation or rule in an item of delegated legislation, give a citation of the Order, Regulations or Rules in accordance with recommendation 5.4 or 5.5 followed by a comma and then the article, regulation or rule number preceded by the abbreviation 'art.', 'reg.' or 'r.' as appropriate. If two or more are cited, use 'arts', 'regs' or 'rr.'.

(b)   The citation of the piece of legislation may be omitted if it has already been cited in the text (not just in a heading) and it is clear which piece of legislation is being referred to. Usually, the citation of the legislation should not be omitted if the last time it was mentioned was in a different chapter or other division of the document or if another piece of legislation has been mentioned since.

(c)   If omitting the citation of the legislation means that the citation of the article, regulation or rule begins a sentence then use 'Article', 'Regulation' or 'Rule' as appropriate (or the plural) instead of an abbreviation.

*Example 5.9*
Law Reform (Miscellaneous Provisions) (Scotland) Act 1990 Commencement (No. 1) Order 1990, art. 3

Companies Act 1985 (Audit Exemption) Regulations 1994, reg. 4
Magistrates' Courts (Discontinuance of Proceedings) Rules 1986, r. 5

*Alternative to recommendation 5.7*

(a)   Omit the punctuation.
(b)   Omit the space before the article, regulation or rule number.
(c)   Use capital 'A' and 'R'.
(d)   Do not abbreviate 'article', 'regulation' or 'rule' at all.
(e)   Put the article, regulation or rule reference before the short title.

### 5.4.1.1   *Citation grammatically part of text statement*

When a citation of an article, regulation or rule is grammatically part of
the text, the form in recommendation 5.7 may be used, followed by a
comma, or a less abbreviated form with the article, regulation or rule
reference first followed by 'of the' and then the citation of the instrument
('of' may be preferred to 'of the' if the instrument is cited by number or an
abbreviated title is used). At the beginning of a sentence, 'Article',
'Regulation' or 'Rule' should be used instead of an abbreviation.

*Example 5.10*
Regulation 2 of the Definition of Subsidiary (Consequential Amend-
ments) Regulations 1990 amends s. 77(3) of the Electricity Act 1989.
Regulation 2 of SI 1990/1395 amends s. 77(3) of the Electricity Act 1989.

### 5.4.2   Paragraphs and further subdivisions

The next subdivision of an article, regulation or rule is called a 'paragraph'
(abbreviation 'para.', plural 'paras') numbered with arabic figures in
parentheses: (1), (2) etc. The parentheses are an essential part of the
reference.

A paragraph may be subdivided into subparagraphs designated by
lower-case letters in parentheses: (a), (b) etc. The parentheses are an
essential part of the reference.

A subparagraph may be divided into subsubparagraphs designated by
lower-case roman numerals in parentheses: (i), (ii) etc. The parentheses
are an essential part of the reference.

*Recommendation 5.8*
To cite a subdivision of an article, regulation or rule, put the paragraph
reference after the article, regulation or rule number without a space,
then, as necessary, the subparagraph reference then the subsubparagraph
reference. The citation of the piece of legislation may be omitted (see

recommendation 5.7(b)), but omitting the article, regulation or rule number, or anything else before the final subdivision reference is not recommended. The article, regulation or rule number is still preceded by 'art.', 'reg.' or 'r.' (or the appropriate word in full at the beginning of a sentence), not 'para.', 'subpara.' or 'subsubpara.'.

*Example 5.11*
Public Offers of Securities Regulations 1995 (SI 1995/1537), reg. 7(2)
POSR 1995, reg. 7(2)(a)
SI 1995/1537, reg. 7(2)(a)(ii)

*Alternative to recommendation 5.8*
Put a space between article, regulation or rule number and paragraph reference and so on.

If the article, regulation or rule number is omitted then the paragraph reference is preceded by 'para.' (plural 'paras'). If both article, regulation or rule number and paragraph reference are omitted then the subparagraph reference is preceded by 'subpara.' (plural 'subparas'). A subsubparagraph reference on its own is preceded by 'subsubpara.' (plural 'subsubparas'). At the beginning of a sentence use a complete word rather than an abbreviation.

### 5.4.3   Intervening division references cannot be omitted

A description in the form 'paragraph (2) of the Public Offers of Securities Regulations 1995' is ambiguous. The intervening article, regulation or rule number must be stated.

### 5.4.4   Two or more divisions of the same article, regulation or rule

When referring to two or more divisions of the same article, regulation or rule, the article, regulation or rule number need not be repeated.

*Example 5.12*
Public Offers of Securities Regulations 1995 (SI 1995/1537), reg. 7(2)(m) and (11)

not 'reg. 7(2)(m) and reg. 7(11)'.

It is wrong to use 'regs' in this situation. Instead of 'and' a comma may be used (for example, reg. 7(2)(m), (11)) but leaving no space (for example, reg. 7(2)(m)(11)) is not recommended.

## 5.4.5   Parts and chapters

As well as being divided into articles, regulations or rules, the main text of a piece of subordinate legislation may be divided into 'parts' numbered with capital roman numerals, I, II etc. The numbering of articles, regulations or rules continues regardless of division into parts.

Parts may be divided into 'chapters', which are numbered with capital roman numerals.

The method of citing parts and chapters of subordinate legislation is the same as for Acts — see section 3.4.6.

*Example 5.13*
Public Offers of Securities Regulations 1995 (SI 1995/1537), part II

## 5.4.6   Schedules

A schedule to an item of subordinate legislation is cited in the same way as a schedule to an Act (see section 3.4.7).

*Example 5.14*
Public Offers of Securities Regulations 1995 (SI 1995/1537), sch. 2, para. 2(3)

## 5.5   RULES OF COURT

Sets of rules of court are among the longest statutory instruments and have a slightly different nomenclature for their subdivisions. The Supreme Court Rules currently in use (Rules of the Supreme Court 1965) are based on rules which were originally issued as 'general orders' of the court, Accordingly they are divided into 'orders' numbered with arabic figures (though in previous versions of the rules they were capital roman numerals). Each order is divided into 'rules', also numbered in arabic figures with the numbering of rules starting at 1 again in each order. A rule may be divided into paragraphs, subparagraphs and subsubparagraphs as described in section 5.4.2. The County Court Rules 1981 follow the same pattern.

*Recommendation 5.9*

   (a)   To cite a rule in a set of rules which is divided into orders, cite the title of the rules, followed by a comma, the abbreviation 'ord.' the number of the order, a comma, the abbreviation 'r.' followed by the number of the rule.

(b)   The Rules of the Supreme Court 1965 are commonly cited as 'RSC 1965' or 'RSC'. The County Court Rules 1981 are commonly cited as 'CCR 1981' or 'CCR'.

(c)   The citation of the title may be omitted as described in recommendation 5.7(b). If this makes the citation of the order begin a sentence then use 'Order' instead of 'ord.'

(d)   Cite subdivisions of a rule in accordance with recommendation 5.8.

*Example 5.15*
County Court Rules 1981, ord. 26, r. 8
CCR, ord. 26, r. 8
Rules of the Supreme Court 1965, ord. 38, r. 2(3)
RSC, ord. 38, r. 2(3)

*Alternative to recommendation 5.9*

(a)   Use 'O.' instead of 'ord.'.
(b)   Use 'Ord.' instead of 'ord.'.
(c)   Omit punctuation.
(d)   Omit spaces after 'ord.' and 'r.'.

In practice, alternatives (a) and (b) are equally popular (and recommendation 5.9 diplomatically chooses neither). It is possible that future rules of court will not be divided into orders.

## 5.6   TABLE OF DELEGATED LEGISLATION

A table of delegated legislation for a document lists every item of delegated legislation cited in the document. Under each item there is a list of all the points in the item cited in the document stating where in the document each point is cited. Nowadays this table is usually called a 'table of statutory instruments'.

A table of statutory instruments can list the legislation either in chronological order by calendar year and SR&O or SI number, or in alphabetical order of title. Sometimes lists in both forms are provided.

When listing is by title, SR&O and SI numbers may be provided, even if they are not given in the main text of the document, to assist in locating the text of each item.

If subordinate legislation from more than one jurisdiction is cited there may be separate lists for each jurisdiction.

## 5.7   FURTHER READING

The Preface to the annual edition of *Statutory Instruments* sets out in detail the arrangements for publishing statutory instruments.

# 6 BOOKS AND ARTICLES

## 6.1 ORIGINATOR

The first element in the citation of a book or article is normally the name of the author. In this chapter, as well as the term 'author', the more general term 'originator' is used. The originator of a book or article is the person, people or organisation responsible for the intellectual content of the book or article. An originator may be, for example, an individual author, two or more individuals as joint authors, or an organisation such as a committee or government department.

If no originator can be identified, the first element in the citation of a book or article will be the title. The use of 'Anonymous' as a substitute for an originator's name in a citation is not recommended.

## 6.2 CITATION OF BOOKS

### 6.2.1 Citation by abbreviated title

Up to the early nineteenth century there were few legal textbooks, and lawyers could be confident that the mere mention of any legal author's name, or an abbreviated version of it, with an abbreviated version of a title would be sufficient to identify a book. In present-day conditions this is unrealistic and citations of books must now give fuller descriptions as explained later in this chapter. Even so, some of the old books are still regularly cited by abbreviation. The books cited in this way probably all come into the category of authorities, that is, books which are accepted as stating authoritatively the common law as it was when they were written.

*Example 6.1*
Sir William Blackstone, *Commentaries on the Laws of England* is cited as:

Bl Com

*Recommendation 6.1*

A number of old authoritative books are given in the List of Recommended Forms of Citation for Law Reports and Other Publications with recommended abbreviations. However, the use of abbreviations for citing books is less familiar than for the citation of law reports and periodicals, and if an old authority is to be cited only occasionally in a document, it may be better to give full details in the citation in accordance with recommendation 6.2.

## 6.2.2  Full citation

### 6.2.2.1  *General form of a full citation*

*Recommendation 6.2*

Unless it is decided to use an abbreviated citation (see recommendation 6.1), a citation of a book should give the following data:

(a)  name of the originator, if any (a person named on the title-page as editor or compiler may be treated as originator of the book if no one else is named as author);

(b)  title of book;

(c)  volume number, if the book was published in two or more separately paginated volumes and only one of them is being cited;

(d)  number of edition, if not the first;

(e)  name of editor and/or translator and/or compiler (if any), if not treated as originator of the book;

(f)  series title and number within series, if any, if the information will assist location of the book;

(g)  place of publication;

(h)  name of publisher;

(i)  year of publication.

The data given in a citation of a book should be taken from the title-page of the book and should reproduce the spelling used there.

If a person described on the title page as editor is treated as the originator of the work, put '(ed.)' (or '(eds)' if there are two or more joint editors) after the originator's name in the citation. Similarly, for a compiler, put '(comp.)'.

The recommended layout and typography for a citation of a book are as illustrated in example 6.2. Further information about each element is given in the following paragraphs.

*Example 6.2*

J.H. Baker, *Manual of Law French*, 2nd ed. (Aldershot: Scolar Press, 1990)

Department of Trade and Industry, *Financial Services in the United Kingdom* (Cmnd 9432) (London: HMSO, 1985)

R.C. I'Anson Banks, *Lindley and Banks on Partnership*, 17th ed. (London: Sweet & Maxwell, 1995)

Sir William Holdsworth, *A History of English Law*, vol. 2 (London: Methuen, 1936)

Eric Stockdale and Silvia Casale (eds), *Criminal Justice under Stress* (London: Blackstone, 1992)

### 6.2.2.2 *Names of individuals*

According to recommendation 6.2, in a citation of a book, the name of an individual author should be in the form in which it appears on the book's title-page, but many people place limits on information they will give in citations about forenames, for example, giving only one forename or giving only the initials of forenames; many do not give any information about forenames at all.

It is common to adopt a rule that where there are more than a certain number of joint authors, only the first one will be named in a citation, followed by 'et al.' or 'and others'. Usually the maximum number of authors to be named is either two or three.

In a list of books and articles arranged alphabetically it is usual to put the forenames or initials of an author's name after the surname so as to make the alphabetical order clear. If it is decided to put forenames after surnames, it may also be decided that this will apply only to the first name when there are joint authors.

If the title of a book includes the name of its author, or of the author of earlier editions, it is normally unnecessary to give an originator's name as well as the title in a citation. In a list of books arranged alphabetically by author, though, it may be necessary to give the originator's name as well as the title so as to make the alphabetical ordering clear.

*Example 6.3*

In a citation:

*Salmond and Heuston on the Law of Torts*, 20th ed. (London: Sweet & Maxwell, 1992)

In an alphabetical list:

Heuston, R.F.V., and Buckley, R.A., *Salmond and Heuston on the Law of Torts*, 20th ed. (London: Sweet & Maxwell, 1992)

Sometimes a rule is adopted that the whole of an author's surname should be in capital letters but the effect is not aesthetically pleasing. In many American law reviews, originators' names are set in capitals and small capitals.

### 6.2.2.3  *Title*

The most common convention, which is recommended here, is to set the title of a book in italic and to give initial capitals to the first and last words of the title and to all other words in the title apart from articles, conjunctions, prepositions and the word 'to' in the infinitive of a verb. (But a preposition or article occurring as part of a name which is usually capitalised, such as Los Angeles, is also capitalised within a book title.) This is known as 'upper- and lower-case'. (In many American law reviews, the letters which would be lower-case in this convention are set in small capitals.) A less common convention is to give an initial capital to the first word and capitalise the rest of the title as if it were ordinary text (that is, giving capital letters only to words, such as proper nouns, that are capitalised wherever they occur in a sentence). This is the convention usually adopted nowadays in library catalogues. There is also a convention of setting book titles wholly in capitals but the effect is not aesthetically pleasing.

The first word, other than an article, of a title should always be given but other words may be omitted if they are not necessary to convey the sense of the title. An omission should be marked by an ellipsis sign (three spaced full points).

### *Example 6.4*

In the List of Recommended Forms of Citation for Law Reports and Other Publications in this book, the title of Thomas Hare's *Reports of Cases Adjudged in the High Court of Chancery* is given as:

*Reports . . . Chancery*

On title-pages, it is usual nowadays not to use punctuation to separate grammatically independent parts of a title but to distinguish the parts by typography or layout. In a citation, it may be necessary to add punctuation for clarity. Usually, a colon is put before an explanatory subtitle.

If all of a subtitle is omitted from a citation (as is common) because it is not necessary to convey the sense of the title, the omission need not be indicated by an ellipsis sign.

### 6.2.2.3  *Volume number*

Give a volume number in arabic figures regardless of the typography used on the title-page. Precede the number with 'vol.' or whatever term is used on the title-page (e.g., 'part' or 'book') using an appropriate abbreviation from table 6.1.

*Table 6.1   Recommended abbreviations for use in citing books and articles*

| Term | Abbreviation |
|---|---|
| appendix | app. |
| article (subdivision of a document) | art. |
| book (subdivision of a work) | bk |
| chapter | ch. |
| circa | c. |
| column | col. or c. |
| columns | coll. or cc. |
| compiled, compiler | comp. |
| edited by, editor | ed. |
| edition | ed. or edn |
| editions | eds or edns |
| editors | eds |
| figure | fig. |
| folio | f. |
| folios | ff. |
| illustration | ill. |
| impression | impr. |
| new series | n.s. |
| no date | n.d. |
| no place | n.p. |
| note | n. |
| notes | nn. |
| number | No. |
| numbers | Nos |
| page | p. |
| pages | pp. |
| part | pt |
| plate | pl. |
| section | sect. |
| series | ser. |
| supplement | suppl. |
| table | tab. |
| translated, translation, translator | transl. |
| volume | vol. |
| volumes | vols |

### 6.2.2.4  Edition

Give an edition number in arabic ordinals — 1st, 2nd, 3rd etc. — regardless of the typography of the title-page. It is unnecessary to specify which impression or reprint of an edition has been consulted unless there is a crucial textual difference in it. It is also unnecessary to reproduce title-page descriptions of editions, such as 'revised and enlarged'. Some people prefer 'edn' to 'ed.' as an abbreviation of 'edition'.

### 6.2.2.5  Place

Only the town where the book was published is given in a citation but further information, such as county (or State in the USA) or country may be added if the location is thought to be unfamiliar or there is risk of confusion with another town of the same name. If more than one place of publication is given on the title-page, only the first-named place need be given in the citation. If no place of publication is named on the title-page, use 'n.p.' (for 'no place').

### 6.2.2.6  Publisher

According to recommendation 6.2, in a citation of a book, the name of the publisher should be in the form in which it appears on the book's title-page. However, the name may be further abbreviated if doing so will not affect identification of the publisher. For example, 'University Press' is commonly abbreviated to 'UP'. Indications of corporate form in publishers' names, such as 'Ltd' and 'plc', are usually omitted in citations.

If more than one publisher is named on the title-page, only the first-named publisher need be given in the citation. If the first-named publisher is foreign, but a local publisher is also named on the title-page, it may be helpful to add the name of the local publisher.

It is usual to omit the name of the publisher when citing a book published before the twentieth century. Many people decide not to give publishers' names for any books they cite. If there is no publisher's name in a citation, the place of publication is followed by a comma instead of a colon.

### 6.2.2.7  Date

Although data for the citation of a book should normally be taken from the title-page, the year of publication will often have to be taken from the next page, known as the verso title-page. It is unnecessary to give season, month or day of publication as well as year in a citation, even if this information is provided on the title-page or its verso.

If the date of publication is not given on the title-page or its verso, use 'n.d.' (for 'no date') or give (in square brackets) the probable year of publication obtained from another source. If there is uncertainty about a date, precede it with 'c.' (for 'circa') or follow it with a question mark. In a citation of a loose-leaf publication, the word 'loose-leaf' is used instead of a publication date. If the whole of a multivolume work is cited and the volumes were published at different times, give the range of publication dates.

*Example 6.5*
*Stroud's Judicial Dictionary of Words and Phrases*, 5th ed. by John S. James (London: Sweet & Maxwell, 1986–94)

*6.2.2.8 Alternative punctuation*
There are several popular alternative systems of punctuation for book citations. The parentheses around the details of publication may be omitted. If so, the place of publication may be preceded by a comma or a full point. A full point may be used instead of a comma after the originator's name.

A space may be inserted between two or more initials of forenames.

## 6.3 CITATION OF ARTICLES

### 6.3.1 Introduction

As in citing a book, the first part of the citation of an article is the name of the originator and the title of the article (see section 6.3.2). It is then necessary to identify the book (see section 6.3.3) or journal (see section 6.3.4) in which the article has been published and to state where the article is located within the book or journal.

### 6.3.2 Originator and title of an article

*Recommendation 6.3*

(a)   In a citation of an article, give the name of the originator as it appears in the heading or at the end of the article and the title of the article as it appears in the heading.

(b)   Put quotation marks at the beginning and end of the title. Give an initial capital to the first word of the title of an article and capitalise the rest of the title as if it were ordinary text (that is, giving capital letters only to proper nouns and other words that are capitalised wherever they occur in a sentence).

(c)   If the title includes a case name, italicise the names of parties in accordance with recommendation 2.1.

(d)   In a list of books and articles arranged alphabetically, it is usual to put the forenames or initials of an author's name after the surname so as to make the alphabetical order clear.

See examples 6.6 to 6.10.

*Alternative to recommendation 6.3*

(a)•  For limitations on information about forenames and maximum number of joint authors to be named see section 6.2.2.2.
(b)   Omit quotation marks from the title.
(c)   Give initial capitals to the first and last words of the title and to all other words in the title apart from articles, conjunctions, prepositions and the word 'to' in the infinitive of a verb. (But also give an initial capital to a preposition or article occurring within a title as part of a name which is usually capitalised, such as Los Angeles.)
(d)   If it is decided to adopt the rule that forenames are placed after surnames, it may be decided to apply it only to the first name when there are joint authors.
(e)   In American law reviews in which book titles are set in capitals and small capitals, article titles are set in upper and lower-case italic without quotation marks.

### 6.3.3   Article in a book

*Recommendation 6.4*
To cite an article in a book, give the originator and the title of the article in accordance with recommendation 6.3 followed by:

— the word 'in'
— the citation of the book in accordance with recommendation 6.2
— the numbers of the first and last pages of the article.

*Example 6.6*
Geoffrey Bindman, 'Freedom of expression' in David Bean (ed.), *Law Reform for All* (London: Blackstone, 1996), pp. 139–51

An introduction or foreword by one author to another's book may be treated as an article in the book.

*Example 6.7*
Frederic William Maitland, 'Introduction' in Otto Gierke, *Political Theories of the Middle Age,* transl. Frederic William Maitland (Cambridge: Cambridge University Press, 1900), pp. vii–xlv

If the book consists entirely of articles by the same originator (apart from an introduction), the originator's name need not be repeated in the citation of the book.

*Example 6.8*
Sir Frederick Pollock, 'English law reporting', in *Essays in the Law* (London: Macmillan, 1922), pp. 241–57

### 6.3.4   Article in a journal

*6.3.4.1   Introduction*
A citation of an article in a journal consists of the name of the originator and the title of the article followed by the citation of the journal, which must identify:

(a)   The name of the journal.
(b)   The volume in which the article appears.
(c)   The page on which the article begins.

Unfortunately, writers in different academic disciplines have established several conventional ways of setting out this information. Lawyers usually cite law journals in the same way as they cite law reports (see section 2.4), and many legal journals in the British Isles have adopted volume-year numbering in imitation of British and Irish law reports.

*6.3.4.2   Legal style*

*Recommendation 6.5*

(a)   To cite an article in a journal, give the originator and title of the article in accordance with recommendation 6.3, followed by the citation of the journal, using an abbreviation of the title in accordance with recommendations 2.10 and 2.11 preceded by the volume year or volume number in accordance with recommendation 2.12.

(b)   If the volume is not numbered by volume year, give the year of publication of the article, in parentheses, after the title of the article and before the journal citation.

(c)   If the article is in more than one part, give the initial page numbers of each part, separated by commas, unless only one part is being cited.

*Example 6.9*
Jill Martin, 'The statutory sub-tenancy: a right against all the world?' (1977) 41 Conv NS 96

P.J. Millett, 'Tracing the proceeds of fraud' (1991) 107 LQR 71
K.W. Wedderburn, 'Shareholders' rights and the rule in *Foss* v *Harbottle*'
[1957] CLJ 194, [1958] CLJ 93

*6.3.4.3   Non-legal style*
In disciplines other than law, the order of data in the citation of a journal
is usually:

—title of journal,
—year of publication,
—volume number,
—page number.

It is common to give the numbers of both first and last pages.
   If the majority of the journals being cited are not law journals, it may be
preferred to cite them in this style.

> *Example 6.10*
> H.J. Byrom, 'Richard Tottell — his life and work', *The Library*, 1947, 4th
> ser., vol. 8, pp. 199–232.

There is an alternative convention in non-legal style that the volume
number is in bold and the abbreviation 'vol.' is omitted. Another alternative is to position the year of publication (usually in parentheses) after the
volume number.

*6.3.4.4   United States journals*
There is a valuable list of standard abbreviations for United States legal
journals in *The Bluebook. A Uniform System of Citation*, 15th ed.
(Cambridge Mass: Harvard Law Review Association, 1991), table T.13.

## 6.4   CITING A POINT IN A BOOK OR ARTICLE

*Recommendation 6.6*

   (a)   To cite a particular page within a book or article give the citation of
the book or article followed by ', p.' or 'at p.' and the page number.
   (b)   To cite a passage extending over two or more pages use 'pp.' instead
of 'p.' and give the first and last pages of the passage. It is not adequate to
state just the first page plus 'ff.' (meaning following pages) or 'et seq.',
either of which invite the reader to read the rest of the volume.
   (c)   Any other identifiable part of a book or article, such as a paragraph,
chapter, appendix or table can be cited in the same way with an

appropriate word or abbreviation in place of 'p.' or 'pp.'. Recommended abbreviations are listed in table 6.1.

(d)   When citing a point in a loose-leaf work, the issue number (which may be called a release number) or date of the page or pages cited must be given.

(e)   If a citation of a point in a book or article immediately follows a citation of the book or article itself, or a citation of another point in the same book or article, the book or article citation can be omitted on the second occasion.

*Example 6.11*
K.W. Wedderburn, 'Shareholders' rights and the rule in *Foss* v *Harbottle*' [1957] CLJ 194 at pp. 214–15
Derek French, Applications to Wind up Companies (London: Black-stone, 1993), ch. 6
M.J. Goodman (general ed.), *Encyclopedia of Health and Safety at Work Law and Practice* (London: Sweet & Maxwell, loose-leaf), para. G2-021 release 103 (February 1996)

## 6.5   ABBREVIATION

If a book or article is cited more than once in a document, the second or third citation need give only the originator's name (surname only if an individual) followed by 'op. cit.' (from the Latin *opus citatum*, meaning 'the work cited from').

*Example 6.12*
For other criticisms of artificial separate personality see M. Wolff, 'On the nature of legal persons' (1938) 54 LQR 494. For references to original German sources see Wolff, op. cit., p. 497, nn. 9 and 10.

This method of abbreviating citations cannot be used if two or more works by the same author have been cited. Readers should not be asked to search back too far in a document to find the full title of a work referred to as 'op. cit.'. If there has been a new chapter or other subdivision of the document since the work was last cited then its title should be given in full again instead of using 'op. cit.'.

A book or article cited frequently in a document may be referred to by an abbreviated citation, for example, using the author's surname and one or more significant words from the title, or the initial letters of the title. Such an abbreviation should be explained when it is first used and in a list of abbreviations.

## 6.6　NAME–DATE SYSTEM

In academic writing in many disciplines, it is usual to refer to authorities using the name-date system (also known as the 'Harvard system'). In a document, an authority is cited by the name of its originator and year of publication. (For an individual author, only the surname is used, though initials of forenames may be added to distinguish two authors with the same surname.) If the originator's name occurs naturally in the text, the year follows in parentheses, but if not, both name and year are in parentheses. If two or more cited items are by the same originator and were published in the same year they are distinguished by adding a, b etc. to the year. At the end of the document, all the authorities are listed in alphabetical order of originator (items by the same originator are listed in date order). In the list at the end of the document, each article or book is cited in full in accordance with recommendation 6.2, 6.4 or 6.5, except that the date of publication is placed immediately after the originator's name.

*Example 6.13*
In the text:

Geldart (1911, p. 93) said that the essence of the realist theory was stated by Maitland (1900, pp. xxv–xxvi). Gierke's views were subsequently used in Fascist political theory (Barker 1934, pp. lxxxiv–lxxxvii).

In the list of references:

Barker, E. (1934), 'Introduction' in Otto Gierke, *Natural Law and the Theory of Society 1550 to 1800*, transl. E. Barker (Cambridge: Cambridge University Press).
Geldart, W.M. (1911), 'Legal personality' 27 LQR 90.
Maitland, Frederic William (1900), 'Introduction' in Otto Gierke, *Political Theories of the Middle Age*, transl. Frederic William Maitland (Cambridge: Cambridge University Press, 1900), pp. vii–xlv.

In the list of references, the year of publication is after the originator's name and is not repeated after the publisher's name.

## 6.7　FURTHER READING

*The Chicago Manual of Style*, 14th ed. (Chicago: University of Chicago Press, 1993). Chapters 15 and 16 contain a very detailed treatment of references to books, articles and other material. There is a briefer and earlier version in Kate L. Turabian, *A Manual for Writers of Term Papers,*

*Theses, and Dissertations*, 5th ed. by Bonnie Birtwistle Honigsblum (Chicago: University of Chicago Press, 1987).

There are three relevant British Standards:

*British Standard Recommendations for Citing and Referencing Published Material* (BS 5605 : 1990).

*British Standard Recommendations for References to Published Materials* (BS 1629 : 1989).

*British Standard Recommendations for Citation of Unpublished Documents* (BS 6371 : 1983).

Very detailed rules for bibliographical description are given in:

*Anglo-American Cataloguing Rules*, 2nd ed. 1988 revision (Ottawa: Canadian Library Association; London: Library Association; Chicago: American Library Association, 1988).

# LIST OF REGNAL YEARS

## INTRODUCTION

The first regnal year of a sovereign's reign begins when the sovereign accedes to the Crown, the second begins on the first anniversary of succession and so on. The practice of dating documents and events in a country by regnal year of the country's sovereign was widely followed in medieval Europe after its use in the Byzantine Empire was decreed by Justinian I in AD 537. Although dating by regnal years was used in England under Anglo-Saxon kings, it was not widely used after the Norman Conquest until the reign of Richard I.

The following list gives the starting date of all regnal years in England from the first of Richard I (the limit of legal memory) to 31 December 1962 when the last surviving use of regnal-year dating — for dating statutes — ended. Unless otherwise stated each regnal year in the list ended on the day before the next one in the list started.

Regnal years are expressed by using an abbreviation of the sovereign's name. The following list gives recommended abbreviations, but others have been used.

The Gregorian or New Style calendar was promulgated by Pope Gregory XIII in 1582 but was not adopted in England until 1752. All dates in the following list before 14 September 1752 are according to the Julian calendar then used in England. However, the list follows the modern practice of dating past events with years beginning on 1 January regardless of the year numbering that would have applied when they occurred. Up to and including 1751, for most governmental and legal purposes in England, the number of the year AD was changed on 25 March (Lady Day) rather than 1 January. Opening the year on 25 March seems to have become the usual practice for governmental, legal and ecclesiastical purposes in England at the end of the twelfth century. In the following list the old official year numbering is also shown for dates from 1 January to 24 March in any year before 1752. In Scotland the beginning of the year was changed from 25 March to 1 January in 1600.

## Further reading

E.B. Fryde et al. (eds), *Handbook of British Chronology*, 3rd ed. (London: Royal Historical Society, 1986).
W.W. Greg, 'Old Style — New Style' in *Collected Papers*, ed. J.C. Maxwell (Oxford: Clarendon Press, 1966), pp. 366–73.

## ENGLISH REGNAL YEARS FROM 1189 TO 1962

### Richard I (Ric 1)

1 Ric 1: 3 Sep 1189
2 Ric 1: 3 Sep 1190
3 Ric 1: 3 Sep 1191
4 Ric 1: 3 Sep 1192
5 Ric 1: 3 Sep 1193
6 Ric 1: 3 Sep 1194
7 Ric 1: 3 Sep 1195
8 Ric 1: 3 Sep 1196
9 Ric 1: 3 Sep 1197
10 Ric 1: 3 Sep 1198

### John (John)

1 John: 27 May 1199
2 John: 27 May 1200
3 John: 27 May 1201
4 John: 27 May 1202
5 John: 27 May 1203
6 John: 27 May 1204
7 John: 27 May 1205
8 John: 27 May 1206
9 John: 27 May 1207
10 John: 27 May 1208
11 John: 27 May 1209
12 John: 27 May 1210
13 John: 27 May 1211
14 John: 27 May 1212
15 John: 27 May 1213
16 John: 27 May 1214
17 John: 27 May 1215
18 John: 27 May 1216

### Henry III (Hen 3)

1 Hen 3: 28 Oct 1216
2 Hen 3: 28 Oct 1217
3 Hen 3: 28 Oct 1218
4 Hen 3: 28 Oct 1219
5 Hen 3: 28 Oct 1220
6 Hen 3: 28 Oct 1221
7 Hen 3: 28 Oct 1222
8 Hen 3: 28 Oct 1223
9 Hen 3: 28 Oct 1224

### Henry III (Hen 3) — *continued*

10 Hen 3: 28 Oct 1225
11 Hen 3: 28 Oct 1226
12 Hen 3: 28 Oct 1227
13 Hen 3: 28 Oct 1228
14 Hen 3: 28 Oct 1229
15 Hen 3: 28 Oct 1230
16 Hen 3: 28 Oct 1231
17 Hen 3: 28 Oct 1232
18 Hen 3: 28 Oct 1233
19 Hen 3: 28 Oct 1234
20 Hen 3: 28 Oct 1235
21 Hen 3: 28 Oct 1236
22 Hen 3: 28 Oct 1237
23 Hen 3: 28 Oct 1238
24 Hen 3: 28 Oct 1239
25 Hen 3: 28 Oct 1240
26 Hen 3: 28 Oct 1241
27 Hen 3: 28 Oct 1242
28 Hen 3: 28 Oct 1243
29 Hen 3: 28 Oct 1244
30 Hen 3: 28 Oct 1245
31 Hen 3: 28 Oct 1246
32 Hen 3: 28 Oct 1247
33 Hen 3: 28 Oct 1248
34 Hen 3: 28 Oct 1249
35 Hen 3: 28 Oct 1250
36 Hen 3: 28 Oct 1251
37 Hen 3: 28 Oct 1252
38 Hen 3: 28 Oct 1253
39 Hen 3: 28 Oct 1254
40 Hen 3: 28 Oct 1255
41 Hen 3: 28 Oct 1256
42 Hen 3: 28 Oct 1257
43 Hen 3: 28 Oct 1258
44 Hen 3: 28 Oct 1259
45 Hen 3: 28 Oct 1260
46 Hen 3: 28 Oct 1261
47 Hen 3: 28 Oct 1262
48 Hen 3: 28 Oct 1263
49 Hen 3: 28 Oct 1264
50 Hen 3: 28 Oct 1265
51 Hen 3: 28 Oct 1266
52 Hen 3: 28 Oct 1267

**Henry III (Hen 3)** — *continued*

53 Hen 3: 28 Oct 1268
54 Hen 3: 28 Oct 1269
55 Hen 3: 28 Oct 1270
56 Hen 3: 28 Oct 1271
57 Hen 3: 28 Oct 1272

**Edward I (Edw 1)**

1 Edw 1: 20 Nov 1272
2 Edw 1: 20 Nov 1273
3 Edw 1: 20 Nov 1274
4 Edw 1: 20 Nov 1275
5 Edw 1: 20 Nov 1276
6 Edw 1: 20 Nov 1277
7 Edw 1: 20 Nov 1278
8 Edw 1: 20 Nov 1279
9 Edw 1: 20 Nov 1280
10 Edw 1: 20 Nov 1281
11 Edw 1: 20 Nov 1282
12 Edw 1: 20 Nov 1283
13 Edw 1: 20 Nov 1284
14 Edw 1: 20 Nov 1285
15 Edw 1: 20 Nov 1286
16 Edw 1: 20 Nov 1287
17 Edw 1: 20 Nov 1288
18 Edw 1: 20 Nov 1289
19 Edw 1: 20 Nov 1290
20 Edw 1: 20 Nov 1291
21 Edw 1: 20 Nov 1292
22 Edw 1: 20 Nov 1293
23 Edw 1: 20 Nov 1294
24 Edw 1: 20 Nov 1295
25 Edw 1: 20 Nov 1296
26 Edw 1: 20 Nov 1297
27 Edw 1: 20 Nov 1298
28 Edw 1: 20 Nov 1299
29 Edw 1: 20 Nov 1300
30 Edw 1: 20 Nov 1301
31 Edw 1: 20 Nov 1302
32 Edw 1: 20 Nov 1303
33 Edw 1: 20 Nov 1304
34 Edw 1: 20 Nov 1305
35 Edw 1: 20 Nov 1306

**Edward II (Edw 2)**

1 Edw 2: 8 Jul 1307
2 Edw 2: 8 Jul 1308
3 Edw 2: 8 Jul 1309
4 Edw 2: 8 Jul 1310
5 Edw 2: 8 Jul 1311
6 Edw 2: 8 Jul 1312
7 Edw 2: 8 Jul 1313
8 Edw 2: 8 Jul 1314
9 Edw 2: 8 Jul 1315

**Edward II (Edw 2)** — *continued*

10 Edw 2: 8 Jul 1316
11 Edw 2: 8 Jul 1317
12 Edw 2: 8 Jul 1318
13 Edw 2: 8 Jul 1319
14 Edw 2: 8 Jul 1320
15 Edw 2: 8 Jul 1321
16 Edw 2: 8 Jul 1322
17 Edw 2: 8 Jul 1323
18 Edw 2: 8 Jul 1324
19 Edw 2: 8 Jul 1325
20 Edw 2: 8 Jul 1326

**Edward III (Edw 3)**

1 Edw 3: 25 Jan 1327 (then called 1326)
2 Edw 3: 25 Jan 1328 (then called 1327)
3 Edw 3: 25 Jan 1329 (then called 1328)
4 Edw 3: 25 Jan 1330 (then called 1329)
5 Edw 3: 25 Jan 1331 (then called 1330)
6 Edw 3: 25 Jan 1332 (then called 1331)
7 Edw 3: 25 Jan 1333 (then called 1332)
8 Edw 3: 25 Jan 1334 (then called 1333)
9 Edw 3: 25 Jan 1335 (then called 1334)
10 Edw 3: 25 Jan 1336 (then called 1335)
11 Edw 3: 25 Jan 1337 (then called 1336)
12 Edw 3: 25 Jan 1338 (then called 1337)
13 Edw 3: 25 Jan 1339 (then called 1338)
14 Edw 3: 25 Jan 1340 (then called 1339)
15 Edw 3: 25 Jan 1341 (then called 1340)
16 Edw 3: 25 Jan 1342 (then called 1341)
17 Edw 3: 25 Jan 1343 (then called 1342)
18 Edw 3: 25 Jan 1344 (then called 1343)
19 Edw 3: 25 Jan 1345 (then called 1344)
20 Edw 3: 25 Jan 1346 (then called 1345)
21 Edw 3: 25 Jan 1347 (then called 1346)
22 Edw 3: 25 Jan 1348 (then called 1347)
23 Edw 3: 25 Jan 1349 (then called 1348)
24 Edw 3: 25 Jan 1350 (then called 1349)
25 Edw 3: 25 Jan 1351 (then called 1350)
26 Edw 3: 25 Jan 1352 (then called 1351)
27 Edw 3: 25 Jan 1353 (then called 1352)
28 Edw 3: 25 Jan 1354 (then called 1353)
29 Edw 3: 25 Jan 1355 (then called 1354)
30 Edw 3: 25 Jan 1356 (then called 1355)
31 Edw 3: 25 Jan 1357 (then called 1356)
32 Edw 3: 25 Jan 1358 (then called 1357)
33 Edw 3: 25 Jan 1359 (then called 1358)
34 Edw 3: 25 Jan 1360 (then called 1359)
35 Edw 3: 25 Jan 1361 (then called 1360)
36 Edw 3: 25 Jan 1362 (then called 1361)
37 Edw 3: 25 Jan 1363 (then called 1362)
38 Edw 3: 25 Jan 1364 (then called 1363)
39 Edw 3: 25 Jan 1365 (then called 1364)
40 Edw 3: 25 Jan 1366 (then called 1365)
41 Edw 3: 25 Jan 1367 (then called 1366)

**Edward III (Edw 3)** — *continued*

42 Edw 3: 25 Jan 1368 (then called 1367)
43 Edw 3: 25 Jan 1369 (then called 1368)
44 Edw 3: 25 Jan 1370 (then called 1369)
45 Edw 3: 25 Jan 1371 (then called 1370)
46 Edw 3: 25 Jan 1372 (then called 1371)
47 Edw 3: 25 Jan 1373 (then called 1372)
48 Edw 3: 25 Jan 1374 (then called 1373)
49 Edw 3: 25 Jan 1375 (then called 1374)
50 Edw 3: 25 Jan 1376 (then called 1375)
51 Edw 3: 25 Jan 1377 (then called 1376)

**Richard II (Ric 2)**

1 Ric 2: 22 Jun 1377
2 Ric 2: 22 Jun 1378
3 Ric 2: 22 Jun 1379
4 Ric 2: 22 Jun 1380
5 Ric 2: 22 Jun 1381
6 Ric 2: 22 Jun 1382
7 Ric 2: 22 Jun 1383
8 Ric 2: 22 Jun 1384
9 Ric 2: 22 Jun 1385
10 Ric 2: 22 Jun 1386
11 Ric 2: 22 Jun 1387
12 Ric 2: 22 Jun 1388
13 Ric 2: 22 Jun 1389
14 Ric 2: 22 Jun 1390
15 Ric 2: 22 Jun 1391
16 Ric 2: 22 Jun 1392
17 Ric 2: 22 Jun 1393
18 Ric 2: 22 Jun 1394
19 Ric 2: 22 Jun 1395
20 Ric 2: 22 Jun 1396
21 Ric 2: 22 Jun 1397
22 Ric 2: 22 Jun 1398
23 Ric 2: 22 Jun 1399

**Henry IV (Hen 4)**

1 Hen 4: 30 Sep 1399
2 Hen 4: 30 Sep 1400
3 Hen 4: 30 Sep 1401
4 Hen 4: 30 Sep 1402
5 Hen 4: 30 Sep 1403
6 Hen 4: 30 Sep 1404
7 Hen 4: 30 Sep 1405
8 Hen 4: 30 Sep 1406
9 Hen 4: 30 Sep 1407
10 Hen 4: 30 Sep 1408
11 Hen 4: 30 Sep 1409
12 Hen 4: 30 Sep 1410
13 Hen 4: 30 Sep 1411
14 Hen 4: 30 Sep 1412

**Henry V (Hen 5)**

1 Hen 5: 21 Mar 1413 (then called 1412)
2 Hen 5: 21 Mar 1414 (then called 1413)
3 Hen 5: 21 Mar 1415 (then called 1414)
4 Hen 5: 21 Mar 1416 (then called 1415)
5 Hen 5: 21 Mar 1417 (then called 1416)
6 Hen 5: 21 Mar 1418 (then called 1417)
7 Hen 5: 21 Mar 1419 (then called 1418)
8 Hen 5: 21 Mar 1420 (then called 1419)
9 Hen 5: 21 Mar 1421 (then called 1420)
10 Hen 5: 21 Mar 1422 (then called 1421)

**Henry VI (Hen 6)**

1 Hen 6: 1 Sep 1422
2 Hen 6: 1 Sep 1423
3 Hen 6: 1 Sep 1424
4 Hen 6: 1 Sep 1425
5 Hen 6: 1 Sep 1426
6 Hen 6: 1 Sep 1427
7 Hen 6: 1 Sep 1428
8 Hen 6: 1 Sep 1429
9 Hen 6: 1 Sep 1430
10 Hen 6: 1 Sep 1431
11 Hen 6: 1 Sep 1432
12 Hen 6: 1 Sep 1433
13 Hen 6: 1 Sep 1434
14 Hen 6: 1 Sep 1435
15 Hen 6: 1 Sep 1436
16 Hen 6: 1 Sep 1437
17 Hen 6: 1 Sep 1438
18 Hen 6: 1 Sep 1439
19 Hen 6: 1 Sep 1440
20 Hen 6: 1 Sep 1441
21 Hen 6: 1 Sep 1442
22 Hen 6: 1 Sep 1443
23 Hen 6: 1 Sep 1444
24 Hen 6: 1 Sep 1445
25 Hen 6: 1 Sep 1446
26 Hen 6: 1 Sep 1447
27 Hen 6: 1 Sep 1448
28 Hen 6: 1 Sep 1449
29 Hen 6: 1 Sep 1450
30 Hen 6: 1 Sep 1451
31 Hen 6: 1 Sep 1452
32 Hen 6: 1 Sep 1453
33 Hen 6: 1 Sep 1454
34 Hen 6: 1 Sep 1455
35 Hen 6: 1 Sep 1456
36 Hen 6: 1 Sep 1457
37 Hen 6: 1 Sep 1458
38 Hen 6: 1 Sep 1459
39 Hen 6: 1 Sep 1460
Between 4 Mar 1461 (then called 1460) and
3 Oct 1470 the throne was held by Edward,
Duke of York (Edward IV).

**Henry VI (Hen 6)** — *continued*

[40 Hen 6: 1 Sep 1461
41 Hen 6: 1 Sep 1462
42 Hen 6: 1 Sep 1463
43 Hen 6: 1 Sep 1464
44 Hen 6: 1 Sep 1465
45 Hen 6: 1 Sep 1466
46 Hen 6: 1 Sep 1467
47 Hen 6: 1 Sep 1468
48 Hen 6: 1 Sep 1469]
49 Hen 6: 1 Sep 1470

**Edward IV**

1 Edw 4: 4 Mar 1471 (then called 1470)
2 Edw 4: 4 Mar 1472 (then called 1471)
3 Edw 4: 4 Mar 1473 (then called 1472)
4 Edw 4: 4 Mar 1474 (then called 1473)
5 Edw 4: 4 Mar 1475 (then called 1474)
6 Edw 4: 4 Mar 1476 (then called 1475)
7 Edw 4: 4 Mar 1477 (then called 1476)
8 Edw 4: 4 Mar 1478 (then called 1477)
9 Edw 4: 4 Mar 1479 (then called 1478)
10 Edw 4: 4 Mar 1480 (then called 1479)
11 Edw 4: 4 Mar 1481 (then called 1480)
12 Edw 4: 4 Mar 1482 (then called 1481)
13 Edw 4: 4 Mar 1483 (then called 1482)
14 Edw 4: 4 Mar 1484 (then called 1483)
15 Edw 4: 4 Mar 1485 (then called 1484)
16 Edw 4: 4 Mar 1486 (then called 1485)
17 Edw 4: 4 Mar 1487 (then called 1486)
18 Edw 4: 4 Mar 1488 (then called 1487)
19 Edw 4: 4 Mar 1489 (then called 1488)
20 Edw 4: 4 Mar 1490 (then called 1489)
21 Edw 4: 4 Mar 1491 (then called 1490)
22 Edw 4: 4 Mar 1492 (then called 1491)
23 Edw 4: 4 Mar 1493 (then called 1492)

**Edward V (Edw 5)**

1 Edw 5: 9 Apr 1483

**Richard III (Ric 3)**

1 Ric 3: 26 Jun 1483
2 Ric 3: 26 Jun 1484
3 Ric 3: 26 Jun 1485

**Henry VII (Hen 7)**

1 Hen 7: 22 Aug 1485
2 Hen 7: 22 Aug 1486
3 Hen 7: 22 Aug 1487
4 Hen 7: 22 Aug 1488
5 Hen 7: 22 Aug 1489
6 Hen 7: 22 Aug 1490

**Henry VII (Hen 7)** — *continued*

7 Hen 7: 22 Aug 1491
8 Hen 7: 22 Aug 1492
9 Hen 7: 22 Aug 1493
10 Hen 7: 22 Aug 1494
11 Hen 7: 22 Aug 1495
12 Hen 7: 22 Aug 1496
13 Hen 7: 22 Aug 1497
14 Hen 7: 22 Aug 1498
15 Hen 7: 22 Aug 1499
16 Hen 7: 22 Aug 1500
17 Hen 7: 22 Aug 1501
18 Hen 7: 22 Aug 1502
19 Hen 7: 22 Aug 1503
20 Hen 7: 22 Aug 1504
21 Hen 7: 22 Aug 1505
22 Hen 7: 22 Aug 1506
23 Hen 7: 22 Aug 1507
24 Hen 7: 22 Aug 1508

**Henry VIII (Hen 8)**

1 Hen 8: 22 Apr 1509
2 Hen 8: 22 Apr 1510
3 Hen 8: 22 Apr 1511
4 Hen 8: 22 Apr 1512
5 Hen 8: 22 Apr 1513
6 Hen 8: 22 Apr 1514
7 Hen 8: 22 Apr 1515
8 Hen 8: 22 Apr 1516
9 Hen 8: 22 Apr 1517
10 Hen 8: 22 Apr 1518
11 Hen 8: 22 Apr 1519
12 Hen 8: 22 Apr 1520
13 Hen 8: 22 Apr 1521
14 Hen 8: 22 Apr 1522
15 Hen 8: 22 Apr 1523
16 Hen 8: 22 Apr 1524
17 Hen 8: 22 Apr 1525
18 Hen 8: 22 Apr 1526
19 Hen 8: 22 Apr 1527
20 Hen 8: 22 Apr 1528
21 Hen 8: 22 Apr 1529
22 Hen 8: 22 Apr 1530
23 Hen 8: 22 Apr 1531
24 Hen 8: 22 Apr 1532
25 Hen 8: 22 Apr 1533
26 Hen 8: 22 Apr 1534
27 Hen 8: 22 Apr 1535
28 Hen 8: 22 Apr 1536
29 Hen 8: 22 Apr 1537
30 Hen 8: 22 Apr 1538
31 Hen 8: 22 Apr 1539
32 Hen 8: 22 Apr 1540
33 Hen 8: 22 Apr 1541
34 Hen 8: 22 Apr 1542

**Henry VIII (Hen 8)** — *continued*

35 Hen 8: 22 Apr 1543
36 Hen 8: 22 Apr 1544
37 Hen 8: 22 Apr 1545
38 Hen 8: 22 Apr 1546

**Edward VI (Edw 6)**

1 Edw 6: 28 Jan 1547 (then called 1546)
2 Edw 6: 28 Jan 1548 (then called 1547)
3 Edw 6: 28 Jan 1549 (then called 1548)
4 Edw 6: 28 Jan 1550 (then called 1549)
5 Edw 6: 28 Jan 1551 (then called 1550)
6 Edw 6: 28 Jan 1552 (then called 1551)
7 Edw 6: 28 Jan 1553 (then called 1552)

**Mary I (M)**
**Philip and Mary (Ph & M)**

Jane succeeded 6 Jul 1553 but was deposed on 19 Jul by Mary I who dated her reign from 6 Jul. Mary married Philip 25 Jul 1554. A royal proclamation styled Philip and Mary king and queen of England and for their joint reign there is a sequence of joint regnal years.

1 M: 19 (or 6) Jul 1553
2 M: 6 Jul 1554
1 & 2 Ph & M: 25 Jul 1554
1 & 3 Ph & M: 6 Jul 1555
2 & 3 Ph & M: 25 Jul 1555
2 & 4 Ph & M: 6 Jul 1556
3 & 4 Ph & M: 25 Jul 1556
3 & 5 Ph & M: 6 Jul 1557
4 & 5 Ph & M: 25 Jul 1557
4 & 6 Ph & M: 6 Jul 1558
5 & 6 Ph & M: 25 Jul 1558

**Elizabeth I (Eliz)**

1 Eliz: 17 Nov 1558
2 Eliz: 17 Nov 1559
3 Eliz: 17 Nov 1560
4 Eliz: 17 Nov 1561
5 Eliz: 17 Nov 1562
6 Eliz: 17 Nov 1563
7 Eliz: 17 Nov 1564
8 Eliz: 17 Nov 1565
9 Eliz: 17 Nov 1566
10 Eliz: 17 Nov 1567
11 Eliz: 17 Nov 1568
12 Eliz: 17 Nov 1569
13 Eliz: 17 Nov 1570
14 Eliz: 17 Nov 1571
15 Eliz: 17 Nov 1572
16 Eliz: 17 Nov 1573

**Elizabeth I (Eliz)** — *continued*

17 Eliz: 17 Nov 1574
18 Eliz: 17 Nov 1575
19 Eliz: 17 Nov 1576
20 Eliz: 17 Nov 1577
21 Eliz: 17 Nov 1578
22 Eliz: 17 Nov 1579
23 Eliz: 17 Nov 1580
24 Eliz: 17 Nov 1581
25 Eliz: 17 Nov 1582
26 Eliz: 17 Nov 1583
27 Eliz: 17 Nov 1584
28 Eliz: 17 Nov 1585
29 Eliz: 17 Nov 1586
30 Eliz: 17 Nov 1587
31 Eliz: 17 Nov 1588
32 Eliz: 17 Nov 1589
33 Eliz: 17 Nov 1590
34 Eliz: 17 Nov 1591
35 Eliz: 17 Nov 1592
36 Eliz: 17 Nov 1593
37 Eliz: 17 Nov 1594
38 Eliz: 17 Nov 1595
39 Eliz: 17 Nov 1596
40 Eliz: 17 Nov 1597
41 Eliz: 17 Nov 1598
42 Eliz: 17 Nov 1599
43 Eliz: 17 Nov 1600
44 Eliz: 17 Nov 1601
45 Eliz: 17 Nov 1602

**James I (Ja 1)**

1 Ja 1: 24 Mar 1603 (then called 1602)
2 Ja 1: 24 Mar 1604 (then called 1603)
3 Ja 1: 24 Mar 1605 (then called 1604)
4 Ja 1: 24 Mar 1606 (then called 1605)
5 Ja 1: 24 Mar 1607 (then called 1606)
6 Ja 1: 24 Mar 1608 (then called 1607)
7 Ja 1: 24 Mar 1609 (then called 1608)
8 Ja 1: 24 Mar 1610 (then called 1609)
9 Ja 1: 24 Mar 1611 (then called 1610)
10 Ja 1: 24 Mar 1612 (then called 1611)
11 Ja 1: 24 Mar 1613 (then called 1612)
12 Ja 1: 24 Mar 1614 (then called 1613)
13 Ja 1: 24 Mar 1615 (then called 1614)
14 Ja 1: 24 Mar 1616 (then called 1615)
15 Ja 1: 24 Mar 1617 (then called 1616)
16 Ja 1: 24 Mar 1618 (then called 1617)
17 Ja 1: 24 Mar 1619 (then called 1618)
18 Ja 1: 24 Mar 1620 (then called 1619)
19 Ja 1: 24 Mar 1621 (then called 1620)
20 Ja 1: 24 Mar 1622 (then called 1621)
21 Ja 1: 24 Mar 1623 (then called 1622)
22 Ja 1: 24 Mar 1624 (then called 1623)
23 Ja 1: 24 Mar 1625 (then called 1624)

## Charles I (Cha 1)

1 Cha 1: 27 Mar 1625
2 Cha 1: 27 Mar 1626
3 Cha 1: 27 Mar 1627
4 Cha 1: 27 Mar 1628
5 Cha 1: 27 Mar 1629
6 Cha 1: 27 Mar 1630
7 Cha 1: 27 Mar 1631
8 Cha 1: 27 Mar 1632
9 Cha 1: 27 Mar 1633
10 Cha 1: 27 Mar 1634
11 Cha 1: 27 Mar 1635
12 Cha 1: 27 Mar 1636
13 Cha 1: 27 Mar 1637
14 Cha 1: 27 Mar 1638
15 Cha 1: 27 Mar 1639
16 Cha 1: 27 Mar 1640
17 Cha 1: 27 Mar 1641
18 Cha 1: 27 Mar 1642
19 Cha 1: 27 Mar 1643
20 Cha 1: 27 Mar 1644
21 Cha 1: 27 Mar 1645
22 Cha 1: 27 Mar 1646
23 Cha 1: 27 Mar 1647
24 Cha 1: 27 Mar 1648 to 30 Jan 1649
(then called 1648)

Charles I was executed on 30 Jan 1649 (then called 1648) and Parliament abolished the monarchy on 7 Feb 1649 (then called 1648) but resolved to restore it on 1 May 1660. The reign of the new king, Charles II, is reckoned to have started when his father was executed.

## Charles II (Cha 2)

12 Cha 2: 30 Jan 1660 (then called 1659)
13 Cha 2: 30 Jan 1661 (then called 1660)
14 Cha 2: 30 Jan 1662 (then called 1661)
15 Cha 2: 30 Jan 1663 (then called 1662)
16 Cha 2: 30 Jan 1664 (then called 1663)
17 Cha 2: 30 Jan 1665 (then called 1664)
18 Cha 2: 30 Jan 1666 (then called 1665)
19 Cha 2: 30 Jan 1667 (then called 1666)
20 Cha 2: 30 Jan 1668 (then called 1667)
21 Cha 2: 30 Jan 1669 (then called 1668)
22 Cha 2: 30 Jan 1670 (then called 1669)
23 Cha 2: 30 Jan 1671 (then called 1670)
24 Cha 2: 30 Jan 1672 (then called 1671)
25 Cha 2: 30 Jan 1673 (then called 1672)
26 Cha 2: 30 Jan 1674 (then called 1673)
27 Cha 2: 30 Jan 1675 (then called 1674)
28 Cha 2: 30 Jan 1676 (then called 1675)
29 Cha 2: 30 Jan 1677 (then called 1676)
30 Cha 2: 30 Jan 1678 (then called 1677)

## Charles II (Cha 2) — continued

31 Cha 2: 30 Jan 1679 (then called 1678)
32 Cha 2: 30 Jan 1680 (then called 1679)
33 Cha 2: 30 Jan 1681 (then called 1680)
34 Cha 2: 30 Jan 1682 (then called 1681)
35 Cha 2: 30 Jan 1683 (then called 1682)
36 Cha 2: 30 Jan 1684 (then called 1683)
37 Cha 2: 30 Jan 1685 (then called 1684)

## James II (Ja 2)

1 Ja 2: 6 Feb 1685 (then called 1684)
2 Ja 2: 6 Feb 1686 (then called 1685)
3 Ja 2: 6 Feb 1687 (then called 1686)
4 Ja 2: 6 Feb 1688 (then called 1687) to 11 Dec 1688
James II fled the country on 11 Dec 1688 which is reckoned to be the end of his reign. Parliament offered the Crown of England to William and Mary on 13 Feb 1689.

## William III and Mary II (Will & Mar)

From 28 Dec 1694 William III (Will 3) alone
1 Will & Mar: 13 Feb 1689 (then called 1688)
2 Will & Mar: 13 Feb 1690 (then called 1689)
3 Will & Mar: 13 Feb 1691 (then called 1690)
4 Will & Mar: 13 Feb 1692 (then called 1691)
5 Will & Mar: 13 Feb 1693 (then called 1692)
6 Will & Mar: 13 Feb 1694 (then called 1693)
6 Will 3: 28 Dec 1694
7 Will 3: 13 Feb 1695 (then called 1694)
8 Will 3: 13 Feb 1696 (then called 1695)
9 Will 3: 13 Feb 1697 (then called 1696)
10 Will 3: 13 Feb 1698 (then called 1697)
11 Will 3: 13 Feb 1699 (then called 1698)
12 Will 3: 13 Feb 1700 (then called 1699)
13 Will 3: 13 Feb 1701 (then called 1700)
14 Will 3: 13 Feb 1702 (then called 1701)

## Anne (Ann)

1 Ann: 8 Mar 1702 (then called 1701)
2 Ann: 8 Mar 1703 (then called 1702)
3 Ann: 8 Mar 1704 (then called 1703)
4 Ann: 8 Mar 1705 (then called 1704)
5 Ann: 8 Mar 1706 (then called 1705)
6 Ann: 8 Mar 1707 (then called 1706)
England and Scotland united 1 May 1707 and their Parliaments were succeeded by the Parliament of Great Britain, which first sat on 23 Oct 1707.
7 Ann: 8 Mar 1708 (then called 1707)
8 Ann: 8 Mar 1709 (then called 1708)
9 Ann: 8 Mar 1710 (then called 1709)

**Anne (Ann)** — *continued*

10 Ann: 8 Mar 1711 (then called 1710)
11 Ann: 8 Mar 1712 (then called 1711)
12 Ann: 8 Mar 1713 (then called 1712)
13 Ann: 8 Mar 1714 (then called 1713)

**George I (Geo 1)**

1 Geo 1: 1 Aug 1714
2 Geo 1: 1 Aug 1715
3 Geo 1: 1 Aug 1716
4 Geo 1: 1 Aug 1717
5 Geo 1: 1 Aug 1718
6 Geo 1: 1 Aug 1719
7 Geo 1: 1 Aug 1720
8 Geo 1: 1 Aug 1721
9 Geo 1: 1 Aug 1722
10 Geo 1: 1 Aug 1723
11 Geo 1: 1 Aug 1724
12 Geo 1: 1 Aug 1725
13 Geo 1: 1 Aug 1726

**George II (Geo 2)**

1 Geo 2: 11 Jun 1727
2 Geo 2: 11 Jun 1728
3 Geo 2: 11 Jun 1729
4 Geo 2: 11 Jun 1730
5 Geo 2: 11 Jun 1731
6 Geo 2: 11 Jun 1732
7 Geo 2: 11 Jun 1733
8 Geo 2: 11 Jun 1734
9 Geo 2: 11 Jun 1735
10 Geo 2: 11 Jun 1736
11 Geo 2: 11 Jun 1737
12 Geo 2: 11 Jun 1738
13 Geo 2: 11 Jun 1739
14 Geo 2: 11 Jun 1740
15 Geo 2: 11 Jun 1741
16 Geo 2: 11 Jun 1742
17 Geo 2: 11 Jun 1743
18 Geo 2: 11 Jun 1744
19 Geo 2: 11 Jun 1745
20 Geo 2: 11 Jun 1746
21 Geo 2: 11 Jun 1747
22 Geo 2: 11 Jun 1748
23 Geo 2: 11 Jun 1749
24 Geo 2: 11 Jun 1750
25 Geo 2: 11 Jun 1751
26 Geo 2: 11 Jun 1752

To change from the Julian (Old Style) to the Gregorian (New Style) calendar, 11 days were omitted from Sep 1752 (2 Sep was followed by 14 Sep), but in order to give 26 Geo 2 a full 365 days it was extended to 21 Jun 1753.

**George II (Geo 2)** — *continued*

27 Geo 2: 22 Jun 1753
28 Geo 2: 22 Jun 1754
29 Geo 2: 22 Jun 1755
30 Geo 2: 22 Jun 1756
31 Geo 2: 22 Jun 1757
32 Geo 2: 22 Jun 1758
33 Geo 2: 22 Jun 1759
34 Geo 2: 22 Jun 1760

**George III (Geo 3)**

1 Geo 3: 25 Oct 1760
2 Geo 3: 25 Oct 1761
3 Geo 3: 25 Oct 1762
4 Geo 3: 25 Oct 1763
5 Geo 3: 25 Oct 1764
6 Geo 3: 25 Oct 1765
7 Geo 3: 25 Oct 1766
8 Geo 3: 25 Oct 1767
9 Geo 3: 25 Oct 1768
10 Geo 3: 25 Oct 1769
11 Geo 3: 25 Oct 1770
12 Geo 3: 25 Oct 1771
13 Geo 3: 25 Oct 1772
14 Geo 3: 25 Oct 1773
15 Geo 3: 25 Oct 1774
16 Geo 3: 25 Oct 1775
17 Geo 3: 25 Oct 1776
18 Geo 3: 25 Oct 1777
19 Geo 3: 25 Oct 1778
20 Geo 3: 25 Oct 1779
21 Geo 3: 25 Oct 1780
22 Geo 3: 25 Oct 1781
23 Geo 3: 25 Oct 1782
24 Geo 3: 25 Oct 1783
25 Geo 3: 25 Oct 1784
26 Geo 3: 25 Oct 1785
27 Geo 3: 25 Oct 1786
28 Geo 3: 25 Oct 1787
29 Geo 3: 25 Oct 1788
30 Geo 3: 25 Oct 1789
31 Geo 3: 25 Oct 1790
32 Geo 3: 25 Oct 1791
33 Geo 3: 25 Oct 1792
34 Geo 3: 25 Oct 1793
35 Geo 3: 25 Oct 1794
36 Geo 3: 25 Oct 1795
37 Geo 3: 25 Oct 1796
38 Geo 3: 25 Oct 1797
39 Geo 3: 25 Oct 1798
40 Geo 3: 25 Oct 1799
41 Geo 3: 25 Oct 1800

Great Britain and Ireland united 1 Jan 1801 and their Parliaments were succeeded by the Parliament of the United Kingdom, which first sat on 22 Jan 1801.

**George III (Geo 3)** — *continued*

42 Geo 3: 25 Oct 1801
43 Geo 3: 25 Oct 1802
44 Geo 3: 25 Oct 1803
45 Geo 3: 25 Oct 1804
46 Geo 3: 25 Oct 1805
47 Geo 3: 25 Oct 1806
48 Geo 3: 25 Oct 1807
49 Geo 3: 25 Oct 1808
50 Geo 3: 25 Oct 1809
51 Geo 3: 25 Oct 1810
52 Geo 3: 25 Oct 1811
53 Geo 3: 25 Oct 1812
54 Geo 3: 25 Oct 1813
55 Geo 3: 25 Oct 1814
56 Geo 3: 25 Oct 1815
57 Geo 3: 25 Oct 1816
58 Geo 3: 25 Oct 1817
59 Geo 3: 25 Oct 1818
60 Geo 3: 25 Oct 1819

**George IV (Geo 4)**

 1 Geo 4: 29 Jan 1820
 2 Geo 4: 29 Jan 1821
 3 Geo 4: 29 Jan 1822
 4 Geo 4: 29 Jan 1823
 5 Geo 4: 29 Jan 1824
 6 Geo 4: 29 Jan 1825
 7 Geo 4: 29 Jan 1826
 8 Geo 4: 29 Jan 1827
 9 Geo 4: 29 Jan 1828
10 Geo 4: 29 Jan 1829
11 Geo 4: 29 Jan 1830

**William IV (Will 4)**

1 Will 4: 26 Jun 1830
2 Will 4: 26 Jun 1831
3 Will 4: 26 Jun 1832
4 Will 4: 26 Jun 1833
5 Will 4: 26 Jun 1834
6 Will 4: 26 Jun 1835
7 Will 4: 26 Jun 1836

**Victoria (Vict)**

1 Vict: 20 Jun 1837
2 Vict: 20 Jun 1838
3 Vict: 20 Jun 1839
4 Vict: 20 Jun 1840
5 Vict: 20 Jun 1841
6 Vict: 20 Jun 1842
7 Vict: 20 Jun 1843
8 Vict: 20 Jun 1844
9 Vict: 20 Jun 1845

**Victoria (Vict)** — *continued*

10 Vict: 20 Jun 1846
11 Vict: 20 Jun 1847
12 Vict: 20 Jun 1848
13 Vict: 20 Jun 1849
14 Vict: 20 Jun 1850
15 Vict: 20 Jun 1851
16 Vict: 20 Jun 1852
17 Vict: 20 Jun 1853
18 Vict: 20 Jun 1854
19 Vict: 20 Jun 1855
20 Vict: 20 Jun 1856
21 Vict: 20 Jun 1857
22 Vict: 20 Jun 1858
23 Vict: 20 Jun 1859
24 Vict: 20 Jun 1860
25 Vict: 20 Jun 1861
26 Vict: 20 Jun 1862
27 Vict: 20 Jun 1863
28 Vict: 20 Jun 1864
29 Vict: 20 Jun 1865
30 Vict: 20 Jun 1866
31 Vict: 20 Jun 1867
32 Vict: 20 Jun 1868
33 Vict: 20 Jun 1869
34 Vict: 20 Jun 1870
35 Vict: 20 Jun 1871
36 Vict: 20 Jun 1872
37 Vict: 20 Jun 1873
38 Vict: 20 Jun 1874
39 Vict: 20 Jun 1875
40 Vict: 20 Jun 1876
41 Vict: 20 Jun 1877
42 Vict: 20 Jun 1878
43 Vict: 20 Jun 1879
44 Vict: 20 Jun 1880
45 Vict: 20 Jun 1881
46 Vict: 20 Jun 1882
47 Vict: 20 Jun 1883
48 Vict: 20 Jun 1884
49 Vict: 20 Jun 1885
50 Vict: 20 Jun 1886
51 Vict: 20 Jun 1887
52 Vict: 20 Jun 1888
53 Vict: 20 Jun 1889
54 Vict: 20 Jun 1890
55 Vict: 20 Jun 1891
56 Vict: 20 Jun 1892
57 Vict: 20 Jun 1893
58 Vict: 20 Jun 1894
59 Vict: 20 Jun 1895
60 Vict: 20 Jun 1896
61 Vict: 20 Jun 1897
62 Vict: 20 Jun 1898
63 Vict: 20 Jun 1899
64 Vict: 20 Jun 1900

## Edward VII (Edw 7)

1 Edw 7: 22 Jan 1901
2 Edw 7: 22 Jan 1902
3 Edw 7: 22 Jan 1903
4 Edw 7: 22 Jan 1904
5 Edw 7: 22 Jan 1905
6 Edw 7: 22 Jan 1906
7 Edw 7: 22 Jan 1907
8 Edw 7: 22 Jan 1908
9 Edw 7: 22 Jan 1909
10 Edw 7: 22 Jan 1910

## George V (Geo 5)

1 Geo 5: 6 May 1910
2 Geo 5: 6 May 1911
3 Geo 5: 6 May 1912
4 Geo 5: 6 May 1913
5 Geo 5: 6 May 1914
6 Geo 5: 6 May 1915
7 Geo 5: 6 May 1916
8 Geo 5: 6 May 1917
9 Geo 5: 6 May 1918
10 Geo 5: 6 May 1919
11 Geo 5: 6 May 1920
12 Geo 5: 6 May 1921
13 Geo 5: 6 May 1922
14 Geo 5: 6 May 1923
15 Geo 5: 6 May 1924
16 Geo 5: 6 May 1925
17 Geo 5: 6 May 1926
18 Geo 5: 6 May 1927
19 Geo 5: 6 May 1928
20 Geo 5: 6 May 1929
21 Geo 5: 6 May 1930
22 Geo 5: 6 May 1931
23 Geo 5: 6 May 1932
24 Geo 5: 6 May 1933
25 Geo 5: 6 May 1934
26 Geo 5: 6 May 1935

## Edward VIII (Edw 8)

1 Edw 8: 20 Jan 1936

## George VI (Geo 6)

1 Geo 6: 11 Dec 1936
2 Geo 6: 11 Dec 1937
3 Geo 6: 11 Dec 1938
4 Geo 6: 11 Dec 1939
5 Geo 6: 11 Dec 1940
6 Geo 6: 11 Dec 1941
7 Geo 6: 11 Dec 1942
8 Geo 6: 11 Dec 1943
9 Geo 6: 11 Dec 1944
10 Geo 6: 11 Dec 1945
11 Geo 6: 11 Dec 1946
12 Geo 6: 11 Dec 1947
13 Geo 6: 11 Dec 1948
14 Geo 6: 11 Dec 1949
15 Geo 6: 11 Dec 1950
16 Geo 6: 11 Dec 1951

## Elizabeth II (Eliz 2)

1 Eliz 2: 6 Feb 1952
2 Eliz 2: 6 Feb 1953
3 Eliz 2: 6 Feb 1954
4 Eliz 2: 6 Feb 1955
5 Eliz 2: 6 Feb 1956
6 Eliz 2: 6 Feb 1957
7 Eliz 2: 6 Feb 1958
8 Eliz 2: 6 Feb 1959
9 Eliz 2: 6 Feb 1960
10 Eliz 2: 6 Feb 1961
11 Eliz 2: 6 Feb 1962
Statutes from 1 Jan 1963 are not dated by
regnal year.

# LIST OF ABBREVIATIONS OF TITLES OF LAW REPORTS AND OTHER PUBLICATIONS

If an abbreviation is the recommended abbreviation then the title of the publication is given in the second column in the same form as in the List of Recommended Forms of Citation for Law Reports and other Publications, which can be consulted for further information such as whether to use volume numbers or volume years.

If an abbreviation is not a recommended abbreviation then the second column shows an = sign followed by the recommended abbreviation, and the entry for the recommended abbreviation in this list should be consulted.

This list covers material published in the British Isles and the English-language reports of the European Courts of Justice and Human Rights. Where an abbreviation in this list is also an abbreviation of a law report in another jurisdiction, a warning ! appears in the second column followed by the title of that report.

Because every possible variation of spacing and punctuation may be encountered, the abbreviations are arranged in alphabetical order letter by letter, ignoring spacing and punctuation. The ampersand (&) is filed before letters of the alphabet. If the only difference between abbreviations (ignoring spacing and punctuation) is in capitalisation then capital letters are filed before lower-case ones. An abbreviation is repeated in the list if it is recommended for two or more different titles, and these repeated entries are either in order of the dates of the publications (if dates are given after the abbreviations) or (if dates are not given) in the titles' alphabetical order. The dates given are volume years if they are used by the publication or years of coverage otherwise. Volume years are given in square brackets (or without brackets if that is the way the publication is cited).

Some commonly occurring variants are not listed. If you are searching for an abbreviation which includes 'Ca' (for 'Case' or 'Cases'), please substitute 'Cas'. If you are searching for an abbreviation which includes 'temp' (for 'tempore'), please substitute 't'.

*Further reading*

The following books have useful lists giving the meaning of abbreviations for law reports and other legal publications, and cover material published outside the British Isles: they do not, however, recommend which abbreviations to use in citations. The work by Raistrick is the most comprehensive.

Colin Fong and Alan J. Edwards, *Australian and New Zealand Legal Abbreviations* (Sydney: Australian Law Librarians' Group New South Wales Branch, 1988).
*Osborn's Concise Law Dictionary*, 8th ed. by Leslie Rutherford and Sheila Bone (London: Sweet & Maxwell, 1993), pp. 355–88.
Donald Raistrick, *Index to Legal Citations and Abbreviations*, 2nd ed. (London: Bowker-Saur, 1993).
University of London Institute of Advanced Legal Studies, *Manual of Legal Citations. Part I: The British Isles* (London: the Institute, 1959); *Part II: The British Commonwealth* (London: the Institute, 1960).

## LIST OF ABBREVIATIONS OF TITLES OF LAW REPORTS AND OTHER PUBLICATIONS

| | |
|---|---|
| A & E | = Ad & El |
| A & E NS | = QB (*Queen's Bench Reports*) |
| A & H | = Arn & H |
| A & N | = Alc & N |
| AB | = Benl (p. 89 to end) |
| Ab Cas | = Craw & D Abr Cas |
| Ab Eq Cas | = Eq Cas Abr |
| Abr Cas | = Craw & D Abr Cas |
| Abr Cas Eq | = Eq Cas Abr |
| AC | *Law Reports. House of Lords.* [1891]– |
| Act | Acton, Thomas Harman, *Reports ... Prize Causes* |
| Acton | = Act |
| Act Pr C | = Act |
| Ad & E | = Ad & El |
| Ad & El | Adolphus, John Leycester, and Ellis, Thomas Flower, *Reports ... King's / Queen's Bench* |
| Adam | Adam, Edwin, *Reports ... High Court of Justiciary* |
| Add | Addams, J., *Reports ... Ecclesiastical Courts* |
| Addams | = Add |
| Addams Ecc | = Add |
| Add Ecc | = Add |
| Add ER | = Add |
| ADIL | = Ann Dig |
| Admin LR | *Administrative Law Reports.* 1989– |
| | ! also *Administrative Law Reports* (Canada) |
| Adolph & E | = Ad & El |
| AER | = All ER |
| Al | Aleyn, John, *Select Cases in B[anco] R[egis]* |
| Al & N | = Alc & N |
| Al & Nap | = Alc & N |
| Alc & N | Alcock, J.C., and Napier, J., *Reports ... King's Bench ... in Ireland* |
| Alc Reg | = Alc Reg Cas |
| Alc Reg C | = Alc Reg Cas |
| Alc Reg Cas | Alcock, J.C., *Registry Cases ... Ireland* |
| Aleyn | = Al |
| Allen | = Al |
| All ER | *All England Law Reports* |
| All ER (EC) | *All England Law Reports European Cases* |
| All ER Rep | *All England Law Reports Reprint* |
| All ER Rev | *All England Law Reports Annual Review* |
| Al N | = Alc & N |
| ALR | *Administrative Law Reports.* 1954–7 |
| | ! also *Australian Law Reports* |
| A M & O | = Arm M & O |
| Amb | Ambler, Charles, *Reports ... Chancery* |
| Ambl | = Amb |

| | |
|---|---|
| A Moo | = separate publication of cases now in 1 Bos & P |
| And | Anderson, Edmund, *Les Reports ... Common-Bank* |
| | also = Andr |
| Anderson | = And |
| Andr | Andrews, George, *Reports ... King's Bench* |
| Andrews | = Andr |
| Anglo-Am L Rev | *Anglo-American Law Review* |
| Ann | = Cas t Hard |
| Annaly | = Cas t Hard |
| Ann Dig | *Annual Digest and Reports of Public International Law Cases* |
| Annual Digest | = Ann Dig |
| Anst | Anstruther, Alexander, *Reports ... Exchequer* |
| App Cas | *Law Reports. Appeal Cases.* (1875–90) |
| Architects' LR | = Arch LR |
| Arch LR | *Architects' Law Reports* |
| Arch PLC | = Arch PL Cas |
| Arch PL Cas | Archbold, J.F., *Abridgment of Cases upon Poor Law*, vol. 3 |
| Ark | = Arkley |
| Arkl | = Arkley |
| Arkley | Arkley, Patrick, *Reports ... High Court and Circuit Courts of Justiciary* |
| Arm & O | = Arm M & O |
| Arm M & O | Armstrong, R., Macartney, J., and Ogle, J.C., *Reports ... Nisi Prius ... in Dublin* |
| Arm Mac & Og | = Arm M & O |
| Arms M & O | = Arm M & O |
| Arn | Arnold, T.J., *Reports ... Common Pleas* |
| Arn & H | Arnold, T.J., and Hodges, W., *Reports ... Queen's Bench* |
| Arn & Hod | = Arn & H |
| Arnot | Arnot, Hugo, *A Collection and Abridgement of Celebrated Criminal Trials in Scotland* |
| Arnot Cr C | = Arnot |
| Asp | Aspinall, James P., *Reports ... Maritime Law* |
| Asp Cas | = Asp |
| Asp Mar Law Cas | = Asp |
| Asp MC | = Asp |
| Asp MCL | = Asp |
| Asp MLC | = Asp |
| Asp Rep Mar LC NS | = Asp |
| Ass | *Liber Assisarum et Placitorum Corone*, see section 2.2.1 |
| ATC | *Annotated Tax Cases* |
| Atk | Atkyns, John Tracy, *Reports ... Chancery* |
| Aust | Austin, R.C., *Reports ... County Courts* |
| Austin CC | = Aust |
| | |
| B | = Beav |
| | also = Bid |
| B & A | = B & Ald |
| B & Ad | Barnewall, Richard Vaughan, and Adolphus, John Leycester, *Reports ... King's Bench* |

| | |
|---|---|
| B & Ald | Barnewall, Richard Vaughan, and Alderson, Edward Hall, *Reports . . . King's Bench* |
| B & Arn | = Barr & Arn |
| B & Aus | = Barr & Aust |
| B & Aust | = Barr & Aust |
| B & B | = Ball & B |
| | also = Brod & Bing |
| B & C | Barnewall, Richard Vaughan, and Cresswell, Cresswell, *Reports . . . King's Bench* |
| B & CPC | = Br & Col Pr Cas |
| B & C Pr Cas | = Br & Col Pr Cas |
| B & CR | *Reports of Bankruptcy and Companies Winding-up Cases* |
| B & D | = Benl & Dal |
| B & F | = Brod & F |
| B & G | = Brownl |
| B & I | *Bankruptcy and Insolvency Reports* |
| B & L | = Br & Lush |
| B & P | = Bos & P |
| B & P NR | = Bos & P NR |
| B & S | Best, William Mawdesley, and Smith, George James Philip, *Reports . . . Queen's Bench* |
| Ba & B | = Ball & B |
| Ba & Be | = Ball & B |
| Bac Abr | Bacon, Matthew, *A New Abridgment of the Law* |
| Bac Chanc | = Bac Rep |
| Bac Rep | *Reports of Cases Decided by Francis Bacon*, Prepared . . . by John Ritchie |
| Bail Ct Cas | = Lownd & M |
| Bail Ct R | = Saund & C |
| Bail Ct Rep | = Saund & C |
| Ball & B | Ball, Thomas, and Beatty, Francis, *Reports . . . Chancery in Ireland* |
| Ban Br | = O Bridg |
| Bank & Ins Rep | = B & I |
| Bank Insol Rep | = B & I |
| Bank LR | *Banking Law Reports* |
| Bankr & Ins R | = B & I |
| Bankr Ins R | = B & I |
| Banks & Ins | = B & I |
| Bar | = Barn KB |
| Bar & Arn | = Barr & Arn |
| Bar & Au | = Barr & Aust |
| Bar & Aust | = Barr & Aust |
| Bar & Cr | = B & C |
| Bar Chy | = Barn Ch |
| Bar N | = Barnes |
| Barn | = Barn Ch |
| | also = Barn KB |
| Barn & Adol | = B & Ad |
| Barn & Ald | = B & Ald |

| | |
|---|---|
| Barn & Cr | = B & C |
| Barn & Cress | = B & C |
| Barnard | = Barn KB |
| 3 Barnard | = Barn Ch |
| Barnard Ch | = Barn Ch |
| Barnard Ch Rep | = Barn Ch |
| Barnard KB | = Barn KB |
| Barn C | = Barn Ch |
| Barn Ch | Barnardiston, Thomas, *Reports ... Chancery* |
| Barn Chy | = Barn Ch |
| Barnes | Barnes, Henry, *Notes of Cases in Points of Practice ...* *Common Pleas* |
| Barn KB | Barnardiston, Thomas, *Reports ... King's Bench* |
| Barr & Arn | Barron, A., and Arnold, T.J., *Reports of Cases of* *Controverted Elections* |
| Barr & Aust | Barron, A., and Austin, A., *Reports of Cases of Controverted* *Elections* |
| Batt | Batty, E., *Reports ... King's Bench ... in Ireland* |
| BCC (1983–9) | *British Company Law Cases* |
| BCC [1990]– | *British Company Cases* |
| BCC | = Bro CC |
| | also = Lownd & M |
| BCLC | *Butterworths Company Law Cases* |
| BCR | = Saund & C |
| | ! also *British Columbia Reports* |
| | ! also *Butterworths Company Reports* (New Zealand) |
| BC Rep | = Saund & C |
| B D & O | Blackham, J., Dundas, W.J., and Osborne, R.W., *Reports ...* *Nisi Prius ... Dublin* |
| Beat | Beatty, F., *Reports ... Chancery in Ireland* |
| Beav | Beavan, Charles, *Reports ... Rolls Court* |
| Beav & W | Beavan, E., and Walford, F., *Parliamentary Cases Relating* *to Railways* |
| Beav & Wal | = Beav & W |
| Beav R & C Cas | = Beav & W |
| Bel | Bellewe, Richard, *Les Ans du Roy Richard le Second* |
| Bel Cas t H VIII | = BNC |
| Bell | Bell, Sydney S., *Cases ... House of Lords on Appeal from ...* *Scotland* |
| | also = Bell CC |
| Bell App | = Bell |
| Bell App Cas | = Bell |
| Bell C | = Bell Oct Cas |
| Bell Cas t Hen 8 | = BNC |
| Bell Cas t R 2 | = Bel |
| Bell CC | Bell, Thomas, *Crown Cases Reserved* |
| Bell Cr Ca | = Bell CC |
| Bell Ct of Sess | = Bell Oct Cas |
| Bell Ct of Sess fol | = Bell Fol Cas |
| Bell Dict Dec | Bell, Sydney S., *Dictionary of the Decisions of the Court of* *Session* |

| | |
|---|---|
| Bellewe | = Bel |
| Bellewe's Cas t Hen VIII | = BNC |
| Bellewe's Cas t R II | = Bel |
| Bell Fol | = Bell Fol Cas |
| Bell Fol Cas | Bell, Robert, *Cases ... Court of Session.* (1794–5) |
| Bell HL | = Bell |
| Bell Oct | = Bell Oct Cas |
| Bell Oct Cas | Bell, Robert, *Cases ... Court of Session.* (1790–2) |
| Bell's App | = Bell |
| Bell Sc App | = Bell |
| Bell's Dict | = Bell Dict Dec |
| Bell's Notes | Bell, Benjamin Robert, 'Supplemental notes', in *Commentaries on the Law of Scotland, Respecting Crimes,* by David Hume |
| Belt Bro | = Bro CC |
| Belt's Sup | = Belt's Supp |
| Belt's Supp | Belt, Robert, *Supplement to the Reports in Chancery of Francis Vesey Senior* |
| Belt Supp | = Belt's Supp |
| Belt Ves Sen | = Belt's Supp |
| Ben | = Benl & Dal (Benloe's section) |
| Ben & D | = Benl & Dal |
| Ben & Dal | = Benl & Dal |
| Bendl | = Benl |
| Ben in Keil | = Benl |
| Benl | Benloe, William, *Reports* also = Benl & Dal (Benloe's section) |
| Benl & Dal | Benloe, William, *Reports*, and Dalison, Sir William, *Reports* |
| Benl New | = Benl |
| Benl Old | = Benl & Dal (Benloe's section) |
| Benne | = 7 Mod |
| Bern | Bernard, W.L., *Irish Church Acts 1869 & 1872 ... together with Reports of Leading Cases* |
| Best & Sm | = B & S |
| Bid | Bidder, Harold Francis, *Locus Standi* |
| Bing | Bingham, Peregrine, *Reports ... Common Pleas* |
| Bing NC | Bingham, Peregrine, *New Cases in the Court of Common Pleas* |
| Bitt Cha Cas | Bittleston, A.H., *Reports in Chambers, Queen's Bench Division* |
| Bitt Chamb Rep | = Bitt Cha Cas |
| Bitt Ch Cas | = Bitt Cha Cas |
| Bitt PC | = Bitt Pr Cas |
| Bitt Prac Cas | = Bitt Pr Cas |
| Bitt Pr Cas | Bittleston, A.H., *Practice under the Judicature Acts* |
| Bitt Rep in Ch | = Bitt Cha Cas |
| Bitt W & P | = New Mag Cas |
| BJAL | *British Journal of Administrative Law* |

| | |
|---|---|
| BJIR | *British Journal of Industrial Relations* |
| Bl | = Bli |
| | also = Bl R |
| Bla | = Bl R |
| Black | Blackerby, S., *Cases in Law* |
| | also = Bl R |
| Black H | = H Bl |
| Black R | = Bl R |
| Blackst | = Bl R |
| Black W | = Bl R |
| Bl Com | Blackstone, Sir William, *Commentaries on the Law of England* |
| Bl D & Osb | = B D & O |
| Bl H | = H Bl |
| Bli | Bligh, Richard, *Reports ... House of Lords* |
| Bligh | = Bli |
| Bligh NS | = Bli NS |
| Bli NS | Bligh, Richard, *Reports ... House of Lords. New Series* |
| Bli OS | = Bli |
| Bl NS | = Bli NS |
| BLR | *Building Law Reports* |
| | ! also *Business Law Reports* (Canada) |
| Bl R | Blackstone, Sir William, *Reports ... Courts of Westminster-Hall* |
| Bl W | = Bl R |
| BM | = Burr |
| BNC | Brooke, Sir Robert, *Some New Cases* |
| | also = Bing NC |
| BNIL | *Bulletin of Northern Ireland Law* |
| Bos & P | Bosanquet, John Bernard, and Puller, Christopher, *Reports ... Common Pleas* |
| Bos & P NR | Bosanquet, John Bernard, and Puller, Christopher, *New Reports ... Common Pleas* |
| Bos & Pul | = Bos & P |
| Bos & Pul NR | = Bos & P NR |
| Bos NR | = Bos & P NR |
| Bosw | Boswell, James, *Decision of the Court of Session upon the Question of Literary Property* |
| Bott | = Bott PL |
| Bott PL | Bott, E., *Laws Relating to the Poor* |
| Bott PL Cas | = Bott PL |
| Bott's PL | = Bott PL |
| Bourke PP | Bourke, R., *Parliamentary Precedents* |
| B PC | = Bro Parl Cas |
| B PL | = Bott PL |
| B PL Cas | = Bott PL |
| BP NR | = Bos & P NR |
| BPR | = Bro Parl Cas |
| Br | = Bruce |
| Br & B | = Brod & Bing |
| Br & Col Pr Cas | = Br & Col Pri Cas |

| | |
|---|---|
| Br & Col Pri Cas | *Prize Cases ... during the Great War* |
| Br & Fr | = Brod & F |
| Br & G | = Brownl |
| Br & Gold | = Brownl |
| Br & Lush | Browning, W.E., and Lushington, Vernon, *Reports ... Admiralty* |
| BRA | *Butterworths' Rating Appeals* |
| Brac | *Bracton's Note Book* |
| Bract | Bracton, Henry de, *De Legibus et Consuetudinibus Angliae* |
| Bracton LJ | *Bracton Law Journal* |
| BR H | = Cas t Hard |
| Bridg | = J Bridg |
| Bridg J | = J Bridg |
| Bridgman J | = J Bridg |
| Bridgman O | = O Bridg |
| Bridg O | = O Bridg |
| Brit J Admin L | = BJAL |
| Br J Criminol | *British Journal of Criminology* |
| Br J Delinquency | *British Journal of Delinquency* |
| Br J Law Soc | *British Journal of Law and Society* |
| Brn | = Brownl |
| Br NC | = BNC |
| Bro | = Bro CC |
| | also = Brooke |
| | also = Brownl |
| Bro & G | = Brownl |
| Bro & Lush | = Br & Lush |
| Bro Abr | Brooke, Sir Robert, *Graunde Abridgement* |
| Bro CC | Brown, William, *Reports ... Chancery* |
| Bro Ch | = Bro CC |
| Brod & B | = Brod & Bing |
| Brod & Bing | Broderip, William John, and Bingham, Peregrine, *Reports ... Common Pleas* |
| Brod & F | Brodrick, George Charles, and Fremantle, W.H., *Collection of the Judgments of ... the Privy Council in Ecclesiastical Cases* |
| Brod & Frem | = Brod & F |
| Bro Ecc Rep | = Brooke |
| Bro NC | = BNC |
| Brooke | Brooke, W.G., *Six Judgments of ... the Privy Council in Ecclesiastical Cases* |
| Brook's New Cases | = BNC |
| Bro Parl Cas | Brown, Josiah, *Reports ... Parliament* |
| Bro PC | = Bro Parl Cas |
| Bro Sup | Brown, M.P., *Supplement to the Dictionary of Decisions of the Court of Session* |
| Bro Supp to Mor | = Bro Sup |
| Bro Syn | Brown, M.P., *General Synopsis of the Decisions of the Court of Session* |
| Bro Synop | = Bro Syn |

| | |
|---|---|
| Broun | Broun, Archibald, *Reports ... High Court and Circuit Courts of Justiciary* |
| Brown | = Bro CC |
| | also = Bro Parl Cas |
| | also = Brownl |
| Brown & Lush | = Br & Lush |
| Brown Ch C | = Bro CC |
| Brownl | Brownlow, Richard, and Goldesborough, John, *Reports* |
| Brownl & Golds | = Brownl |
| Brown's Supp | = Bro Sup |
| Brown's Syn | = Bro Syn |
| Brown Sup | = Bro Sup |
| Brown Syn | = Bro Syn |
| Br Sup | = Bro Sup |
| Br Syn | = Bro Syn |
| Bru | = Bruce |
| Bruce | Bruce, Alexander, *Decisions of the Lords of Council and Session* |
| B S | = Bro Sup |
| BTC | *British Tax Cases* |
| BTLC | *Butterworths Trading Law Cases* |
| BTR | *British Tax Review* |
| | also = BTRLR |
| BTRLR | *Brewing Trade Review Law Reports* |
| Buch | Buchanan, W., *Reports ... Remarkable Cases* |
| Buchan | = Buch |
| Buch Cas | = Buch |
| Buck | Buck, J.W., *Cases in Bankruptcy* |
| Build LR | = BLR |
| Bulst | Bulstrode, Edward, *Reports ... King's Bench* |
| Bun | = Bunb |
| Bunb | Bunbury, William, *Reports ... Exchequer* |
| Bunbury | = Bunb |
| Bur | = Burr |
| Burr | Burrow, Sir James, *Reports ... King's Bench* |
| Burr Adm | = Burrell |
| Burrell | Burrell, Sir William, *Reports ... Admiralty* |
| Burr SC | Burrow, Sir James, *Decisions ... upon Settlement-Cases* |
| Bus LB | *Greens Business Law Bulletin* |
| BVC | *British Value Added Tax Cases* |
| BWCC | *Butterworths' Workmen's Compensation Cases* |
| BWCC Supp | = *Butterworths' Workmen's Compensation Cases* (referring to Supplement) |
| BY | = BYIL |
| BYBIL | = BYIL |
| BYIL | *British Year Book of International Law* |
| | |
| C & A | = Cooke & A |
| C & D | = Corb & D |
| C & D CC | = Craw & D |
| C & E | = Cab & El |

| | |
|---|---|
| C & F | = Cl & F |
| C & J | = Cr & J |
| C & K | = Car & K |
| C & L | = Con & L |
| C & M | = Car & M |
| | also = Cr & M |
| C & Mar | = Car & M |
| C & O | = 3 Ry & Can Cas |
| C & P | = Car & P |
| | also = Cr & Ph |
| C & R | = Clif & R |
| | also = Cock & R |
| C & S | = Clif & S |
| Ca | see Cas |
| Cab & E | = Cab & El |
| Cab & El | Cababé, Michael, and Ellis, Charles Gregson, *Reports . . . Queen's Bench* |
| Cab & Ell | = Cab & El |
| Cairns' Dec | Reilly, F.S., *Albert Life Assurance Company Arbitration Act 1871: Lord Cairns' Decisions* |
| Cal | = Calth |
| Cald | = Cald MC |
| Cald Mag Cas | = Cald MC |
| Cald MC | Caldecott, Thomas, *Reports of Cases Relative to the Duty and Office of a Justice of the Peace* |
| Calth | Calthrop, Sir Henry, *Reports of Special Cases Touching . . . the City of London* |
| Calthrop | = Calth |
| Camb LJ | = CLJ |
| Cambrian Law Rev | *Cambrian Law Review* |
| Camp | Campbell, John, 1st Baron Campbell, *Reports . . . Nisi Prius* |
| Camp NP | = Camp |
| CAR | = Cr App R |
| | ! also *Commonwealth Arbitration Reports* (Australia) |
| Car & K | Carrington, F.A., and Kirwan, A.V., *Reports . . . Nisi Prius* |
| Car & Kir | = Car & K |
| Car & M | Carrington, F.A., and Marshman, J.R., *Reports . . . Nisi Prius* |
| Car & Ol | = 3 Ry & Can Cas |
| Car & P | Carrington, F.A., and Payne, J., *Reports . . . Nisi Prius* |
| Car H & A | = New Sess Cas |
| Carp Pat Cas | Carpmael, W., *Law Reports of Patent Cases* |
| Carp PC | = Carp Pat Cas |
| Carr Ham & Al | = New Sess Cas |
| Cart | Carter, S., *Reports . . . Common Pleas* |
| Carter | = Cart |
| Carth | Carthew, Thomas, *Reports . . . King's Bench* |
| Carthew | = Carth |
| Cartm | Austen-Cartmell, James, *Abstract of Reported Cases Relating to Trade Marks* |
| Cary | Cary, Sir George, *Reports . . . Chancery* |

| | |
|---|---|
| Cas Arg & Dec | = Chan Cas |
| Cas BR | = 12 Mod |
| Cas BR t Wm III | = 12 Mod |
| Cas Ch | = 9 Mod |
| Cas CL | = Leach |
| Cas CR | = 12 Mod |
| Cas Eq | = Gilb Ch |
| Cas Eq Abr | = Eq Cas Abr |
| Cases t Talbot | = Cas t Talb |
| Cas FT | = Cas t Talb |
| Cas in Ch | = Ch Cas |
| Cas KB | = 8 Mod |
| Cas KB t H | = Kel W |
| Cas KB t Hardwicke | = Kel W |
| Cas L & Eq | = Gilb KB |
| | also = 10 Mod |
| Cas L Eq | = 10 Mod |
| Cas Prac CP | = Cooke |
| Cas Pract KB | = Cas Pr KB |
| Cas Pra KB | = Cas Pr KB |
| Cas Pr KB | *Cases of Practice in the Court of King's Bench* |
| Cas Sett | *Cases and Resolutions ... Concerning Settlements and Removals* |
| Cas Six Cir | *Reports of Cases ... on Six Circuits in Ireland* |
| Cass LGB | Casson, William Augustus, *Decisions of the Local Government Board* |
| Cas temp | see Cas t |
| Cas t F | = Rep t Finch |
| Cas t Finch | = Rep t Finch |
| Cas t Geo 1 | = 8 and 9 Mod |
| Cas t H | = Cas t Hard |
| Cas t Hard | *Cases Argued and Adjudged in the Court of King's Bench ... [tempore] Hardwicke* |
| Cas t Holt | = 11 Mod |
| Cas t King | = Sel Cas t King |
| Cas t Lee | = Lee |
| Cas t Mac | = 10 Mod |
| Cas t Maccl | = 10 Mod |
| Cas t N | = Eden |
| Cas t Nap | = Dr t Nap |
| Cas t North | = Eden |
| Cas t QA | = 11 Mod |
| Cas t Q Anne | = 11 Mod |
| Cas t Sugd | = Dr t Sug |
| Cas t T | = Cas t Talb |
| Cas t Talb | *Cases in Equity during the Time of the Late Lord Chancellor Talbot* |
| Cas t Wm 3 | = 12 Mod |
| Ca t | see Cas t |
| Ca temp | see Cas t |
| CB | *Common Bench Reports* |

| | |
|---|---|
| CB NS | *Common Bench Reports, New Series* |
| CB Rep | = CB |
| CCC | = Ch Cas in Ch |
| | also = Cox CC |
| | ! also *Canadian Criminal Cases* |
| CCC Cas | = CCC Sess Pap |
| CC Chron | = Co Ct Chr |
| CCC Sess Pap | *Central Criminal Court Sessions Papers* |
| CC Ct Cas | = CCC Sess Pap |
| CCLR | *Consumer Credit Law Reports* |
| CEC | *European Community Cases* |
| CFLQ | *Child and Family Law Quarterly* |
| CG | Department of Health and Social Security, *Reported Decisions of the Commissioner under the National Insurance and Family Allowances Acts* (referring to a case number) |
| Ch | *Law Reports. Chancery Division.* [1891]– |
| C H & A | = New Sess Cas |
| Ch & P | = Cha & P |
| Cha & P | Chambers, T.G., and Pretty, A.H.F., *Finance (1909-10) Act 1910. Reports of Cases ... on the Interpretation of Part I* |
| Chan Cas | = Ch Cas |
| Chan Rep | = Rep Ch |
| Chan Rep C | = Rep Ch |
| Char Cha Cas | Charley, W.T., *Reports ... Judges' Chambers* |
| Char Cham Cas | = Char Cha Cas |
| Charl Cha Cas | = Char Cha Cas |
| Charl Pr Cas | = Char Pr Cas |
| Char Pr Cas | Charley, W.T., *Reports of Cases ... Illustrative of the New System of Practice and Pleading* |
| Ch Cas | *Cases Argued and Decreed in the High Court of Chancery* |
| Ch Cas Ch | = Ch Cas in Ch |
| Ch Cas in Ch | *Choyce Cases in Chancery* |
| ChD | *Law Reports. ... Chancery Division.* (1875–90) |
| Chit | Chitty, J., *Reports ... Practice and Pleading* |
| Cho Ca Ch | = Ch Cas in Ch |
| C Home | = Cl Home |
| Ch Pre | = Prec Ch |
| ChR | = Rep Ch |
| Ch Rep | = Rep Ch |
| Ch Rob | = C Rob |
| CI | Department of Health and Social Security, *Reported Decisions of the Commissioner under the Social Security and National Insurance (Industrial Injuries) Acts* (referring to a case number) |
| CJQ | *Civil Justice Quarterly* |
| CL | *Current Law Monthly Digest* |
| Cl & F | Clark, C., and Finnelly, W., *Reports ... House of Lords* |
| Cl & Fin | = Cl & F |
| CL&P | *Computer Law and Practice* |
| Clark & Finnelly | = Cl & F |

| | |
|---|---|
| Clay | Clayton, John, *Reports and Pleas of Assises at Yorke* |
| CLC | *CCH Commercial Law Cases* |
| CLC | *Current Law Consolidation* |
| Cleary Reg Cas | Cleary, A.P., *Registration Cases* |
| Cl Home | Home, Alexander, *Decisions of the Court of Session* |
| Clif | Clifford, H., *Report of the Two Cases of Controverted Elections of the Borough of Southwark* |
| Clif & R | Clifford, F., and Rickards, A.G., *Cases ... Court of Referees.* [*Locus Standi.*] |
| Clif & Rick | = Clif & R |
| Clif & S | Clifford, F., and Stephens, P.S., *Practice of the Court of Referees ... Locus Standi of Petitioners* |
| Clif & Steph | = Clif & S |
| Clif El | = Clif |
| Cliff | = Clif |
| Cliff & Rick | = Clif & R |
| Cliff & Steph | = Clif & S |
| CLJ | *Cambridge Law Journal* |
| CLR | = Com Law Rep |
| | ! also *Commonwealth Law Reports* (Australia) |
| | ! also *Construction Law Reports* (Canada) |
| CLSR | *Computer Law and Security Report* |
| CLY | *Current Law Year Book* |
| CLY | *Scottish Current Law Year Book* |
| CLYB | = CLY |
| C M & H | = Cox M & H |
| C M & R | = Cr M & R |
| CMLR | *Common Market Law Reports* |
| CMLR D | *Common Market Law Reports* (referring to Restrictive Practices Supplement) |
| CML Rev | *Common Market Law Review* |
| CMLR M | *Common Market Law Reports* (referring to Merger Decisions) |
| CMR | = Cr M & R |
| Co | = Co Rep |
| Cob St Tr | = St Tr |
| Cock & R | Cockburn, Sir Alexander, and Rowe, William Carpenter, *Cases of Controverted Elections* |
| Cock & Rowe | = Cock & R |
| Cockb & R | = Cock & R |
| Cockb & Rowe | = Cock & R |
| Co Ct Chr | *County Courts Chronicle* |
| Co Ct Rep | *Reports of County Court Cases* |
| COD | *Crown Office Digest* |
| Co Ent | Coke, Sir Edward, *Book of Entries* |
| C of S 5th series | = F |
| Co G | = Cooke |
| Co Inst | Coke, Sir Edward, *Institutes of the Laws of England*, bk 2–4 |
| Co Law | *Company Lawyer* |
| Col CC | = Coll |
| Co Litt | Coke, Sir Edward, *Institutes of the Laws of England*, bk 1 |

| | |
|---|---|
| Coll | Collyer, John, *Reports ... Chancery*. [Vice-Chancellor.] |
| Coll CC | = Coll |
| Coll CR | = Coll |
| Colles | Colles, Richard, *Reports ... Parliament* |
| Colles PC | = Colles |
| Coll NC | = Coll |
| Coll PC | = Colles |
| Colly | = Coll |
| Colquit | = 1 Mod |
| Colt | Coltman, F.J., *Registration Cases* |
| Com | Comyns, Sir John, *Reports ... King's Bench, Common Pleas and Exchequer* |
| Comb | Comberbach, Roger, *Report of Several Cases ... King's Bench* |
| Com B | = CB |
| Comberbach | = Comb |
| Com B Rep | = CB |
| Com Cas | *Reports of Commercial Cases* |
| Com Dig | Comyns, Sir John, *A Digest of the Laws of England* |
| Com Law Rep | *Common Law Reports* |
| Com LR | *Commercial Law Reports* |
| Comp & Law | *Computers and Law* |
| Comp L & P | = CL&P |
| Comp Lawyer | = Co Law |
| Com Rep | = Com |
| Comyns | = Com |
| Con & L | Connor, Henry, and Lawson, James Anthony, *Reports ... Chancery*. [Ireland.] |
| Con & Law | = Con & L |
| Con LR | *Construction Law Reports* |
| Conr | Conroy, J., *Custodiam Reports* |
| Consist | = Hag Con |
| Const | = 4th ed. of Bott PL |
| Const LJ | *Construction Law Journal* |
| Consum LJ | *Consumer Law Journal* |
| Consum LJ CS | *Consumer Law Journal* (referring to Current Survey) |
| Conv (1916–36) | *Conveyancer* |
| Conv [1978]– | *Conveyancer and Property Lawyer*. 1978– |
| Conv NS | *Conveyancer and Property Lawyer*. 1937–77 |
| Coo & Al | = Cooke & A |
| Cooke | Cooke, Sir George, *Reports ... Common Pleas* |
| Cooke & A | Cooke, J.R., and Alcock, J.C., *Reports ... King's Bench ... in Ireland* |
| Cooke & Al | = Cooke & A |
| Cooke CP | = Cooke |
| Cooke Pr Cas | = Cooke |
| Coop | = G Coop |
| Coop CC | = Coop t Cott |
| Coop CP | = Coop t Cott |
| Coop G | = G Coop |

| | |
|---|---|
| Coop PC | = Coop Pr Cas |
| Coop Pr Cas | Cooper, Charles Purton, *Reports of Some Cases Adjudged in the Courts of the Lord Chancellor, Master of the Rolls and Vice-Chancellor* |
| Coop t Brough | Cooper, Charles Purton, *Select Cases Decided by Lord Brougham* |
| Coop t Cott | Cooper, Charles Purton, *Reports of Cases in Chancery Decided by Lord Cottenham* |
| Corb & D | Corbett, V., and Daniell, E.R., *Reports of Cases of Controverted Elections* |
| Corb & Dan | = Corb & D |
| Co Rep | Coke, Sir Edward, *Reports* |
| Coup | Couper, Charles T., *Reports ... High Court and Circuit Courts of Justiciary* |
| Couper | = Coup |
| Court Sess Cas 1st Series | = S |
| Court Sess Cas 2nd Series | = D |
| Court Sess Cas 3rd Series | = M |
| Court Sess Cas 4th Series | = R (Rettie, M., *Cases ... Court of Session, Court of Justiciary and House of Lords*) |
| Court Sess Cas 5th Series | = F |
| Court Sess Cas 6th Series | = SC |
| Cowp | Cowper, Henry, *Reports ... King's Bench* |
| Cox | Cox, Samuel Compton, *Cases ... Equity* <br> also = Cox CC |
| Cox & A | Cox, E.W., and Atkinson, H.T., *Registration Appeal Cases* |
| Cox & Atk | = Cox & A |
| Cox & M'C | = Cox M & H |
| Cox CC | Cox, E.W., *Reports of Cases in Criminal Law* |
| Cox Cr Cas | = Cox CC |
| Cox Cty Ct Cas | = Co Ct Rep |
| Cox Eq Cas | = Cox |
| Cox Jt Stk | Cox, E.W., *Reports of all the Cases ... Relating to the Law of Joint-Stock Companies* |
| Cox M & H | Cox, E.W., Macrae, D.C., and Hertslet, C.J.B., *Reports of County Courts Cases* |
| Cox Mag Cas | = Cox MC |
| Cox MC | Cox, E.W., *Reports of all the Cases ... Relating to Magistrates* |
| CP | Department of Health and Social Security, *Reported Decisions of the Commissioner under the National Insurance and Family Allowances Acts* (referring to a case number) |
| CPC | = Coop Pr Cas |
| CP Coop | = Coop Pr Cas |

| | |
|---|---|
| CP Cooper | = Coop Pr Cas |
| CPD | *Law Reports. Common Pleas Division.* (1875–80) |
| Cr & D | = Craw & D |
| Cr & D Ab Cas | = Craw & D Abr Cas |
| Cr & Dix | = Craw & D |
| | also = Craw & D Abr Cas |
| Cr & Dix Ab Cas | = Craw & D Abr Cas |
| Cr & J | Crompton, Charles, and Jervis, John, *Reports . . .* |
| | *Exchequer* |
| Cr & M | Crompton, Charles, and Meeson, R., *Reports . . . Exchequer* |
| Cr & Ph | Craig, R.D., and Phillips, T.J., *Reports . . . Chancery* |
| Cr & St | = 1 Pat |
| Craig & Ph | = Cr & Ph |
| Craig St & Paton | = 1 Pat |
| Cr App R | *Criminal Appeal Reports* |
| Cr App Rep | = Cr App R |
| Cr App R (S) | *Criminal Appeal Reports (Sentencing)* |
| Craw & D | Crawford, G., and Dix, E.S., *Reports . . . Circuits, in Ireland* |
| Craw & D Abr C | = Craw & D Abr Cas |
| Craw & D Abr Cas | Crawford, G., and Dix, E.S., *Abridged Notes of Cases* |
| Cress | Cresswell, R.N., *Reports . . . Court for Relief of Insolvent* |
| | *Debtors* |
| Cress Ins Cas | = Cress |
| Cress Insol Cas | = Cress |
| Cress Insolv Cas | = Cress |
| Crim LB | *Greens Criminal Law Bulletin* |
| Crim LR | *Criminal Law Review* |
| Crim L Rev | = Crim LR |
| Cripps Cas | Cripps, H.W., *Reports of New Cases . . . Relating to the* |
| | *Church and Clergy* |
| Cripps' Cas | = Cripps Cas |
| Cripps Ch Cas | = Cripps Cas |
| Cripps' Church Cas | = Cripps Cas |
| Cr M & R | Crompton, Charles, Meeson, R., and Roscoe, H., *Reports . . .* |
| | *Exchequer* |
| Cr MR | = Cr M & R |
| Cro | = Keil |
| C Rob | Robinson, Chr., *Reports . . . Admiralty* |
| C Rob App | Robinson, Chr., *Reports . . . Admiralty* (referring to an |
| | appendix) |
| Cro Car | Croke, Sir George, *Reports . . . Charles [I]* |
| Crockf | = Crockford |
| Crockford | *Reports . . . Maritime Law* |
| Cro Eliz | Croke, Sir George, *Reports . . . Elizabeth [I]* |
| Cro Jac | Croke, Sir George, *Reports . . . James [I]* |
| Croke | = Keil |
| Cromp & Jer | = Cr & J |
| Cromp & M | = Cr & M |
| Cromp & Mees | = Cr & M |
| Cromp M & R | = Cr M & R |
| Cr S & P | = 1 Pat |

| | |
|---|---|
| Cr St & P | = 1 Pat |
| CS | Department of Health and Social Security, *Reported Decisions of the Commissioner under the National Insurance and Family Allowances Acts* (referring to a case number) |
| C S & P | = 1 Pat |
| CSG | Department of Health and Social Security, *Reported Decisions of the Commissioner under the National Insurance and Family Allowances Acts* (referring to a case number) |
| CSI | Department of Health and Social Security, *Reported Decisions of the Commissioner under the Social Security and National Insurance (Industrial Injuries) Acts* (referring to a case number) |
| CSP, CSS, CSU | Department of Health and Social Security, *Reported Decisions of the Commissioner under the National Insurance and Family Allowances Acts* (referring to a case number) |
| C t N | = Eden |
| Cty Ct Chron | = Co Ct Chr |
| Cty Ct R | = Co Ct Rep |
| CU | Department of Health and Social Security, *Reported Decisions of the Commissioner under the National Insurance and Family Allowances Acts* (referring to a case number) |
| Cun | Cunningham, Timothy, *Reports . . . King's Bench* |
| Cunn | = Cun |
| Curt | Curteis, W.C., *Reports . . . Ecclesiastical Courts* |
| Curt Ecc | = Curt |
| CWG | Department of Health and Social Security, *Reported Decisions of the Commissioner under the National Insurance and Family Allowances Acts* (referring to a case number) |
| CWI | Department of Health and Social Security, *Reported Decisions of the Commissioner under the Social Security and National Insurance (Industrial Injuries) Acts* (referring to a case number) |
| CWP, CWS, CWU | Department of Health and Social Security, *Reported Decisions of the Commissioner under the National Insurance and Family Allowances Acts* (referring to a case number) |
| D | Dunlop, A., *Cases . . . Court of Session*. [Session Cases, 2nd series.] |
| | also = Den |
| | also = Dy |
| D & B | = Dears & B |
| D & C | = Dow & Cl |
| D & Ch | = Deac & Ch |
| D & E | = TR |
| D & G | Diprose, J., and Gammon, J., *Reports of Law Cases Affecting Friendly Societies* |

| | |
|---|---|
| D & J | = De G & J |
| D & J B | = De G & J Bcy |
| D & L | = Dowl & L |
| D & M | = Dav & Mer |
| D & Mer | = Dav & Mer |
| D & P | = 2 Den |
| D & R | = Dowl & Ry KB |
| D & R MC | = Dowl & Ry MC |
| D & R NP | = Dowl & Ry NP |
| D & R NPC | = Dowl & Ry NP |
| D & S | = Dea & Sw |
| | also = Drew & Sm |
| D & Sm | = De G & Sm |
| D & W | = Dr & Wal |
| | also = Dr & War |
| Dal | = Benl & Dal (Dalison's section) |
| Dale | Dale, James Murray, *Legal Ritual* |
| Dalr | Dalrymple, Sir Hew, *Decisions of the Court of Session* |
| Dan | Daniell, Edmund Robert, *Reports ... Exchequer* |
| Dan & L | = Dans & L |
| Dan & Ll | = Dans & L |
| Daniell | = Dan |
| Dans & L | Danson, F.M., and Lloyd, J.H., *Mercantile Cases* |
| Das | = 2 B & I |
| Dav | Davies, Sir John, *Les Reports ... Courts del Roy en Ireland* |
| Dav & M | = Dav & Mer |
| Dav & Mer | Davison, H., and Merivale, H., *Reports ... Queen's Bench* |
| Davies | = Dav |
| Dav Ir | = Dav |
| Davis | = Dav |
| Dav Pat Cas | Davies, J., *Collection of the Most Important Cases Respecting Patents* |
| Dav PC | = Dav Pat Cas |
| Davy | = Dav |
| Davys | = Dav |
| Day | Day, Samuel Henry, *Election Cases* |
| Day Elect Cas | = Day |
| DCLD | *Discrimination Case Law Digest* |
| Dea & Ch | = Deac & Ch |
| Dea & Sw | Deane, James Parker, and Swabey, M.C. Merttins, *Reports ... Ecclesiastical Courts* |
| Deac | Deacon, E.E., *Reports ... Bankruptcy* |
| Deac & C | = Deac & Ch |
| Deac & Ch | Deacon, E.E., and Chitty, E., *Reports ... Bankruptcy* |
| Deac & Chit | = Deac & Ch |
| Deane | = Dea & Sw |
| Deane Ecc Rep | = Dea & Sw |
| Dears | Dearsly, Henry Richard, *Crown Cases Reserved* |
| Dears & B | Dearsly, Henry Richard, and Bell, Thomas, *Crown Cases Reserved* |
| Dears & B CC | = Dears & B |

| | |
|---|---|
| Dears & Bell | = Dears & B |
| Dears CC | = Dears |
| Deas & A | Deas, G., and Anderson, J., *Cases ... Court of Session [etc.]* |
| Deas & And | = Deas & A |
| Decisions and Reports | = DR |
| De Col | De Colyar, H.A., *Reports ... County Courts* |
| De Coly | = De Col |
| De G | De Gex, John P., *Reports ... Bankruptcy* |
| De G & J | De Gex, John P., and Jones, H. Cadman, *Reports ... Chancery* |
| De G & J B | = De G & J Bcy |
| De G & J Bcy | De Gex, John P., and Jones, H. Cadman, *Reports ... Bankruptcy Appeals* |
| De G & Jo | = De G & J |
| De G & Sm | De Gex, John P., and Smale, John, *Reports ... Chancery*. [Vice-Chancellor.] |
| De Gex | = De G |
| De G F & J | De Gex, John P., Fisher, F., and Jones, H. Cadman, *Reports ... Chancery* |
| De G F & J Bcy | De Gex, John P., Fisher, F., and Jones, H. Cadman, *Bankruptcy Appeals* |
| De G J & S | De Gex, John P., Jones, H. Cadman, and Smith, R. Horton, *Reports ... Chancery* |
| De G J & S Bcy | De Gex, John P., Jones, H. Cadman, and Smith, R. Horton, *Reports ... Bankruptcy Appeals* |
| De G J & Sm | = De G J & S |
| De G M & G | De Gex, John P., Macnaghten, S., and Gordon, A., *Reports ... Chancery* |
| De G M & G Bcy | De Gex, John P., Macnaghten, S., and Gordon, A., *Reports ... Bankruptcy Appeals* |
| Del | Delane, William Frederick Augustus, *Collection of Decisions in the Courts for Revising the Lists of Electors* |
| Delane | = Del |
| Den | Denison, Stephen Charles, *Crown Cases Reserved* |
| Den & P | = 2 Den |
| Den CC | = Den |
| Denning LJ | *Denning Law Journal* |
| D F & J | = De G F & J |
| D F & J B | = De G F & J Bcy |
| D Falc | Falconer, David, *Decisions of the Court of Session* |
| D G | = De G |
| D (HL) | Dunlop, A., *Cases ... Court of Session*. [Session Cases, 2nd series.] (referring to House of Lords section) |
| Dick | Dickens, John, *Reports ... Chancery* |
| Dickens | = Dick |
| Diprose & Gammon | = D & G |
| Dirl | Dirleton, Lord (Sir John Nisbet), *Decisions of the Lords of Council and Session* |
| D J & S | = De G J & S |
| D J & S B | = De G J & S Bcy |
| DM | = Dav & Mer |

| | |
|---|---|
| D M & G | = De G M & G |
| D M & G B | = De G M & G Bcy |
| D NS | = Dowl NS |
| Dod | = Dods |
| Dods | Dodson, John, *Reports ... Admiralty* |
| Dods App | Dodson, John, *Reports ... Admiralty* (referring to an appendix) |
| Don Ir Land Cas | Donnell, R., *Reports ... Irish Land Courts* |
| Donn | Donnelly, Ross, *Minutes of Cases ... Chancery* |
| Donnelly | = Donn |
| Donn Ir Land Cas | = Don Ir Land Cas |
| Doug | = Doug El Cas |
| | also = Doug KB |
| Doug El Cas | Douglas, Sylvester, Baron Glenbervie, *History of the Cases of Controverted Elections* |
| Doug KB | Douglas, Sylvester, Baron Glenbervie, *Reports ... King's Bench* |
| Dougl | = Doug KB |
| Dow | Dow, P., *Reports ... House of Lords* |
| | also = Dowl Pr Cas |
| Dow & Cl | Dow, P., and Clark, C., *Reports ... House of Lords* |
| Dow & Clark | = Dow & Cl |
| Dow & L | = Dowl & L |
| Dow & Ry | = Dowl & Ry KB |
| Dow & Ry KB | = Dowl & Ry KB |
| Dow & Ry MC | = Dowl & Ry MC |
| Dow & Ry NP | = Dowl & Ry NP |
| Dowl | = Dowl Pr Cas |
| Dowl & L | Dowling, A.S., and Lowndes, J.J., *Reports ... [Bail Court]* |
| Dowl & R | = Dowl & Ry KB |
| Dowl & R MC | = Dowl & Ry MC |
| Dowl & Ry KB | Dowling, J., and Ryland, A., *Reports of Cases Argued ... King's Bench* |
| Dowl & Ry MC | Dowling, J., and Ryland, A., *Reports of Cases Relating to the Duty and Office of Magistrates* |
| Dowl & Ry NP | Dowling, J., and Ryland, A., *Cases ... Nisi Prius* |
| Dowl NS | Dowling, A.S., and Dowling, V., *Reports ... [Bail Court]* |
| Dowl PR | = Dowl Pr Cas |
| Dowl Pr Cas | Dowling, A.S., *Reports ... [Bail Court]* |
| Dow NS | = Dow & Cl |
| | also = Dowl NS |
| Dow Pr Cas | = Dowl Pr Cas |
| D PC | = Dowl Pr Cas |
| DR | Council of Europe, European Commission of Human Rights, *Decisions and Reports* |
| | also = DRA |
| Dr | = Drew |
| Dr & Nap | = Dr t Nap |
| Dr & Sm | = Drew & Sm |
| Dr & Sug | = Dr t Sug |
| Dr & Wal | Drury, W.B., and Walsh, F.W., *Reports ... Chancery.* [Ireland.] |

| | |
|---|---|
| Dr & War | Drury, W.B., and Warren, R.R., *Reports ... Chancery.* [Ireland.] |
| DRA | *De-rating and Rating Appeals* |
| Drew | Drewry, C. Stewart, *Reports ... Chancery.* [Vice-Chancellor.] |
| Drew & Sm | Drewry, C. Stewart, and Smale, J. Jackson, *Reports ... Chancery.* [Vice-Chancellor.] |
| Drewry | = Drew |
| Drink | Drinkwater, W.L., *Reports ... Common Pleas* |
| Drinkwater | = Drink |
| Dr t Nap | Drury, W.B., *Select Cases ... Chancery, during the time of Lord Chancellor Napier.* [Ireland.] |
| Dr t Sug | Drury, W.B., *Reports ... Chancery, during the time of Lord Chancellor Sugden.* [Ireland.] |
| Dru & Nap | = Dr t Nap |
| Dru & Sug | = Dr t Sug |
| Dru & Wal | = Dr & Wal |
| Dru & War | = Dr & War |
| Drury | = Dr t Nap |
| | also = Dr t Sug |
| Drury t Nap | = Dr t Nap |
| Drury t Sug | = Dr t Sug |
| DULJ | *Dublin University Law Journal* |
| Dunc Mer Cas | Duncan, J.A., *Annual Review of Mercantile Cases* |
| Dunl | = D |
| Dunl Ct of Sess | = D |
| Dunlop | = D |
| Dunn | Dunning, John, 1st Baron Ashburton, *Reports ... King's Bench* |
| Dunning | = Dunn |
| Durie | Durie, Lord (Sir Alexander Gibson), *Decisions of the Lords of Council and Session* |
| Durn & E | = TR |
| Dy | Dyer, Sir James, *Reports* |
| Dyer | = Dy |
| | |
| E | = East |
| E & A | = Notes of Cas |
| | also = Sp Ecc & Ad |
| E & B | = El & Bl |
| E & Bl | = El & Bl |
| E & E | = El & El |
| E & P | *International Journal of Evidence and Proof* |
| E & Y | = Eag & Y |
| E & Y Tithe Cas | = Eag & Y |
| Ea | = East |
| Eag & Y | Eagle, F.K., and Younge, E., *Collection ... of Cases ... Relating to Tithes* |
| Eag & Yo | = Eag & Y |
| East | East, Edward Hyde, *Reports ... King's Bench* |
| East PC | East, Edward Hyde, *Treatise of the Pleas of the Crown* |

| | |
|---|---|
| E B & E | = El Bl & El |
| Ec & Mar | = Notes of Cas |
| Ec & Mar Cas | = Notes of Cas |
| ECC | *European Commercial Cases* |
| Ecc & Ad | = Sp Ecc & Ad |
| Eccl & Ad | = Sp Ecc & Ad |
| ECLR | *European Competition Law Review* |
| ECR. [1954–6]–<br>   [1957–8] | Court of Justice of the European Coal and Steel Community, *Reports* |
| ECR. [1959]– | Court of Justice of the European Communities, *Reports* |
| ECR-SC | Court of First Instance, *European Court Reports: Reports of European Community Staff Cases* |
| Ed | = Eden<br>also = Edgar |
| Eden | Eden, Robert Henley, *Reports ... Chancery* |
| Edgar | Edgar, John, *Decisions of the Court of Session* |
| Edw | Edwards, Thomas, *Reports ... Admiralty* |
| Edw Adm | = Edw |
| Edwards | = Edw |
| Edw Tho | = Edw |
| EG | *Estates Gazette* |
| EGCS | *Estates Gazette Case Summaries* |
| EGD | *Estates Gazette Digest of Land and Property Cases* |
| EGLR | *Estates Gazette Law Reports* |
| EHRR | *European Human Rights Reports* |
| EIPR | *European Intellectual Property Review* |
| EIPR D | *European Intellectual Property Review* (referring to the News Section) |
| El | = Elchies |
| El & Bl | Ellis, Thomas Flower, and Blackburn, Colin, *Reports ... Queen's Bench* |
| El & El | Ellis, Thomas Flower, and Ellis, Francis, *Reports ... Queen's Bench* |
| El B & E | = El Bl & El |
| El B & El | = El Bl & El |
| El Bl & El | Ellis, Thomas Flower, Blackburn, Colin, and Ellis, Francis, *Reports ... Queen's Bench* |
| Elch | = Elchies |
| Elchies | Elchies, Lord (Patrick Grant), *Decisions of the Court of Session* |
| Ell & Bl | = El & Bl |
| Ell & Ell | = El & El |
| Ell B & E | = El Bl & El |
| Ell B & Ell | = El Bl & El |
| ELR | *Employment Law Report*<br>also = EL Rev |
| EL Rev | *European Law Review* |
| EMLR | *Entertainment and Media Law Reports* |
| Eng Judg | *Decisions of the English Judges during the Usurpation* |
| Eng Pr Cas | = Rosc Pri Cas |

| | |
|---|---|
| Eng R & C Cas | = Ry & Can Cas |
| Eng Rep | = ER |
| Ent LR | *Entertainment Law Review* |
| Ent LR E | *Entertainment Law Review* (referring to the News Section) |
| Env Liability | *Environmental Liability* |
| Env Liability CS | *Environmental Liability* (referring to the Current Survey) |
| Env LR | *Environmental Law Reports* |
| Env LR D | *Environmental Law Reports* (referring to the Digest) |
| EPC | = Rosc Pri Cas |
| EPL | *European Public Law* |
| EPOR | *European Patent Office Reports* |
| Eq Ab | = Eq Cas Abr |
| Eq Cas Abr | *General Abridgment of Cases in Equity* |
| Eq R | = Eq Rep |
| Eq Rep | *Equity Reports* <br> also = Gilb Ch |
| ER | *English Reports* <br> also = East |
| Esp | 'Espinasse, Isaac, *Reports ... Nisi Prius* |
| Eur Ass Arb | Marrack, R., *European Assurance Arbitration before Lord Westbury* |
| Eur Court <br> HR Series A | *Publications of the European Court of Human Rights.* <br> *Series A. Judgments and Decisions* |
| Eur Court <br> HR Series B | *Publications of the European Court of Human Rights.* <br> *Series B. Pleadings, Oral Arguments and Documents* |
| Euro CL | *European Current Law Monthly Digest* |
| Euro CLY | *European Current Law Year Book* |
| Ex | *Exchequer Reports* |
| Exch | = Ex |
| Exch Cas | *Reports ... Court of Exchequer, Scotland* |
| Exch Rep W H & G | = Ex |
| ExD | *Law Reports. Exchequer Division.* (1875–80) |
| | |
| F | Fraser, H.J.E., *Cases ... Court of Session, Court of Justiciary and House of Lords.* [Session Cases, 5th series.] <br> ! also *Federal Reporter* (USA) |
| F & F | Foster, T. Campbell, and Finlason, W.F., *Reports ... Nisi Prius* |
| F & Fitz | = Falc & F |
| F & S | = Fox & S <br> also = Fox & S Reg |
| Fac Coll | = FC |
| Fac Dec | *Faculty Decisions. Octavo Series* |
| Falc | = D Falc |
| Falc & F | Falconer, T., and Fitzherbert, E.H., *Cases of Controverted Elections* |
| Falc & Fitz | = Falc & F |
| Fam | *Law Reports. Family Division.* [1972]– |
| Fam Law | *Family Law* |
| Fam Law R | = FLR |
| Fam LB | *Greens Family Law Bulletin* |

| | |
|---|---|
| Far | = early ed. of 7 Mod |
| Farr | = early ed. of 7 Mod |
| Farrant | Farrant, R.D., *Digest of Manx Cases* |
| Farresley | = early ed. of 7 Mod |
| Fawc Ref | Fawcett, J.H., *Treatise on the Court of Referees* |
| FBC | = Fonbl |
| FC (1752–1808) | *Faculty Collection. Old Series* |
| FC (1808–25) | *Faculty Collection. New Series* |
| FCR | *Family Court Reporter* |
| F Ct of Sess | = F |
| F Dict | = Fol Dic |
| Ferg | = Ferg Cons |
| | also = Kilk |
| Ferg Cons | Fergusson, James, *Reports . . . Consistorial Court of Scotland* |
| F (HL) | Fraser, H.J.E., *Cases . . . Court of Session, Court of Justiciary and House of Lords*. [Session Cases, 5th series.] (referring to House of Lords cases) |
| Fin | = Rep t Finch |
| Finch | = Rep t Finch |
| | also = Prec Ch |
| Finch Cas Contr | Finch, Gerard Brown, *A Selection of Cases on the English Law of Contract* |
| Fin Dig | = Finl Dig |
| Fin H | = Rep t Finch |
| Finl Dig | Finlay, J., *Digest . . . Irish Reported Cases* |
| Fin LR | = FLR (*Financial Law Reports*) |
| Fin Pr | = Prec Ch |
| Fin T | = Prec Ch |
| Fitz-G | = Fitzg |
| Fitzg | Fitz-Gibbons, John, *Reports . . . King's Bench* |
| | also = Fitzg Land R |
| Fitzg Land R | Fitzgibbon, H.M., *Irish Land Reports* |
| Fitzg Reg Cas | Fitzgibbon, H.M., *Irish Registration Appeal Cases* |
| F (J) | Fraser, H.J.E., *Cases . . . Court of Session, Court of Justiciary and House of Lords*. [Session Cases, 5th series.] (referring to Justiciary cases) |
| F (JC) | = F (J) |
| Fl & K | Flanagan, S.W., and Kelly, C., *Reports . . . Rolls Court*. [Ireland.] |
| FLR (1980–3) or [1984]– | *Family Law Reports* |
| FLR 1985–9 | *Financial Law Reports* ! also *Federal Law Reports* (Australia) |
| Fol Dic | Kames, Lord (Henry Home), and Woodhouselee, Lord (Alexander Fraser Tytler), *Decisions in the Court of Session . . . in the Form of a Dictionary* |
| Fol Dict | = Fol Dic |
| Fol PL Cas | Foley, Robert, *Laws Relating to the Poor . . . with Cases* |
| Fonbl | Fonblanque, John William Martin, *Reports . . . Courts of the Commissioners in Bankruptcy* |

| | |
|---|---|
| For | = Cas t Talb |
| | also = Forr |
| Forb | = Forbes |
| Forbes | Forbes, W., *Journal of the Session Containing the Decisions of the Lords of Council and Session* |
| Forr | Forrest, Robert, *Reports . . . Exchequer* |
| | also = Cas t Talb |
| Forrest | = Forr |
| Forrester | = Cas t Talb |
| Fors Cas & Op | Forsyth, William, *Cases and Opinions on Constitutional Law* |
| Fort | Fortescue Aland, Sir John, 1st Baron Fortescue of Credan, *Reports . . . Courts of Westminster-Hall* |
| Fortes | = Fort |
| Fortescue | = Fort |
| Fortes Rep | = Fort |
| Fost | Foster, Sir Michael, *Report of Some Proceedings . . . and of Other Crown Cases* |
| Fost & Fin | = F & F |
| Foster | = Fost |
| Fount | Fountainhall, Lord (Sir John Lauder), *Decisions of the Lords of Council and Session* |
| Fox & S | Fox, M.C., and Smith, T.B.C., *Reports . . . King's Bench.* [Ireland.] |
| Fox & S Ir | = Fox & S |
| Fox & Sm | = Fox & S |
| | = Fox & S Reg |
| Fox & Sm RC | = Fox & S Reg |
| Fox & S Reg | Fox, J.S., and Smith, C.L., *Registration Cases* |
| Fras | Fraser, S., *Reports . . . Cases of Controverted Elections* |
| Fraser | = F |
| Fr Chy | = Freem Ch |
| Fr EC | = Fras |
| Free | = Freem Ch |
| Free CC | = Freem Ch |
| Free Ch | = Freem Ch |
| Free KB | = Freem KB |
| 1 Freeman | = Freem KB |
| 2 Freeman | = Freem Ch |
| Freem Ch | Freeman, Richard, *Reports . . . Chancery* |
| Freem Chy | = Freem Ch |
| Freem KB | Freeman, Richard, *Reports . . . King's Bench and Common Pleas* |
| Frewen | Frewen, Gerard L., *Judgments of the Court of Criminal Appeal.* [Irish Free State, Republic of Ireland.] |
| FSR | *Fleet Street Reports* |
| | |
| G | = Gal |
| G & D | = Gal & Dav |
| G & J | = Gl & J |
| Gal | Gale, C.J., *Reports . . . Exchequer* |

| | |
|---|---|
| Gal & Dav | Gale, C.J., and Davison, H., *Reports . . . Queen's Bench* |
| Gale | = Gal |
| Gaz Bank | = Gaz Bcy |
| Gaz Bcy | *Gazette of Bankruptcy* |
| Gazette | *Gazette* |
| G Coop | Cooper, George, *Cases . . . Chancery* |
| G Cooper | = G Coop |
| Geo Coop | = G Coop |
| Gib Dec | = Durie |
| Gif | = Giff |
| Giff | Giffard, J.W. de Longueville, *Reports . . . Chancery.* [Vice-Chancellor.] |
| Gil | = Gilb Ch |
| Gil | = Gilb KB |
| Gil & Fal | Gilmour, Sir John (Lord Craigmillar), and Falconer, Sir David (Lord Newton), *Collection of Decisions of the Lords of Council and Session* |
| Gilb | = Gilb Ch |
| | also = Gilb KB |
| Gilb Cas | = Gilb KB |
| Gilb Ch | Gilbert, J., *Reports of Cases in Equity* |
| Gilb Eq | = Gilb Ch |
| Gilb KB | Gilbert, J., *Cases . . . King's Bench* |
| Gilb Rep | = Gilb Ch |
| Gilm | = Gil & Fal |
| Gilm & F | = Gil & Fal |
| Gl & J | Glyn, T.C., and Jameson, R.S., *Cases in Bankruptcy* |
| Glan El Cas | Glanville, J., *Reports . . . Commons in Parliament* |
| Glanv El Cas | = Glan El Cas |
| Glas | Glascock, W., *Miscellaneous Reports* |
| Glasc | = Glas |
| Glascock | = Glas |
| Glyn & J | = Gl & J |
| Glyn & Jam | = Gl & J |
| Godb | Godbolt, John, *Reports . . . Courts of Record at Westminster* |
| Godbolt | = Godb |
| Gold | = Gould |
| Goldes | = Gould |
| Good Pat | = Good Pat Cas |
| Good Pat Cas | Goodeve, T.M., *Abstract of Reported Cases Relating to Letters Patent for Inventions* |
| Gould | Gouldsborough, J., *Reports . . . All the Courts at Westminster* |
| Gouldsb | = Gould |
| Gouldsborough | = Gould |
| Gow | Gow, Niel, *Reports . . . Nisi Prius* |
| Grant | = Elchies |
| Greer | Greer, E., *Irish Land Acts. Monthly Law Reports* |
| Greer LC | Greer, E., *Irish Land Acts: One Hundred and Ninety Reports of Leading Cases* |

| | |
|---|---|
| Griffin's Patent Cases | = Grif Pat Cas |
| Griff PC | = Grif Pat Cas |
| Grif Pat Cas | Griffin, Ralph, *Abstract of Reported Cases Relating to Letters Patent for Inventions* |
| Grif PL Cas | Griffith, E., *Cases of Supposed Exemption from Poor Rates* |
| Guth Sh Cas | Guthrie, W., *Select Cases ... Sheriff Courts* |
| GWD | *Greens Weekly Digest* |
| Gwil | = Gwill |
| Gwill | Gwillim, Sir Henry, *Collection of Acts ... with Reports of Cases ... Respecting Tithes* |
| Gwil Tithe Cas | = Gwill |
| | |
| H | = Hare |
| H & B | = Hud & B |
| H & C | = Hurl & C |
| H & H | = Horn & H |
| H & J | = Hayes & J |
| H & M | = Hay & M |
| | also = Hem & M |
| H & N | = Hurl & N |
| H & P | = Hop & Ph |
| H & R | = Har & Ruth |
| H & T | = H & Tw |
| H & Tw | Hall, Frederick J., and Twells, Philip, *Reports ... Chancery* |
| H & W | = Har & Woll |
| | also = Hurl & W |
| Ha | = Hare |
| Ha & Tw | = H & Tw |
| Hag Adm | Haggard, John, *Reports ... Admiralty* |
| Hag Con | Haggard, John, *Reports ... Consistory Court* |
| Hag Con App | Haggard, John, *Reports ... Consistory Court* (referring to an appendix) |
| Hag Cons | = Hag Con |
| Hag Ecc | Haggard, John, *Reports ... Ecclesiastical Courts* |
| Hag Ecc App | Haggard, John, *Reports ... Ecclesiastical Courts* (referring to an appendix) |
| Hag Ecc Supp | Haggard, John, *Reports ... Ecclesiastical Courts* (referring to the supplement) |
| Hagg | = Hag Adm |
| Hagg Ecc | = Hag Ecc |
| Hailes | Hailes, Lord (Sir David Dalrymple), *Decisions of the Lords of Council and Session* |
| Hale Cr Prec | Hale, W.H., *Series of Precedents and Proceedings in Criminal Causes* |
| Hale Ecc | Hale, W.H., *Precedents in Causes of Office against Churchwardens and Others* |
| Hale PC | Hale, Sir Matthew, *Historia Placitorum Coronae. The History of the Pleas of the Crown* |
| Hall & Tw | = H & Tw |
| Har & Ruth | Harrison, O.B.C., and Rutherford, H., *Reports ... Common Pleas* |

| | |
|---|---|
| Har & W | = Har & Woll |
| Har & Woll | Harrison, S.B., and Wollaston, F.L., *Reports . . . King's Bench and Bail Court* |
| Harc | Harcarse, Lord (Sir Roger Hog), *Decisions of the Court of Session* |
| Hard | = Hardres |
| | also = Kel W |
| Hardr | = Hardres |
| Hardres | Hardres, Sir Thomas, *Reports . . . Exchequer* |
| Hardw | = Cas t Hard |
| Hare | Hare, Thomas, *Reports . . . Chancery*. [Vice-Chancellor.] |
| Harr & Woll | = Har & Woll |
| Hats | Hatsell, John, *Precedents of Proceedings in the House of Commons* |
| Hats Pr | = Hats |
| Hawk PC | Hawkins, William, *Treatise of the Pleas of the Crown* |
| Hay | = Hayes |
| Hay & J | = Hayes & J |
| Hay & Jo | = Hayes & J |
| Hay & M | *Decisions . . . Admiralty during the Time of Sir George Hay, and of Sir James Marriott* |
| Hay & Mar | = Hay & M |
| Hay & Marr | = Hay & M |
| Hayes | Hayes, Edmund, *Reports . . . Exchequer in Ireland* |
| Hayes & J | Hayes, Edmund, and Jones, Thomas, *Reports . . . Exchequer in Ireland* |
| Hayes & Jo | = Hayes & J |
| Hayes Exch | = Hayes |
| H B | = H Bl |
| H Bl | Blackstone, Henry, *Reports . . . Common Pleas* |
| H Black | = H Bl |
| HBR | Hansell, Miles Edward, *Reports of Bankruptcy and Companies Winding-up Cases* |
| Hem & M | Hemming, George W., and Miller, Alexander Edward, *Reports . . . Chancery*. [Vice-Chancellor.] |
| Het | Hetley, Sir Thomas, *Reports* |
| Hetl | = Het |
| Hetley | = Het |
| HLC | = HL Cas |
| HL Cas | *House of Lords Cases* |
| HLR | *Housing Law Reports* |
| Hob | Hobart, Sir Henry, *Reports* |
| Hob R | = Hob |
| Hodg | = Hodges |
| Hodges | Hodges, W., *Reports . . . Common Pleas* |
| Hog | Hogan, W., *Reports . . . Rolls Court in Ireland* |
| | also = Harc |
| Ho Lords C | = HL Cas |
| Holt | Holt, Sir John, *The Judgements . . . in . . . Ashby v. White . . . and . . . Paty* |

|  |  |
|---|---|
|  | also = Holt NP |
| Holt Adm | Holt, William, *Admiralty Court Cases on the Rule of the Road* |
| Holt Adm Cas | = Holt Adm |
| Holt Eq | Holt, William, *Equity Reports*. [Vice-Chancellor.] |
| Holt KB | Holt, Sir John, *Report of All the Cases Determined by Sir John Holt* |
| Holt NP | Holt, Francis Ludlow, *Reports . . . Nisi Prius* |
| Home | = Cl Home |
| Home Cl | = Cl Home |
| Home Ct of Sess | = Cl Home |
| Hop & C | Hopwood, C.H., and Coltman, F.J., *Registration Cases* |
| Hop & Colt | = Hop & C |
| Hop & Ph | Hopwood, C.H., and Philbrick, F.A., *Registration Cases* |
| Ho Pl | = How Po Cas |
| Hopw & C | = Hop & C |
| Hopw & P | = Hop & Ph |
| Horn & H | Horn, H., and Hurlstone, E.T., *Reports . . . Exchequer* |
| Hov Supp | Hovenden, John Eykyn, *A Supplement to Vesey Junior's Reports of Cases in Chancery* |
| How C | = How Ch Pr |
| How Ch Pr | Howard, Gorges Edmond, *Rules and Practice of the High Court of Chancery in Ireland* |
| How Ch Pr S | Howard, Gorges Edmond, *Rules and Practice of the High Court of Chancery in Ireland* (referring to Supplement) |
| How EE | Howard, Gorges Edmond, *Treatise on the Rules and Practice of the Equity Side of the Exchequer in Ireland* |
| How Po Cas | Howard, Gorges Edmond, *Several Special Cases on the Laws against the Further Growth of Popery in Ireland* |
| How St Tr | = St Tr |
| Hub | = Hob |
| Hud & B | Hudson, W.E., and Brooke, J., *Reports . . . King's Bench . . . in Ireland* |
| Hud & Br | = Hud & B |
| Hume | Hume, David, *Decisions of the Court of Session* |
| Hunt's AC | Hunt, W., *Collection of Cases on the Annuity Act* |
| Hurl & C | Hurlstone, Edwin Tyrrell, and Coltman, Francis Joseph, *Exchequer Reports* |
| Hurl & Colt | = Hurl & C |
| Hurl & Gord | = 10 and 11 Ex |
| Hurl & N | Hurlstone, Edwin Tyrrell, and Norman, J.P., *Exchequer Reports* |
| Hurl & Nor | = Hurl & N |
| Hurl & W | Hurlstone, Edwin Tyrrell, and Walmsley, T., *Reports . . . Exchequer* |
| Hurl & Walm | = Hurl & W |
| Hut | Hutton, Sir Richard, *Reports* |
| Hutt | = Hut |
| Hutton | = Hut |
| Hux Judg | = Sec Bk Judg |
| Hy Bl | = H Bl |

| | |
|---|---|
| I&NL&P | *Immigration and Nationality Law and Practice* |
| ICCLR | *International Company and Commercial Law Review* |
| ICCLR C | *International Company and Commercial Law Review* (referring to the News Section) |
| IChR | *Irish Chancery Reports* |
| ICLQ | *International and Comparative Law Quarterly* |
| ICLR | *Irish Common Law Reports* |
| ICR | *Industrial Cases Reports* |
| ICSID Reports | *ICSID Reports* |
| IEqR | *Irish Equity Reports* |
| IHRR | *International Human Rights Reports* |
| IJEL | *Irish Journal of European Law* |
| IL | = Fitzg Land R |
| IL&P | *Insolvency Law and Practice* |
| ILJ | *Industrial Law Journal* |
| ILQ | *International Law Quarterly* |
| ILR<br>   vols 1–9 (1942–84) | *Insurance Law Reports* |
| ILR<br>   vols 17– | *International Law Reports* |
| ILR<br>   vols 1–13 (1838–50) | *Irish Law Reports*<br>! also *Canadian Insurance Law Reporter* |
| ILRM | *Irish Law Reports Monthly* |
| ILT | *Irish Law Times* |
| ILT & SJ | *Irish Law Times and Solicitors' Journal* |
| ILT Jo | = ILT & SJ |
| ILTR | *Irish Law Times Reports* |
| Imm AR | *Immigration Appeals* |
| Ind C Aw | *Industrial Court Decisions* |
| Indust C Aw | = Ind C Aw |
| InsL&P | *Insurance Law and Practice* |
| Int & Comp LQ | = ICLQ |
| Int Cas | = Rowe |
| Int ILR | *International Insurance Law Review* |
| Int LR | = ILR (*International Law Reports*) |
| Int Rev Law Econ | *International Review of Law and Economics* |
| IPD | *Intellectual Property Decisions* |
| IR | *Irish Reports* |
| Ir Ch R | = IChR |
| IR Ch Rep | = IChR |
| Ir Cir Rep | = Cas Six Cir |
| IR volume number CL | *Irish Reports. Common Law* |
| Ir CLR | = ICLR |
| Ir Com Law Rep | = ICLR |
| Ir Eccl | = Milw |
| IR volume number Eq | *Irish Reports. Equity* |
| Ir Eq R | = IEqR |
| Ir Eq Rep | = IEqR |
| Irish Jurist | *Irish Jurist. 1966–* |
| Ir Jur | *Irish Jurist. 1935–65* |

| | |
|---|---|
| Ir Jur Rep | *Irish Jurist Reports* |
| Ir Law Rec NS | = Law Rec NS |
| IRLB | *Industrial Relations Law Bulletin* |
| IRLIB | *Industrial Relations Legal Information Bulletin* |
| IRLR | *Industrial Relations Law Reports* |
| Ir LR | = LR Ir |
| Ir L Rec 1st ser | = Law Rec |
| Ir L Rec NS | = Law Rec NS |
| Ir L Rep | = ILR (*Irish Law Reports*) |
| IrLTR | = ILTR |
| IrR | = IR |
| IR R & L | *Irish Reports. Registry Appeals . . . and Appeals in the Court for Land Cases Reserved* |
| IrR Reg App | = IR R & L |
| Irv | Irvine, Alex. Forbes, *Reports . . . High Court and Circuit Courts of Justiciary* |
| Ir WCC | = Shill WC |
| Ir WLR | = IWLR |
| ITR | *Industrial Tribunal Reports* |
| IWLR | *Irish Weekly Law Reports* |
| | |
| J | = Sc Jur |
| J & C | = Jones & C |
| J & H | = John & H |
| J & La T | = Jones & La T |
| J & S | = Jebb & S |
| J & W | = Jac & W |
| Jac | Jacob, Edward, *Reports . . . Chancery* |
| Jac & W | Jacob, Edward, and Walker, John, *Reports . . . Chancery* |
| Jacob | = Jac |
| JALT | *Journal of the Association of Law Teachers* |
| JBL | *Journal of Business Law* |
| J Bridg | Bridgman, Sir John, *Reports* |
| J Bus L | = JBL |
| JC | *Session Cases. Cases Decided in the Court of Justiciary. 1917–* |
| J Ch Law | = JCL (*Journal of Child Law*) |
| JCL | *Journal of Child Law* |
| JCL | *Journal of Criminal Law* |
| JCMS | *Journal of Common Market Studies* |
| J Crim L | = JCL (*Journal of Criminal Law*) |
| Jebb | Jebb, R., *Cases . . . Criminal . . . Ireland* |
| Jebb & B | Jebb, R., and Bourke, R., *Reports . . . Queen's Bench, in Ireland* |
| Jebb & S | Jebb, R., and Symes, A.R., *Reports . . . Queen's Bench and Exchequer Chamber in Ireland* |
| Jebb CC | = Jebb |
| Jebb Cr & Pr Cas | = Jebb |
| JEL | *Journal of Environmental Law* |
| JELP | *Journal of Employment Law and Practice* |
| Jenk | Jenkins, David, *Eight Centuries of Reports* |

| | |
|---|---|
| Jenk Cent | = Jenk |
| JIBL | *Journal of International Banking Law* |
| JIBL N | *Journal of International Banking Law* (referring to News Section) |
| JIFDL | *Journal of International Franchising and Distribution Law* |
| JJ | *Jersey Judgments* |
| J Kel | = Kel |
| J Kelyng | = Kel |
| J Law Soc | *Journal of Law and Society* |
| J Law Soc Sc | = JLSS |
| J Legal Hist | *Journal of Legal History* |
| JLH | = J Legal Hist |
| JLR | *Jersey Law Reports* |
| JLR N | *Jersey Law Reports* (referring to the Notes of Cases) |
| JLS | = JLSS |
| J L Soc Scotland | = JLSS |
| JLSS | *Journal of the Law Society of Scotland* |
| JML&P | *Journal of Media Law and Practice* |
| Jo | = Jones |
| Jo & Car | = Jones & C |
| Jo & Lat | = Jones & La T |
| Jo Ex Ir | = Jones |
| Joh | = John |
| John | Johnson, Henry Robert Vaughan, *Reports . . . Chancery.* [Vice-Chancellor.] |
| John & H | Johnson, Henry Robert Vaughan, and Hemming, George W., Reports . . . Chancery. [Vice-Chancellor.] |
| Johns | = John |
| Johns & Hem | = John & H |
| Johns V-C | = John |
| 1 Jon | = W Jones |
| 2 Jon | = T Jones |
| Jon & Car | = Jones & C |
| Jones | Jones, Thomas, *Reports . . . Exchequer, in Ireland* |
| 1 Jones | = W Jones |
| 2 Jones | = T Jones |
| Jones & C | Jones, Thomas, and Carey, H., *Reports . . . Exchequer in Ireland* |
| Jones & La T | Jones, Thomas, and La Touche, Edmond Digges, *Reports . . . Chancery.* [Ireland.] |
| Jones T | = T Jones |
| Jones W | = W Jones |
| Jon Ex | = Jones |
| JP | *Justice of the Peace Reports* |
| JPIL | *Journal of Personal Injury Litigation* |
| JP Jo | = JPN |
| JPL | *Journal of Planning and Environment Law* |
| JPN | *Justice of the Peace and Local Government Law* |
| JP Sm | = Smith KB |
| JR | *Juridical Review* |

|                |                                                                                          |
| -------------- | ---------------------------------------------------------------------------------------- |
|                | also = Jur                                                                                |
| J Shaw         | Shaw, John, *Reports . . . High Court and Circuit Courts of Justiciary*                   |
| J Shaw Just    | = J Shaw                                                                                  |
| J Soc Pub TL   | = JSPTL                                                                                   |
| JSPTL          | *Journal of the Society of Public Teachers of Law*                                        |
| JSSL           | *Journal of Social Security Law*                                                           |
| JSSL D         | *Journal of Social Security Law* (referring to the Digest)                                |
| JSWFL          | *Journal of Social Welfare and Family Law*                                                 |
| JSWL           | *Journal of Social Welfare Law*                                                            |
| Jur            | *Jurist*. 1838–55                                                                          |
| Jur NS         | *Jurist*. 1856–67                                                                          |
| Jur Sc         | = Sc Jur                                                                                   |
| JWTL           | *Journal of World Trade Law*                                                               |
|                |                                                                                          |
| K              | = Keny                                                                                    |
| K & G          | = Keane & Gr                                                                              |
| K & J          | = Kay & J                                                                                 |
| K & O          | = Kn & O                                                                                  |
| K & W          | = Fol Dic                                                                                 |
| K & W Dic      | = Fol Dic                                                                                 |
| Kames Dict Dec | = Fol Dic                                                                                 |
| Kames Rem Dec  | Kames, Lord (Henry Home), *Remarkable Decisions of the Court of Session*                  |
| Kames Sel Dec  | Kames, Lord (Henry Home), *Select Decisions of the Court of Session*                      |
| Kam Rem        | = Kames Rem Dec                                                                           |
| Kam Sel        | = Kames Sel Dec                                                                           |
| Kam Sel Dec    | = Kames Sel Dec                                                                           |
| Kay            | Kay, Edward E., *Reports . . . Chancery*. [Vice-Chancellor.]                              |
| Kay & J        | Kay, Edward E., and Johnson, Henry Robert Vaughan, *Reports . . . Chancery*. [Vice-Chancellor.] |
| KB             | *Law Reports. King's Bench Division*. [1901]–[1952] 1                                     |
| Ke             | = Keen                                                                                    |
| Keane & Gr     | Keane, D.D., and Grant, J., *Registration Cases*                                          |
| Keb            | Keble, Joseph, *Reports . . . King's Bench*                                               |
| Keble          | = Keb                                                                                     |
| Keen           | Keen, Benjamin, *Reports . . . Rolls Court*                                               |
| Keil           | Keilwey, Robert, *Reports*                                                                |
| Keilw          | = Keil                                                                                    |
| Keilwey        | = Keil                                                                                    |
| Kel            | Kelyng, Sir John, *Reports of Divers Cases in Pleas of the Crown*                         |
| 1 Kel          | = Kel                                                                                     |
| 2 Kel          | = Kel W                                                                                   |
| Kel J          | = Kel                                                                                     |
| Kel W          | Kelynge, William, *Report . . . Chancery, the King's Bench*                               |
| Kelyng J       | = Kel                                                                                     |
| Ken            | = Keny                                                                                    |
| Keny           | Kenyon, Lloyd, 1st Baron Kenyon, *Notes of Cases . . . King's Bench*                      |

| | |
|---|---|
| Keny Ch | = 3 Keny |
| Keyl | = Keil |
| Kilk | Kilkerran, Lord (Sir James Fergusson), *Decisions of the Court of Session* |
| Kilkerran | = Kilk |
| KILR | *Knight's Industrial Law Reports* |
| King | = Sel Cas t King |
| King Cas temp | = Sel Cas t King |
| KIR | *Knight's Industrial Reports* |
| Kn | Knapp, J.W., *Reports . . . Privy Council* |
| Kn & O | Knapp, J.W., and Ombler, E., *Cases of Controverted Elections* |
| Kn & Omb | = Kn & O |
| Kn AC | = Kn |
| Knapp | = Kn |
| Knapp & O | = Kn & O |
| Knapp PCC | = Kn |
| Konst & W Rat App | Konstam, E.M., and Ward, H.R., *Reports of Rating Appeals* |
| Konst Rat App | Konstam, E.M., *Reports of Rating Appeals* |
| | |
| L & C | = Le & Ca |
| L & C CC | = Le & Ca |
| L & G t Plunk | = Ll & G t Plunk |
| L & G t S | = Ll & G t Sug |
| L & G t Sug | = Ll & G t Sug |
| L & G t Sugd | = Ll & G t Sug |
| L & M | = Lownd & M |
| L & T | = Long & T |
| L & W | = Ll & W |
| L & Welsb | = Ll & W |
| LA | = Legal Action |
| La | = Lane |
| LAG Bulletin | *LAG Bulletin* |
| Land Com Rep | = Roche D & K |
| Lane | Lane, Richard, *Reports . . . Exchequer* |
| LAR | *Lloyd's Arbitration Reports* |
| Lat | Latch, Jean, *Plusieurs tres-bons Cases . . . Bank le Roy* |
| Latch | = Lat |
| Lauder | = Fount |
| Law J Rep abbreviation for section | see the entry in this list for LJ OS followed by the same abbreviation |
| Law J Rep NS abbreviation for section | see the entry in this list for LJ followed by the same abbreviation |
| Law Libr | *Law Librarian* |
| Law Rec | *Law Recorder* |
| Law Rec NS | *Law Recorder. New Series* |
| Law Rec OS | = Law Rec |
| Law Rep volume number | see the entry in this list for LR volume number followed by the same abbreviation |

abbreviation
for division

| | |
|---|---|
| Laws Reg Cas | Lawson, W., *Notes of Decisions under the Representation of the People Acts and the Registration Acts* |
| Law Teach | *Law Teacher* |
| LC | = SLCR |
| LDB | *Legal Decisions Affecting Bankers* |
| Ld Ken | = Keny |
| Ld Ray | = Ld Raym |
| Ld Raym | Raymond, Sir Robert, 1st Baron Raymond, *Reports . . . King's Bench and Common Pleas* |
| Le & Ca | Leigh, E. Chandos, and Cave, Lewis W., *Crown Cases Reserved* |
| Leach | Leach, Thomas, *Cases in Crown Law* |
| Leach CC | = Leach |
| Lee | Lee, Sir George, *Reports . . . Arches and Prerogative Courts of Canterbury* |
| Lee & H | = Cas t Hard |
| Lee's Cas t Hard | = Cas t Hard |
| Lee t H | = Cas t Hard |
| Lee t Hard | = Cas t Hard |
| Legal Action | *Legal Action* |
| Leg Rep | *Legal Reporter* |
| Leigh | = Ley |
| Leigh & C | = Le & Ca |
| Leo | Leonard, William, *Reports . . . Courts at Westminster* |
| Leon | = Leo |
| Leonard | = Leo |
| Lev | Levinz, Sir Creswell, *Reports* |
| Lew CC | = Lewin |
| Lewin | Lewin, Sir Gregory A., *Report . . . Crown Side on the Northern Circuit* |
| Lewin CC | = Lewin |
| Ley | Ley, Sir James, *Reports . . . Court of Wards [etc.]* |
| LGR | *Knight's Local Government Reports* |
| LG Rev | *Local Government Review* |
| Lib Ass | *Liber Assisarum et Placitorum Corone*, see section 2.2.1 |
| Lil | Lilly, John, *Reports and Pleadings of Cases in Assise* |
| Lilly | = Lil |
| Lilly Assise | = Lil |
| Lit | *Litigation* |
| | also = Litt |
| Lit Rep | = Litt |
| Litt | Littleton, Edw., Baron de Mounslow, *Reports . . . Common Bank & Exchequer* |
| Littleton | = Lit |
| Liverpool L Rev | *Liverpool Law Review* |
| LJ | *Law Journal* |
| LJ Adm | *Law Journal Reports*. 1832–1946. Admiralty |
| LJ Bank | = LJ Bcy |
| LJ Bankr | = LJ Bcy |

| | |
|---|---|
| LJ Bcy | *Law Journal Reports*. 1832–1946. Bankruptcy |
| LJ Bk | = LJ Bcy |
| LJCCA | *Law Journal Newspaper County Court Appeals* |
| LJCCR | *Law Journal County Courts Reporter* |
| LJ Ch | *Law Journal Reports*. 1832–1946. Chancery |
| LJ Chanc | = LJ Ch |
| LJ CP | *Law Journal Reports*. 1832–1946. Common Pleas |
| LJ Ecc | *Law Journal Reports*. 1832–1946. Ecclesiastical Cases |
| LJ Eccl | = LJ Ecc |
| LJ Eccles | = LJ Ecc |
| LJ Eq | = LJ Ch |
| LJ Ex | *Law Journal Reports*. 1832–1946. Exchequer |
| LJ Exch | = LJ Ex |
| LJ Ex Eq | *Law Journal Reports*. 1832–1946. Exchequer in Equity |
| LJ IFS | *Law Journal Irish Free State Section* |
| LJ Ir | *Law Journal Irish Section* |
| LJ KB | *Law Journal Reports*. 1832–1946. King's Bench |
| LJ MC | *Law Journal Reports*. 1832–1946. Magistrates' Cases |
| LJ NC | *Law Journal*. 1832–1946 (Notes of Cases section) |
| LJNCCR | *Law Journal County Court Reports* |
| L Jo | = LJ |
| LJ OS Ch | *Law Journal ... Reports*. 1822–31. Chancery |
| LJ OS CP | *Law Journal ... Reports*. 1822–31. Common Pleas |
| LJ OS Ex | *Law Journal ... Reports*. 1822–31. Exchequer |
| LJ OS KB | *Law Journal ... Reports*. 1822–31. King's Bench |
| LJ OS MC | *Law Journal ... Reports*. 1822–31. Magistrates' Cases |
| LJ P | *Law Journal Reports*. 1832–1946. Probate, Divorce and Admiralty |
| LJ P & M | *Law Journal Reports*. 1832–1946. Probate and Matrimonial Cases |
| LJ PC | *Law Journal Reports*. 1832–1946. Privy Council |
| LJ P D & A | = LJ P |
| LJ P M & A | *Law Journal Reports*. 1832–1946. Probate, Matrimonial and Admiralty |
| LJ Prob & D | = LJ P & M |
| LJ Prob & M | = LJ P & M |
| LJ Prob M & A | = LJ P M & A |
| LJ QB | *Law Journal Reports*. 1832–1946. Queen's Bench |
| LJR | *Law Journal Reports*. [1947]–[1949] |
| Ll & G t Plunk | Lloyd, B.C., and Goold, F., *Selection of Cases ... Chancery in Ireland, during the time of Lord Chancellor Plunket* |
| Ll & G t Sug | Lloyd, B.C., and Goold, F., *Reports ... Chancery in Ireland, during the time of Lord Chancellor Sugden* |
| Ll & W | Lloyd, J.H., and Welsby, W.N., *Mercantile Cases* |
| Ll & Wels | = Ll & W |
| Ll List LR | = Ll L Rep |
| Ll LLR | = Ll L Rep |
| Ll LR | = Ll L Rep |
| Ll L Rep | *Lloyd's List Law Reports*. 1919–50 |
| Lloyd Pr Cas NS | = Ll Pri Cas NS |
| Lloyd Pr Cas | = Ll Pri Cas |

| | |
|---|---|
| Lloyd's Rep | *Lloyd's Law Reports* |
| Ll PC | = Ll Pri Cas |
| Ll Pri Cas | *Lloyd's Reports of Prize Cases* |
| Ll Pri Cas NS | *Lloyd's Reports of Prize Cases*, 2nd Series |
| Ll Rep | = Ll L Rep |
| | also = Lloyd's Rep |
| L M & P | = Lownd M & P |
| LMCLQ | *Lloyd's Maritime and Commercial Law Quarterly* |
| Lofft | Lofft, Capel, *Reports . . . King's Bench* |
| Long & T | Longfield, R., and Townsend, J.F., *Reports . . . Exchequer in Ireland* |
| Longf & T | = Long & T |
| Lonq Quinto | A yearbook of 5 Edw 4, see section 2.2.1 |
| Lownd & M | Lowndes, J.J., and Maxwell, P.B., *Bail Court Cases* |
| Lownd M & P | Lowndes, J.J., Maxwell, P.B., and Pollock, C.E., *Reports . . . Queen's Bench Practice Court* |
| LQR | *Law Quarterly Review* |
| LR volume number A & E | *Law Reports. High Court of Admiralty, and Ecclesiastical Courts.* (1865–75) |
| LR volume number Adm & Ecc | = LR volume number A & E |
| LRC | *Law Reports of the Commonwealth* |
| LR volume number CC | = LR volume number CCR |
| LRC (Comm) | *Law Reports of the Commonwealth. Commercial Law Reports* |
| LRC (Const) | *Law Reports of the Commonwealth. Constitutional Law Reports* |
| LR volume number CCR | *Law Reports. . . . Court for Crown Cases Reserved.* (1865–75) |
| LRC (Crim) | *Law Reports of the Commonwealth. Criminal Law Reports* |
| LR volume number Ch | = LR volume number Ch App |
| LR volume number Ch App | *Law Reports. Chancery Appeal Cases.* (1865–75) |
| LR volume number ChD | = ChD |
| LR volume number CP | *Law Reports. Court of Common Pleas.* (1865–75) |
| LR volume number E & I App | = LR volume number HL |
| LR volume number Eng & Ir App | = LR volume number HL |
| LR volume number Eq | *Law Reports. Equity Cases.* (1865–75) |
| LR volume number Eq Cas | = LR volume number Eq |
| LR volume number Ex | *Law Reports. Court of Exchequer.* (1865–75) |
| LR volume number Ex (Ch) | = LR volume number Ex (referring to a case in the Court of Exchequer Chamber) |

| | |
|---|---|
| LR volume number Exch | = LR volume number Ex |
| LR volume number HL | *Law Reports. English and Irish Appeal Cases.* (1866–75) |
| LR volume number HL Sc | = LR volume number Sc & Div |
| LR volume number IA | = LR volume number Ind App |
| LR volume number Ind App | *Law Reports. Indian Appeals.* (1873–1950) |
| LR Ind App Supp | *Law Reports. Indian Appeals. Supplementary Volume* |
| LR Ind App Supp Vol | = LR Ind App Supp |
| LR Ir | *Law Reports (Ireland)* |
| LRLR | *Lloyd's Reinsurance Law Reports* |
| LR volume number P & D | *Law Reports. Courts of Probate and Divorce.* (1865–75) |
| LR volume number P & M | = LR volume number P & D |
| LR volume number PC | *Law Reports. Privy Council Appeals.* (1865–75) |
| LR volume number PC App | = LR volume number PC |
| LR volume number Prob & D | = LR volume number P & D |
| LR volume number Prob & M | = LR volume number P & D |
| LR volume number QB | *Law Reports. Court of Queen's Bench.* (1865–75) |
| LR volume number QBD | = QBD |
| LR volume number RP | *Reports of Restrictive Practices Cases* |
| LR volume number Sc & Div | *Law Reports. Scotch and Divorce Appeal Cases before the House of Lords.* (1866–75) |
| LS | *Legal Studies* |
| LS Gaz | *Law Society's Gazette* |
| LSR | *Locus Standi Reports* |
| LT | *Law Times Reports* |
| L Teach | = Law Teach |
| LT J | = LT Jo |
| LT Jo | *Law Times.* 1859 to 1965 |
| LT Jour | = LT Jo |
| LT NS | = LT |
| LT OS | *Law Times.* 1843 to 1859 |
| LTRA | *Selected List of Lands Tribunal Rating Appeals* |
| LT Rep | = LT OS |
| LT Rep NS | = LT |
| Luc | = early ed. of 10 Mod |
| Lucas | = early ed. of 10 Mod |
| Lud EC | = Lud El Cas |
| Lud El Cas | Luders, A., *Reports . . . Controverted Elections* |

| | |
|---|---|
| Lumley PLC | = Lum PL Cas |
| Lum PL Cas | Lumley, W.G., *Abridgment of Cases upon Poor Law*, vols 1 and 2 |
| Lush | Lushington, Vernon, *Reports ... Admiralty* |
| Lut | Lutwyche, Sir Edward, *Un Livre des Entries ... auxi ... Report* |
| Lut RC | = Lut Reg Cas |
| Lut Reg Cas | Lutwyche, A.J.P., *Reports ... Court of Common Pleas.* [Registration Cases.] |
| Lutw | = Lut |
| Lutw Reg Cas | = Lut Reg Cas |
| Lutwyche | = Lut |
| Lyne (Wall) | = Wal Lyn |
| | |
| M | Macpherson, Norman, *Cases ... Court of Session, Teind Court and House of Lords.* [Session Cases, 3rd series.] |
| M & A | = Mont & A |
| M & B | = Mont & B |
| M & C | = Mont & Ch |
| | also = My & Cr |
| M & G | = Mac & G |
| | also = 6 Madd |
| | also = Man & G |
| M & Gord | = Mac & G |
| M & H | = Mur & H |
| M & K | = My & K |
| M & M | = Mood & M |
| M & M'A | = Mont & M |
| M & P | = Moo & P |
| M & R | = Macl & R |
| | also = Man & Ry KB |
| | also = Mood & R |
| M & R MC | = Man & Ry MC |
| M & Rob | = Mood & R |
| M & S | Maule, George, and Selwyn, William, *Reports ... King's Bench* |
| | also = CB |
| | also = Moo & S |
| M & Sc | = Moo & S |
| M & Scott | = Moo & S |
| M & W | Meeson, R., and Welsby, W.N., *Reports ... Exchequer* |
| Mac & G | Macnaghten, Steuart, and Gordon, Alexander, *Reports ... Chancery* |
| Mac & Gor | = Mac & G |
| Mac & H | = Macr & H |
| Mac & R | = Macl & R |
| Mac & Rob | = Macl & R |
| MacCarthy | MacCarthy, J.H., *Leading Cases in Land Purchase Law* |
| Mac CC | = MacG |
| Maccl | = 10 Mod |

| | |
|---|---|
| MacDev | MacDevitt, E.O., *Land Cases.* [Ireland.] |
| Macf | Macfarlane, Robert, Lord Ormidale, *Reports ... Court of Session* |
| Macfarlane | = Macf |
| MacG | MacGillivray, E.J., *Copyright Cases* |
| MacG CC | = MacG |
| MacG Cop Cas | = MacG |
| Macl & R | Maclean, Charles Hope, and Robinson, George, *Cases ... House of Lords* |
| Macl & Rob | = Macl & R |
| Maclaurin | = Macl Rem Cas |
| Maclean & Robinson | = Macl & R |
| Macl Rem Cas | MacLaurin, J., *Arguments and Decisions in Remarkable Cases before the High Court of Justiciary* |
| Macn & G | = Mac & G |
| Mac Pat Cas | = Macr Pat Cas |
| Mac PC | = Macr Pat Cas |
| Macph | = M |
| Macph Ct of Sess | = M |
| Macph (HL) | = M (HL) |
| Macq | Macqueen, J.F., *Reports of Scotch Appeals ... House of Lords* |
| Macq HL Cas | = Macq |
| Macq H of L Cas | = Macq |
| Macr | = Macr Pat Cas |
| Macr & H | Macrae, D.C., and Hertslet, C.J.B., *Reports ... Insolvency* |
| Macr Pat Cas | Macrory, E., *Reports of Cases Relating to Letters Patent for Inventions* |
| Macr P Cas | = Macr Pat Cas |
| Mad | = Madd |
| Mad & Gel | = 6 Madd |
| Madd | Maddock, Henry, *Reports ... Vice-Chancellor* |
| Madd & G | = 6 Madd |
| Man | Manning, W.M., *Proceedings in Courts of Revision* |
| Man & G | Manning, James, and Granger, T.C., *Cases ... Common Pleas* |
| Man & Ry | = Man & Ry KB |
| Man & Ry KB | Manning, James, and Ryland, Archer, *Reports ... King's Bench* |
| Man & Ry Mag Cas | = Man & Ry MC |
| Man & Ry MC | Manning, James, and Ryland, Archer, *Reports of Cases Relating to the Duty and Office of Magistrates* |
| Man & Sc | = CB |
| Man El Cas | = Man |
| Man Gr & S | = CB |
| Mann EC | = Man |
| Mans | Manson, E., *Reports ... Bankruptcy and Companies Winding-up* |
| Manson | = Mans |
| Mar | = March NC |
| March | = March NC |

| | |
|---|---|
| March NC | March, John, *Reports: or, New Cases* |
| March NR | = March NC |
| Mar LC | = Crockford |
| Marr | = Hay & M |
| Marsh | Marshall, C., *Reports ... Common Pleas* |
| Marshall | = Marsh |
| Mau & Sel | = M & S |
| Maxwell | Maxwell, T.H., *Irish Land Purchase Cases* |
| M CC | = Mood CC |
| McCle | = M'Cle |
| McCle & Yo | = M'Cle & Yo |
| McF R | = Macf |
| M'Cle | M'Cleland, Thomas, *Reports ... Exchequer* |
| M'Cle & Y | M'Cleland, Thomas, and Younge, Edward, *Reports ... Exchequer* |
| M'Cle & Yo | = M'Cle & Y |
| M'Clel | = M'Cle |
| M'Clel & Y | = M'Cle & Y |
| M D & D | = Mont D & De G Bcy |
| M D & De G | = Mont D & De G Bcy |
| M Dict | = Mor |
| Med LR | *Medical Law Reports* |
| Med Sci Law | *Medicine Science and the Law* |
| Mees & Wels | = M & W |
| Meg | Megone, William Bernard, *Reports of Cases under the Companies Acts* |
| Megone | = Meg |
| Mer | Merivale, J.H., *Reports ... Chancery* |
| M G & S | = CB |
| M (HL) | Macpherson, Norman, *Cases ... Court of Session, Teind Court and House of Lords.* [Session Cases, 3rd series.] (referring to House of Lords cases) |
| M IA | = Moo Ind App |
| Millin | Millin, S.S., *Digest ... Decisions ... Relating to Petty Sessions in Ireland* |
| Milw | Milward, C.R., *Reports ... Court of Prerogative in Ireland* |
| Milw Ir Ecc Rep | = Milw |
| MLB | *Manx Law Bulletin* |
| MLR | *Manx Law Reports* |
| MLR | *Modern Law Review* |
| Mo | = Mod |
| | also = Moo |
| | also = Moo Ind App |
| | also = Moo KB |
| | also = Moo PC |
| Mo & R | = Mood & R |
| Mo & Sc | = Moo & S |
| Mod | *Modern Reports* |
| Mod Cas | = 6 Mod |
| Mod Cas L & Eq | = 8 & 9 Mod |
| Mod Cas per Far | = early ed. of 7 Mod |

| | |
|---|---|
| Mod Cas t Holt | = 7 Mod |
| Mod LR | = MLR (*Modern Law Review*) |
| Mod Rep | = Mod |
| Mo IA | = Moo Ind App |
| Mol | Molloy, P., *Reports . . . Chancery in Ireland* |
| Moll | = Mol |
| Mont | Montagu, B., *Reports . . . Bankruptcy* |
| Mont & A | Montagu, B., and Ayrton, S., *Reports . . . Bankruptcy* |
| Mont & Ayr | = Mont & A |
| Mont & B | Montagu, B., and Bligh, R., *Reports . . . Bankruptcy* |
| Mont & Bl | = Mont & B |
| Mont & Bligh | = Mont & B |
| Mont & C | = Mont & Ch |
| Mont & Ch | Montagu, B., and Chitty, E., *Reports . . . Bankruptcy* |
| Mont & Chit | = Mont & Ch |
| Mont & M | Montagu, B., and MacArthur, J., *Reports . . . Bankruptcy* |
| Mont & MacA | = Mont & M |
| Mont & McA | = Mont & M |
| Mont D & D | = Mont D & De G Bcy |
| Mont D & De G | = Mont D & De G Bcy |
| Mont D & De G Bcy | Montagu, B., Deacon, E.E., and De Gex, J., *Reports . . . Bankruptcy* |
| Moo | Moore, J.B., *Reports . . . Common Pleas* |
| Moo & M | = Mood & M |
| Moo & Mal | = Mood & M |
| Moo & P | Moore, J.B., and Payne, J., *Reports . . . Common Pleas* |
| Moo & Pay | = Moo & P |
| Moo & R | = Mood & R |
| Moo & Rob | = Mood & R |
| Moo & S | Moore, J.B., and Scott, J., *Cases . . . Common Pleas* |
| Moo A | = separate publication of cases now in 1 Bos & P |
| Moo CC | = Mood CC |
| Mood | = Mood CC |
| Mood & M | Moody, William, and Malkin, Benjamin Heath, *Reports . . . Nisi Prius* |
| Mood & R | Moody, William, and Robinson, Frederic, *Reports . . . Nisi Prius* |
| Mood CC | Moody, William, *Crown Cases Reserved* |
| Moo F | = Moo KB |
| Moo Ind App | Moore, Edmund F., *Reports . . . Privy Council, on Appeal from . . . the East Indies* |
| Moo JB | = Moo |
| Moo KB | Moore, Sir Francis, *Cases* |
| Moo NS | = Moo PC NS |
| Moo PC | Moore, Edmund F., *Reports . . . Privy Council* |
| Moo PCC | = Moo PC |
| Moo PCC NS | = Moo PC NS |
| Moo PC NS | Moore, Edmund F., *Reports . . . Privy Council*. [New Series.] |
| Moore | = Moo PC |
| Moore CP | = Moo |
| Moore Ind App | = Moo Ind App |

| | |
|---|---|
| Moore KB | = Moo KB |
| Moore NS | = Moo PC NS |
| Moore PC | = Moo PC |
| Moore PCC | = Moo PC |
| Moore PCC NS | = Moo PC NS |
| Mor | Morison, W.M., *Decisions of the Court of Session . . . in the Form of a Dictionary* |
| Mor Dic | = Mor |
| Mor Dict | = Mor |
| Morr | Morrell, C.F., *Reports of Cases under the Bankruptcy Act 1883* |
| Morrell | = Morr |
| Mor Syn | Morison, W.M., *Synopsis of . . . Decisions of the Court of Session* |
| Mos | Mosely, William, *Reports . . . Chancery* |
| Mosely | = Mos |
| M PC | = Moo PC |
| Mun | = Mun App |
| Mun App | *Appeals from Munitions Tribunals* |
| Mun App Sc | *Munitions of War Acts 1915–1916. Scottish Appeal Reports* |
| Mur | Murray, J., *Reports . . . Jury Court* |
| Mur & H | Murphy, F.S., and Hurlstone, E.T., *Reports . . . Exchequer* |
| Mur & Hurl | = Mur & H |
| Murp & H | = Mur & H |
| Murr | = Mur |
| My & Cr | Mylne, J.W., and Craig, R.D., *Reports . . . Chancery* |
| My & K | Mylne, J.W., and Keen, Benjamin, *Reports . . . Chancery* |
| Myl & Cr | = My & Cr |
| Myl & K | = My & K |
| Mylne & C | = My & Cr |
| Mylne & K | = My & K |
| | |
| N & M | = Nev & M KB |
| N & M MC | = Nev & M MC |
| N & P | = Nev & P KB |
| N & P MC | = Nev & P MC |
| N Ben | = Benl |
| N Benl | = Benl |
| NC | = Bing NC |
| | also = Notes of Cas |
| NCC | = Y & C Ch Cas |
| Nel | = Nels |
| | also = Rep t Finch |
| Nels | Nelson, W., *Reports . . . Chancery* |
| | also = Rep t Finch |
| Nels 8vo | = Nels |
| Nels F | = Rep t Finch |
| Nels Fol | = Rep t Finch |
| Nelson | = Nels |
| Nelson's Rep | = Rep t Finch |

| | |
|---|---|
| Nev & Man | = Nev & M KB |
| Nev & M KB | Nevile, S., and Manning, W.M., *Reports of Cases Argued and Determined in the Court of King's Bench* |
| Nev & M Mag Cas | = Nev & M MC |
| Nev & M MC | Nevile, S., and Manning, W.M., *Reports of Cases Relating to the Duty and Office of Magistrates* |
| Nev & P | = Nev & P KB |
| Nev & P KB/QB | Nevile, S., and Perry, T.E., *Reports . . . King's / Queen's Bench* |
| Nev & P Mag Cas | = Nev & P MC |
| Nev & P MC | Nevile, S., and Perry, T.E., *Reports of Cases Relating to the Office of Magistrates* |
| New Benl | = Benl |
| New LJ | = NLJ |
| New Mag Cas | *Reports of New Magistrates' Cases* |
| New Pract Cas | = New Pr Cas |
| New Pr Cas | *New Practice Cases* |
| New Rep | *New Reports* |
| New Sess Cas | *New Sessions Cases* |
| N H & C | = 1 and 2 Ry & Can Cas |
| NI | *Northern Ireland Law Reports* |
| Nic Ha C | = 1 and 2 Ry & Can Cas |
| Nicholl H & C | = 1 and 2 Ry & Can Cas |
| NIJB | *Northern Ireland Law Reports Bulletin of Judgments* |
| NILQ | *Northern Ireland Legal Quarterly* |
| NLC | New Law Publishing |
| NLJ | *New Law Journal* |
| NLJ Practitioner | *New Law Journal* (referring to Practitioner section) |
| NLJ Rep | = NLJ; NLJ Practitioner in vol. 138 |
| Nolan | Nolan, M., *Reports of Cases Relating to the Duty and Office of a Justice of the Peace* |
| No of Cas | = Notes of Cas |
| Not Cas | = Notes of Cas |
| Notes of Cas | *Notes of Cases in the Ecclesiastical and Maritime Courts* |
| Noy | Noy, William, *Reports* |
| NPC | = New Pr Cas |
| NR | = Bos & P NR |
| | also = New Rep |
| | ! also *National Reporter* (Canada) |
| NSC | = New Sess Cas |
| | |
| O Benl | = Benl & Dal (Benloe's section) |
| O Bridg | Bridgman, Sir Orlando, Reports |
| OBSP | *Old Bailey Sessions Papers* |
| OGLTR | *Oil and Gas Law and Taxation Review* |
| OGLTR D | *Oil and Gas Law and Taxation Review* (referring to News Section) |
| OJLS | = Oxford J Legal Stud |
| Old Benloe | = Benl & Dal (Benloe's section) |
| Oliv B & L | = 5–7 Ry & Can Cas |

| | |
|---|---|
| O'M & H | O'Malley, E.L., and Hardcastle, H., *Reports ... Election Petitions* |
| O'Mal & H | = O'M & H |
| OPLR | *Occupational Pensions Law Reports* |
| OR | = RPC |
| | ! also *Ontario Reports* |
| Orl Bridg | = O Bridg |
| Ow | Owen, Thomas, *Reports ... King's Bench and Common Pleas* |
| Owen | = Ow |
| Oxford J Legal Stud | *Oxford Journal of Legal Studies* |
| | |
| P | *Law Reports. Probate, Divorce and Admiralty Division.* [1891]–[1971] |
| P & C | = 4 New Sess Cas |
| P & CR | *Property, Planning and Compensation Reports* |
| P & D | = Per & Dav |
| P & K | = Per & K |
| P & R | = Pig & R |
| PAD | *Planning Appeal Decisions* |
| Pal | = Palm |
| Palm | Palmer, Sir Gefrey, *Reports* |
| Palmer | = Palm |
| Par | = Park |
| Park | Parker, Sir Thomas, *Reports ... Exchequer* |
| Parker | = Park |
| Pat | Paton, Thomas S., *Reports ... House of Lords ... Scotland* |
| Pat Abr | = Pat PL Cas |
| Pat App | = Pat |
| Pater App | = Paters |
| Paters | Paterson, J., *Reports of Scotch Appeals ... House of Lords* |
| Paters App | = Paters |
| Pat PL Cas | Paterson, J., *Abridgment of Cases upon Poor Law*, vol. 4 |
| PC | = Br & Col Pri Cas |
| P Cas | = Br & Col Pri Cas |
| PCB | *Private Client Business* |
| PCC | *Palmer's Company Cases* |
| PD | *Law Reports. Probate Division.* (1875–90) |
| Pea | = Peake |
| Peake | Peake, Thomas, *Cases Determined at Nisi Prius* |
| Peake Add Cas | Peake, Thomas, *Additional Cases ... Nisi Prius* |
| Peake NP | = Peake |
| Peake NPC | = Peake |
| Peake's Add Cas | = Peake Add Cas |
| Peck | Peckwell, R.H., *Cases of Controverted Elections* |
| Peck Elec Cas | = Peck |
| Peere Wms | = P Wms |
| Per & Dav | Perry, T.E., and Davison, H., *Reports ... Queen's Bench* |
| Per & K | Perry, H.J., and Knapp, J.W., *Cases of Controverted Elections* |
| Per & Kn | = Per & K |

| | |
|---|---|
| Per Insolv | Perry, T., *Reports ... Court for the Relief of Insolvent Debtors* |
| Perry Ins | = Per Insolv |
| Ph | Phillips, T.J., *Reports ... Chancery* |
| | also = Phil Ecc |
| | also = Ph El Cas |
| Ph El Cas | Philipps, John, *Election Cases* |
| Phil | = Ph |
| | also = Phil Ecc |
| Phil | = Ph El Cas |
| Phil Ecc | Phillimore, Joseph, *Reports ... Ecclesiastical Courts* |
| Phil Ecc Judg | = Phil Judg |
| Phil Ecc R | = Phil Ecc |
| Phil El Cas | = Ph El Cas |
| Phil Judg | Phillimore, Sir Robert, *Principal Ecclesiastical Judgments* |
| Phill | = Ph |
| Phill Ecc | = Phil Ecc |
| Phillim | = Phil Ecc |
| Phillim Eccl Jud | = Phil Judg |
| Phillips | = Ph |
| Pig & R | Pigott, G., and Rodwell, H., *Reports ... Court of Common Pleas.* [Registration Cases.] |
| PIQR | *Personal Injuries and Quantum Reports* |
| PIQR P | *Personal Injuries and Quantum Reports* (referring to the Personal Injuries section) |
| PIQR Q | *Personal Injuries and Quantum Reports* (referring to the Quantum section) |
| Pitc | Pitcairn, Robert, *Criminal Trials in Scotland* |
| PL | *Public Law* |
| Pl & Pr Cas | *Pleading and Practice Cases* |
| Plow | Plowden, Edmund, *Commentaries, or Reports* |
| Plow App | Plowden, Edmund, *Commentaries, or Reports* (referring to the appendix) |
| Plowd | = Plow |
| Plowden | = Plow |
| PLR | *Estates Gazette Planning Law Reports* |
| PN | *Professional Negligence* |
| P NP | = Peake |
| Pol | = Pollex |
| Poll | = Pollex |
| Pollex | Pollexfen, Sir Henry, *Arguments and Reports ... in Some Special Cases* |
| Pop | Popham, Sir John, *Reports and Cases* |
| Poph | = Pop |
| Popham | = Pop |
| Pow R & D | Power, D., Rodwell, H., and Dew, E.L., *Reports ... Controverted Elections* |
| PPLR | *Public Procurement Law Review* |
| PPLR CS | *Public Procurement Law Review* (referring to the Current Survey) |
| Pr | = Price |

P R & D = Pow R & D
Pr Ch = Prec Ch
Prec Ch *Precedents in Chancery*
Pres Fal = D Falc
Pres Falc = D Falc
Pr Exch = Price
Pri = Price
Price Price, George, *Reports ... Exchequer*
Price Notes PC = Price Pr Cas
Price PC = Price Pr Cas
Price Pr Cas Price, George, *Notes of Points in Practice Rules*
Prid & C = 4 New Sess Cas
Prid & Co = 4 New Sess Cas
Prop LB *Greens Property Law Bulletin*
P Shaw = Shaw Just
PW = P Wms
P Wms Peere Williams, William, *Reports ... Chancery*

QB (1841–52) *Queen's Bench Reports*
QB [1891]–[1900] or *Law Reports. Queen's Bench Division.* [1891]–[1900] and
  [1952] 2– [1952] 2–
QBD *Law Reports. ... Queen's Bench Division.* (1875–90)
QBR = QB (*Queen's Bench Reports*)
Quinto A yearbook of 5 Edw 4, see section 2.2.1

R (1873–98, Scotland) Rettie, M., *Cases ... Court of Session, Court of Justiciary*
  *and House of Lords.* [Session Cases, 4th series]
R (1893–5, England) *Reports, the*
R & Can Cas = Ry & Can Cas
R & Can Tr Cas = Traff Cas
R & C C = Ry & Can Cas
R & IT *Rating and Income Tax*
R & M = Rick & M
   = Russ & M
   = Ry & M
R & My = Russ & M
R & R = Russ & Ry
R & R CC = Russ & Ry
R & S = Rick & S
R & VR = RVR
RA (1950–61) = LTRA
RA [1962]– *Rating Appeals*
R(A) (1972–6) Department of Health and Social Security, *Reported Decisions of the Commissioner under the National Insurance and Family Allowances Acts* (referring to A series)
R(A) (1977– ) Department of Social Security, *Reported Decisions of the Social Security Commissioner* (referring to A series)
Rail & Can Cas = Ry & Can Cas
Rail Cas = Ry & Can Cas
Railway Cas = Ry & Can Cas

| | |
|---|---|
| Railw Cas | = Ry & Can Cas |
| Rast | Rastell, William, *A Collection of Entries* |
| Ray Tithe Cas | = Rayn |
| Raym | = Ld Raym |
| | = T Raym |
| Raym Ld | = Ld Raym |
| Raym Sir T | = T Raym |
| Rayn | Rayner, J., *Cases at Large Concerning Tithes* |
| Ray Sir T | = T Raym |
| Ray Ti Cas | = Rayn |
| R Ct of Sess | = R (Rettie, M., *Cases ... Court of Session, Court of Justiciary and House of Lords.* [Session Cases, 4th series]) |
| Real Prop Cas | *Reports of Cases ... Real Property and Conveyancing* |
| Re LR | *Reinsurance Law Reports* |
| Rep | = Co Rep |
| Rep Cas Eq | = Gilb Ch |
| Rep Cas Pr | = Cooke |
| Rep Ch | *Reports of Cases ... in the Court of Chancery* |
| Rep Com Cas | = Com Cas |
| Rep Eq | = Gilb Ch |
| Rep in Ch | = Rep Ch |
| Rep in Cha | = Bitt Cha Cas |
| Rep of Sel Cas in Ch | = Kel W |
| Reports | = Co Rep |
| Rep QA | = 11 Mod |
| Rep t F | = Rep t Finch |
| Rep t Finch | *Reports ... Chancery during the Time Sir Heneage Finch ... was Lord Chancellor* |
| Rep t Hard | = Cas t Hard |
| Rep t QA | = 11 Mod |
| Rep Yorke Ass | = Clay |
| Reserv Cas | *Rules and Orders of the Common Law Judges and Reserved Cases* |
| R(F) (1960–76) | Department of Health and Social Security, *Reported Decisions of the Commissioner under the National Insurance and Family Allowances Acts* (referring to F series) |
| R(F) (1977– ) | Department of Social Security, *Reported Decisions of the Social Security Commissioner* (referring to F series) |
| R(FC) | Department of Social Security, *Reported Decisions of the Social Security Commissioner* (referring to FC series) |
| R(FIS) | Department of Social Security, *Reported Decisions of the Social Security Commissioner* (referring to FIS series) |
| R(G) (1951–76) | Department of Health and Social Security, *Reported Decisions of the Commissioner under the National Insurance and Family Allowances Acts* (referring to G series) |
| R(G) (1977– ) | Department of Social Security, *Reported Decisions of the Social Security Commissioner* (referring to G series) |

| | |
|---|---|
| R (HL) | Rettie, M., *Cases ... Court of Session, Court of Justiciary and House of Lords*. [Session Cases, 4th series.] (referring to House of Lords cases) |
| R(I) (1951–76) | Department of Health and Social Security, *Reported Decisions of the Commissioner under the Social Security and National Insurance (Industrial Injuries) Acts* |
| R(I) (1977– ) | Department of Social Security, *Reported Decisions of the Social Security Commissioner* (referring to I series) |
| Rick & M | Rickards, A.G., and Michael, M.J., *Cases ... Court of Referees*. [*Locus Standi*.] |
| Rick & S | Rickards, A.G., and Saunders, R.C., *Cases ... Court of Referees*. [*Locus Standi*.] |
| Ridg | = Ridge t Hard |
| Ridg Ap | = Ridg Parl Rep |
| Ridge t Hard | Ridgeway, W., *Reports ... King's Bench and Chancery during the Time in which Lord Hardwicke Presided* |
| Ridg L & S | Ridgeway, W., Lapp, W., and Schoales, J., *Irish Term Reports* |
| Ridg Parl Rep | Ridgeway, W., *Reports ... High Court of Parliament in Ireland* |
| Ridg PC | = Ridg Parl Rep |
| Ridg t H | = Ridge t Hard |
| Ridg t Hard | = Ridge t Hard |
| Ridgw | = Ridg Parl Rep |
| Ridgw Ap | = Ridg Parl Rep |
| R(IS) | Department of Social Security, *Reported Decisions of the Social Security Commissioner* (referring to IS series) |
| Ritch | = Bac Rep |
| R (J) | Rettie, M., *Cases ... Court of Session, Court of Justiciary and House of Lords*. [Session Cases, 4th series.] (referring to Justiciary cases) |
| R L & S | = Ridg L & S |
| R L & W | = Rob L & W |
| RLR | *Road Law Reports* |
| R(M) | Department of Social Security, *Reported Decisions of the Social Security Commissioner* (referring to M series) |
| Road Law | *Road Law* |
| Rob | = C Rob |
| | also = Robert |
| | also = Robin |
| | also = W Rob |
| Rob A | = C Rob |
| Rob Adm Rep | = W Rob |
| Rob App | = Robin |
| | also = Robert |
| Rob Cas | = Robert |
| Rob Chr | = C Rob |
| Rob E | = Rob Ecc |
| Rob Ecc | Robertson. J.E.P., *Reports ... Ecclesiastical Courts* |
| Rob Eccl | = Rob Ecc |
| Rob Ecc Rep | = Rob Ecc |

| | |
|---|---|
| Robert | Robertson, David, *Reports of Cases on Appeal from Scotland ... House of Peers* |
| Robert Ap | = Robert |
| Robert App | = Robert |
| Roberts | Roberts, J., *Divorce Bills in the Imperial Parliament* |
| Robin | Robinson, G., *Cases ... House of Lords ... Scotland* |
| Robin App | = Robin |
| Robin Sc App | = Robin |
| Robinson | = C Rob |
| | also = W Rob |
| Rob Jun | = W Rob |
| Rob L & W | Roberts, W.H., Leeming, H., and Wallis, J.E., *Reports ... on the Law and Practice of the New County Courts* |
| Rob Sc App | = Robert |
| Roche D & K | Roche, C.R., Dillon, L., and Kehoe, D., *Reports ... Irish Land Commission* |
| Roll | = Rolle |
| Roll Abr | Rolle, Henry, *Abridgment des Plusieurs Cases* |
| Rolle | Rolle, Henry, *Reports ... Banke le Roy* |
| Roll R | = Rolle |
| Roll Rep | = Rolle |
| Rom | Romilly, Sir Samuel, *Notes of Cases* |
| Rosc PC | = Rosc Pri Cas |
| Rosc Pri Cas | Roscoe, E.S., *Reports of Prize Cases* |
| Rose | Rose, George, *Cases in Bankruptcy* |
| Ross LC Comm | Ross, George, *Leading Cases in the Commercial Law of England and Scotland* |
| Ross LC Land | Ross, George, *Leading Cases in the Law of Scotland ... Land Rights* |
| Rowe | Rowe, R.R., *Reports of Interesting Cases* |
| R(P) (1951–76) | Department of Health and Social Security, *Reported Decisions of the Commissioner under the National Insurance and Family Allowances Acts* (referring to P series) |
| R(P) (1977– ) | Department of Social Security, *Reported Decisions of the Social Security Commissioner* (referring to P series) |
| RPC | *Reports of Patent, Design and Trade Mark Cases* |
| RR | *Revised Reports* |
| RRC | *Ryde's Rating Cases* |
| R(S) (1951–76) | Department of Health and Social Security, *Reported Decisions of the Commissioner under the National Insurance and Family Allowances Acts* (referring to S series) |
| R(S) (1977– ) | Department of Social Security, *Reported Decisions of the Social Security Commissioner* (referring to S series) |
| R(SB) | Department of Social Security, *Reported Decisions of the Social Security Commissioner* (referring to SB series) |
| R(SSP) | Department of Social Security, *Reported Decisions of the Social Security Commissioner* (referring to SSP series) |
| R t F | = Rep t Finch |
| R t H | = Cas T Hard |

| | |
|---|---|
| R t QA | = 11 Mod |
| RTR | *Road Traffic Reports* |
| R(U) (1951–76) | Department of Health and Social Security, *Reported Decisions of the Commissioner under the National Insurance and Family Allowances Acts* (referring to U series) |
| R(U) (1977– ) | Department of Social Security, *Reported Decisions of the Social Security Commissioner* (referring to U series) |
| Russ | Russell, James, *Reports ... Chancery* |
| Russ & M | Russell, James, and Mylne, J.W., *Reports ... Chancery* |
| Russ & Mylne | = Russ & M |
| Russ & R | = Russ & Ry |
| Russ & Ry | Russell, William Oldnall, and Ryan, Edward, *Crown Cases Reserved* |
| Russ t Eld | = Russ |
| RVR | *Rating and Valuation Reporter* |
| Ry & Can Cas | *Cases Relating to Railways and Canals* |
| Ry & Can Tr Cas | = Traff Cas |
| Ry & Can Traff Cas | = Traff Cas |
| Ry & M | Ryan, Edward, and Moody, William, *Reports ... Nisi Prius* |
| Ry & Mood | = Ry & M |
| Ry Cas | = Ry & Can Cas |
| Ryde | = Ryde Rat App |
| Ryde & K | = Ryde & K Rat App |
| Ryde & K Rat App | Ryde, W.C., and Konstam, E.M., *Reports of Rating Appeals* |
| Ryde Rat App | Ryde, E., and Ryde, A.L., *Reports ... Court of General Assessment* |
| | |
| S | Shaw, Patrick, *Cases ... Court of Session* also = Shaw App |
| S & A | = Saund & A |
| S & B | = Saund & B also = Smith & B |
| S & C | = Saund & C |
| S & D | = S |
| S & G | = Sm & G |
| S & L | = Sch & L |
| S & M | = Shaw & M |
| S & S | = Sau & S also = Sea & S also = Sim & St |
| S & Sm | = Sea & S |
| S & T | = Sw & Tr |
| Salk | Salkeld, William, *Reports ... King's Bench* |
| Sau & S | Sausse, M.R., and Scully, V., *Reports ... Rolls Court.* [Ireland.] |
| Sau & Sc | = Sau & S |
| Saund | Saunders, Sir Edmund, *Reports ... King's Bench* |
| Saund & A | Saunders, R.C., and Austin, E., *Court of Referees.* [*Locus Standi.*] |

| | |
|---|---|
| Saund & B | Saunders, R.C., and Bidder, H.F., *Court of Referees*. [*Locus Standi*.] |
| Saund & C | Saunders, T.W., and Cole, H.T., *Bail Court Reports* |
| Saund & M | Saunders, T.W., and Macrae, D.C., *County Court Cases* |
| Saund BC | = Saund & C |
| Sausse & Sc | = Sau & S |
| Sav | Savile, Sir John, *Les Reports . . . Common Bank* |
| Say | Sayer, Joseph, *Reports . . . King's Bench* |
| Sayer | = Say |
| S Bell | = Bell |
| SC | *Session Cases. Cases Decided in the Court of Session* |
| Sc | Scott, J., *Cases . . . Common Pleas* |
| SCC | = Sel Cas t King |
| SCCR | *Scottish Criminal Case Reports* |
| SCCR Supp | *Scottish Criminal Case Reports Supplement (1950–80)* |
| Sch & L | Schoales, J., and Lefroy, T., *Reports . . . Chancery in Ireland* |
| Sch & Lef | = Sch & L |
| SC (HL) | *Session Cases. Cases Decided in the House of Lords* |
| SC (J) | *Session Cases. Cases Decided in the Court of Justiciary.* 1907–16 |
| Sc Jur | *Scottish Jurist* |
| SCL | = Sel Cas t King |
| SCLR | *Scottish Civil Law Reports* |
| ScLR | = SLR |
| Sc NR | Scott, J., *New Reports . . . Common Pleas* |
| Sco | = Sc |
| Sco NR | = Sc NR |
| Scot Jur | = Sc Jur |
| Scot Law Rep | = SLR |
| Scot L Rev | Scottish Law Review section of *Scottish Law Review and Sheriff Court Reports* |
| Scott | = Sc |
| Scott NR | = Sc NR |
| ScRR | *Scots Revised Reports* |
| Sea & S | Searle, Richard, and Smith, James Charles, *Monthly Reports . . . Court of Probate and in the Court for Divorce and Matrimonial Causes* |
| Sea & Sm | = Sea & S |
| Searle & Sm | = Sea & S |
| Sec Bk Judg | Huxley, George, *A Second Book of Judgments* |
| Sel Cas Ch | = 3 Ch Cas |
| Sel Cas Ch (t King) | = Sel Cas t King |
| Sel Cas NP | *Select Cases at Nisi Prius . . . in Dublin* |
| Sel Cas t King | *Select Cases Argued and Adjudged . . . before . . . Lord Chancellor King* |
| Select Cas Ch | = 3 Ch Cas |
| Sess Cas | *Sessions Cases . . . Chiefly Touching Settlements* |
| Sess Cas KB | = Sess Cas |
| Sett & Rem | = Cas Sett |
| Sh | = S |
| | = Show KB |

|  |  |
|---|---|
|  | = Show Parl Cas |
| Sh & Macl | = Shaw & M |
| Sh & McL | = Shaw & M |
| Sh & M'L | = Shaw & M |
| Sh App | = Shaw App |
| Shaw | = Shaw Just |
| Shaw & M | Shaw, Patrick, and Maclean, Charles Hope, *Cases . . . House of Lords . . . Scotland* |
| Shaw App | Shaw, Patrick, *Cases . . . House of Lords . . . Scotland* |
| Shaw J | = J Shaw |
| Shaw Just | Shaw, Patrick, *Cases . . . Court of Justiciary* |
| Shaw P | = Shaw Just |
|  | = Shaw Teind |
| Shaw T Cas | = Shaw Teind |
| Shaw Teind | Shaw, Patrick, and others, *Cases . . . Court of Teinds* |
| Shaw Teind Ct | = Shaw Teind |
| Sh Ct of Sess | = S |
| Sh Ct Rep | Sheriff Court Reports section of *Scottish Law Review and Sheriff Court Reports* |
| Shep Touch | Sheppard, William, *Touchstone of Common Assurances* |
| Sher Ct Rep | = Sh Ct Rep |
| Shill WC | Shillman, B., *Irish Workmen's Compensation Cases* |
| Sh Just | = Shaw Just |
| Show | = Show KB |
| Show KB | Shower, Sir Bartholomew, *Reports . . . King's Bench* |
| Show Parl Cas | Shower, Sir Bartholomew, *Cases in Parliament* |
| Show PC | = Show Parl Cas |
| Shower PC | = Show Parl Cas |
| Sh Sc App | = Shaw App |
| Sh Teind Ct | = Shaw Teind |
| Sid | Siderfin, Thomas, *Reports . . . Bank le Roy* |
| Sim | Simons, Nicholas, *Reports . . . Chancery.* [Vice-Chancellor.] |
| Sim & S | = Sim & St |
| Sim & St | Simons, Nicholas, and Stuart, John, *Reports . . . Chancery.* [Vice-Chancellor.] |
| Sim & Stu | = Sim & St |
| Sim NS | Simons, Nicholas, *Reports . . . Chancery.* [Vice-Chancellor. New Series.] |
| Six Circ | = Cas Six Cir |
| SJ | *Solicitors Journal*<br>also = Sc Jur |
| SJ LB | *Solicitors Journal* (referring to Lawbrief) |
| S Jur | = Sc Jur |
| S Just | = J Shaw<br>also = Shaw Just |
| Skin | Skinner, Robert, *Reports . . . King's Bench* |
| Skinner | = Skin |
| SLCR | *Scottish Land Court Reports* |
| SLG | *Scottish Law Gazette* |
| SLJ | *Scottish Law Journal and Sheriff Court Record* |
| SLM | *Scottish Law Magazine and Sheriff Court Reporter* |

| | |
|---|---|
| SLR | *Scottish Law Reporter* |
| | also = Scot L Rev |
| | ! also *Singapore Law Reports* |
| SL Rev | = Scot L Rev |
| SLT | *Scots Law Times* |
| SLT (Land Ct) | *Scots Law Times* Scottish Land Court Reports |
| SLT (Lands Tr) | *Scots Law Times* Lands Tribunal for Scotland Reports |
| SLT (Lyon Ct) | *Scots Law Times* Lyon Court Reports |
| SLT (News) | *Scots Law Times* News |
| SLT (Notes) | *Scots Law Times* Notes of Recent Decisions |
| SLT (PL) | *Scots Law Times* Poor Law Reports |
| SLT (Sh Ct) | *Scots Law Times* Sheriff Court Reports |
| Sm | = Smith KB |
| | also = Smith Reg Cas |
| Sm & Bat | = Smith & B |
| Sm & G | Smale, John, and Giffard, J.W. de Longueville, *Reports . . . Chancery*. [Vice-Chancellor.] |
| Sm & Giff | = Sm & G |
| Smith | = Smith KB |
| Smith & B | Smith, T.B.C., and Batty, E., *Reports . . . King's Bench in Ireland* |
| Smith KB | Smith, J.P., *Reports . . . King's Bench* |
| Smith LC | Smith, John William, *Selection of Leading Cases on Various Branches of the Law* |
| Smith Reg Cas | Smith, C.L., *Registration Cases* |
| Smith's LC | = Smith LC |
| Sm LC | = Smith LC |
| Smy | Smythe, H., *Reports . . . Common Pleas . . . in Ireland* |
| Smy & B | Smythe, H., and Bourke, R., *The Queen v. Milles and the Queen v. Carroll* |
| Smythe | = Smy |
| SN | *Session Notes* |
| Sol J | = SJ |
| Sol Jo | = SJ |
| Sp | = Sp Ecc & Ad |
| | also = Sp Pri Cas |
| Sp Ecc & Ad | Spinks, Thomas, *Ecclesiastical and Admiralty Reports* |
| Sp Ecc & Ad App | Spinks, Thomas, *Ecclesiastical and Admiralty Reports* (referring to the appendix) |
| SPEL | *Scottish Planning and Environmental Law* |
| Spinks | = Sp Pri Cas |
| Spk Ecc & Ad | = Sp Ecc & Ad |
| SPLP | *Scottish Planning Law and Practice* |
| Sp PC | = Sp Pri Cas |
| Sp Pri Cas | Spinks, Thomas, *Reports . . . Admiralty Prize Court* |
| ST | = St Tr |
| St | = Stair |
| Stair | Stair, Lord (Sir James Dalrymple), *Decisions of the Lords of Council and Session* |
| Stair Rep | = Stair |

| | |
|---|---|
| Star | = Stark |
| Stark | Starkie, Thomas, *Reports ... Nisi Prius* |
| State Tr | = St Tr |
| State Tr NS | = St Tr NS |
| Stat LR | *Statute Law Review* |
| STC | *Simon's Tax Cases* |
| STC (SCD) | *Simon's Tax Cases Special Commissioners' Decisions* |
| St Eccl Cas | = Stil |
| STI | *Simon's Tax Intelligence* |
| Stil | Stillingfleet, E., *Ecclesiastical Cases* |
| Still Eccl Cas | = Stil |
| Sto & G | Stone, Arthur Paul, and Graham, W., *Courts of Referees.* [*Locus Standi.*] |
| Str | Strange, Sir John, *Reports* |
| Stra | = Str |
| St Tr | Cobbett, William, and Howell, T.B., *Complete Collection of State Trials* |
| St Tri | = St Tr |
| St Tr NS | *Reports of State Trials, New Series* |
| Stuart | = Stu M & P |
| Stuart M & P | = Stu M & P |
| Stu M & P | Stuart, R., Milne, J.S., and Peddie, W., *Reports ... Court of Session [etc.]* |
| Stu Mil & Ped | = Stu M & P |
| Sty | Style, William, *Narrationes Modernae, or Modern Reports* |
| Style | = Sty |
| Sw | Swabey, M.C. Merttins, *Reports ... Admiralty* also = Swans |
| Sw & Tr | Swabey, M.C. Merttins, and Tristram, Thomas Hutchinson, *Reports ... Probate ... Divorce and Matrimonial Causes* |
| Swab | = Sw |
| Sw Ad | = Sw |
| Swan | = Swans |
| Swan Ch | = Swans |
| Swans | Swanston, Clement Tudway, *Reports ... Chancery* |
| Swanst | = Swans |
| Swin | Swinton, Archibald, *Reports ... High Court and Circuit Courts of Justiciary* |
| Swin Reg App | Swinton, Archibald, *Digest of Decisions in the Registration Appeal Court at Glasgow* |
| SWTI | *Simon's Weekly Tax Intelligence* |
| Syme | Syme, David, *Reports ... High Court of Justiciary* |
| | |
| T & G | = Tyr & G |
| T & M | Temple, L., and Mew, G., *Reports ... Court of Criminal Appeal* |
| T & R | = Turn & R |
| Tal | = Cas t Talb |
| Talb | = Cas t Talb |
| Tam | = Taml |

| | |
|---|---|
| Taml | Tamlyn, John, *Reports ... Chancery*. [Rolls Court.] |
| Tamlyn | = Taml |
| Taun | = Taunt |
| Taunt | Taunton, William Pyle, *Reports ... Common Pleas* |
| Tax | *Taxation* |
| Tax Cas | = TC |
| TC | *Reports of Tax Cases* |
| TC Leaflet No. | unbound parts of *Reports of Tax Cases* |
| Temp & M | = T & M |
| Term Rep | = TR |
| Times LR | = TLR |
| T Jo | = T Jones |
| T Jones | Jones, Sir Thomas, *Reports ... King's Bench and Common Pleas* |
| TLR | *Times Law Reports* |
| To Jo | = T Jones |
| Toml Supp Br | = 8 Bro Parl Cas |
| Tot | = Toth |
| Toth | Tothill, William, *Transactions ... Chancery* |
| Tothill | = Toth |
| Town St Tr | Townsend, William C., *Modern State Trials* |
| TR (1785–1800) | *Term Reports* |
| TR [1939]–[1981] | *Taxation Reports* |
| Traf Cas | = Traff Cas |
| Traff Cas | *Traffic Cases* |
| T Ray | = T Raym |
| T Raym | Raymond, Sir Thomas, *Reports* |
| Tr Consist J | Tristram, T.H., *Principal Judgments ... Consistory Courts* |
| Trist | = Tr Consist J |
| TrL | *Trading Law* |
| TrLR | *Trading Law Reports* |
| TruLI | *Trust Law International* |
| Trust L & P | *Trust Law and Practice* |
| Tur & Rus | = Turn & R |
| Turn & R | Turner, George, and Russell, James, *Reports ... Chancery* |
| Turn & Russ | = Turn & R |
| Tyr | Tyrwhitt, R.P., *Reports ... Exchequer* |
| Tyr & G | Tyrwhitt, R.P., and Granger, T.C., *Reports ... Exchequer* |
| Tyr & Gr | = Tyr & G |
| Tyr & Gra | = Tyr & G |
| Tyrw | = Tyr |
| Tyrw & G | = Tyr & G |
| | |
| ULR | = Util LR |
| Util LR | *Utilities Law Review* |
| | |
| V & B | = Ves & B |
| V & S | = Vern & S |
| VATTR | *Value Added Tax Tribunals Reports* |
| Vaug | = Vaugh |
| Vaugh | Vaughan, Sir John, *Reports* |

| | |
|---|---|
| Vent | Ventris, Sir Peyton, *Reports* |
| Vern | Vernon, Thomas, *Cases ... Chancery* |
| Vern & S | Vernon, G.W., and Scriven, J.B., *Irish Reports* |
| Vern & Sc | = Vern & S |
| Vern & Scr | = Vern & S |
| Ves | = Ves Jr |
| Ves & B | Vesey, Francis, Junior, and Beames, John, *Reports ... Chancery* |
| Ves & Bea | = Ves & B |
| Ves Jr | Vesey, Francis, Junior, *Reports ... Chancery* |
| Ves Jun | = Ves Jr |
| Ves Jun Supp | = Hov Supp |
| Ves Sen | Vesey, Francis, Senior, *Reports ... Chancery* |
| Ves Sen Supp | = Belt's Supp |
| Vin Abr | Viner, Charles, *A General Abridgment of Law and Equity* |
| Vin Supp | Viner, Charles, *Abridgment of the Modern Determinations in the Courts ... being a Supplement to Viner's Abridgment* |
| | |
| W & B | = Wolf & B |
| W & D | = Wolf & D |
| W & S | = Wils & S |
| W & S App | = Wils & S |
| Wall | = Wal Lyn |
| Wallis by Lyne | = Wal Lyn |
| Wal Lyn | Wallis, J., *Reports ... Chancery in Ireland* |
| Water Law | *Water Law* |
| W Bl | = Bl R |
| W Black | = Bl R |
| WCC | *Workmen's Compensation Cases* |
| Web Pat Cas | Webster, T., *Reports and Notes of Cases on Letters Patent for Inventions* |
| Web PC | = Web Pat Cas |
| Weekly Rep | = WR |
| Welsh | = Welsh Reg Cas |
| Wels H & G | = Ex |
| Welsh Reg Cas | Welsh, T., *Registry Cases* |
| West | = West HL |
| | also = West t Hard |
| West Ch | = West t Hard |
| West HL | West, Martin John, *Cases ... House of Lords* |
| West t H | = West t Hard |
| West t Hard | West, Martin John, *Reports ... Chancery ... from the Original Manuscripts of Lord Chancellor Hardwicke* |
| West Ti Cas | Western, T.G., *Cases Relating to Tithes of the City of London* |
| West Tithe Cas | = West Ti Cas |
| White | White, James C., *Reports ... High Court and Circuit Courts of Justiciary* |
| Wight | Wightwick, John, *Reports ... Exchequer* |
| Wightw | = Wight |

| Will | = Willes |
|---|---|
| Willes | Willes, Sir John, *Reports ... Common Pleas* |
| Williams | = P Wms |
| Williams Cas Eq | = Cas t Talb |
| Williams P | = P Wms |
| Will Woll & D | Willmore, G., Wollaston, F.L., and Davison, H., *Reports ... King's Bench ... and ... Bail Court* |
| Will Woll & Dav | = Will Woll & D |
| Will Woll & H | Willmore, G., Wollaston, F.L., and Hodges, W., *Reports ... Queen's Bench ... and ... Bail Court* |
| Wilm | Wilmot, Sir John Eardley, *Notes* |
| Wils | = Wils Ch also = Wils KB |
| Wils & S | Wilson, James, and Shaw, Patrick, *Cases ... House of Lords ... Scotland* |
| Wils & Sh | = Wils & S |
| Wils CC | = Wils Ch |
| Wils Ch | Wilson, John, *Reports ... Chancery* |
| Wils Ex | Wilson, John, *Reports ... Exchequer in Equity* |
| Wils Exch | = Wils Ex |
| Wils Ex Eq | = Wils Ex |
| Wils KB | Wilson, George, *Reports ... Courts at Westminster* |
| Win | = Winch |
| Winch | Winch, Sir Humphry, *Reports* |
| W Jo | = W Jones |
| W Jones | Jones, Sir William, *Reports* |
| W Kelynge | = Kel W |
| WLR | *Weekly Law Reports* ! also *Western Law Reporter* (Canada 1905–16) |
| Wm Bl | = Bl R |
| Wm Rob | = W Rob |
| Wms | = P Wms |
| Wms P | = P Wms |
| Wms Saund | = Saund |
| WN | *Weekly Notes* |
| Wol | = Woll |
| Wolf & B | Wolferstan, F.S.P., and Bristowe, S.B., *Reports ... Election Committees* |
| Wolf & D | Wolferstan, F.S.P., and Dew, E.L., *Reports ... Controverted Elections* |
| Woll | Wollaston, F.L., *Reports ... Bail Court* |
| Wood | Wood, H., *Collection of Decrees ... in Tithe-causes* |
| Wood Tit Cas | = Wood |
| Wood Tithe Cas | = Wood |
| WPC | = Woll |
| W P Cas | = Woll |
| WR | *Weekly Reporter* also = West t Hard |
| W Rep | = West t Hard |
| W Rob | Robinson, William, *Reports ... Admiralty* |
| W W & D | = Will Woll & D |

W W & H                = Will Woll & H

Y                      Younge, Edward, *Reports ... Exchequer in Equity*
Y & C CC               = Y & C Ch
Y & C Ch               Younge, Edward, and Collyer, John, *Reports ... Chancery.*
                       [Vice-Chancellor.]
Y & C Ch Cas           = Y & C Ch
Y & C Ex               Younge, Edward, and Collyer, John, *Reports ... Exchequer*
                       *in Equity*
Y & J                  Younge, Edward, and Jervis, John, *Reports ... Exchequer*
YB                     Yearbook, see sections 2.2.1 and 2.4.4
YB Eur L               = YEL
Yearb Eur Law          = YEL
YEL                    *Yearbook of European Law*
Yel                    Yelverton, Sir Henry, *Reports ... King's Bench*
Yelv                   = Yel
Yelverton              = Yel
YLCT                   *Yearbook of Law Computers and Technology*
You                    = Y
You & Coll Ch          = Y & C Ch
You & Coll Ex          = Y & C Ex
Younge                 = Y
Younge & Coll Ch       = Y & C Ch
Younge & Coll Ex       = Y & C Ex

# LIST OF RECOMMENDED FORMS OF CITATION FOR LAW REPORTS AND OTHER PUBLICATIONS

In each entry the 'recommended citation' gives the recommended abbreviation for the publication (see section 2.4.2.1) and also shows whether to use a volume number (see section 2.4.2.4), a volume year in square brackets — indicated by '[volume year]' — or a volume year without brackets (see section 2.4.2.5). If a volume number should be used there is a reminder that the year of a decision or publication of an article should be given in parentheses. If a volume year should be used, information is given on whether and when a volume number is also required.

For example, the entry for *All England Law Reports* gives the recommended citation as:

[volume year] volume number All ER page number

showing that a typical citation would be:

[1994] 4 All ER 42

The entry for Adolphus, John Leycester, and Ellis, Thomas Flower, *Reports ... King's / Queen's Bench* gives the recommended citation as:

(year of decision) volume number Ad & El page number

showing that a typical citation would be:

(1840) 12 Ad & El 139

The 'Notes' at the end of an entry give any other information which might be useful for citing the publication, including its location in the *English Reports* (ER) if it is included in that collection. More details will be found in Wallace Breem and Sally Phillips, *Bibliography of Common-wealth Law Reports* (London: Mansell, 1991) in which each report is given a number. The Breem and Phillips (Br & Ph) number for a report is given at the end of its entry in the following list.

The list is in alphabetical order of the first words of entries, ignoring apostrophes (') and opening quotation marks ('). A hyphen is treated as a space separating two words. The first word of an entry may be an author's surname or the first word of the title of a publication (ignoring an initial article). If the same word occurs as a surname and as the first word of a title then the entries in which it is a surname are listed first. Entries with the same surname are in alphabetical order of forename or initials. Entries for an individual as sole author are listed before entries for the same person as the first of two or more joint authors. Entries for the same author or authors are in alphabetical order of title (ignoring initial articles).

This list is limited to material published in the British Isles and the English-language reports of the European Courts of Justice and Human Rights. For citation of material not in the list see recommendations 2.10 and 2.12.

*Abbreviations used in the list*

| | |
|---|---|
| app. | appendix |
| bk | book |
| Br & Ph | Wallace Breem and Sally Phillips, *Bibliography of Commonwealth Law Reports* (London: Mansell, 1991) (referring to an item number) |
| c. | circa |
| ed. | edited, edition, editor |
| eds | editions |
| ER | *English Reports* |
| f. | folio |
| n.d. | no date |
| p. | page |
| q.v. | *quod vide* (which see) |
| suppl. | supplement |
| transl. | translated, translation, translator |
| vol. | volume |
| vols | volumes |

## LIST OF RECOMMENDED FORMS OF CITATION FOR LAW REPORTS AND OTHER PUBLICATIONS

*Abridgment of Cases upon Poor Law*; for vols 1 and 2 see Lumley, W.G.; for vol. 3 see Archbold, J.F., for vol. 4 see Paterson, J.

*Accountant Tax Cases*; see *Annotated Tax Cases*.

Acton, Thomas Harman, *Reports . . . Prize Causes*.
    Recommended citation: (year of decision) volume number Act page number.
    Published: 2 vols 1811–12. Covering: 1809–11. Notes: In 12 ER. Br & Ph 809.

Adam, Edwin, *Reports . . . High Court of Justiciary*.
    Recommended citation: (year of decision) volume number Adam page number.
    Published: 7 vols 1895–1919. Covering: 1893–1916. Br & Ph 1596.

Addams, J., *Reports . . . Ecclesiastical Courts*.
    Recommended citation: (year of decision) volume number Add page number.
    Published: 3 vols 1823–7. Covering: 1822–6. Notes: In 162 ER. Br & Ph 481.

*Administrative Law Reports*. 1954–7.
    Recommended citation: [volume year] ALR page number.
    Published: [1954-5], [1955-6], [1956-7]. Notes: Published in *British Journal of Administrative Law*.

*Administrative Law Reports*. 1989– .
    Recommended citation: (year of decision) volume number Admin LR page number.
    Published: 1989– .

*Admiralty and Ecclesiastical Cases*; see *Law Reports. High Court of Admiralty, and Ecclesiastical Courts*.

Adolphus, John Leycester, and Ellis, Thomas Flower, *Reports . . . King's / Queen's Bench*.
    Recommended citation: (year of decision) volume number Ad & El page number.
    Published: 12 vols 1835–42. Covering: 1834–40. Notes: In 110 ER (vol. 1), 111 ER (vols 2–5), 112 ER (vols 6–9), 113 ER (vols 10–12). See also *Queen's Bench Reports* by the same reporters covering 1841–52. Br & Ph 538.

Alcock, J.C., *Registry Cases . . . Ireland*.
    Recommended citation: (year of decision) volume number Alc Reg Cas page number.
    Published: 3 vols 1837–41. Covering: 1832–41. Br & Ph 1416.

Alcock, J.C., and Napier, J., *Reports . . . King's Bench . . . in Ireland*.
    Recommended citation: (year of decision) Alc & N page number.
    Published: 1 vol. 1834. Covering: 1831–3. Br & Ph 1357.

Aleyn, John, *Select Cases in B[anco] R[egis]*.
    Recommended citation: (year of decision) Al page number.
    Published: 1 vol. 1681, 2nd ed. 1688. Covering: 1646–9. Notes: 1st ed. in 82 ER. Br & Ph 539.

*All England Law Reports*.
    Recommended citation: [volume year] volume number All ER page number.
    Published: [1936]– . Notes: [1936] 3 vols, [1937]–[1940] 4 vols a year, [1941] 3 vols, [1942]–[1953] 2 vols a year, [1954]–[1990] 3 vols a year, [1991]– 4 vols a year. Br & Ph 313.

*All England Law Reports Annual Review*.
    Recommended citation: All ER Rev volume year without brackets page number.
    Published: 1982– .

*All England Law Reports European Cases.*
Recommended citation: [volume year] All ER (EC) page number.
Published: [1995]– .
*All England Law Reports Reprint.*
Recommended citation: [volume year] All ER Rep page number; Ext page
number for pages in extension vols.
Published: 36 vols 1957–68. Covering: 1558–1935. Notes: The date in square
brackets in the citation of a volume indicates the period covered by the volume.
The volumes are [1558-1774], [1775-1802], [1803-13], [1814-23], [1824-34],
[1835-42], [1843-60], [1861-73], [1874-80], [1881-5], [1886-90], [1891-4], [1895-
9], [1900-3], [1904-7], [1908-10], [1911-13], [1914-15], [1916-17], [1918-19] and
then single years from [1920] to [1935]. 16 'extension volumes' were published
in Australia 1968–71 containing additional pages for each of the volumes in the
original work. The reports have new headnotes but are otherwise reprinted from
nominate reports or, for the period 1843–1935, from the *Law Times Reports*. Br
& Ph 314.
Ambler, Charles, *Reports ... Chancery.*
Recommended citation: (year of decision) Amb page number.
Published: 1 vol. 1790, 2nd ed. by John Elijah Blunt 1828. Covering: 1737–84.
Notes: 2nd ed. in 27 ER. Br & Ph 370.
Anderson, Edmund, *Les Reports ... Common-Bank.*
Recommended citation: (year of decision) volume number And page number.
Published: 2 vols 1664–5. Covering: 1534–1605. Notes: In 123 ER. In law French.
Br & Ph 432.
Andrews, George, *Reports ... King's Bench.*
Recommended citation: (year of decision) Andr page number.
Published: 1 vol. 1754, 2nd ed. by George William Vernon 1791. Covering:
1738–9. Notes: 2nd ed. in 95 ER. Page numbers in the appendix are roman
numerals. Br & Ph 540.
*Anglo-American Law Review.*
Recommended citation: (year of publication of article) volume number Anglo-Am
L Rev page number.
Published: 1972– .
*Annaly's Hardwicke*; see *Cases Argued and Adjudged in the Court of King's Bench
... [tempore] Hardwicke.*
*Annotated Tax Cases.*
Recommended citation: (year of decision) volume number ATC page number.
Published: 54 vols 1922–75. Covering: 1922–75. Notes: Volumes 1–5 titled
*Accountant Tax Cases* (same form of citation). Br & Ph 890.
*Annual Digest and Reports of Public International Law Cases.*
Recommended citation: (year of decision) volume number Ann Dig page number.
Published: 16 vols 1932–55. Notes: Volumes 1–7 (1932–40) titled *Annual Digest
of Public International Law Cases* (same form of citation). From vol. 17 titled
*International Law Reports* (q.v.).
*Annual Digest of Public International Law Cases*; see *Annual Digest and Reports
of Public International Law Cases.*
*Anonymous, at the end of Benloe*; see Benloe, William, *Reports.*
Anstruther, Alexander, *Reports ... Exchequer.*
Recommended citation: (year of decision) volume number Anst page number.
Published: 3 vols 1796–7, 2nd ed. 1817. Covering: 1792–7. Notes: 2nd ed. in 145
ER. Paginated continuously, vol. 2 starting on p. 343, vol. 3 on p. 627. Br & Ph 491.

*Appeal Cases.* (1875–90); see *Law Reports. Appeal Cases.* (1875–90).

*Appeal Cases.* [1891]– ; see *Law Reports. House of Lords.* [1891]– .

*Appeals from Munitions Tribunals.*
　　Recommended citation: (year of decision) volume number Mun App page number.
　　Published: 4 vols 1916–20. Covering: 1916–20. Notes: Also known as 'Munitions Appeal Reports'. Br & Ph 842.

Archbold, J.F., *Abridgment of Cases upon Poor Law*, vol. 3.
　　Recommended citation: (year of decision) Arch PL Cas page number.
　　Published: 1 vol. 1858. Covering: 1842–58. Notes: For vols 1 and 2 see Lumley, W.G.; for vol. 4 see Paterson, J. Br & Ph 920.

*Architects' Law Reports.*
　　Recommended citation: (year of decision) volume number Arch LR page number.
　　Published: 4 vols 1904–9. Br & Ph 714.

Arkley, Patrick, *Reports . . . High Court and Circuit Courts of Justiciary.*
　　Recommended citation: (year of decision) Arkley page number.
　　Published: 1 vol. 1849. Covering: 1846–8. Br & Ph 1597.

Armstrong, R., Macartney, J., and Ogle, J.C., *Reports . . . Nisi Prius . . . in Dublin.*
　　Recommended citation: (year of decision) Arm M & O page number.
　　Published: 1 vol. 1843. Covering: 1840–2. Br & Ph 1368.

Arnold, T.J., *Reports . . . Common Pleas.*
　　Recommended citation: (year of decision) volume number Arn page number.
　　Published: 2 vols 1840. Covering: 1838–9. Br & Ph 461.

Arnold, T.J., and Hodges, W., *Reports . . . Queen's Bench.*
　　Recommended citation: (year of decision) Arn & H page number.
　　Published: 1 vol. 1841. Covering: 1840–1. Br & Ph 625.

Arnot, Hugo, *A Collection and Abridgement of Celebrated Criminal Trials in Scotland.*
　　Recommended citation: (year of decision) Arnot page number.
　　Published: 1 vol. 1785. Covering: 1536–1784.

Ashburton, 1st Baron; see Dunning, John.

Aspinall, James P., *Reports . . . Maritime Law.*
　　Recommended citation: (year of decision) volume number Asp page number.
　　Published: 19 vols 1873–1943. Covering: 1870–1940. Notes: Volume 20 is an index. Br & Ph 810.

Atkyns, John Tracy, *Reports . . . Chancery.*
　　Recommended citation: (year of decision) volume number Atk page number.
　　Published: 3 vols 1765–8, 3rd ed. by Francis Williams Sanders 1794. Covering: 1736–55. Notes: 3rd ed. in 26 ER. Br & Ph 371.

Austen-Cartmell, James, *Abstract of Reported Cases Relating to Trade Marks.*
　　Recommended citation: (year of decision) Cartm page number.
　　Published: 1 vol. 1893. Covering: 1876–92. Br & Ph 762.

Austin, R.C., *Reports . . . County Courts.*
　　Recommended citation: (year of decision) Aust page number.
　　Published: 1 vol. 1869. Covering: 1867–9. Br & Ph 471.


Bacon, Matthew, *A New Abridgment of the Law.*
　　Recommended abbreviation: Bac Abr.
　　Published: 5 vols 1736–66, 7th ed. by Sir Henry Gwillim and Charles Dodd in 8 vols 1832.

Ball, Thomas, and Beatty, Francis, *Reports ... Chancery in Ireland.*
Recommended abbreviation: (year of decision) volume number Ball & B page number.
Published: 2 vols 1813–24, 3rd ed. of vol. 1 1823. Covering: 1807–14. Br & Ph 1332.

*Banking Law Reports.*
Recommended citation: (year of decision) volume number Bank LR page number.
Published: 1992– . Notes: The publisher's suggested form of citation includes a year in square brackets as well as the volume number but this is not recommended, as explained in section 2.4.2.6.

*Bankruptcy and Insolvency Reports.*
Recommended citation: (year of decision) volume number B & I page number.
Published: 2 vols 1855. Covering: 1853–5. Notes: Volume 2 ed. J.B. Dasent. Br & Ph 689.

*Bannister's Bridgman*; see Bridgman, Sir Orlando, *Reports.*
Barnardiston, Thomas, *Reports ... Chancery.*
Recommended citation: (year of decision) Barn Ch page number.
Published: 1 vol. 1742. Covering: 1740–1. Notes: In 27 ER. Br & Ph 373.

Barnardiston, Thomas, *Reports ... King's Bench.*
Recommended citation: (year of decision) volume number Barn KB page number.
Published: 2 vols 1744. Covering: 1726–34. Notes: In 94 ER. Br & Ph 541.

Barnes, Henry, *Notes of Cases in Points of Practice ... Common Pleas.*
Recommended citation: (year of decision) Barnes page number.
Published: 1 vol. 1741, 3rd ed. 1790. Covering: 1732–60. Notes: 3rd ed. in 94 ER. Br & Ph 433.

Barnewall, Richard Vaughan, and Adolphus, John Leycester, *Reports ... King's Bench.*
Recommended citation: (year of decision) volume number B & Ad page number.
Published: 5 vols 1831–5. Covering: 1830–4. Notes: In 109 ER (vols 1 and 2) and 110 ER (vols 3–5). Br & Ph 542.

Barnewall, Richard Vaughan, and Alderson, Edward Hall, *Reports ... King's Bench.*
Recommended citation: (year of decision) volume number B & Ald page number.
Published: 5 vols 1818–22. The first 216 pp. of vol. 1 were by Selwyn and Barnewall. Covering: 1817–22. Notes: In 106 ER. Br & Ph 543.

Barnewall, Richard Vaughan, and Cresswell, Cresswell, *Reports ... King's Bench.*
Recommended citation: (year of decision) volume number B & C page number.
Published: 10 vols 1823–32. Covering: 1822–30. Notes: In 107 ER (vols 1–4), 108 ER (vols 5–8) and 109 ER (vols 9–10). Br & Ph 544.

Barron, A., and Arnold, T.J., *Reports of Cases of Controverted Elections.*
Recommended citation: (year of decision) Barr & Arn page number.
Published: 1 vol. 1846. Covering: 1843–6. Br & Ph 843.

Barron, A., and Austin, A., *Repoi ـs of Cases of Controverted Elections.*
Recommended citation: (year of decision) Barr & Aust page number.
Published: 1 vol. 1844. Covering: 1842. Br & Ph 844.

Batty, E., *Reports ... King's Bench ... in Ireland.*
Recommended citation: (year of decision) Batt page number.
Published: 1 vol. 1828. Covering: 1825–6. Br & Ph 1358.

Beatty, F., *Reports ... Chancery in Ireland.*
Recommended citation: (year of decision) Beat page number.
Published: 1 vol. 1847. Covering: 1813–30. Br & Ph 1333.

Beavan, Charles, *Reports . . . Rolls Court.*
Recommended citation: (year of decision) volume number Beav page number.
Published: 36 vols 1840–69. Covering: 1838–66. Notes: In 48 ER (vols 1 and 2),
49 ER (vols 3–7), 50 ER (vols 8–12), 51 ER (vols 13–17), 52 ER (vols 18–22), 53
ER (vols 23–6), 54 ER (vols 27–31) and 55 ER (vols 32–6). Br & Ph 664.

Beavan, E., and Walford, F., *Parliamentary Cases Relating to Railways.*
Recommended citation: (year of decision) Beav & W page number.
Published: 1 vol. 1847. Covering: 1846. Br & Ph 939.

Bell, Benjamin Robert, 'Supplemental notes', in *Commentaries on the Law of
Scotland, Respecting Crimes*, by David Hume.
Recommended citation: (year of decision) Bell's Notes page number.
Published: 1844.

Bell, Robert, *Cases . . . Court of Session.* (1790–2).
Recommended citation: (year of decision) Bell Oct Cas page number.
Published: 1 vol. 1794. Covering: 1790–2. Notes: Known as 'Bell's Octavo Cases'
from the format of the volume. See also next entry. Br & Ph 1611.

Bell, Robert, *Cases . . . Court of Session.* (1794–5).
Recommended citation: (year of decision) Bell Fol Cas page number.
Published: 1 vol. 1796. Covering: 1794–5. Notes: Known as 'Bell's Folio Cases'
from the format of the volume. See also preceding entry. Br & Ph 1612.

Bell, Sydney S., *Dictionary of the Decisions of the Court of Session.*
Recommended citation: (year of decision) volume number Bell Dict Dec page
number.
Published: 2 vols 1841–2. Covering: 1808–33. Br & Ph 1613.

Bell, Sydney S., *Cases . . . House of Lords on Appeal from . . . Scotland.*
Recommended citation: (year of decision) volume number Bell page number.
Published: 7 vols 1843–52. Covering: 1842–50. Notes: Also known as 'Bell's
Appeal Cases'. Br & Ph 1654.

Bell, Thomas, *Crown Cases Reserved.*
Recommended citation: (year of decision) Bell CC page number.
Published: 1 vol. 1861. Covering: 1858–60. Notes: In 169 ER. Br & Ph 717.

Bellewe, Richard, *Les Ans du Roy Richard le Second.*
Recommended citation: (year of decision) Bel page number.
Published: 1 vol. 1585. Covering: 1378–1400. Notes: In 72 ER. There is also an
1869 ed. by Hugh Cooke. In law French. Br & Ph 545.

*Bell's Appeal Cases*; see Bell, Sydney S., *Cases . . . House of Lords on Appeal from
. . . Scotland.*

*Bell's Folio Cases*; see Bell, Robert, *Cases . . . Court of Session.* (1794–5).

*Bell's Octavo Cases*; see Bell, Robert, *Cases . . . Court of Session.* (1790–2).

Belt, Robert, *Supplement to the Reports in Chancery of Francis Vesey Senior.*
Recommended citation: (year of decision) Belt's Supp page number.
Published: 1 vol. 1817, 2nd ed. 1825. Covering: 1747–56. Notes: 2nd ed. in 28 ER.
Br & Ph 374.

Benloe, William, *Reports.*
Recommended citation: (year of decision) Benl page number.
Published: 1 vol. 1661. Covering: 1531–1628. Notes: In 73 ER. In law French. The
work is sometimes known as 'New Benloe'. The author's name is also spelt
Bendloe, Bendloes (on the original title-page of these reports), Bendlowes (in the
*Dictionary of National Biography*), Bendoes or Benlowes. From p. 89 to the end
the reports are not by Benloe and used to be known as 'Anonymous, at the end
of Benloe' (which used to be cited as AB). Br & Ph 546.

Benloe, William, *Reports*, and Dalison, Sir William, *Reports*.
Recommended citation: (year of decision) Benl & Dal Benloe page number; Dalison page number.
Published: 1 vol. 1689. Covering: 1486–1580. Notes: In 123 ER. In law French. The two parts are separately paginated. Benloe's part is also known as 'Old Benloe'. Benloe is also sometimes spelt Bendloe, Bendloes, Bendlowes (in the *Dictionary of National Biography*), Bendoes or Benlowes. Dalison is also spelt Dallison. Br & Ph 434.

Bernard, W.L., *Irish Church Acts 1869 & 1872 . . . together with Reports of Leading Cases*.
Recommended citation: (year of decision) Bern page number.
Published: 1871, [4th ed.] in 1 vol. 1876. Covering: 1870–5. Br & Ph 1387.

Best, William Mawdesley, and Smith, George James Philip, *Reports . . . Queen's Bench*.
Recommended citation: (year of decision) volume number B & S page number.
Published: 10 vols 1862–71. Covering: 1861–9. Notes: Volumes 1–6 in 121 ER (vols 1 and 2) and 122 ER (vols 3–6). Part of vol. 1 was by Ellis, Best and Smith. Br & Ph 547.

Bidder, Harold Francis, *Locus Standi*.
Recommended citation: (year of decision) Bid page number.
Published: 1 vol. 1937. Covering: 1920–36. Br & Ph 790.

Bingham, Peregrine, *New Cases in the Court of Common Pleas*.
Recommended citation: (year of decision) volume number Bing NC page number.
Published: 6 vols 1835–41. Covering: 1834–40. Notes: In 131 ER (vol. 1), 132 ER (vols 2–5) and 133 ER (vol. 6). See also Bingham, Peregrine, *Reports . . . Common Pleas*. Br & Ph 435.

Bingham, Peregrine, *Reports . . . Common Pleas*.
Recommended citation: (year of decision) volume number Bing page number.
Published: 10 vols 1824–34. Covering: 1822–34. Notes: In 130 ER (vols 1–6) and 131 ER (vols 7–10). See also Bingham, Peregrine, *New Cases in the Court of Common Pleas*. Br & Ph 436.

Bittleston, A.H., *Practice under the Judicature Acts*.
Recommended citation: (year of decision) Bitt Pr Cas page number.
Published: 1 vol. 1876. Covering: 1875–6. Notes: Bittleston, A.H., *Reports in Chambers, Queen's Bench Division*, published 1884, is sometimes regarded as a second volume of this work. Br & Ph 870.

Bittleston, A.H., *Reports in Chambers, Queen's Bench Division*.
Recommended citation: (year of decision) Bitt Cha Cas page number.
Published: 1 vol. 1884. Covering: 1883–4. Notes: Sometimes regarded as vol. 2 of Bittleston, A.H., *Practice under the Judicature Acts*, published 1876. Br & Ph 869.

Blackerby, S., *Cases in Law*.
Recommended citation: (year of decision) Black page number.
Published: 1 vol. 1717, 3rd ed. 1734. Described on the title-page as the Second Part of The Justice of the Peace, His Companion. Covering: 1327–1716. Br & Ph 637.

Blackham, J., Dundas, W.J., and Osborne, R.W., *Reports . . . Nisi Prius . . . Dublin*.
Recommended citation: (year of decision) B D & O page number.
Published: 1 vol. 1849. Covering: 1846–8. Br & Ph 1369.

Blackstone, Henry, *Reports . . . Common Pleas.*
Recommended citation: (year of decision) volume number H Bl page number.
Published: 2 vols 1788–96, 4th ed. 1827. Covering: 1788–96. Notes: 4th ed. in 126
ER. There is also a 5th ed., 1837, by F.W. Meymott. Br & Ph 437.
Blackstone, Sir William, *Commentaries on the Law of England.*
Recommended abbreviation: Bl Com.
Published: 4 vols 1765–9, many other editions.
Blackstone, Sir William, *Reports . . . Courts of Westminster-Hall.*
Recommended citation: (year of decision) volume number Bl R page number.
Published: 2 vols 1781, 2nd ed. by Charles Heneage Elsley 1828. Covering:
1746–79. Notes: 2nd ed. in 96 ER. Paginated continuously, vol. 2 beginning on
p. 681. Br & Ph 548.
Bligh, Richard, *Reports . . . House of Lords.*
Recommended citation: (year of decision) volume number Bli page number.
Published: 4 vols 1823–7. Covering: 1819–21. Notes: In 4 ER. See also Bligh,
Richard, *Reports . . . House of Lords. New Series.* Br & Ph 524.
Bligh, Richard, *Reports . . . House of Lords. New Series.*
Recommended citation: (year of decision) volume number Bli NS page number.
Published: 11 vols 1829–38. Covering: 1827–37. Notes: In 4 ER (vols 1–3), 5 ER
(vols 4–9) and 6 ER (vols 10 and 11). See also Bligh, Richard, *Reports . . . House
of Lords.* Br & Ph 523.
Bosanquet, John Bernard, and Puller, Christopher, *New Reports . . . Common
Pleas.*
Recommended citation: (year of decision) volume number Bos & P NR page
number.
Published: 2 vols 1806–8, 2nd ed. 1826. Covering: 1804–7. Notes: In 127 ER. See
also Bosanquet, John Bernard, and Puller, Christopher, *Reports . . . Common
Pleas.* Br & Ph 438.
Bosanquet, John Bernard, and Puller, Christopher, *Reports . . . Common Pleas.*
Recommended citation: (year of decision) volume number Bos & P page number.
Published: 3 vols 1800–4, 3rd ed. 1826. Covering: 1796–1804. Notes: 3rd ed. in
126 ER (vols 1 and 2) and 127 ER (vol. 3). In vol. 1, pp. 471 onwards are cases
reported by A. Moore which were also published separately in 1800. See also
Bosanquet, John Bernard, and Puller, Christopher, *New Reports . . . Common
Pleas.* Br & Ph 439.
Boswell, James, *Decision of the Court of Session upon the Question of Literary
Property.*
Recommended citation: (year of decision) Bosw page number.
Published: 1 vol. 1774.
Bott, E., *Laws Relating to the Poor.*
Recommended citation: (year of decision) volume number Bott PL (for the 1833
supplement: Pratt) page number.
Published: 6th ed. by John Tidd Pratt in 2 vols with a supplement 1827–33.
Covering: 1560–1833. Notes: 1st ed. published anonymously 1771. Br & Ph 921.
Bourke, R., *Parliamentary Precedents.*
Recommended citation: (year of decision) Bourke PP page number.
Published: 1857, 2nd ed. in 1 vol. 1857. Covering: 1839–57. Br & Ph 847.
Bracton, Henry de, *De Legibus et Consuetudinibus Angliae.*
Recommended abbreviation: Bract.
Written about 1250–9. Notes: The author's name is also spelt Bratton or
Bretton.

*Bracton Law Journal.*
Recommended citation: (year of publication of article) volume number Bracton LJ page number.
Published: 1965– .
*Bracton's Note Book.*
Recommended citation: (year of decision) volume number Brac page number.
Published: 3 vols 1887 ed. F.W. Maitland from a manuscript which seems to be by Henry de Bracton (or Bratton or Bretton) (died 1268). Covering: 1217–40.
*Brewing Trade Review Law Reports.*
Recommended citation: (year of decision) volume number BTRLR page number.
Published: 31 vols 1914–58. Br & Ph 783.
Bridgman, Sir John, *Reports.*
Recommended citation: (year of decision) J Bridg page number.
Published: 1 vol. 1659. Covering: 1613–21. Notes: In 123 ER. An earlier ed. of 1651 or 1652 is listed in some bibliographies. Br & Ph 440.
Bridgman, Sir Orlando, *Reports.*
Recommended citation: (year of decision) O Bridg page number.
Published: 1 vol. 1823 ed. S. Bannister. Covering: 1660–7. Notes: In 124 ER. Also called 'Bannister's Bridgman'. Br & Ph 441.
*British and Colonial Prize Cases*; see *Prize Cases ... during the Great War.*
*British Company Cases.*
Recommended citation: [volume year] BCC page number.
Published: [1990]– . Notes: Continuation of *British Company Law Cases* (q.v.).
*British Company Law Cases.*
Recommended citation: (year of decision) volume number BCC page number.
Published: 5 vols 1985–9. Covering: 1983–9. Notes: Continued by *British Company Cases* (q.v.).
*British Journal of Administrative Law.*
Recommended citation: (year of publication of article) volume number BJAL page number.
Published: 3 vols 1954–7. Notes: Merged with *Public Law.* Includes Administrative Law Reports (see separate entry).
*British Journal of Criminology.*
Recommended citation: (year of publication of article) volume number Br J Criminol page number.
Published: 1960– . Notes: Continuation of *British Journal of Delinquency* (q.v.).
*British Journal of Delinquency.*
Recommended citation: (year of publication of article) volume number Br J Delinquency page number.
Published: 10 vols 1950–60. Notes: Continued as *British Journal of Criminology* (q.v.).
*British Journal of Industrial Relations.*
Recommended citation: (year of publication of article) volume number BJIR page number.
Published: 1963– .
*British Journal of Law and Society.*
Recommended citation: (year of publication of article) volume number Br J Law Soc page number.
Published: 8 vols 1974–81. Notes: From vol. 9 titled *Journal of Law and Society* (q.v.).

*British Tax Cases.*
    Recommended citation: [volume year] BTC page number.
    Published: [1982]– . Br & Ph 891.
*British Tax Review.*
    Recommended citation: [volume year] BTR page number.
    Published: [1956]– .
*British Value Added Tax Cases.* (1973–90).
    Recommended citation: (year of decision) volume number BVC page number.
    Published: 5 vols 1985–91. Covering: 1973–90. Notes: For citation of later vols
    see next entry.
*British Value Added Tax Cases.* [1991]– .
    Recommended citation: [volume year] BVC page number.
    Published: [1991]– . Notes: For citation of earlier vols see preceding entry.
*British Year Book of International Law.*
    Recommended citation: (year of decision or of publication of article) volume
    number BYIL page number.
    Published: 1920– .
Broderip, William John, and Bingham, Peregrine, *Reports ... Common Pleas.*
    Recommended citation: (year of decision) volume number Brod & Bing page
    number.
    Published: 3 vols 1820–2. Covering: 1819–22. Notes: In 129 ER. The first 218 pp.
    of vol. 1 were by Taunton and Broderip. Br & Ph 442.
Brodrick, George Charles, and Fremantle, W.H., *Collection of the Judgments of ...*
    *the Privy Council in Ecclesiastical Cases.*
    Recommended citation: (year of decision) Brod & F page number.
    Published: 1 vol. 1865. Covering: 1840–64. Br & Ph 735.
Brooke, Sir Robert, *Graunde Abridgement.*
    Recommended abbreviation: Bro Abr.
    Published: 2 vols 1574, 3rd ed. 1586. Notes: In law French. The author's surname
    is also spelt Broke (in the *Dictionary of National Biography*) or Brook.
Brooke, Sir Robert, *Some New Cases.*
    Recommended citation: (year of decision) BNC page number.
    Published: 1 vol. in law French 1578, English translation by John March
    1651. Covering: 1515–58. Notes: March's translation in 73 ER. For the first
    edition the cases were extracted by Richard Bellewe from the *Graunde*
    *Abridgement* by Sir Robert Brooke and so it became known as 'Petit', 'Petty'
    or 'Little' Brooke to distinguish it from the Abridgement. In the law French
    editions, the cases are in chronological order; in March's version they are under
    subject headings. There is also an 1873 ed. containing both the law French and
    English versions. The author's surname is also spelt Broke (in the *Dictionary*
    *of National Biography*) or Brook (on the title-page of the 1651 ed.).
    Br & Ph 549.
Brooke, W.G., *Six Judgments of ... the Privy Council in Ecclesiastical Cases.*
    Recommended citation: (year of decision) Brooke page number.
    Published: 1 vol. 1872. Covering: 1850–72. Br & Ph 736.
Broun, Archibald, *Reports ... High Court and Circuit Courts of Justiciary.*
    Recommended citation: (year of decision) volume number Broun page number.
    Published: 2 vols 1844–6. Covering: 1842–5. Br & Ph 1598.
Brown, Josiah, *Reports ... Parliament.*
    Recommended citation: (year of decision) volume number Bro Parl Cas page
    number.

Published: 7 vols 1779–83, 2nd ed. by T.E. Tomlins in 8 vols 1803. Covering: 1702–1800. Notes: 2nd ed. in 1 ER (vols 1–3), 2 ER (vols 4–6) and 3 ER (vols 7 and 8). The pagination of the 1st and 2nd eds is completely different. In the 1st ed. the cases are arranged chronologically, in the 2nd under subject headings. Br & Ph 525.

Brown, M.P., *General Synopsis of the Decisions of the Court of Session.*
Recommended citation: (year of decision) volume number Bro Syn page number.
Published: 4 vols 1829. Covering: 1540–1827. Br & Ph 1647.

Brown, M.P., *Supplement to the Dictionary of Decisions of the Court of Session.*
Recommended citation: (year of decision) volume number Bro Sup page number.
Published: 5 vols 1826. Covering: 1622–1794. Br & Ph 1648.

Brown, William, *Reports ... Chancery.*
Recommended citation: (year of decision) volume number Bro CC page number.
Published: 4 vols 1785–94, [5th] ed. by Robert Belt 1820. Covering: 1778–94. Notes: Belt's ed. in 28 ER (vol. 1) and 29 ER (vols 2–4). The 4th ed. by R.H. Eden 1819 used to be considered equally important. Br & Ph 375.

Browning, W.E., and Lushington, Vernon, *Reports ... Admiralty.*
Recommended citation: (year of decision) Br & Lush page number.
Published: 1 vol. 1868. Covering: 1863–5. Notes: In 167 ER. Br & Ph 347.

Brownlow, Richard, and Goldesborough, John, *Reports.*
Recommended citation: (year of decision) volume number Brownl page number.
Published: 2 vols 1651–2, 3rd ed. of vol. 1 and 2nd ed. of vol. 2 1675. Covering: 1569–1624. Notes: In 123 ER. Volume 2 is by Brownlow alone. Br & Ph 443.

Bruce, Alexander, *Decisions of the Lords of Council and Session.*
Recommended citation: (year of decision) Bruce page number.
Published: 1 vol. 1720. Covering: 1714–15. Notes: Known as 'Bruce and Home's Decisions' when bound together with vol. 1 of Kames, Lord (Henry Home), *Remarkable Decisions of the Court of Session.* Br & Ph 1614.

Buchanan, W., *Reports ... Remarkable Cases.*
Recommended citation: (year of decision) Buch page number.
Published: 1 vol. 1813. Covering: 1806–13. Br & Ph 1649.

Buck, J.W., *Cases in Bankruptcy.*
Recommended citation: (year of decision) Buck page number.
Published: 1 vol. 1820. Covering: 1816–20. Br & Ph 690.

*Building Law Reports.*
Recommended citation: (year of decision) volume number BLR page number.
Published: 1976– . Br & Ph 715.

*Bulletin of Northern Ireland Law.*
Recommended citation: [volume year] issue number BNIL item number.
Published: [1981]– .

Bulstrode, Edward, *Reports ... King's Bench.*
Recommended citation: (year of decision) volume number Bulst page number.
Published: 3 vols 1657–9, 2nd ed. 1688. Covering: 1610–25. Notes: In 80 ER (vols 1 and 2) and 81 ER (vol. 3). Br & Ph 550.

Bunbury, William, *Reports ... Exchequer.*
Recommended citation: (year of decision) Bunb page number.
Published: 1 vol. 1755, 2nd ed. 1793. Covering: 1713–41. Notes: In 145 ER. The reports were edited by George Wilson. Br & Ph 492.

Burrell, Sir William, *Reports ... Admiralty.*
Recommended citation: (year of decision) Burrell page number.
Published: 1 vol. 1885 ed. Reginald G. Marsden. Covering: 1584–1774. Notes: Extracts in 167 ER. Br & Ph 356.

Burrow, Sir James, *Decisions ... upon Settlement-Cases.*
Recommended citation: (year of decision) Burr SC page number.
Published: 2 vols 1768, Continuation in 2 vols 1772–[6?], 2nd ed. in 1 vol. 1786.
Covering: 1733–76. Notes: Pagination is continuous. The 1st ed. was titled *A Series of the Decisions ... upon Settlement-Cases.* Br & Ph 774.
Burrow, Sir James, *Reports ... King's Bench.*
Recommended citation: (year of decision) volume number Burr page number.
Published: 5 vols 1766–80, 5th ed. 1812. Covering: 1757–71. Notes: In 80 ER (vols 1–3) and 81 ER (vols 4 and 5). Also known as 'Burrow's Mansfield' (which used to be cited as BM) after Lord Mansfield who was Chief Justice during the period reported. Br & Ph 551.
*Burrow's Mansfield*; see Burrow, Sir James, *Reports ... King's Bench.*
*Butterworths Company Law Cases.*
Recommended citation: [volume year] number if there is more than 1 volume for the year BCLC page number.
Published: [1983]– . Notes: [1983]–[1993] 1 vol. a year, [1994]– 2 vols a year. Br & Ph 820.
*Butterworths' Rating Appeals.*
Recommended citation: (year of decision) BRA (1913–1925) or BRA (1926–1931) page number.
Published: 2 sets of 2 vols 1925–32. Covering: 1913–31. Notes: Each set of 2 vols is paginated continuously. Br & Ph 892.
*Butterworths Trading Law Cases.*
Recommended citation: [volume year] BTLC page number.
Published: [1986]– .
*Butterworths' Workmen's Compensation Cases.*
Recommended citation: (year of decision) volume number BWCC page number; Supp page number for Supplement in vols 24–41.
Published: 41 vols 1909–50. Br & Ph 747.


Cababé, Michael, and Ellis, Charles Gregson, *Reports ... Queen's Bench.*
Recommended citation: (year of decision) Cab & El page number.
Published: 1 vol. 1885. Covering: 1882–5. Br & Ph 552.
Caldecott, Thomas, *Reports of Cases Relative to the Duty and Office of a Justice of the Peace.*
Recommended citation: (year of decision) Cald MC page number.
Published: 1 vol. 1797, new ed. 1800. Covering: 1776–85. Br & Ph 801.
Calthrop, Sir Henry, *Reports of Special Cases Touching ... the City of London.*
Recommended citation: (year of decision) Calth page number.
Published: 1 vol. 1655, 2nd ed. 1670. Covering: 1609–18. Notes: 2nd ed. in 80 ER. There is also an 1872 ed. Br & Ph 716.
*Cambrian Law Review.*
Recommended citation: (year of publication of article) volume number Cambrian Law Rev page number.
Published: 1970– .
*Cambridge Law Journal.* 1923 to 1953.
Recommended citation: (year of publication of article) volume number CLJ page number.
Published: 11 vols 1923–53. Notes: For citation of later vols see next entry.

*Cambridge Law Journal.* 1954–.
Recommended citation: [volume year] CLJ page number.
Published: [1954]–. There were two vols for 1972 identified as [1972A] and [1972B]. Notes: For citation of earlier vols see preceding entry.
Campbell, John, 1st Baron Campbell, *Reports ... Nisi Prius.*
Recommended citation: (year of decision) volume number Camp page number.
Published: 4 vols 1809–16. Covering: 1807–16. Notes: In 170 ER (vols 1–3) and 171 ER (vol. 4). Some bibliographies list later editions. Br & Ph 642.
Carpmael, W., *Law Reports of Patent Cases.*
Recommended citation: (year of decision) volume number Carp Pat Cas page number.
Published: 3 vols 1843–51. Covering: 1602–1842. Br & Ph 763.
Carrington, F.A., and Kirwan, A.V., *Reports ... Nisi Prius.*
Recommended citation: (year of decision) volume number Car & K page number.
Published: 3 vols 1845–53. Covering: 1843–53. Notes: In 174 ER (vol. 1) and 175 ER (vols 2 and 3). Br & Ph 643.
Carrington, F.A., and Marshman, J.R., *Reports ... Nisi Prius.*
Recommended citation: (year of decision) Car & M page number.
Published: 1 vol. 1843. Covering: 1840–2. Notes: In 174 ER. Br & Ph 644.
Carrington, F.A., and Payne, J., *Reports ... Nisi Prius.*
Recommended citation: (year of decision) volume number Car & P page number.
Published: 9 vols 1825–41. Covering: 1823–41. Notes: In 171 ER (vol. 1), 172 ER (vols 2–6) and 173 ER (vols 7–9). Br & Ph 645.
Carter, S., *Reports ... Common Pleas.*
Recommended citation: (year of decision) Cart page number.
Published: 1 vol. 1688. Covering: 1664–76. Notes: In 124 ER. Originally published under the author's initials only. Br & Ph 444.
Carthew, Thomas, *Reports ... King's Bench.*
Recommended citation: (year of decision) Carth page number.
Published: 1 vol. 1728, 2nd ed. 1741. Covering: 1686–1701. Notes: 2nd ed. in 90 ER. Br & Ph 553.
Cary, Sir George, *Reports ... Chancery.*
Recommended citation: (year of decision) Cary page number.
Published: 1 vol. 1650, 3rd ed. 1820. Covering: 1557–1602. Notes: 1st ed. in 21 ER. There is also an 1872 ed. Br & Ph 376.
*Cases and Resolutions ... Concerning Settlements and Removals.*
Recommended citation: (year of decision) Cas Sett page number.
Published: 4th ed. in 1 vol. 1742. Covering: 1685–1733. Notes: Also known as 'Cases of Settlement' and 'Cases of Settlements and Removals'. Br & Ph 775.
*Cases Argued and Adjudged in the Court of King's Bench ... [tempore] Hardwicke.*
Recommended citation: (year of decision) Cas t Hard page number.
Published: 1 vol. 1769, 2nd ed. by Thomas Lee 1815. Covering: 1733–8. Notes: 2nd ed. in 95 ER. Sometimes called 'Annaly's Hardwicke' after John Gore, 1st Baron Annaly, who prepared an index and who was thought to have been the reporter. Br & Ph 554.
*Cases Argued and Decreed in the High Court of Chancery.*
Recommended citation: (year of decision) volume number Ch Cas page number.
Published: 3 vols 1697–1702(?), 3rd ed. 1735. Covering: 1660–97. Notes: In 22 ER. Known as 'Cases in Chancery'. Volume 3 is sometimes called 'Select Cases in Chancery'. Br & Ph 377.
*Cases in Chancery*; see *Cases Argued and Decreed in the High Court of Chancery.*

*Cases in Equity during the Time of the Late Lord Chancellor Talbot.*
 Recommended citation: (year of decision) Cas t Talb page number.
 Published: 1 vol. 1741, 3rd ed. by John Griffith Williams 1792. Covering: 1733–8.
 Notes: 3rd ed. in 25 ER. The reporter was Alexander Forrester. Br & Ph 379.
*Cases of Practice in the Court of King's Bench.*
 Recommended citation: (year of decision) Cas Pr KB page number.
 Published: 1 vol. 1778. Covering: 'From the Reign of Queen Eliz. to the 14th of
 K. George III'.
*Cases of Settlement*; see *Cases and Resolutions ... Concerning Settlements and Removals.*
*Cases of Settlements and Removals*; see *Cases and Resolutions ... Concerning Settlements and Removals.*
*Cases Relating to Railway, Canal, and Joint Stock Companies*; see *Cases Relating to Railways and Canals.*
*Cases Relating to Railways and Canals.*
 Recommended citation: (year of decision) volume number Ry & Can Cas page number.
 Published: 7 vols 1840–55. Covering: 1835–54. Notes: Volume 7 titled *Cases Relating to Railway, Canal, and Joint Stock Companies*. Volumes 1 and 2 by Henry Iltid Nicholl, Thomas Hare and John Monson Carrow, vol. 3 by Carrow and Lionel Oliver, vol. 4 by Carrow, Oliver, Edward Beavan and Thomas E.P. Lefroy, vols 5–7 by Oliver, Beavan and Lefroy. Br & Ph 941.
*Cases tempore Northington*; see Eden, Robert Henley, *Reports ... Chancery.*
Casson, William Augustus, *Decisions of the Local Government Board.*
 Recommended citation: (year of decision) volume number Cass LGB page number.
 Published: 8 vols 1904–11. Notes: Volume 9 is an index.
*CCH Commercial Law Cases.*
 Recommended citation: [volume year] CLC page number.
*Central Criminal Court Sessions Papers.*
 Recommended citation: (year of decision) volume number CCC Sess Pap page number.
 Published: 158 vols 1834–1913. Br & Ph 718.
Chambers, T.G., and Pretty, A.H.F., *Finance (1909-10) Act 1910. Reports of Cases ... on the Interpretation of Part I.*
 Recommended citation: (year of decision) volume number Cha & P page number.
 Published: 2 vols 1913–14. Covering: 1911–14. Br & Ph 894.
*Chancery Appeal Cases*; see *Law Reports. Chancery Appeal Cases.* (1865–75).
*Chancery Division.* (1875–90); see *Law Reports. ... Chancery Division.* (1875–90).
*Chancery Division.* [1891]– ; see *Law Reports. Chancery Division.* [1891]– .
Charley, W.T., *Reports ... Judges' Chambers.*
 Recommended citation: (year of decision) volume number Char Cha Cas page number.
 Published: 2 vols 1876–7. Covering: 1875–6. Br & Ph 871.
Charley, W.T., *Reports of Cases ... Illustrative of the New System of Practice and Pleading.*
 Recommended citation: (year of decision) volume number Char Pr Cas page number.
 Published: 3 vols 1876–81. Covering: 1875–8. Br & Ph 872.
*Child and Family Law Quarterly.*
 Recommended citation: [volume year] CFLQ page number.
 Published: [1995]– . Notes: Previously titled *Journal of Child Law* (q.v.).

Chitty, J., *Reports ... Practice and Pleading.*
Recommended citation: (year of decision) volume number Chit page number.
Published: 2 vols 1820–3. Covering: 1770–1822. Br & Ph 359.

*Choyce Cases in Chancery.*
Recommended citation: (year of decision) Ch Cas in Ch page number.
Published: 1652, new ed. 1672. Covering: 1557–1606. Notes: 1672 ed. in 21 ER. There is also an 1870 ed. using the text of the 1672 ed. The reports were originally published as the second part of *The Practice of the High Court of Chancery Unfolded* so the first page of the reports is 105. Br & Ph 380.

*Civil Justice Quarterly.*
Recommended citation: (year of publication of article) volume number CJQ page number.
Published: 1982– .

Clark, C., and Finnelly, W., *Reports ... House of Lords.*
Recommended citation: (year of decision) volume number Cl & F page number.
Published: 12 vols 1835–47. Covering: 1831–46. Notes: In 6 ER (vols 1–3), 7 ER (vols 4–7) and 8 ER (vols 8–12). Br & Ph 526.

Clayton, John, *Reports and Pleas of Assises at Yorke.*
Recommended citation: (year of decision) Clay page number.
Published: 1 vol. 1651. Covering: 1631–50. Br & Ph 646.

Cleary, A.P., *Registration Cases.*
Recommended citation: (year of decision) Cleary Reg Cas page number.
Published: 1 vol. 1887. Covering: 1886–7. Br & Ph 1417.

Clifford, F., and Rickards, A.G., *Cases ... Court of Referees.* [*Locus Standi.*]
Recommended citation: (year of decision) volume number Clif & R page number.
Published: 3 vols 1876–85. Covering: 1873–84. Br & Ph 791.

Clifford, F., and Stephens, P.S., *Practice of the Court of Referees ... Locus Standi of Petitioners.*
Recommended citation: (year of decision) volume number Clif & S page number.
Published: 2 vols 1870–3. Covering: 1867–72. Br & Ph 792.

Clifford, H., *Report of the Two Cases of Controverted Elections of the Borough of Southwark.*
Recommended citation: (year of decision) Clif page number.
Published: 1 vol. 1797, [new ed.] 1802. Covering: 1796–7. Br & Ph 848.

Cobbett, William, and Howell, T.B., *Complete Collection of State Trials.*
Recommended citation: (year of decision) volume number St Tr column number.
Published: 33 vols 1809–26, 2nd ed. 1816–28. Covering: 1163–1820. Notes: Volumes 1–10 by Cobbett, vols. 11–21 by T.B. Howell, vols 22–33 by Thomas Jones Howell, vol. 34 is an index. Within the work the columns (2 to a page) are referred to as 'pages'. Cobbett and Howell's work superseded earlier works with the same title ed. by T. Salmon (4 vols 1719 and suppl.), S. Emlyn (10 vols 1730–66) and Hargrave (11 vols 1775–81) which were all in folio format whereas Cobbett and Howell's work is in octavo format.

Cockburn, Sir Alexander, and Rowe, William Carpenter, *Cases of Controverted Elections.*
Recommended citation: (year of decision) Cock & R page number.
Published: 1 vol. 1833. Covering: 1833. Br & Ph 849.

Coke, Sir Edward, *Book of Entries.*
Recommended abbreviation: Co Ent.
Published: 1 vol. 1614, 2nd ed. 1671.

Coke, Sir Edward, *Institutes of the Laws of England.*
Recommended citation: Co Litt for bk 1; volume number Co Inst for bk 2–4.
Published: 4 vols 1628–44, 7th ed. of vols 2–4 1797, many other eds of vol. 1.
Notes: Volume 1 subtitled Commentary upon Littleton (i.e., on Sir Thomas
Littleton's *Tenores Novelli*).
Coke, Sir Edward, *Reports.*
Recommended citation: (year of decision) volume number Co Rep folio number.
Published: 13 vols 1600–97, new ed. (in English) by John Henry Thomas and
John Farquhar Fraser 1826. Covering: 1572–1616. Notes: 1826 ed. in 76 ER (vols
1–4) and 77 ER (vols 5–13). Until recently Coke's *Reports* were known simply as
'the Reports'. The 1st ed. of vols 1–11 (1600–15) was in law French but the only
published eds of vols 12 and 13 have been in English transl. Br & Ph 555.
Colles, Richard, *Reports . . . Parliament.*
Recommended citation: (year of decision) Colles page number.
Published: 1 vol. 1789. Covering: 1697–1713. Notes: In 1 ER. Described on its
title-page as a supplement to Brown, Josiah, *Reports . . . Parliament.* Br & Ph 527.
Collyer, John, *Reports . . . Chancery.* [Vice-Chancellor.]
Recommended citation: (year of decision) volume number Coll page number.
Published: 2 vols 1845–7. Covering: 1844–6. Notes: In 63 ER. Br & Ph 667.
Coltman, F.J., *Registration Cases.*
Recommended citation: (year of decision) Colt page number.
Published: 1 vol. 1886. Covering: 1879–85. Br & Ph 878.
Comberbach, Roger, *Report of Several Cases . . . King's Bench.*
Recommended citation: (year of decision) Comb page number.
Published: 1 vol. 1724. Covering: 1685–99. Notes: In 90 ER. Br & Ph 556.
*Commercial Cases*; see *Reports of Commercial Cases.*
*Commercial Law Cases*; see *CCH Commercial Law Cases.*
*Commercial Law Reports.*
Recommended citation: [volume year] Com LR page number.
Published: [1980]–[1983]. The volume for [1980] has only 14 pages and is usually
bound with [1981]. Br & Ph 821.
*Common Bench Reports.*
Recommended citation: (year of decision) volume number CB page number.
Published: 18 vols 1846–56. Covering: 1845–56. Notes: In 135 ER (vols 1 and 2),
136 ER (vols 3–6), 137 ER (vols 7–9), 138 ER (vols 10–13) and 139 ER (vols 14–18).
The reporters were James Manning, T.C. Granger and John Scott (vols 1-8),
Manning and Scott (vol. 9) and Scott (vols 10–18). See also *Common Bench
Reports, New Series.* Br & Ph 445.
*Common Bench Reports, New Series.*
Recommended citation: (year of decision) volume number CB NS page number.
Published: 20 vols 1857–66. Covering: 1856–66. Notes: In 140 ER (vols 1–4), 141
ER (vols 5–8), 142 ER (vols 9–12), 143 ER (vols 13–16) and 144 ER (vols 17–20).
The reporter was John Scott. See also *Common Bench Reports.* Br & Ph 446.
*Common Law Reports.*
Recommended citation: (year of decision) volume number Com Law Rep page
number.
Published: 3 vols 1854–5. Covering: 1853–5. Br & Ph 317.
*Common Market Law Reports.*
Recommended citation: [volume year] number if there is more than 1 vol. for the
year CMLR page number; Dpage number for Restrictive Practices Supplement
in [1967]–[1978] 1; Mpage number for Merger Decisions in [1992]–[1994].

Published: [1962]– . Notes: [1962]–[1973] 1 vol. a year, [1974]–[1977] 2 vols a year, [1978]–[1987] 3 vols a year, [1988]–[1991] 4 vols a year, [1992]– 5 vols a year. Volumes 4 and 5 contain Antitrust Reports, called Antitrust Supplement in [1988]–[1990], Antitrust from [1991] on.

*Common Market Law Review.*
Recommended citation: (year of publication of article) volume number CML Rev page number.
Published: 1963– . Notes: The publisher suggests that the citation should be volume number CML Rev volume year without brackets page number. Volumes 1–6 are for 2 years each, 1963–4 to 1968–9.

*Common Pleas Cases.* (1865–75); see *Law Reports. Court of Common Pleas.* (1865–75).

*Common Pleas Division.* (1875–80); see *Law Reports. Common Pleas Division.* (1875–80).

*Company Lawyer.*
Recommended citation: (year of publication of article) volume number Co Law page number.
Published: 1980– .

*Computer Law and Practice.*
Recommended citation: (year of publication of article) volume number CL&P page number.
Published: 1984– .

*Computer Law and Security Report.*
Recommended citation: (year of decision or of publication of article) volume number (issue number in vols 1–6) CLSR page number.
Published: 1985– . Notes: Alternatively vols 1–6 may be cited by [volume year] issue number CLSR page number. Each of vols 1–6 is for two years from [1985-6] to [1990-1].

*Computers and Law.* 1974–89.
Recommended citation: (year of decision or of publication of article) Comp & Law issue number page number.
Published: 62 issues summer 1974–December 1989. Notes: For citation of later vols see next entry. Issues 1 and 2 were titled *Society for Computers and Law Limited Newsletter.*

*Computers and Law.* 1990– .
Recommended citation: (year of decision or of publication of article) volume number (issue number) Comp & Law page number.
Published: 1990– . Notes: For citation of earlier vols see preceding entry.

Comyns, Sir John, *A Digest of the Laws of England.*
Recommended abbreviation: Com Dig.
Published: 5 vols 1762–7, 5th ed. by Anthony Hammond in 8 vols 1822.

Comyns, Sir John, *Reports . . . King's Bench, Common Pleas and Exchequer.*
Recommended citation: (year of decision) volume number Com page number.
Published: 1 vol. 1744, 2nd ed. in 2 vols by Samuel Rose 1792. Covering: 1695–1741. Notes: 2nd ed. in 92 ER. The vols are paginated continuously, vol. 2 beginning on p. 422. Br & Ph 557.

Connor, Henry, and Lawson, James Anthony, *Reports . . . Chancery.* [Ireland.]
Recommended citation: (year of decision) volume number Con & L page number.
Published: 2 vols 1842–4. Covering: 1841–3. Br & Ph 1334.

Conroy, J., *Custodiam Reports.*
Recommended citation: (year of decision) Conr page number.
Published: 1 vol. 1795. Covering: 1652–1788. Br & Ph 873.

*Construction Law Journal.*
Recommended citation: (year of decision or of publication of article) volume number Const LJ page number.
Published: 1984– .
*Construction Law Reports.*
Recommended citation: (year of decision) volume number Con LR page number.
Published: 1985– .
*Consumer Credit Law Reports.*
Recommended citation: [volume year] CCLR page number.
Published: [1980]– . Notes: Published in loose-leaf form for filing in F.A.R. Bennion and Paul Dobson, *Consumer Credit Control.* Br & Ph 822.
*Consumer Law Journal.*
Recommended citation: [volume year] Consum LJ page number; CS page number for Current Survey section.
Published: [1993]– .
*Conveyancer.*
Recommended citation: (year of publication of article) volume number Conv page number.
Published: 21 vols 1916–36. Notes: Volume 22 is an index. Continued as *Conveyancer and Property Lawyer* (q.v.).
*Conveyancer and Property Lawyer.* 1937–77.
Recommended citation: (year of publication of article) volume number Conv NS page number.
Published: 41 vols 1937–77. Notes: Continuation of *Conveyancer* (q.v.). For citation of later vols see next entry.
*Conveyancer and Property Lawyer.* 1978– .
Recommended citation: [volume year] Conv page number.
Published: [1978]– . Notes: For citation of earlier vols see preceding entry.
Cooke, Sir George, *Reports ... Common Pleas.*
Recommended citation: (year of decision) Cooke page number.
Published: 1742, 2nd ed. 1747, 3rd ed. by Thomas Townsend Bucknill in 1 vol. 1872. Covering: 1706–47. Notes: 3rd ed. in 125 ER. Br & Ph 447.
Cooke, J.R., and Alcock, J.C., *Reports ... King's Bench ... in Ireland.*
Recommended citation: (year of decision) Cooke & A page number.
Published: 1 vol. 1835. Covering: 1833–4. Br & Ph 1359.
Cooper, Charles Purton, *Reports of Cases in Chancery Decided by Lord Cottenham.*
Recommended citation: (year of decision) volume number Coop t Cott page number.
Published: 2 vols 1846–8. Covering: 1846–8. Notes: In 47 ER. Br & Ph 424.
Cooper, Charles Purton, *Reports of Some Cases Adjudged in the Courts of the Lord Chancellor, Master of the Rolls and Vice-Chancellor.*
Recommended citation: (year of decision) Coop Pr Cas page number.
Published: 1 vol. 1841. Covering: 1837–8. Notes: In 47 ER. Also known as 'Cooper's Practice Cases'. Br & Ph 425.
Cooper, Charles Purton, *Select Cases Decided by Lord Brougham.*
Recommended citation: (year of decision) Coop t Brough page number.
Published: 1 vol. 1835. Covering: 1833–4. Notes: In 47 ER. Br & Ph 426.
Cooper, George, *Cases ... Chancery.*
Recommended citation: (year of decision) G Coop page number.
Published: 1 vol. 1815. Covering: 1792–1815. Notes: In 35 ER. Br & Ph 381.

*Cooper's Practice Cases*; see Cooper, Charles Purton, *Reports of Some Cases Adjudged in the Courts of the Lord Chancellor, Master of the Rolls and Vice-Chancellor.*

Corbett, V., and Daniell, E.R., *Reports of Cases of Controverted Elections.*
Recommended citation: (year of decision) Corb & D page number.
Published: 1 vol. 1821. Covering: 1819. Br & Ph 851.

Council of Europe, European Commission of Human Rights, *Decisions and Reports.*
Recommended citation: (year of decision) volume number DR page number.
Published: 1975– . Notes: After vol. 75 divided into two series with either -A or -B added to volume number. Series A contains original texts, series B translations.

*County Court Reports*; see *Reports of County Court Cases.*

*County Courts Chronicle.*
Recommended citation: (year of decision) volume number Co Ct Chr page number.
Published: 47 vols 1847–1920. Covering: 1847–1920. Notes: In vols 5, 7, 12 and 13 the law reports are separately paginated. Br & Ph 473.

Couper, Charles T., *Reports . . . High Court and Circuit Courts of Justiciary.*
Recommended citation: (year of decision) volume number Coup page number.
Published: 5 vols 1871–87. Covering: 1868–85. Br & Ph 1599.

Court of First Instance, *European Court Reports: Reports of European Community Staff Cases.*
Recommended citation: [volume year] ECR-SC I-A-page number, I-B-page number or II-page number.
Published: [1994]– .

Court of Justice of the European Coal and Steel Community, *Reports.*
Recommended citation: [volume year] ECR page number.
Published: [1954-6]–[1957-8]. Notes: Continued as Court of Justice of the European Communities, *Reports.*

Court of Justice of the European Communities, *Reports.*
Recommended citation: [volume year] ECR page number, from [1990] the page number is preceded by I- or II-.
Published: [1959]– . Notes: From [1990] in two sections: section I Court of Justice Reports, section II Court of First Instance Reports. Also called 'European Court Reports'. Continuation of Court of Justice of the European Coal and Steel Community, *Reports.*

Cowper, Henry, *Reports . . . King's Bench.*
Recommended citation: (year of decision) volume number Cowp page number.
Published: 1 vol. 1783, 2nd ed. in 2 vols 1800. Covering: 1774–8. Notes: In 98 ER. Paginated continuously, vol. 2 beginning on p. 420. Br & Ph 558.

Cox, E.W., *Reports of all the Cases . . . Relating to Magistrates.*
Recommended citation: (year of decision) volume number Cox MC page number.
Published: 27 vols 1862–1919. Covering: 1859–1919. Br & Ph 786.

Cox, E.W., *Reports of all the Cases . . . Relating to the Law of Joint-Stock Companies.*
Recommended citation: (year of decision) volume number Cox Jt Stk page number.
Published: 5 vols 1867–73. Covering: 1864–72. Br & Ph 823.

Cox, E.W., *Reports of Cases in Criminal Law.*
Recommended citation: (year of decision) volume number Cox CC page number.
Published: 31 vols 1846–1948. Notes: Volumes 1–13 ed. Cox, vol. 14 ed. Cox and John Thompson, vol. 15 ed. Thompson and R. Cunningham Glen, vols 16–20 ed.

Glen, vol. 21 ed. Basil Crump, vols 22–7 ed. W. de Bracy Herbert, vols 28–30 ed. J. Turnley Luscombe, vol. 31 ed. Luscombe and Robert Calburn.

Cox, E.W., and Atkinson, H.T., *Registration Appeal Cases.*
Recommended citation: (year of decision) Cox & A page number.
Published: 1 vol. 1846. Covering: 1843–6. Br & Ph 879.

Cox, E.W., Macrae, D.C., and Hertslet, C.J.B., *Reports of County Courts Cases.*
Recommended citation: (year of decision) volume number Cox M & H page number.
Published: 1 vol. 1852. Notes: For vols 2 and 3, see Saunders, T.W., and Macrae, D.C., *County Court Cases.* Br & Ph 472.

Cox, Samuel Compton, *Cases ... Equity.*
Recommended citation: (year of decision) volume number Cox page number.
Published: 2 vols 1816. Covering: 1783–96. Notes: In 29 ER (vol. 1) and 30 ER (vol. 2). Br & Ph 382.

*Cox's County Court Reports*; see *Reports of County Court Cases.*

*Cox's County Courts Equity and Bankruptcy Cases*; see *Reports of County Court Cases.*

Craig, R.D., and Phillips, T.J., *Reports ... Chancery.*
Recommended citation: (year of decision) Cr & Ph page number.
Published: 1 vol. 1842. Covering: 1840–1. Notes: In 41 ER. Br & Ph 383.

Craigmillar, Lord; see Gilmour, Sir John.

Crawford, G., and Dix, E.S., *Abridged Notes of Cases.*
Recommended citation: (year of decision) Craw & D Abr Cas page number.
Published: 1 vol. ? Covering: 1837–8. Br & Ph 1309.

Crawford, G., and Dix, E.S., *Reports ... Circuits, in Ireland.*
Recommended citation: (year of decision) volume number Craw & D page number.
Published: 3 vols 1841–7. Covering: 1839–46. Br & Ph 1348.

Cresswell, R.N., *Reports ... Court for Relief of Insolvent Debtors.*
Recommended citation: (year of decision) Cress page number.
Published: 1 vol. 1830. Covering: 1827–9. Br & Ph 691.

*Criminal Appeal Reports.* 1908–94.
Recommended citation: (year of decision) volume number Cr App R page number.
Published: 99 vols 1908–94. Notes: For citation of later vols see next entry. Br & Ph 719.

*Criminal Appeal Reports.* 1995– .
Recommended citation: [volume year] volume number Cr App R page number.
Published: [1995]– . Notes: 2 vols a year. For citation of earlier vols see preceding entry. Br & Ph 719.

*Criminal Appeal Reports (Sentencing).* 1979–95.
Recommended citation: (year of decision) volume number Cr App R (S) page number.
Published: 16 vols 1979–95. Notes: For citation of later vols see next entry. Br & Ph 720.

*Criminal Appeal Reports (Sentencing).* [1996]– .
Recommended citation: [volume year] volume number Cr App R (S) page number.
Published: [1996]– . Notes: 2 vols a year. For citation of earlier vols see preceding entry.

*Criminal Law Review.*
Recommended citation: [volume year] Crim LR page number.
Published: [1954]– .
Cripps, H.W., *Reports of New Cases . . . Relating to the Church and Clergy.*
Recommended citation: (year of decision) Cripps Cas page number.
Published: 1 vol. 1850. Covering: 1847–50. Br & Ph 737.
Croke, Sir George, *Reports . . . Charles [I].*
Recommended citation: (year of decision) Cro Car page number.
Published: 1 vol. 1657, 4th ed. by Thomas Leach 1792. Covering: 1625–41. Notes:
1792 ed. in 79 ER. Translated into English by Sir Harbottle Grimston from a law
French manuscript. See note to Croke, Sir George, *Reports . . . Elizabeth [I].* Br
& Ph 559.
Croke, Sir George, *Reports . . . Elizabeth [I].*
Recommended citation: (year of decision) Cro Eliz page number.
Published: 1 vol. 1661, 4th ed. by Thomas Leach 1790. Covering: 1582–1603.
Notes: 1790 ed. in 78 ER. Translated into English by Sir Harbottle Grimston
from a law French manuscript. Described on the title-page of the 1st ed. as 'The
First Part — though last publish't — of the Reports of Sir George Croke', the 2nd
and 3rd parts being Croke, Sir George, *Reports . . . James [I]* and Croke, Sir
George, *Reports . . . Charles [I].* Br & Ph 559.
Croke, Sir George, *Reports . . . James [I].*
Recommended citation: (year of decision) Cro Jac page number.
Published. 1 vol. 1659, 4th ed. by Thomas Leach 1791. Covering: 1603–25. Notes:
1791 ed. in 79 ER. Translated into English by Sir Harbottle Grimston from a law
French manuscript. See note to Croke, Sir George, *Reports . . . Elizabeth [I].* Br
& Ph 559.
Crompton, Charles, and Jervis, John, *Reports . . . Exchequer.*
Recommended citation: (year of decision) volume number Cr & J page number.
Published: 2 vols 1832–3. Covering: 1830–2. Notes: In 148 ER (vol. 1) and 149 ER
(vol. 2). Br & Ph 493.
Crompton, Charles, and Meeson, R., *Reports . . . Exchequer.*
Recommended citation: (year of decision) volume number Cr & M page number.
Published: 2 vols 1834–5. Covering: 1832–4. Notes: In 149 ER. Br & Ph 494.
Crompton, Charles, Meeson, R., and Roscoe, H., *Reports . . . Exchequer.*
Recommended citation: (year of decision) volume number Cr M & R page
number.
Published: 2 vols 1835–6. Covering: 1834–5. Notes: In 149 ER (vol. 1) and 150 ER
(vol. 2). Br & Ph 495.
*Crown Cases Reserved*; see *Law Reports. . . . Court for Crown Cases Reserved.*
*Crown Office Digest.*
Recommended citation: [volume year] COD page number.
Published: [1988]– . Notes: [1988] and [1989] are in 1 vol. with continuous
pagination, [1989] beginning at p. 161.
Cunningham, Timothy, *Reports . . . King's Bench.*
Recommended citation: (year of decision) Cun page number.
Published: 1 vol. 1766, 2nd ed. 1770. Covering: 1734–6. Notes: 1st ed. in 94 ER.
Originally published anonymously. There is also a 3rd ed. by Thomas Townsend
Bucknill 1871. Br & Ph 560.
*Current Law Consolidation.*
Recommended citation: (year of decision) CLC item number.
Published: 1 vol. 1952. Covering: 1947–51.

*Current Law Monthly Digest.*
Recommended citation: [volume year] issue number CL item number.
Published: [1947]– . Notes: 12 issues a year. Issues of *Current Law Monthly Digest* should not be cited after being replaced by a *Current Law Year Book.*
*Current Law Year Book.*
Recommended citation: [volume year] CLY item number.
Published: [1947]– . Notes: The vols for [1947]–[1951] have been replaced by *Current Law Consolidation* which should be cited instead.
Curteis, W.C., *Reports ... Ecclesiastical Courts.*
Recommended citation: (year of decision) volume number Curt page number.
Published: 3 vols 1840–4. Covering: 1834–44. Notes: In 163 ER. Page numbers in the appendix to vol. 3 are roman numerals. Br & Ph 482.


Dale, James Murray, *Legal Ritual.*
Recommended citation: (year of decision) Dale page number.
Published: 1 vol. 1871. Covering: 1868–71. Br & Ph 738.
Dalison, Sir William, *Reports*; see Benloe, William, *Reports*, and Dalison, Sir William, *Reports.*
Dalrymple, Sir David; see Hailes, Lord.
Dalrymple, Sir Hew, *Decisions of the Court of Session.*
Recommended citation: (year of decision) Dalr page number.
Published: 1 vol. 1758. Covering: 1698–1718. Br & Ph 1616.
Dalrymple, Sir James; see Stair, Lord.
Daniell, Edmund Robert, *Reports ... Exchequer.*
Recommended citation: (year of decision) Dan page number.
Published: 1 vol. 1824. Covering: 1817–23. Notes: Extracts in 159 ER. Br & Ph 496.
Danson, F.M., and Lloyd, J.H., *Mercantile Cases.*
Recommended citation: (year of decision) Dans & L page number.
Published: 1 vol. 1830. Covering: 1828–9. Br & Ph 826.
Davies, J., *Collection of the Most Important Cases Respecting Patents.*
Recommended citation: (year of decision) Dav Pat Cas page number.
Published: 1 vol. 1816. Covering: 1785–1816. Br & Ph 764.
Davies, Sir John, *Les Reports ... Courts del Roy en Ireland.*
Recommended citation: (year of decision) Dav page number.
Published: 1 vol. 1615, 3rd ed. 1674. Covering: 1604–12. Notes: 1674 ed. in 80 ER. In law French except for one case in English. An English translation was published in 1762. The author's name is sometimes spelt Davis (in the *English Reports*) or Davys. Br & Ph 1360.
Davison, H., and Merivale, H., *Reports ... Queen's Bench.*
Recommended citation: (year of decision) Dav & Mer page number.
Published: 1 vol. 1844. Covering: 1843–4. Br & Ph 626.
Davys, Sir John; see Davies, Sir John.
Day, Samuel Henry, *Election Cases.*
Recommended citation: (year of decision) Day page number.
Published: 1 vol. 1894. Covering: 1892–3. Br & Ph 852.
De Colyar, H.A., *Reports ... County Courts.*
Recommended citation: (year of decision) De Col page number.
Published: 1 vol. 1883. Covering: 1867–82. Br & Ph 474.
De Gex, John P., *Reports ... Bankruptcy.*
Recommended citation: (year of decision) volume number De G page number.
Published: 2 vols 1852. Covering: 1844–50. Br & Ph 692.

De Gex, John P., Fisher, F., and Jones, H. Cadman, *Bankruptcy Appeals.*
Recommended citation: (year of decision) De G F & J Bcy page number.
Published: 1 part 1862. Covering: 1859–61. Br & Ph 693.
De Gex, John P., Fisher, F., and Jones, H. Cadman, *Reports ... Chancery.*
Recommended citation: (year of decision) volume number De G F & J page number.
Published: 4 vols 1861–70. Covering: 1859–62. Notes: In 45 ER. Br & Ph 385.
De Gex, John P., and Jones, H. Cadman, *Reports ... Bankruptcy Appeals.*
Recommended citation: (year of decision) De G & J Bcy page number.
Published: 1 vol. 1861. Covering: 1857–9. Br & Ph 694.
De Gex, John P., and Jones, H. Cadman, *Reports ... Chancery.*
Recommended citation: (year of decision) volume number De G & J page number.
Published: 4 vols 1858–61. Covering: 1857–9. Notes: In 44 ER (vols 1–3) and 45 ER (vol. 4). Br & Ph 384.
De Gex, John P., Jones, H. Cadman, and Smith, R. Horton, *Reports ... Bankruptcy Appeals.*
Recommended citation: (year of decision) De G J & S Bcy page number.
Published: 1 vol. 1874. Covering: 1862–5. Br & Ph 695.
De Gex, John P., Jones, H. Cadman, and Smith, R. Horton, *Reports ... Chancery.*
Recommended citation: (year of decision) volume number De G J & S page number.
Published: 4 vols 1865–73. Covering: 1862–5. Notes: In 46 ER. Br & Ph 386.
De Gex, John P., Macnaghten, S., and Gordon, A., *Reports ... Bankruptcy Appeals.*
Recommended citation: (year of decision) De G M & G Bcy page number.
Published: 1 vol. 1851–7. Covering: 1851–5. Br & Ph 696.
De Gex, John P., Macnaghten, S., and Gordon, A., *Reports ... Chancery.*
Recommended citation: (year of decision) volume number De G M & G page number.
Published: 8 vols 1853–64. Covering: 1851–7. Notes: In 42 ER (vols 1 and 2), 43 ER (vols 3–6) and 44 ER (vols 7 and 8). Br & Ph 387.
De Gex, John P., and Smale, John, *Reports ... Chancery.* [Vice-Chancellor.]
Recommended citation: (year of decision) volume number De G & Sm page number.
Published: 5 vols 1849–53. Covering: 1846–52. Notes: In 63 ER (vol. 1) and 64 ER (vols 2–5). Br & Ph 668.
*De-rating and Rating Appeals.*
Recommended citation: (year of decision) volume number DRA page number.
Published: 29 vols n.d. (no later than 1934)–1962. Covering: 1930–61. Notes: Volumes 1–3 titled *English De-rating Appeals*, vols 4 and 5–? titled *De-rating Appeals: English and Scottish Appeals*, vols ?–17–? (before 29) titled *De-rating and Rating Appeals. English and Scottish.* Br & Ph 897, 911.
*De-rating Appeals*; see *De-rating and Rating Appeals.*
Deacon, E.E., *Reports ... Bankruptcy.*
Recommended citation: (year of decision) volume number Deac page number.
Published: 4 vols 1837–41. Covering: 1835–40. Br & Ph 697.
Deacon, E.E., and Chitty, E., *Reports ... Bankruptcy.*
Recommended citation: (year of decision) volume number Deac & Ch page number.
Published: 4 vols 1833–7. Covering: 1832–5. Br & Ph 698.
Deane, James Parker, and Swabey, M.C. Merttins, *Reports ... Ecclesiastical Courts.*

Recommended citation: (year of decision) Dea & Sw page number.
Published: 1 vol. 1858. Covering: 1855–7. Notes: In 164 ER. Br & Ph 483.
Dearsly, Henry Richard, *Crown Cases Reserved.*
Recommended citation: (year of decision) Dears page number.
Published: 1 vol. 1856. Covering: 1852–6. Notes: In 169 ER. Br & Ph 721.
Dearsly, Henry Richard, and Bell, Thomas, *Crown Cases Reserved.*
Recommended citation: (year of decision) Dears & B page number.
Published: 1 vol. 1858. Covering: 1856–8. Notes: In 169 ER. Br & Ph 722.
Deas, G., and Anderson, J., *Cases ... Court of Session [etc.].*
Recommended citation: (year of decision) volume number Deas & A page number.
Published: 5 vols 1829–33. Covering: 1829–32. Br & Ph 1650.
*Decisions ... Admiralty during the Time of Sir George Hay, and of Sir James Marriott.*
Recommended citation: (year of decision) Hay & M page number.
Published: 1 vol. 1801. Covering: 1776–9. Notes: In 165 ER. Br & Ph 351.
*Decisions and Reports of the European Commission of Human Rights*; see Council of Europe, European Commission of Human Rights, *Decisions and Reports.*
*Decisions of the Court of Session*; see *Faculty Collection. Old Series; Faculty Decisions. Octavo Series.*
*Decisions of the English Judges during the Usurpation.*
Recommended citation: (year of decision) Eng Judg page number.
Published: 1 vol. 1762. Covering: 1655–61. Br & Ph 1622.
*Decisions of the First and Second Divisions of the Court of Session*; see *Faculty Collection. New Series.*
Delane, William Frederick Augustus, *Collection of Decisions in the Courts for Revising the Lists of Electors.*
Recommended citation: (year of decision) Del page number.
Published: 1 vol. 1834, 2nd ed. 1836. Covering: 1832–5. Br & Ph 880.
Denison, Stephen Charles, *Crown Cases Reserved.*
Recommended citation: (year of decision) volume number Den page number.
Published: 2 vols 1850–2. Covering: 1844–52. Notes: In 169 ER. Volume 2 was completed by Robert Rouiere Pearce. Br & Ph 723.
*Denning Law Journal.*
Recommended citation: [volume year] Denning LJ page number.
Published: [1986]– .
Department of Health and Social Security, *Reported Decisions of the Commissioner under the National Insurance and Family Allowances Acts.*
Recommended citation: case number for cases before 1951; R followed (without a space) by abbreviation for series report number for cases from 1951.
Published: 7 vols 1955–78. Covering: 1948–76. Notes: The series are: (A) (attendance allowance from 1972); (F) (child benefit from 1960); (G) (maternity benefit, widow's benefit, guardian's allowance, child's special allowance and death grant); (P) (retirement pension); (S) (sickness benefit, invalidity benefit and non-contributory invalidity pension); (U) (unemployment benefit). Report numbers are in the form 1/69, 2/69 etc., where 69 means the case was in 1969. Case numbers are in the same form prefixed by C (for English cases), CS (for Scottish cases) or CW (for Welsh cases) and the series letter. Volumes 1 and 2 titled *Reported Decisions of the Commissioner under the National Insurance Acts.* The department responsible for vols 1 and 2 was the Ministry of Pensions and National Insurance. No responsible department is listed on the title-pages

of vols 3 and 4. Before a bound volume was published, each decision was published separately with the same form of citation. For citation of later vols see Department of Social Security, *Reported Decisions of the Social Security Commissioner*. Br & Ph 927.

Department of Health and Social Security, *Reported Decisions of the Commissioner under the National Insurance (Industrial Injuries) Acts*; see Department of Health and Social Security, *Reported Decisions of the Commissioner under the Social Security and National Insurance (Industrial Injuries) Acts*.

Department of Health and Social Security, *Reported Decisions of the Commissioner under the Social Security and Child Benefit Acts*; see Department of Social Security, *Reported Decisions of the Social Security Commissioner*.

Department of Health and Social Security, *Reported Decisions of the Commissioner under the Social Security and National Insurance (Industrial Injuries) Acts*. Recommended citation: case number for cases before 1951; R(I) report number for cases from 1951.

Published: 7 vols 1955–78. Covering: 1948–76. Notes: Report numbers are in the form 1/69, 2/69 etc., where 69 means the case was in 1969. Case numbers are in the same form prefixed by CI (for English cases), CSI (for Scottish cases) or CWI (for Welsh cases). Volumes 1–6 titled *Reported Decisions of the Commissioner under the National Insurance (Industrial Injuries) Acts* (same form of citation). The department responsible for vols 1 and 2 was the Ministry of Pensions and National Insurance. No responsible department is listed on the title-pages of vols 3 and 4. Before a bound volume was published, each decision was published separately with the same form of citation. For citation of later vols see Department of Social Security, *Reported Decisions of the Social Security Commissioner*. Br & Ph 928.

Department of Social Security, *Reported Decisions of the Social Security Commissioner*. Recommended citation: R followed (without a space) by abbreviation for series report number

Published: 1980 (vol. 8)– . Covering: 1977– . Notes: Report numbers are in the form 1/89, 2/89 etc., where 89 means the case was in 1989. The series are: (A) (attendance allowance); (F) (child benefit); (FC) (family credit from 1990); (FIS) (family income supplements from 1981); (G) (maternity benefit, widow's benefit, invalid care allowance from 1986, guardian's allowance, child's special allowance and, until 1984, death grant); (I) (industrial injuries); (IS) (income support from 1990); (M) (mobility allowance from 1978); (P) (retirement pension); (S) (sickness benefit, invalidity benefit, non-contributory invalidity pension until 1985 and, from 1986, severe disablement allowance); (SB) (supplementary benefit from 1981); (SSP) (statutory sick pay from 1985); (U) (unemployment benefit). Volume 8 titled *Reported Decisions of the Commissioner under the Social Security and Child Benefit Acts*. The department responsible for vols 8–11 was the Department of Health and Social Security. Before a bound volume is published, each decision is published separately with the same form of citation. For citation of earlier vols see Department of Health and Social Security, *Reported Decisions of the Commissioner under the National Insurance and Family Allowances Acts*; Department of Health and Social Security, *Reported Decisions of the Commissioner under the Social Security and National Insurance (Industrial Injuries) Acts*. Br & Ph 927.

Dickens, John, *Reports . . . Chancery*. Recommended citation: (year of decision) Dick page number.

Published: 2 vols 1803. Covering: 1559–1798. Notes: In 21 ER. The vols are paginated continuously, vol. 2 beginning at p. 431. Br & Ph 388.

Diprose, J., and Gammon, J., *Reports of Law Cases Affecting Friendly Societies.*
Recommended citation: (year of decision) D & G page number.
Published: 1 vol. 1897. Covering: 1801–97. Br & Ph 744.

Dirleton, Lord (Sir John Nisbet), *Decisions of the Lords of Council and Session.*
Recommended citation: (year of decision) Dirl page number.
Published: 1 vol. 1698. Covering: 1665–77. Br & Ph 1617.

*Discrimination Case Law Digest.*
Recommended citation: (year of decision) DCLD issue number.

Dodson, John, *Reports . . . Admiralty.*
Recommended citation: (year of decision) volume number Dods page number; App page number for appendices.
Published: 2 vols 1815–28. Covering: 1811–22. Notes: In 165 ER. Page numbers in the appendix to vol. 1 are roman numerals. Br & Ph 348.

Donnell, R., *Reports . . . Irish Land Courts.*
Recommended citation: (year of decision) Don Ir Land Cas page number.
Published: 1 vol. 1873, 2nd ed. 1876. Covering: 1871–6. Br & Ph 1401.

Donnelly, Ross, *Minutes of Cases . . . Chancery.*
Recommended citation: (year of decision) Donn page number.
Published: 1 vol. 1837. Covering: 1836–7. Notes: In 47 ER. Br & Ph 427.

Douglas, Sylvester, Baron Glenbervie, *History of the Cases of Controverted Elections.*
Recommended citation: (year of decision) volume number Doug El Cas page number.
Published: 4 vols 1775–7, 2nd ed. 1802. Covering: 1774–6. Br & Ph 853.

Douglas, Sylvester, Baron Glenbervie, *Reports . . . King's Bench.*
Recommended citation: (year of decision) volume number Doug KB page number.
Published: 4th ed. in 4 vols by William Frere and Henry Roscoe 1813–31. Earlier eds (1st 1783) were of vols 1 and 2 only. Covering: 1778–85. Notes: In 99 ER. Volumes 3 and 4 are by William Frere and Henry Roscoe. Br & Ph 561.

Dow, P., *Reports . . . House of Lords.*
Recommended citation: (year of decision) volume number Dow page number.
Published: 6 vols 1814–19. Covering: 1812–18. Notes: In 3 ER. Br & Ph 528.

Dow, P., and Clark, C., *Reports . . . House of Lords.*
Recommended citation: (year of decision) volume number Dow & Cl page number.
Published: 2 vols 1830–2. Covering: 1827–32. Notes: In 6 ER. Volume 1 was by Dow alone. Br & Ph 529.

Dowling, A.S., *Reports . . . [Bail Court].*
Recommended citation: (year of decision) volume number Dowl Pr Cas page number.
Published: 9 vols 1833–42. Covering: 1830–41. Br & Ph 360.

Dowling, A.S., and Dowling, V., *Reports . . . [Bail Court].*
Recommended citation: (year of decision) volume number Dowl NS page number.
Published: 2 vols 1841–3. Covering: 1841–3. Br & Ph 361.

Dowling, A.S., and Lowndes, J.J., *Reports . . . [Bail Court].*
Recommended citation: (year of decision) volume number Dowl & L page number.
Published: 7 vols 1845–51. Covering: 1843–9. Br & Ph 362.

Dowling, J., and Ryland, A., *Cases ... Nisi Prius.*
Recommended citation: (year of decision) Dowl & Ry NP page number.
Published: 1 vol. 1823. Covering: 1822–3. Notes: In 171 ER. Br & Ph 647.

Dowling, J., and Ryland, A., *Reports of Cases Argued ... King's Bench.*
Recommended citation: (year of decision) volume number Dowl & Ry KB page number.
Published: 9 vols 1822–31. Covering: 1821–7. Br & Ph 627.

Dowling, J., and Ryland, A., *Reports of Cases Relating to the Duty and Office of Magistrates.*
Recommended citation: (year of decision) volume number Dowl & Ry MC page number.
Published: 4 vols 1823–31. Covering: 1822–7. Notes: A 2nd ed. of vol.1, 1835, is listed by Breem and Phillips. Br & Ph 802.

Drewry, C. Stewart, *Reports ... Chancery.* [Vice-Chancellor.]
Recommended citation: (year of decision) volume number Drew page number.
Published: 4 vols 1853–60. Covering: 1852–9. Notes: In 61 ER (vols 1–3) and 62 ER (vol. 4). Br & Ph 669.

Drewry, C. Stewart, and Smale, J. Jackson, *Reports ... Chancery.* [Vice-Chancellor.]
Recommended citation: (year of decision) volume number Drew & Sm page number.
Published: 2 vols 1862–7. Covering: 1859–65. Notes: In 62 ER. Br & Ph 670.

Drinkwater, W.L., *Reports ... Common Pleas.*
Recommended citation: (year of decision) Drink page number.
Published: 1 vol. 1841. Covering: 1840–1. Br & Ph 462.

Drury, W.B., *Reports ... Chancery, during the time of Lord Chancellor Sugden.* [Ireland.]
Recommended citation: (year of decision) Dr t Sug page number.
Published: 1 vol. 1851. Covering: 1843–4. Br & Ph 1335.

Drury, W.B., *Select Cases ... Chancery, during the time of Lord Chancellor Napier.* [Ireland.]
Recommended citation: (year of decision) Dr t Nap page number.
Published: 1 vol. 1860. Covering: 1858–9. Br & Ph 1336.

Drury, W.B., and Walsh, F.W., *Reports ... Chancery.* [Ireland.]
Recommended citation: (year of decision) volume number Dr & Wal page number.
Published: 2 vols 1839–42. Covering: 1837–40. Br & Ph 1337.

Drury, W.B., and Warren, R.R., *Reports ... Chancery.* [Ireland.]
Recommended citation: (year of decision) volume number Dr & War page number.
Published: 4 vols 1843–4. Covering: 1841–3. Br & Ph 1338.

*Dublin University Law Journal.*
Recommended citation: (year of publication of article) volume number DULJ page number.

Duncan, J.A., *Annual Review of Mercantile Cases.*
Recommended citation: (year of decision) volume number Dunc Mer Cas page number.
Published: 2 vols 1886–7. Covering: 1885–6. Br & Ph 827.

Dunlop, A., *Cases ... Court of Session.* [Session Cases, 2nd series.]
Recommended citation: (year of decision) volume number D page number; (HL) page number for House of Lords cases in vols 13–24.
Published: 24 vols 1839–62. Covering: 1838–62. Br & Ph 1618.

Dunning, John, 1st Baron Ashburton, *Reports ... King's Bench.*
Recommended citation: (year of decision) Dunn page number.
Published: 1 vol. 1885. Covering: 1753–4. Br & Ph 628.
Durie, Lord (Sir Alexander Gibson), *Decisions of the Lords of Council and Session.*
Recommended citation: (year of decision) Durie page number.
Published: 1 vol. 1690. Covering: 1621–42. Br & Ph 1619.
Durnford, C., and East, E.H., *Term Reports*; see *Term Reports.*
Dyer, Sir James, *Reports.*
Recommended citation: (year of decision) Dy folio number.
Published: 1 vol. in law French 1585, English transl. by John Vaillant in 3 vols 1794 reproducing foliation of French original. Covering: 1513–82. Notes: Vaillant's transl. in 73 ER. Br & Ph 562.

Eagle, F.K., and Younge, E., *Collection ... of Cases ... Relating to Tithes.*
Recommended citation: (year of decision) volume number Eag & Y page number.
Published: 4 vols 1826. Covering: 1204–1825. Br & Ph 934.
East, Edward Hyde, *Reports ... King's Bench.*
Recommended citation: (year of decision) volume number East page number.
Published: 16 vols 1801–14. Covering: 1800–12. Notes: In 102 ER (vols 1–6), 103 ER (vols 7–11) and 104 ER (vols 12–16). Br & Ph 563.
East, Edward Hyde, *Treatise of the Pleas of the Crown.*
Recommended citation: volume number East PC page number.
Published: 2 vols 1803 reprinted 1972. Notes: The vols are paginated continuously, vol. 2 beginning at p. 481.
Eden, Robert Henley, *Reports ... Chancery.*
Recommended citation: (year of decision) volume number Eden page number.
Published: 1818, 2nd ed., 2 vols, 1827. Covering: 1757–66. Notes: In 28 ER. From manuscripts of the Earl of Northington LC and so also known as 'Cases *tempore* Northington' and used to be cited as C t N. Br & Ph 389.
Edgar, John, *Decisions of the Court of Session.*
Recommended citation: (year of decision) Edgar page number.
Published: 1 vol. 1742. Covering: 1724–5. Notes: Known as 'Edgar and Falconer' when bound with Falconer, David, *Decisions of the Court of Session.* Br & Ph 1620.
Edwards, Thomas, *Reports ... Admiralty.*
Recommended citation: (year of decision) Edw page number.
Published: 1 vol. 1812. Covering: 1808–12. Notes: In 165 ER. Pages in the appendix are numbered with roman numerals in the *English Reports* but were originally unnumbered. Br & Ph 349.
Elchies, Lord (Patrick Grant), *Decisions of the Court of Session.*
Recommended citation: (year of decision) volume number Elchies page number.
Published: 2 vols 1813. Covering: 1733–54. Br & Ph 1621.
Ellis, Thomas Flower, and Blackburn, Colin, *Reports ... Queen's Bench.*
Recommended citation: (year of decision) volume number El & Bl page number.
Published: 8 vols 1853–9. Covering: 1852–8. Notes: In 118 ER (vols 1–3), 119 ER (vols 4–7) and 120 ER (vol. 8). Br & Ph 564.
Ellis, Thomas Flower, Blackburn, Colin, and Ellis, Francis, *Reports ... Queen's Bench.*
Recommended citation: (year of decision) El Bl & El page number.
Published: 1 vol. 1860. Covering: 1858. Notes: In 120 ER. Br & Ph 565.

Ellis, Thomas Flower, and Ellis, Francis, *Reports ... Queen's Bench.*
Recommended citation: (year of decision) volume number El & El page number.
Published: 3 vols 1863–7. Covering: 1858–61. Notes: In 120 ER (vol. 1) and 121
ER (vols 2 and 3). Br & Ph 566.
*Employment Law Report.*
Recommended citation: [volume year] ELR page number.
Published: [1990]– . Notes: Volumes for [1990]–[1993] titled *Employment Law
Reports* (same form of citation).
*English and Irish Appeal Cases.* (1866–75); scc *Law Reports. English and Irish
Appeal Cases.* (1866–75).
*English De-rating Appeals*; see *De-rating and Rating Appeals.*
*English Reports.*
Recommended citation: (year of decision) full reference for original report,
volume number ER page number.
Published: 176 vols 1900–30. Notes: For example, *Foss* v *Harbottle* (1843) 2 Hare
461, 67 ER 189. Volumes 177 and 178 (1932) contain a table of cases. Br & Ph 318.
*Entertainment and Media Law Reports.*
Recommended citation: [volume year] EMLR page number.
Published: [1993]– .
*Entertainment Law Review.*
Recommended citation: [volume year] Ent LR page number; E-page number for
News Section.
Published: [1990]– .
*Environmental Law Reports.*
Recommended citation: [volume year] Env LR page number; Dpage number for
Digest.
Published: [1993]– .
*Environmental Liability.*
Recommended citation: [volume year] Env Liability page number; CSpage
number for Current Survey section.
Published: [1993]– .
*Equity Cases*; see *Law Reports. Equity Cases.* (1865–75).
*Equity Cases Abridged*; see *General Abridgment of Cases in Equity.*
*Equity Reports.*
Recommended citation: (year of decision) volume number Eq Rep page number.
Published: 3 vols 1854–5. Covering: 1853–5. Br & Ph 320.
'Espinasse, Isaac, *Reports ... Nisi Prius.*
Recommended citation: (year of decision) volume number Esp page number.
Published: 6 vols 1796–1811, 2nd ed. of vols 1 and 2 1801–3, new ed. of vol. 3 1819
with pagination of unknown 2nd ed. indicated. Covering: 1793–1807. Notes: In
170 ER (using 1801 ed. of vol. 1, 1803 ed. of vol. 2 and 1819 ed. of vol. 3 but with
pagination of unknown 2nd ed.). Some copies of the 2nd ed. of vol. 1 are dated
1803. Pagination of vols 1 and 2 is continuous, vol. 2 beginning at p. 465. The
apostrophe is often omitted from the author's surname. Br & Ph 648.
*Estates Gazette.* 1858–1987.
Recommended citation: (year of decision or of publication of article) volume
number EG page number.
Published: 284 vols 1858–1987. Notes: For citation of later vols see next entry.
*Estates Gazette.* 1988– .
Recommended citation: [volume year] issue number EG page number.
Published: [1988]– . Notes: For citation of earlier vols see preceding entry.

*Estates Gazette Case Summaries.*
 Recommended citation: [volume year] EGCS case number.
 Published: [1988]– .
*Estates Gazette Digest of Land and Property Cases.*
 Recommended citation: [volume year] EGD page number.
 Published: [1901]–[1984]. Br & Ph 778.
*Estates Gazette Law Reports.*
 Recommended citation: [volume year] volume number EGLR page number.
 Published: [1975]– . Notes: 2 vols a year. Volumes for years before [1985]
 published retrospectively back to [1975] so far. Br & Ph 779.
*Estates Gazette Planning Law Reports.*
 Recommended citation: [volume year] volume number PLR page number.
 Published: [1988]– . Notes: 3 vols a year.
*European Assurance Arbitration before Lord Westbury*; see Marrack, R., *European Assurance Arbitration before Lord Westbury.*
*European Commercial Cases.*
 Recommended citation: [volume year] ECC page number.
 Published: [1978]– .
*European Community Cases.*
 Recommended citation: [volume year] volume number CEC page number.
 Published: [1989]– . Notes: 2 vols a year.
*European Competition Law Review.*
 Recommended citation: [volume year] ECLR page number.
 Published: [1980]– .
*European Court Reports*; see Court of Justice of the European Communities, *Reports.*
*European Current Law Monthly Digest.*
 Recommended citation: [volume year] issue number Euro CL item number.
 Published: [1992]– . Notes: 12 issues a year. Issues of *European Current Law Monthly Digest* should not be cited after being replaced by a *European Current Law Year Book.*
*European Current Law Year Book.*
 Recommended citation: [volume year] Euro CLY item number.
 Published: [1992]– .
*European Human Rights Reports.*
 Recommended citation: (year of decision) volume number EHRR page number.
 Published: 1980– .
*European Intellectual Property Review.*
 Recommended citation: [volume year] EIPR page number; D-page number for News Section.
 Published: [1978]– . Notes: The publisher's suggested form of citation gives the issue number after [volume year] but this is superfluous.
*European Law Review.*
 Recommended citation: (year of publication of article) volume number EL Rev page number.
 Published: 1976– .
*European Patent Office Reports.*
 Recommended citation: [volume year] EPOR page number.
 Published: [1986]– . Notes: A supplementary set of 3 vols was published in 1989, cited [1979-85] EPOR vol. A page number, [1979-85] EPOR vol. B page number, [1979-85] EPOR vol. C page number, though the vols are paginated continuously, vol. B beginning on p. 241 and vol. C beginning on p. 629.

*European Public Law.*
Recommended citation: [volume year] EPL page number.
Published: [1995]– .
*Exchequer Cases.* (1840–53); see *Reports . . . Court of Exchequer, Scotland.*
*Exchequer Cases.* (1865–75); see *Law Reports. Court of Exchequer.* (1865–75).
*Exchequer Division.* (1875–80); see *Law Reports. Exchequer Division.* (1875–80).
*Exchequer Reports.*
Recommended citation: (year of decision) volume number Ex page number.
Published: 11 vols 1849–56. Covering: 1847–56. Notes: In 154 ER (vols 1–4), 155 ER (vols 5–8) and 156 ER (vols 9–11). The reporters were W.N. Welsby, E.T. Hurlstone and J. Gordon (vols 1–9), E.T. Hurlstone and J. Gordon (vols 10 and 11). Br & Ph 497.

*Faculty Collection. New Series.*
Recommended citation: date of decision without brackets FC.
Published: c. 7 vols (depending on binding) 1811–28. Covering: 1808–25. Notes: Also called 'Decisions of the First and Second Divisions of the Court of Session'; 'Faculty Decisions. New Series'; 'Faculty of Advocates Reports. New Series'. Br & Ph 1623.
*Faculty Collection. Old Series.*
Recommended citation: date of decision without brackets FC.
Published: c. 14 vols (depending on binding) 1760–1810. Covering: 1752–1808. Notes: Also called 'Decisions of the Court of Session'; 'Faculty Decisions. Old Series'; 'Faculty of Advocates Reports. Old Series'; 'Old Faculty Reports'. Br & Ph 1624.
*Faculty Decisions. New Series*; see *Faculty Collection. New Series.*
*Faculty Decisions. Octavo Series.*
Recommended citation: (year of decision) volume number Fac Dec page number.
Published: 16 vols 1826–41. Covering: 1825–41. Notes: Also called 'Decisions of the Court of Session'; 'Faculty of Advocates Reports. Octavo Series'. Br & Ph 1625.
*Faculty Decisions. Old Series*; see *Faculty Collection. Old Series.*
*Faculty of Advocates Reports. New Series*; see *Faculty Collection. New Series.*
*Faculty of Advocates Reports. Octavo Series*; see *Faculty Decisions. Octavo Series.*
*Faculty of Advocates Reports. Old Series*; see *Faculty Collection. Old Series.*
Falconer, David, *Decisions of the Court of Session.*
Recommended citation: (year of decision) volume number D Falc page number.
Published: 2 vols 1753. Covering: 1744–51. Notes: Known as 'Edgar and Falconer' when bound with Edgar, John, *Decisions of the Court of Session.* Br & Ph 1626.
Falconer, T., and Fitzherbert, E.H., *Cases of Controverted Elections.*
Recommended citation: (year of decision) Falc & F page number.
Published: 1 vol. 1839. Covering: 1835–8. Br & Ph 854.
*Family Court Reporter.*
Recommended citation: [volume year] number if there is more than 1 vol. for the year FCR page number.
Published: [1987]– . Notes: [1987]–[1991] 1 vol. a year, [1992] and [1993] 2 vols a year, [1994]– 3 vols a year.
*Family Division*; see *Law Reports. Family Division.* [1972]– .

*Family Law*. 1971–83.
Recommended citation: (year of decision or of publication of article) volume number Fam Law page number.
Published: 13 vols 1971–83. Notes: For citation of later vols see next entry.
*Family Law*. 1984– .
Recommended citation: [volume year] Fam Law page number.
Published: [1984]– . Notes: For citation of earlier vols see preceding entry.
*Family Law Reports*. 1980–3.
Recommended citation: (year of decision) volume number FLR page number.
Published: 4 vols 1980–3. Notes: For citation of later vols see next entry. Br & Ph 742.
*Family Law Reports*. 1984– .
Recommended citation: [volume year] number if there is more than 1 vol. for the year FLR page number.
Published: [1984]– . Notes: [1984] and [1985] 1 vol. a year, [1986]– 2 vols a year. For citation of earlier vols see preceding entry. Br & Ph 742.
Farrant, R.D., *Digest of Manx Cases*.
Recommended citation: (year of decision) Farrant page number.
Published: 1 vol. 1948. Covering: 1927–47. Br & Ph 1427.
Fawcett, J.H., *Treatise on the Court of Referees*.
Recommended citation: (year of decision) Fawc Ref page number.
Published: 1 vol. 1866. Br & Ph 793.
Fergusson, James, *Reports . . . Consistorial Court of Scotland*.
Recommended citation: (year of decision) Ferg Cons page number.
Published: 1 vol. 1817. Covering: 1691–1817. Br & Ph 1678.
Fergusson, Sir James; see Kilkerran, Lord.
*Financial Law Reports*.
Recommended citation: volume year without brackets FLR page number.
Published: 1985–1989.
Finch, Gerard Brown, *A Selection of Cases on the English Law of Contract*.
Recommended citation: (year of decision) Finch Cas Contr page number.
Published: 1 vol. 1886, 2nd ed. by R.T. Wright and W.W. Buckland 1896.
Finlay, J., *Digest . . . Irish Reported Cases*.
Recommended citation: (year of decision) Finl Dig page number.
Published: 1 vol. 1830. Covering: 1769–71 (original reports). Br & Ph 1338A.
Fitz-Gibbons, John, *Reports . . . King's Bench*.
Recommended citation: (year of decision) Fitzg page number.
Published: 1 vol. 1732. Covering: 1728–33. Notes: In 94 ER. The author's name is also spelt Fitzgibbon. Br & Ph 567.
Fitzgibbon, H.M., *Irish Land Reports*.
Recommended citation: (year of decision) volume number Fitzg Land R page number.
Published: 25 vols 1897–1920. Br & Ph 1407.
Fitzgibbon, H.M., *Irish Registration Appeal Cases*.
Recommended citation: (year of decision) Fitzg Reg Cas page number.
Published: 1 vol. 1895. Covering: 1894. Br & Ph 1418.
Fitzgibbon, John; see Fitz-Gibbons, John.
Flanagan, S.W., and Kelly, C., *Reports . . . Rolls Court*. [Ireland.]
Recommended citation: (year of decision) Fl & K page number.
Published: 1 vol. 1843. Covering: 1840–2. Br & Ph 1371.
*Fleet Street Patent Law Reports*; see *Fleet Street Reports*.

*Fleet Street Reports.*
Recommended citation: [volume year] FSR page number.
Published: [1963]–. Notes: Volumes for [1963] to [1977] titled *Fleet Street Patent Law Reports* (same form of citation). Br & Ph 765.

Foley, Robert, *Laws Relating to the Poor ... with Cases.*
Recommended citation: (year of decision) Fol PL Cas page number.
Published: 1 vol. 1739, 4th ed. 1756. Covering: 1556–1730. Br & Ph 923.

*Folio Dictionary*; see Kames, Lord (Henry Home), and Woodhouselee, Lord (Alexander Fraser Tytler), *Decisions in the Court of Session ... in the Form of a Dictionary.*

Fonblanque, John William Martin, *Reports ... Courts of the Commissioners in Bankruptcy.*
Recommended citation: (year of decision) Fonbl page number.
Published: 1 vol. 1851–2. Covering: 1849–52. Br & Ph 699.

Forbes, W., *Journal of the Session Containing the Decisions of the Lords of Council and Session.*
Recommended citation: (year of decision) Forbes page number.
Published: 1 vol. 1714, [new ed.] 1763. Covering: 1705–13. Br & Ph 1627.

Forrest, Robert, *Reports ... Exchequer.*
Recommended citation: (year of decision) Forr page number.
Published: 1 vol. 1802. Covering: 1800–1. Notes: 1802 ed. in 145 ER. There is also an 1884 ed. Br & Ph 498.

Forsyth, William, *Cases and Opinions on Constitutional Law.*
Recommended citation: (year of decision) Fors Cas & Op page number.
Published: 1 vol. 1869.

Fortescue Aland, Sir John, 1st Baron Fortescue of Credan, *Reports ... Courts of Westminster-Hall.*
Recommended citation: (year of decision) Fort page number.
Published: 1 vol. 1748. Covering: 1695–1738. Notes: In 92 ER. Br & Ph 568.

Foster, Sir Michael, *Report of Some Proceedings ... and of Other Crown Cases.*
Recommended citation: (year of decision) Fost page number.
Published: 1 vol. 1762, 3rd ed. by Michael Dodson 1792. Covering: 1743–61. Notes: Extracts from 3rd ed. in 168 ER. Br & Ph 724.

Foster, T. Campbell, and Finlason, W.F., *Reports ... Nisi Prius.*
Recommended citation: (year of decision) volume number F & F page number.
Published: 4 vols 1860–7. Covering: 1856–67. Notes: In 175 ER (vols 1 and 2) and 176 ER (vols 3 and 4). Br & Ph 649.

Fountainhall, Lord (Sir John Lauder), *Decisions of the Lords of Council and Session.*
Recommended citation: (year of decision) volume number Fount page number.
Published: 2 vols 1759–61. Covering: 1678–1712. Br & Ph 1628.

Fox, J.S., and Smith, C.L., *Registration Cases.*
Recommended citation: (year of decision) Fox & S Reg page number.
Published: 1 vol. 1895. Covering: 1886–95. Br & Ph 881.

Fox, M.C., and Smith, T.B.C., *Reports ... King's Bench.* [Ireland.]
Recommended citation: (year of decision) volume number Fox & S page number.
Published: 2 vols 1825. Covering: 1822–4. Br & Ph 1361.

Fraser, H.J.E., *Cases ... Court of Session, Court of Justiciary and House of Lords.* [Session Cases, 5th series.]
Recommended citation: (year of decision) volume number F page number; (J) page number for Justiciary cases; (HL) page number for House of Lords cases.
Published: 8 vols 1899–1906. Covering: 1898–1906. Br & Ph 1629.

Fraser, S., *Reports . . . Cases of Controverted Elections.*
Recommended citation: (year of decision) volume number Fras page number.
Published: 2 vols 1793. Covering: 1776–7. Br & Ph 855.
Freeman, Richard, *Reports . . . Chancery.*
Recommended citation: (year of decision) Freem Ch page number.
Published: 1 vol. 1742, 2nd ed. by J.E. Hovenden 1823. Covering: 1660–1706.
Notes: 2nd ed. in 22 ER. Known as 2 Freeman — 1 Freeman being Freeman,
Richard, *Reports . . . King's Bench and Common Pleas*, with which this work was
originally published. Br & Ph 391.
Freeman, Richard, *Reports . . . King's Bench and Common Pleas.*
Recommended citation: (year of decision) Freem KB page number.
Published: 1 vol. 1742, 2nd ed. by Edward Smirke 1826. Covering: 1670–1704.
Notes: In 89 ER. Known as 1 Freeman — 2 Freeman being Freeman, Richard,
*Reports . . . Chancery*, with which this work was originally published. Br & Ph
569.
Frewen, Gerard L., *Judgments of the Court of Criminal Appeal.* [Irish Free State,
Republic of Ireland.]
Recommended citation: (year of decision) volume number Frewen page
number.
Published: n.d.– . Covering: 1924– . Notes: Volume 1 is undated but includes
cases up to 1978. Volume 3 is by Eithne Casey.

Gale, C.J., *Reports . . . Exchequer.*
Recommended citation: (year of decision) volume number Gal page number.
Published: 2 vols 1836–8. Covering: 1835–6. Br & Ph 517.
Gale, C.J., and Davison, H., *Reports . . . Queen's Bench.*
Recommended citation: (year of decision) volume number Gal & Dav page
number.
Published: 3 vols 1842–3. Covering: 1841–3. Br & Ph 629.
*Gazette.*
Recommended citation: (year of decision or of publication of article) volume
number (issue number) Gazette page number.
Published: 1994 (vol. 91)– . Notes: Volumes 1–90 titled *Law Society's Gazette*
(q.v.).
*Gazette of Bankruptcy.*
Recommended citation: (year of decision) volume number Gaz Bcy page number.
Published: 4 vols 1862–3. Covering: 1861–3. Br & Ph 700.
*General Abridgment of Cases in Equity.*
Recommended citation: (year of decision) volume number Eq Cas Abr page
number.
Published: 2 vols 1732–56, 5th ed. of vol. 1 1793, 2nd ed. of vol. 2 1769. Covering:
1667–1744. Notes: In 21 ER (vol. 1) and 22 ER (vol. 2). Known as 'Equity Cases
Abridged'. Volume 2 was first published with the 4th ed. of vol. 1. There is also
a Dublin ed. 1793 and some bibliographies list an 1869 ed. of vol. 2. Br & Ph 390.
Gibson, Sir Alexander; see Durie, Lord.
Giffard, J.W. de Longueville, *Reports . . . Chancery.* [Vice-Chancellor.]
Recommended citation: (year of decision) volume number Giff page number.
Published: 2 vols 1860–71. Covering: 1856–65. Notes: In 65 ER (vol. 1) and 66 ER
(vols 2–5). Br & Ph 671.
Gilbert, J., *Cases . . . King's Bench.*
Recommended citation: (year of decision) Gilb KB page number.

Published: 1 vol. 1740 (Dublin), new ed. 1760 (London), new ed. 1792 (Dublin). Covering: 1713–15. Notes: 1760 ed. in 93 ER. The full title is *Cases in Law and Equity: Argued, Debated and Adjudged in the King's Bench and Chancery*, but in fact it does not contain any Chancery cases. Br & Ph 570.

Gilbert, J., *Reports of Cases in Equity.*
Recommended citation: (year of decision) Gilb Ch page number.
Published: 1 vol. 1734, 2nd ed. 1742. Covering: 1705–27. Notes: 2nd ed. in 25 ER. Br & Ph 392.

Gilmour, Sir John (Lord Craigmillar), and Falconer, Sir David (Lord Newton), *Collection of Decisions of the Lords of Council and Session.*
Recommended citation: (year of decision) Gil & Fal page number.
Published: 1 vol. 1701. Covering: 1661–6 and 1681–6. Br & Ph 1630.

Glanville, J., *Reports … Commons in Parliament.*
Recommended citation: (year of decision) Glan El Cas page number.
Published: 1 vol. 1775. Covering: 1623–4. Br & Ph 856.

Glascock, W., *Miscellaneous Reports.*
Recommended citation: (year of decision) Glas page number.
Published: 1 vol. 1832. Covering: 1831–2. Br & Ph 1310.

Glenbervie, Baron; see Douglas, Sylvester.

Glyn, T.C., and Jameson, R.S., *Cases in Bankruptcy.*
Recommended citation: (year of decision) volume number Gl & J page number.
Published: 2 vols 1824–8. Covering: 1819–28. Br & Ph 701.

Godbolt, John, *Reports … Courts of Record at Westminster.*
Recommended citation: (year of decision) Godb page number.
Published: 1 vol. 1652, 2nd ed. 1653. Covering: 1575–1638. Notes: In 78 ER. Br & Ph 571.

Goodeve, T.M., *Abstract of Reported Cases Relating to Letters Patent for Inventions.*
Recommended citation: (year of decision) Good Pat Cas page number.
Published: 1 vol. 1884. Covering: 1785–1883. Br & Ph 766.

Gouldsborough, J., *Reports … All the Courts at Westminster.*
Recommended citation: (year of decision) Gould page number.
Published: 1 vol. 1653, 2nd ed. 1682. Covering: 1586–1602. Notes: 2nd ed. in 75 ER. Br & Ph 572.

Gow, Niel, *Reports … Nisi Prius.*
Recommended citation: (year of decision) Gow page number.
Published: 1 vol. 1828. Covering: 1818–20. Notes: In 171 ER. Br & Ph 655.

Grant, Patrick; see Elchies, Lord.

*Greens Business Law Bulletin.*
Recommended citation: (year of decision) Bus LB issue number hyphen page number.
Published: February 1993– .

*Greens Criminal Law Bulletin.*
Recommended citation: (year of decision) Crim LB issue number hyphen page number.
Published: February 1993– .

*Greens Family Law Bulletin.*
Recommended citation: (year of decision) Fam LB issue number hyphen page number.
Published: January 1993– .

*Greens Property Law Bulletin.*
Recommended citation: (year of decision) Prop LB issue number hyphen page number.
Published: February 1993– .

*Greens Weekly Digest.*
Recommended citation: volume year without brackets GWD issue number hyphen item number.
Published: 1986– .

Greer, E., *Irish Land Acts. Monthly Law Reports.*
Recommended citation: (year of decision) volume number Greer page number.
Published: 5 vols 1899–1903. Covering: 1897–1903. Br & Ph 1406.

Greer, E., *Irish Land Acts: One Hundred and Ninety Reports of Leading Cases.*
Recommended citation: (year of decision) Greer LC page number.
Published: 1 vol. 1897 and appendix 1898. Covering: 1872–98. Br & Ph 1404.

Griffin, Ralph, *Abstract of Reported Cases Relating to Letters Patent for Inventions.*
Recommended citation: (year of decision) Grif Pat Cas page number.
Published: 1 vol. 1887. Covering: 1866–87. Notes: Another work by Griffin, titled *Patent Cases Decided by the Comptroller-General and Law Officers of the Crown* (1888), is sometimes described as being a second volume of this work but citations never use volume numbers. Br & Ph 767.

Griffith, E., *Cases of Supposed Exemption from Poor Rates.*
Recommended citation: (year of decision) Grif PL Cas page number.
Published: 1 vol. 1831. Covering: 1821–31. Br & Ph 924.

Guthrie, W., *Select Cases ... Sheriff Courts.*
Recommended citation: (year of decision) volume number Guth Sh Cas page number.
Published: 2 vols 1879–94. Covering: 1861–85. Br & Ph 1668.

Gwillim, Sir Henry, *Collection of Acts ... with Reports of Cases ... Respecting Tithes.*
Recommended citation: (year of decision) volume number Gwill page number.
Published: 4 vols 1801, 2nd ed. by C. Ellis 1825. Covering: 1224–1824. Br & Ph 935.


Haggard, John, *Reports ... Admiralty.*
Recommended citation: (year of decision) volume number Hag Adm page number.
Published: 3 vols 1825–40. Covering: 1822–38. Notes: In 166 ER. Br & Ph 350.

Haggard, John, *Reports ... Consistory Court.*
Recommended citation: (year of decision) volume number Hag Con page number; App page number for appendices.
Published: 2 vols 1822. Covering: 1789–1821. Notes: In 161 ER. Br & Ph 484.

Haggard, John, *Reports ... Ecclesiastical Courts.*
Recommended citation: (year of decision) volume number Hag Ecc page number; App page number for appendices; Supp page number for supplement.
Published: 4 vols 1829–34. Covering: 1827–33. Notes: In 162 ER. Br & Ph 485.

Hailes, Lord (Sir David Dalrymple), *Decisions of the Lords of Council and Session.*
Recommended citation: (year of decision) volume number Hailes page number.
Published: 2 vols 1826. Covering: 1766–91. Notes: The pagination is continuous, vol. 2 starting at p. 561.

Hale, Sir Matthew, *Historia Placitorum Coronae. The History of the Pleas of the Crown.*

Recommended citation: volume number Hale PC page number.
Published: 2 vols 1736 reprinted 1971. Notes: There were also editions by George Wilson 1778 and T. Dogherty 1800.
Hale, W.H., *Precedents in Causes of Office against Churchwardens and Others.*
Recommended citation: (year of decision) Hale Ecc page number.
Published: 1 vol. 1841. Covering: 1583–1736. Br & Ph 739.
Hale, W.H., *Series of Precedents and Proceedings in Criminal Causes.*
Recommended citation: (year of decision) Hale Cr Prec page number.
Published: 1 vol. 1847. Covering: 1475–1640. Br & Ph 725.
Hall, Frederick J., and Twells, Philip, *Reports ... Chancery.*
Recommended citation: (year of decision) volume number H & Tw page number.
Published: 2 vols 1850–1. Covering: 1849–50. Notes: In 47 ER. Br & Ph 428.
Hansell, Miles Edward, *Reports of Bankruptcy and Companies Winding-up Cases.*
Recommended citation: [volume year] HBR page number.
Published: [1915]–[1917]. Br & Ph 702.
Harcarse, Lord (Sir Roger Hog), *Decisions of the Court of Session.*
Recommended citation: (year of decision) Harc page number.
Published: 1 vol. 1757. Covering: 1681–91. Br & Ph 1633.
Hardres, Sir Thomas, *Reports ... Exchequer.*
Recommended citation: (year of decision) Hardres page number.
Published: 1 vol. 1693, 2nd ed. 1792. Covering: 1655–69. Notes: 2nd ed. in 145 ER. Br & Ph 499.
Hare, Thomas, *Reports ... Chancery.* [Vice-Chancellor.]
Recommended citation: (year of decision) volume number Hare page number.
Published: 11 vols 1843–58. Covering: 1841–53. Notes: In 66 ER (vol. 1), 67 ER (vols 2–6) and 68 ER (vols 7–11). Page numbers in appendices are roman numerals. Br & Ph 672.
Harrison, O.B.C., and Rutherford, H., *Reports ... Common Pleas.*
Recommended citation: (year of decision) Har & Ruth page number.
Published: 1 vol. 1868. Covering: 1865–6. Br & Ph 463.
Harrison, S.B., and Wollaston, F.L., *Reports ... King's Bench and Bail Court.*
Recommended citation: (year of decision) volume number Har & Woll page number.
Published: 2 vols 1836–7. Covering: 1835–6. Br & Ph 630.
Hatsell, John, *Precedents of Proceedings in the House of Commons.*
Recommended citation: (year of decision) volume number Hats page number.
Published: 1 vol. 1781, new ed. in 4 vols 1818. Covering: 1290–1818. Br & Ph 857.
Hawkins, William, *Treatise of the Pleas of the Crown.*
Recommended citation: volume number Hawk PC page number.
Published: 2 vols 1716–21, reprinted 1973.
Hayes, Edmund, *Reports ... Exchequer in Ireland.*
Recommended citation: (year of decision) Hayes page number.
Published: 1 vol. 1837. Covering: 1830–2. Br & Ph 1351.
Hayes, Edmund, and Jones, Thomas, *Reports ... Exchequer in Ireland.*
Recommended citation: (year of decision) Hayes & J page number.
Published: 1 vol. 1843. Covering: 1832–4. Br & Ph 1352.
Hemming, George W., and Miller, Alexander Edward, *Reports ... Chancery.* [Vice-Chancellor.]
Recommended citation: (year of decision) volume number Hem & M page number.
Published: 2 vols 1864–6. Covering: 1862–5. Notes: In 71 ER. Br & Ph 673.

Hetley, Sir Thomas, *Reports.*
  Recommended citation: (year of decision) Het page number.
  Published: 1 vol. 1657. Covering: 1627–32. Notes: In 124 ER. Br & Ph 448.
Hobart, Sir Henry, *Reports.*
  Recommended citation: (year of decision) Hob page number.
  Published: 1641, 5th ed. by Edward Chilton 1724. Covering: 1603–25. Notes: In
  80 ER. Br & Ph 573.
Hodges, W., *Reports ... Common Pleas.*
  Recommended citation: (year of decision) volume number Hodges page number.
  Published: 3 vols 1836–9. Covering: 1835–7. Br & Ph 464.
Hog, Sir Roger; see Harcarse, Lord.
Hogan, W., *Reports ... Rolls Court in Ireland.*
  Recommended citation: (year of decision) volume number Hog page number.
  Published: 2 vols 1828–38. Covering: 1816–34. Br & Ph 1372.
Holt, Francis Ludlow, *Reports ... Nisi Prius.*
  Recommended citation: (year of decision) Holt NP page number.
  Published: 1 vol. 1818. Covering: 1815–17. Notes: In 171 ER. Br & Ph 656.
Holt, Sir John, *The Judgements ... in ... Ashby v. White ... and ... Paty.*
  Recommended citation: (year of decision) Holt page number.
  Published: 1 vol. 1837.
Holt, Sir John, *Report of All the Cases Determined by Sir John Holt.*
  Recommended citation: (year of decision) Holt KB page number.
  Published: 1 vol. 1738. Covering: 1688–1711. Notes: In 90 ER. Br & Ph 574.
Holt, William, *Admiralty Court Cases on the Rule of the Road.*
  Recommended citation: (year of decision) Holt Adm page number.
  Published: 1 vol. 1867. Covering: 1863–7. Br & Ph 357.
Holt, William, *Equity Reports.* [Vice-Chancellor.]
  Recommended citation: (year of decision) volume number Holt Eq page number.
  Published: 2 vols 1845. Covering: 1845. Notes: In 71 ER. Br & Ph 684.
Home, Alexander, *Decisions of the Court of Session.*
  Recommended citation: (year of decision) Cl Home page number.
  Published: 1 vol. 1757, 2nd ed. 1791. Covering: 1735–44. Notes: The reporter was
  Clerk of Session and is known as Clerk Home. Br & Ph 1615.
Home, Henry; see Kames, Lord.
Hopwood, C.H., and Coltman, F.J., *Registration Cases.*
  Recommended citation: (year of decision) volume number Hop & C page number.
  Published: 2 vols 1873–9. Covering: 1868–78. Br & Ph 882.
Hopwood, C.H., and Philbrick, F.A., *Registration Cases.*
  Recommended citation: (year of decision) Hop & Ph page number.
  Published: 1 vol. 1868. Covering: 1863–7. Br & Ph 883.
Horn, H., and Hurlstone, E.T., *Reports ... Exchequer.*
  Recommended citation: (year of decision) volume number Horn & H page number.
  Published: 2 vols 1840. Covering: 1838–9. Br & Ph 518.
*House of Lords Cases.*
  Recommended citation: (year of decision) volume number HL Cas page number.
  Published: 11 vols 1849–66. Covering: 1847–66. Notes: In 9 ER (vols 1 and 2), 10
  ER (vols 3–6) and 11 ER (vols 7–11). Volumes 1 and 2 by C. Clark and W. Finnelly;
  vols 3–11 by C. Clark. Volume 12 is an index. Br & Ph 530.
*Housing Law Reports.*
  Recommended citation: (year of decision) volume number HLR page number.
  Published: 1982– . Br & Ph 745.

Hovenden, John Eykyn, *A Supplement to Vesey Junior's Reports of Cases in Chancery.*
Recommended citation: (year of decision) volume number Hov Supp page number.
Published: 2 vols 1827. Covering: 1789–1817. Notes: In 34 ER. Br & Ph 393.

Howard, Gorges Edmond, *Rules and Practice of the High Court of Chancery in Ireland.*
Recommended citation: (year of decision) How Ch Pr page number; S page number for Supplement.
Published: 1 vol. 1772, supplement [1775]. Covering: 1619–1775. Notes: Though the title-page of the Supplement is dated 1774 it includes 'addenda' referring to cases decided in 1775. Br & Ph 1339.

Howard, Gorges Edmond, *Several Special Cases on the Laws against the Further Growth of Popery in Ireland.*
Recommended citation: (year of decision) How Po Cas page number.
Published: 1 vol. 1775. Covering: 1720–73. Br & Ph 1388A.

Howard, Gorges Edmond, *Supplement to the Rules and Practice of the High Court of Chancery in Ireland*; see Howard, Gorges Edmond, *Rules and Practice of the High Court of Chancery in Ireland.*

Howard, Gorges Edmond, *Treatise on the Rules and Practice of the Equity Side of the Exchequer in Ireland.*
Recommended citation: (year of decision) volume number How EE page number.
Published: 2 vols 1760. Notes: Pagination is continuous, vol. 2 beginning at p. 465. A 2nd ed. 1793 is listed in bibliographies. Br & Ph 1353.

Hudson, W.E., and Brooke, J., *Reports ... King's Bench ... in Ireland.*
Recommended citation: (year of decision) volume number Hud & B page number.
Published: 2 vols 1829–46. Covering: 1827–31. Br & Ph 1362.

Hume, David, *Decisions of the Court of Session.*
Recommended citation: (year of decision) Hume page number.
Published: 1 vol. 1839. Covering: 1781–1822. Br & Ph 1634.

Hunt, W., *Collection of Cases on the Annuity Act.*
Recommended citation: (year of decision) Hunt's AC page number.
Published: 1794, 2nd ed. 1 vol. 1796. Covering: 1776–96. Br & Ph 685.

Hurlstone, Edwin Tyrrell, and Coltman, Francis Joseph, *Exchequer Reports.*
Recommended citation: (year of decision) volume number Hurl & C page number.
Published: 4 vols 1863–8. Covering: 1862–6. Notes: Volumes 1–3 in 158 ER (vol. 1) and 159 ER (vols 2 and 3). Br & Ph 500.

Hurlstone, Edwin Tyrrell, and Norman, J.P., *Exchequer Reports.*
Recommended citation: (year of decision) volume number Hurl & N page number.
Published: 7 vols 1857–62. Covering: 1856–62. Notes: In 156 ER (vol. 1), 157 ER (vols 2–5) and 158 ER (vols 6 and 7). Br & Ph 501.

Hurlstone, Edwin Tyrrell, and Walmsley, T., *Reports ... Exchequer.*
Recommended citation: (year of decision) Hurl & W page number.
Published: 1 vol. 1841. Covering: 1840–1. Br & Ph 519.

Hutton, Sir Richard, *Reports.*
Recommended citation: (year of decision) Hut page number.
Published: 1 vol. 1656, 2nd ed. 1682. Covering: 1612–39. Notes: In 123 ER. Br & Ph 449.

Huxley, George, *A Second Book of Judgments.*
Recommended citation: Sec Bk Judg title item number.
Published: 1 vol. 1674, 2nd ed. 1675. Covering: ?1424–1622. Notes: A collection of court judgments which are in Latin. On the title-page of the 1st ed. the spelling 'Judgements' is used. Br & Ph 339.

*ICSID Reports.*
Recommended citation: (year of decision) volume number ICSID Reports page number.
Published: 1993– .
*Immigration and Nationality Law and Practice.*
Recommended citation: (year of publication of article) volume number I&NL&P page number.
Published: 1986– .
*Immigration Appeals.*
Recommended citation: [volume year] Imm AR page number.
Published: [1972]– . Br & Ph 746.
*Indian Appeals*; see *Law Reports. Indian Appeals.* (1873–1950).
*Industrial Cases Reports.*
Recommended citation: [volume year] ICR page number.
Published: [1972]– . Notes: Volumes for [1972] to [1974] titled *Industrial Court Reports* (same form of citation). Br & Ph 752.
*Industrial Court Decisions.*
Recommended citation: (year of decision) volume number Ind C Aw page number.
Published: 53 vols 1920–72. Br & Ph 751.
*Industrial Court Reports*; see *Industrial Cases Reports.*
*Industrial Law Journal.*
Recommended citation: (year of publication of article) volume number ILJ page number.
Published: 1972– .
*Industrial Relations Law Bulletin.*
Recommended citation: (year of decision or of publication of article) issue number IRLB page number.
Published: January 1993 (No. 464)– . Notes: Earlier vols titled *Industrial Relations Legal Information Bulletin* (q.v.).
*Industrial Relations Law Reports.*
Recommended citation: [volume year] IRLR page number.
Published: [1972]– . Br & Ph 754.
*Industrial Relations Legal Information Bulletin.*
Recommended citation: (year of decision or of publication of article) issue number IRLIB page number.
Published: 463 issues 1974?–December 1992. Notes: From issue 464 titled *Industrial Relations Law Bulletin* (q.v.). Numbering of the issues started with No. 46 dated 6 August 1975.
*Industrial Tribunal Reports.*
Recommended citation: (year of decision) volume number ITR page number.
Published: 13 vols 1966–78. Notes: Volumes 1–5 titled *Industrial Tribunals* (same form of citation). Br & Ph 755.
*Industrial Tribunals*; see *Industrial Tribunal Reports.*

*Insolvency Law and Practice.*
Recommended citation: (year of publication of article) volume number IL&P page number.
Published: 1985– .
*Insurance Law and Practice.*
Recommended citation: (year of publication of article) volume number InsL&P page number.
Published: 1991– .
*Insurance Law Reports.*
Recommended citation: (year of decision) volume number ILR page number.
Published: 9 vols 1982–4. Covering: 1942–84. Br & Ph 829.
*Intellectual Property Decisions.*
Recommended citation: (year of decision) IPD item number.
Published: 1978– . Notes: The first two digits of the item number are the volume number.
*International and Comparative Law Quarterly.*
Recommended citation: (year of publication of article) volume number ICLQ page number.
Published: 1952– .
*International Company and Commercial Law Review.*
Recommended citation: [volume year] ICCLR page number; C-page number for News Section.
Published: [1990]– . Notes: The publisher's suggested form of citation gives the issue number after [volume year] but this is superfluous.
*International Human Rights Reports.*
Recommended citation: (year of decision) volume number IHRR page number.
Published: 1994– .
*International Insurance Law Review.*
Recommended citation: [volume year] Int ILR page number.
Published: [1993]– .
*International Journal of Evidence and Proof.*
Recommended citation: (year of publication of article) issue number E & P page number.
Published: 1996–.
*International Law Quarterly.*
Recommended citation: (year of publication of article) volume number ILQ page number.
Published: 4 vols 1947–51.
*International Law Reports.*
Recommended citation: (year of decision) volume number ILR page number.
Published: 1956 (vol. 17)– . Notes: For vols 1–16 see *Annual Digest and Reports of Public International Law Cases.*
*International Review of Law and Economics.*
Recommended citation: (year of publication of article) volume number Int Rev Law Econ page number.
Published: 1981– .
*Irish Chancery Reports.*
Recommended citation: (year of decision) volume number IChR page number.
Published: 17 vols 1852–67. Covering: 1850–66. Notes: Sometimes regarded as a division of the second series of the *Irish Reports.* Br & Ph 1311.

*Irish Common Law Reports.*
Recommended citation: (year of decision) volume number ICLR page number.
Published: 17 vols 1852–67. Covering: 1850–66. Notes: Sometimes regarded as a
division of the second series of the *Irish Reports*. Br & Ph 1312.

*Irish Equity Reports.*
Recommended citation: (year of decision) volume number IEqR page number.
Published: 13 vols 1838–52. Covering: 1838–50. Notes: Sometimes regarded as a
division of the first series of the *Irish Reports*. Initially published as a division of
the third series of the *Law Recorder*. Br & Ph 1313.

*Irish Journal of European Law.*
Recommended citation: (year of publication of article) volume number IJEL page
number.
Published: 1992– .

*Irish Jurist.* 1935–65.
Recommended citation: [volume year] Ir Jur page number.
Published: [1935]–[1965].

*Irish Jurist.* 1966– .
Recommended citation: (year of publication of article in parentheses) volume
number Irish Jurist page number.
Published: 1966– .

*Irish Jurist Reports.*
Recommended citation: [volume year] Ir Jur Rep page number.
Published: [1935]–[1965]. Br & Ph 1316.

*Irish Law Journal Reports*; see *Irish Weekly Law Reports.*

*Irish Law Reports.*
Recommended citation: (year of decision) volume number ILR page number.
Published: 13 vols 1839–52. Covering: 1838–50. Notes: Sometimes regarded as a
division of the first series of the *Irish Reports*. Initially published as a division of
the third series of the *Law Recorder*. Br & Ph 1317.

*Irish Law Reports Monthly.*
Recommended citation: [volume year] number if there is more than 1 vol. for the
year ILRM page number.
Published: [1981]– . Notes: [1981]–[1993] 1 vol. a year, [1994]– 2 vols a year. Volumes
of previously unreported cases for years before 1981 are also being published and
vols for [1976-7], [1978], [1979] and [1980] have appeared. Br & Ph 1318.

*Irish Law Times.*
Recommended citation: (year of decision or of publication of article) volume
number ILT page number.
Published: 1983– .

*Irish Law Times and Solicitors' Journal.*
Recommended citation: (year of decision or of publication of article) volume
number ILT & SJ page number.
Published: 114 vols 1867–1980.

*Irish Law Times Reports.*
Recommended citation: (year of decision) volume number ILTR page number.
Published: 110 vols 1867–1980. Covering: 1867–1980. Notes: Volumes 1–4 are in
the *Irish Law Times and Solicitors' Journal*, from which they are not separately
paginated. Br & Ph 1319.

*Irish Reports.*
Recommended citation: [volume year] number if there is more than one volume
for the year IR page number.

Published: [1894]– . Notes: [1894]–[1925] 2 vols a year, [1926]–[1989] 1 vol. a year, [1990]–[1992] 2 vols a year, [1993]– 3 vols a year. Sometimes regarded as the fifth series of the *Irish Reports*. For the first series see *Irish Equity Reports* and *Irish Law Reports*. For the second series see *Irish Chancery Reports* and *Irish Common Law Reports*. For the third series see *Irish Reports. Common Law*, *Irish Reports. Equity* and *Irish Reports. Registry Appeals ... and Appeals in the Court for Land Cases Reserved*. For the fourth series see *Law Reports (Ireland)*. Br & Ph 1321.

*Irish Reports. Common Law.*
Recommended citation: (year of decision) IR volume number CL page number.
Published: 11 vols 1867–78. Covering: 1866–78. Notes: Sometimes regarded as a division of the third series of the *Irish Reports*. Br & Ph 1322.

*Irish Reports. Equity.*
Recommended citation: (year of decision) IR volume number Eq page number.
Published: 11 vols 1867–78. Covering: 1866–78. Notes: Sometimes regarded as a division of the third series of the *Irish Reports*. Br & Ph 1340.

*Irish Reports. Registry Appeals ... and Appeals in the Court for Land Cases Reserved.*
Recommended citation: (year of decision) IR R & L page number.
Published: 1 vol. 1886. Covering: 1868–76. Notes: Sometimes regarded as a division of the third series of the *Irish Reports*. Br & Ph 1420.

*Irish Weekly Law Reports.*
Recommended citation: (year of decision) volume number IWLR page number.
Published: 8 vols 1895–1902. Notes: Volumes 7 and 8 titled *Irish Law Journal Reports* (same form of citation). Br & Ph 1323.

Irvine, Alex. Forbes, *Reports ... High Court and Circuit Courts of Justiciary.*
Recommended citation: (year of decision) volume number Irv page number.
Published: 5 vols 1855–68. Covering: 1851–68. Br & Ph 1600.


Jacob, Edward, *Reports ... Chancery.*
Recommended citation: (year of decision) Jac page number.
Published: 1 vol. 1828. Covering: 1821–2. Notes: In 37 ER. Br & Ph 394.

Jacob, Edward, and Walker, John, *Reports ... Chancery.*
Recommended citation: (year of decision) volume number Jac & W page number.
Published: 2 vols 1821–3. Covering: 1819–21. Notes: In 37 ER. Br & Ph 395.

Jebb, R., *Cases ... Criminal ... Ireland.*
Recommended citation: (year of decision) Jebb page number.
Published: 1 vol. 1841. Covering: 1822–40. Br & Ph 1380.

Jebb, R., and Bourke, R., *Reports ... Queen's Bench, in Ireland.*
Recommended citation: (year of decision) Jebb & B page number.
Published: 1 vol. 1843. Covering: 1841–2. Br & Ph 1363.

Jebb, R., and Symes, A.R., *Reports ... Queen's Bench and Exchequer Chamber in Ireland.*
Recommended citation: (year of decision) volume number Jebb & S page number.
Published: 2 vols 1840–2. Covering: 1838–41. Br & Ph 1364.

Jenkins, David, *Eight Centuries of Reports.*
Recommended citation: (year of decision) Jenk page number.
Published: 1 vol. in law French 1661. English transl. by Theodore Barlow (called 2nd ed.) 1734, 3rd ed. (English) 1771 or 1777. Covering: 1220–1623. Notes: 3rd ed. in 145 ER. There is a 4th ed. by C.F. Morrell 1885. Br & Ph 502.

*Jersey Judgments.* (1950–76).
Recommended citation: (year of decision) volume number JJ page number.
Published: 2 vols 1967–77. Covering: 1950–76. Notes: For citation of later vols see next entry. Br & Ph 306.

*Jersey Judgments.* 1977–1984.
Recommended citation: year without brackets JJ page number.
Published: 1977–1984. Notes: For citation of earlier vols see preceding entry. Br & Ph 306.

*Jersey Law Reports.*
Recommended citation: volume year without brackets JLR page number; N-page number for Notes of Cases section.
Published: 1985-6– . Notes: All vols except 1985-6 and 1987-8 are for single years.

Johnson, Henry Robert Vaughan, *Reports ... Chancery.* [Vice-Chancellor.]
Recommended citation: (year of decision) John page number.
Published: 1 vol. 1860. Covering: 1858–60. Notes: In 70 ER. Br & Ph 674.

Johnson, Henry Robert Vaughan, and Hemming, George W., *Reports ... Chancery.* [Vice-Chancellor.]
Recommended citation: (year of decision) volume number John & H page number.
Published: 2 vols 1861–3. Covering: 1859–62. Notes: In 70 ER. Br & Ph 675.

Jones, Thomas, *Reports ... Exchequer, in Ireland.*
Recommended citation: (year of decision) volume number Jones page number.
Published: 2 vols 1838–47. Covering: 1834–8. Br & Ph 1354.

Jones, Thomas, and Carey, H., *Reports ... Exchequer in Ireland.*
Recommended citation: (year of decision) Jones & C page number.
Published: 1 vol. 1840. Covering: 1838–9. Br & Ph 1355.

Jones, Thomas, and La Touche, Edmond Digges, *Reports ... Chancery.* [Ireland.]
Recommended citation: (year of decision) volume number Jones & La T page number.
Published: 3 vols 1846–9. Covering: 1844–6. Br & Ph 1341.

Jones, Sir Thomas, *Reports ... King's Bench and Common Pleas.*
Recommended citation: (year of decision) T Jones page number.
Published: 1 vol. in law French 1692, 2nd ed. with English transl. 1729. Covering: 1667–85. Notes: 2nd ed. in 84 ER. Br & Ph 575.

Jones, Sir William, *Reports.*
Recommended citation: (year of decision) W Jones page number.
Published: 1 vol. 1675. Covering: 1620–41. Notes: In 82 ER. In law French. Br & Ph 576.

*Journal of Business Law.*
Recommended citation: [volume year] JBL page number.
Published: [1957]– .

*Journal of Child Law.*
Recommended citation: (year of publication of article) volume number JCL page number.
Published: 1988– . Notes: As from vol. 7, No. 2 (June 1995), titled *Child and Family Law Quarterly* (q.v.).

*Journal of Common Market Studies.*
Recommended citation: (year of publication of article) volume number JCMS page number.
Published: 1962– .

*Journal of Criminal Law.*
Recommended citation: (year of publication of article) volume number JCL page number.
Published: 1937– .
*Journal of Employment Law and Practice.*
Recommended citation: (year of publication of article) volume number JELP page number.
*Journal of Environmental Law*
Recommended citation: (year of decision or of publication of article) volume number JEL page number.
Published: 1989– .
*Journal of International Banking Law.*
Recommended citation: [volume year] JIBL page number; N-page number for News Section.
Published: [1986]– . Notes: The publisher's suggested form of citation gives the issue number after [volume year] but this is superfluous.
*Journal of International Franchising and Distribution Law.*
Recommended citation: (year of publication of article) volume number JIFDL page number.
Published: 1986– .
*Journal of Law and Society.*
Recommended citation: (year of publication of article) volume number J Law Soc page number.
Published: 1982 (vol. 9)– . Notes: Volumes 1 to 8 titled *British Journal of Law and Society* (q.v.).
*Journal of Legal History.*
Recommended citation: (year of publication of article) volume number J Legal Hist page number.
Published: 1980– .
*Journal of Media Law and Practice.*
Recommended citation: (year of publication of article) volume number JML&P page number.
Published: 1980– .
*Journal of Personal Injury Litigation.*
Recommended citation: [volume year] JPIL page number.
Published: [1994]– .
*Journal of Planning and Environment Law.*
Recommended citation: [volume year] JPL page number.
Published: [1948]– . Notes: Volumes for [1948] to [1953] titled *Journal of Planning Law* (same form of citation). Volumes for [1954] to [1972] titled *Journal of Planning and Property Law* (same form of citation).
*Journal of Planning and Property Law*; see *Journal of Planning and Environment Law.*
*Journal of Planning Law*; see *Journal of Planning and Environment Law.*
*Journal of Social Security Law.*
Recommended citation: (year of decision or of publication of article) volume number JSSL page number; Dpage number for Digest section.
Published: 1994– .
*Journal of Social Welfare and Family Law.*
Recommended citation: [volume year] JSWFL page number.
Published: [1991]– . Notes: Earlier vols titled *Journal of Social Welfare Law* (q.v.).

*Journal of Social Welfare Law.*
Recommended citation: [volume year] JSWL page number.
Published: [1978-79]–[1990]. Notes: All vols other than [1978-79] were for a single year. From [1991] titled *Journal of Social Welfare and Family Law* (q.v.).

*Journal of the Association of Law Teachers.*
Recommended citation: (year of publication of article) volume number JALT page number.
Published: 4 vols 1967–70. Notes: For vol. 1 the issue number must be given after the volume number. From vol. 5 titled *Law Teacher* (q.v.).

*Journal of the Law Society of Scotland.*
Recommended citation: (year of publication of article) volume number JLSS page number.
Published: 1956– .

*Journal of the Society of Public Teachers of Law.* [1924]–[1938].
Recommended citation: [volume year] JSPTL page number.
Published: [1924]–[1938]. Notes: For citation of later vols see next entry.

*Journal of the Society of Public Teachers of Law.* 1947–80.
Recommended citation: (year of publication of article) volume number JSPTL page number.
Published: 15 vols 1947–80. Notes: For citation of earlier vols see preceding entry. Succeeded by *Legal Studies* (q.v.).

*Journal of World Trade Law.*
Recommended citation: (year of publication of article) volume number JWTL page number.
Published: 21 vols 1967–87. Notes: From vol. 22 titled *Journal of World Trade* and published in Switzerland.

*Juridical Review.* 1889–1955.
Recommended citation: (year of publication of article) volume number JR page number.
Published: 67 vols 1889–1955. Notes: For citation of later vols see next entry.

*Juridical Review.* 1956– .
Recommended citation: [volume year] JR page number.
Published: [1956]– . Notes: For citation of earlier vols see preceding entry.

*Jurist.* 1838–55.
Recommended citation: (year of decision) volume number Jur page number.
Published: 18 vols 1838–55. Notes: For citation of later vols see next entry. Br & Ph 321.

*Jurist.* 1856–67.
Recommended citation: (year of decision) volume number Jur NS page number.
Published: 12 vols 1856–67. Notes: For citation of earlier vols see preceding entry. Br & Ph 322.

*Justice of the Peace*; see *Justice of the Peace and Local Government Law.*

*Justice of the Peace and Local Government Law.*
Recommended citation: (year of decision or of publication of article) volume number JPN page number.
Published: 1837– . Notes: For citation of the 'Reports' section of vols 1–66 see *Justice of the Peace Reports*. Until vol. 91, No. 6 (5 February 1927), and from vol. 135, No. 47 (20 November 1971) to vol. 157, No. 46 (13 November 1993) titled *Justice of the Peace*. From vol. 91, No. 7 (12 February 1927) to vol. 135, No. 46 (13 November 1971) titled *Justice of the Peace and Local Government Review*. *Local Government Review* (q.v.) then became a separate publication.

*Justice of the Peace and Local Government Review*; see *Justice of the Peace and Local Government Law.*
*Justice of the Peace and Local Government Review Reports*; see *Justice of the Peace Reports.*
*Justice of the Peace Reports.*
  Recommended citation: (year of decision) volume number JP page number.
  Published: 1837– . Notes: From 1837 to 1902 the reports were published in the *Justice of the Peace* (vols 1–66). Volumes 91–146 titled *Justice of the Peace and Local Government Review Reports.* Br & Ph 788.
*Justiciary Cases*; see *Session Cases. Cases Decided in the Court of Justiciary.*


Kames, Lord (Henry Home), *Remarkable Decisions of the Court of Session.*
  Recommended citation: (year of decision) volume number Kames Rem Dec page number.
  Published: 2 vols 1728–66. Covering: 1716–28. Notes: Volume 1 is known as 'Bruce and Home's Decisions' when bound together with Bruce, Alexander, *Decisions of the Lords of Council and Session.* Br & Ph 1635.
Kames, Lord (Henry Home), *Select Decisions of the Court of Session.*
  Recommended citation: (year of decision) Kames Sel Dec page number.
  Published: 1 vol. 1780. Covering: 1752–68. Br & Ph 1636.
Kames, Lord (Henry Home), and Woodhouselee, Lord (Alexander Fraser Tytler), *Decisions in the Court of Session ... in the Form of a Dictionary.*
  Recommended citation: (year of decision) volume number Fol Dic page number.
  Published: 5 vols 1741–1804, 2nd ed. of vols 1 and 2 1791. Covering: 1540–1796. Notes: Known as the 'Folio Dictionary'. Volumes 1 and 2 were by Kames, vols 3 and 4 by Woodhouselee, vol. 5 by T. McGrugar. Br & Ph 1651.
Kay, Edward E., *Reports ... Chancery.* [Vice-Chancellor.]
  Recommended citation: (year of decision) Kay page number.
  Published: 1 vol. 1854. Covering: 1853–4. Notes: In 69 ER. Page numbers in the appendix are roman numerals. Br & Ph 676.
Kay, Edward E., and Johnson, Henry Robert Vaughan, *Reports ... Chancery.* [Vice-Chancellor.]
  Recommended citation: (year of decision) volume number Kay & J page number.
  Published: 4 vols 1855–9. Covering: 1854–8. Notes: In 69 ER (vols 1–3) and 70 ER (vol. 4). Br & Ph 677.
Keane, D.D., and Grant, J., *Registration Cases.*
  Recommended citation: (year of decision) Keane & Gr page number.
  Published: 1 vol. 1863. Covering: 1854–62. Br & Ph 884.
Keble, Joseph, *Reports ... King's Bench.*
  Recommended citation: (year of decision) volume number Keb page number.
  Published: 3 vols 1685. Covering: 1661–79. Notes: In 83 ER (vol. 1) and 84 ER (vols 2 and 3). Br & Ph 577.
Keen, Benjamin, *Reports ... Rolls Court.*
  Recommended citation: (year of decision) volume number Keen page number.
  Published: 2 vols 1837–9. Covering: 1836–8. Notes: In 48 ER. Br & Ph 665.
Keilwey, Robert, *Reports.*
  Recommended citation: (year of decision) Keil page number.
  Published: 1 vol. 1602, 3rd ed. 1688. Covering: 1496–1531. Notes: 3rd ed. in 72 ER. In law French. The author's name is sometimes spelt Keilway or Keylway. Pages 204–6 contain reports by Sir William Dalison, and pp. 207–396 reports by William Benloe. Br & Ph 578.

Kelyng, Sir John, *Reports of Divers Cases in Pleas of the Crown.*
Recommended citation: (year of decision) Kel page number.
Published: 1 vol. 1708. Covering: 1662–9. Notes: 1st ed. in 84 ER. There is also a 3rd ed. by R.L. Loveland 1873. Br & Ph 726.

Kelynge, William, *Report ... Chancery, the King's Bench.*
Recommended citation: (year of decision) Kel W page number.
Published: 1 vol. 1740, 2nd ed. 1764. Covering: 1730–5. Notes: 2nd ed. in 25 ER. There is also an 1873 ed. using the text of the 2nd ed. The Earl of Hardwicke was successively Chief Justice and Lord Chancellor during the period reported and the reports used to be cited as Cas KB t Hardwicke or as Hard. Br & Ph 396.

Kenyon, Lloyd, 1st Baron Kenyon, *Notes of Cases ... King's Bench.*
Recommended citation: (year of decision) volume number Keny page number.
Published: 2 vols paginated as 3, ed. by Job Walden Hanmer 1819–25. Covering: 1753–9. Notes: In 96 ER. The part treated as vol. 3 contains Chancery cases. Br & Ph 580.

Kilkerran, Lord (Sir James Fergusson), *Decisions of the Court of Session.*
Recommended citation: (year of decision) Kilk page number.
Published: 1 vol. 1775. Covering: 1738–52. Br & Ph 1637.

*King's Bench Division*; see *Law Reports. King's Bench Division.* [1901]–[1952].

Knapp, J.W., *Reports ... Privy Council.*
Recommended citation: (year of decision) volume number Kn page number.
Published: 3 vols 1831–6. Covering: 1829–36. Notes: In 12 ER. Br & Ph 660.

Knapp, J.W., and Ombler, E., *Cases of Controverted Elections.*
Recommended citation: (year of decision) Kn & O page number.
Published: 1 vol. 1837. Covering: 1834–5. Br & Ph 858.

*Knight's Industrial and Commercial Reports*; see *Knight's Industrial Reports.*

*Knight's Industrial Law Reports.*
Recommended citation: (year of decision) volume number KILR page number.
Published: 1 vol. 1975. Br & Ph 757.

*Knight's Industrial Reports.*
Recommended citation: (year of decision) volume number KIR page number.
Published: 17 vols 1967–74. Notes: Volumes 1–9 (1967–71) titled *Knight's Industrial and Commercial Reports* (same form of citation). Br & Ph 756.

*Knight's Local Government and Magisterial Reports*; see *Knight's Local Government Reports.*

*Knight's Local Government Reports.*
Recommended citation: (year of decision) volume number LGR page number.
Published: 1903–. Notes: Volumes 26 to 71 titled *Knight's Local Government and Magisterial Reports* (same form of citation). Br & Ph 789.

Konstam, E.M., *Reports of Rating Appeals.*
Recommended citation: (year of decision) volume number Konst Rat App page number.
Published: 2 vols 1909–12. Covering: 1904–8. Br & Ph 901.

Konstam, E.M., and Ward, H.R., *Reports of Rating Appeals.*
Recommended citation: (year of decision) Konst & W Rat App page number.
Published: 1 vol. 1912. Covering: 1909–12. Br & Ph 902.


*LAG Bulletin.*
Recommended citation: (year of decision or of publication of article) month and year of issue without brackets LAG Bulletin page number.

Published: April 1972–December 1983. Notes: 2 earlier issues dated January and February 1972 were titled *Legal Action Group Circular*. Issues from 1984 on titled *Legal Action* (q.v.).

*Lands Tribunal Rating Appeals*; see *Selected List of Lands Tribunal Rating Appeals*.

Lane, Richard, *Reports . . . Exchequer*.
Recommended citation: (year of decision) Lane page number.
Published: 1 vol. 1657. Covering: 1605–11. Notes: 1st ed. in 145 ER. There is a 2nd ed. 1884 by C.F. Morrell. Br & Ph 503.

Latch, Jean, *Plusieurs tres-bons Cases . . . Bank le Roy*.
Recommended citation: (year of decision) Lat page number.
Published: 1 vol. 1661. Covering: 1625–8. Notes: In 82 ER. In law French. Br & Ph 581.

Lauder, Sir John; see Fountainhall, Lord.

*Law Journal*.
Recommended citation: (year of decision or of publication of article) volume number LJ page number; NC page number for Notes of Cases section.
Published: 115 vols 1866–1965.

*Law Journal County Court Reports*.
Recommended citation: (year of decision) volume number LJNCCR page number.
Published: 14 vols 1934–48. Covering: 1934–47. Notes: See also *Law Journal County Courts Reporter*. Br & Ph 478.

*Law Journal County Courts Reporter*.
Recommended citation: (year of decision) volume number LJCCR page number.
Published: 30 vols 1912–33. Covering: 1912–33. Notes: Published in the *Law Journal*. See also *Law Journal County Court Reports*. Br & Ph 477.

*Law Journal Irish Free State Section*.
Recommended citation: [volume year] LJ IFS page number.
Published: [1931]–[1932]. Notes: From [1933] titled *Law Journal Irish Section* (q.v.).

*Law Journal Irish Section*.
Recommended citation: [volume year] LJ Ir page number.
Published: [1933]–[1934]. Notes: Earlier vols and pages 1–72 of [1933] titled *Law Journal Irish Free State Section* (q.v.).

*Law Journal Newspaper County Court Appeals*.
Recommended citation: (year of decision) LJCCA page number.
Published: 1 vol. 1935. Covering: 1935. Notes: Supplement to the *Law Journal* of 28 December 1935. Br & Ph 479.

*Law Journal . . . Reports*. 1822–31.
Recommended citation: (year of decision) volume number LJ OS abbreviation for section page number.
Published: 9 vols n.d.–1831. Covering: 1822–31. Notes: The sections are Ch (Chancery), CP (Common Pleas), Ex (Exchequer in vol. 9), KB (King's Bench) and MC (Magistrates' Cases in vols 5–9). Continued as *Law Journal Reports* (q.v.) of which it is regarded as the 'old series'. Br & Ph 323.

*Law Journal Reports*. 1832–1946.
Recommended citation: (year of decision) volume number LJ abbreviation for section page number.
Published: 115 vols 1832–1946. Notes: The abbreviations for sections are: Adm (Admiralty in vols 35–44), Bcy (Bankruptcy in vols 1–49), CP (Common Pleas in

vols 1–44), Ch (Chancery in vols 1–115), Eccl (Ecclesiastical in vols 35–44), Ex
(Exchequer in vols 1–44), Ex Eq (Exchequer in Equity in vols 2 and 4–10), KB
(King's Bench in vols 1–6 and 70–115), MC (Magistrates' Cases in vols 1–65), P
(Probate, Divorce and Admiralty in vols 1–115), P & M (Probate and Matrimonial
Courts in vols 27, 28 and 35–44), PC (Privy Council in vols 35–115), P M & A
(Probate, Matrimonial and Admiralty in vols 29–34), QB (Queen's Bench in vols
7–69). Continuation of *Law Journal ... Reports* (1822–31) (q.v.) of which it is
regarded as the 'new series'. The title-page of vol. 1 is numbered vol. 10 (i.e., of
*Law Journal ... Reports*. 1822–31). For citation of later vols see next entry. Br
& Ph 324.

*Law Journal Reports*. [1947]–[1949].
Recommended citation: [volume year] LJR page number.
Published: [1947]–[1949]. Notes: For citation of earlier vols see preceding entry.
Br & Ph 324.

*Law Librarian*.
Recommended citation: (year of publication of article) volume number Law Libr
page number.
Published: 1970– .

*Law Quarterly Review*.
Recommended citation: (year of publication of article) volume number LQR page
number.
Published: 1885– .

*Law Recorder*.
Recommended citation: (year of decision) volume number Law Rec page
number.
Published: 4 vols 1828–32. Covering: 1827–31. Br & Ph 1324.

*Law Recorder. New Series*.
Recommended citation: (year of decision) volume number Law Rec NS page
number.
Published: 6 vols 1833–8. Covering: 1833–8. Br & Ph 1325.

*Law Reports. Admiralty and Ecclesiastical Cases*; see *Law Reports. High Court of
Admiralty, and Ecclesiastical Courts*.

*Law Reports. Appeal Cases*. (1875–90).
Recommended citation: (year of decision) volume number App Cas page number.
Published: 15 vols 1876–90. Covering: 1875–90. Notes: A division of the 2nd
series of the *Law Reports*. Br & Ph 531.

*Law Reports. Appeal Cases*. [1891]– ; see *Law Reports. House of Lords*. [1891]– .

*Law Reports. Chancery Appeal Cases*. (1865–75).
Recommended citation: (year of decision) LR volume number Ch App page
number.
Published: 10 vols 1866–75. Covering: 1865–75. Notes: A division of the 1st series
of the *Law Reports*. Br & Ph 398.

*Law Reports. ... Chancery Division*. (1875–90).
Recommended citation: (year of decision) volume number ChD page number.
Published: 45 vols 1876–90. Covering: 1875–90. Notes: A division of the 2nd
series of the *Law Reports*. Br & Ph 399.

*Law Reports. Chancery Division*. [1891]– .
Recommended citation: [volume year] number if there is more than 1 vol. for the
year Ch page number.
Published: [1891]– . Notes: [1891]–[1894] 3 vols a year, [1895]–[1924] 2 vols a
year, [1925] and [1926] 1 vol. a year, [1927] 2 vols, [1928] 1 vol., [1929]–[1932] 2

vols a year, [1933]–[1968] 1 vol. a year, [1969] 2 vols, [1970]–[1995] 1 vol. a year. If it is not known how many vols there will be for a year then the first is printed with 1 Ch in the running head but if no further vols are published for the year then 1 is omitted from citations for that year. The subtitle for [1891]–[1941] was 'Supreme Court of Judicature. Cases Determined in the Chancery Division'. A division of the 3rd series of the *Law Reports*. Br & Ph 397.

*Law Reports. Common Pleas Cases.* (1865–75); see *Law Reports. Court of Common Pleas.* (1865–75).

*Law Reports. Common Pleas Division.* (1875–80).
Recommended citation: (year of decision) volume number CPD page number. Published: 5 vols 1876–80. Covering: 1875–80. Notes: A division of the 2nd series of the *Law Reports*. Br & Ph 450.

*Law Reports. . . . Court for Crown Cases Reserved.* (1865–75).
Recommended citation: (year of decision) LR volume number CCR page number.
Published: 2 vols 1872–5. Covering: 1865–75. Notes: A division of the 1st series of the *Law Reports*. Br & Ph 727.

*Law Reports. Court of Common Pleas.* (1865–75).
Recommended citation: (year of decision) LR volume number CP page number. Published: 10 vols 1866–75. Covering: 1865–75. Notes: Spine title may be 'Law Reports. Common Pleas' or 'Law Reports. Common Pleas Cases'. A division of the 1st series of the *Law Reports*. Br & Ph 451.

*Law Reports. Court of Exchequer.* (1865–75).
Recommended citation: (year of decision) LR volume number Ex page number. Published: 10 vols 1866–75. Covering: 1865–75. Notes: Spine title may be 'Law Reports. Exchequer' or 'Law Reports. Exchequer Cases'. A division of the 1st series of the *Law Reports*. Br & Ph 504.

*Law Reports. Court of Queen's Bench.* (1865–75).
Recommended citation: (year of decision) LR volume number QB page number. Published: 10 vols 1866–75. Covering: 1865–75. Notes: Spine title may be 'Law Reports. Queen's Bench' or 'Law Reports. Queen's Bench Cases'. A division of the 1st series of the *Law Reports*. Br & Ph 582.

*Law Reports. Courts of Probate and Divorce.* (1865–75).
Recommended citation: (year of decision) LR volume number P & D page number.
Published: 3 vols 1869–75. Covering: 1865–75. Notes: Spine title may be 'Law Reports. Probate and Divorce Cases'. A division of the 1st series of the *Law Reports*. Br & Ph 327.

*Law Reports. Crown Cases Reserved*; see *Law Reports. . . . Court for Crown Cases Reserved.*

*Law Reports. English and Irish Appeal Cases.* (1866–75).
Recommended citation: (year of decision) LR volume number HL page number. Published: 7 vols 1866–75. Covering: 1866–75. Notes: A division of the 1st series of the *Law Reports*. Br & Ph 532.

*Law Reports. Equity Cases.* (1865–75).
Recommended citation: (year of decision) LR volume number Eq page number. Published: 20 vols 1866–75. Covering: 1865–75. Notes: A division of the 1st series of the *Law Reports*. Br & Ph 400.

*Law Reports. Exchequer Cases.* (1865–75); see *Law Reports. Court of Exchequer.* (1865–75).

*Law Reports. Exchequer Division.* (1875–80).

Recommended citation: (year of decision) volume number ExD page number.
Published: 5 vols 1876–80. Covering: 1875–80. Notes: A division of the 2nd series of the *Law Reports*. Br & Ph 505.

*Law Reports. Family Division.* [1972]– .
Recommended citation: [volume year] Fam page number.
Published: [1972]– . Notes: A division of the 3rd series of the *Law Reports*. Br & Ph 743.

*Law Reports. High Court of Admiralty, and Ecclesiastical Courts.* (1865–75).
Recommended citation: (year of decision) LR volume number A & E page number.
Published: 4 vols 1867–75. Covering: 1865–75. Notes: Spine title may be 'Law Reports. Admiralty and Ecclesiastical Cases'. A division of the 1st series of the *Law Reports*. Br & Ph 328.

*Law Reports. House of Lords.* [1891]– .
Recommended citation: [volume year] number if there is more than 1 vol. for the year AC page number.
Published: [1891]– . Notes: Spine title may be 'Law Reports. Appeal Cases'. [1891]–[1915] 1 vol. a year, [1916] 2 vols, [1917]–[1920] 1 vol. a year, [1921] and [1922] 2 vols a year, [1923]–[1966] 1 vol. a year, [1967] 2 vols, [1968] 1 vol., [1969] 2 vols, [1970]–[1982] 1 vol. a year, [1983] 2 vols, [1984]–[1989] 1 vol. a year, [1990]–[1992] 2 vols a year, [1993] 1 vol., [1994] and [1995] 2 vols a year. If it is not known how many vols there will be for a year then the first is printed with 1 AC in the running head but if no further vols are published for the year then 1 is omitted from citations for that year. A division of the 3rd series of the *Law Reports*. Br & Ph 533.

*Law Reports. Indian Appeals.* (1873–1950).
Recommended citation: (year of decision) LR volume number Ind App page number.
Published: 77 vols 1874–1950. Covering: 1873–1950. Br & Ph 993.

*Law Reports. Indian Appeals. Supplementary Volume.*
Recommended citation: (year of decision) LR Ind App Supp page number.
Published: 1 vol. 1880. Covering: 1872–3. Br & Ph 993.

*Law Reports. King's Bench Division.* [1901]–[1952].
Recommended citation: [volume year] number if there is more than 1 vol. for the year KB page number.
Published: [1901]–[1952] 1. Notes: [1901]–[1911] 2 vols a year, [1912]–[1915] 3 vols a year, [1916]–[1919] 2 vols a year, [1920] and [1921] 3 vols a year, [1922]–[1942] 2 vols a year, [1943]–[1947] 1 vol. a year, [1948]–[1952] 2 vols a year (but [1952] 2 is QB). [1943]–[1947] have 1 KB in the running head but the 1 is omitted in citation. A division of the 3rd series of the *Law Reports*. See also *Law Reports. Queen's Bench Division.* [1891]–[1900] and [1952] 2– . Br & Ph 331.

*Law Reports. Privy Council Appeals.* (1865–75).
Recommended citation: (year of decision) LR volume number PC page number.
Published: 6 vols 1867–75. Covering: 1865–75. Notes: A division of the 1st series of the *Law Reports*. Br & Ph 661.

*Law Reports. Probate and Divorce Cases.* (1865–75); see *Law Reports. Courts of Probate and Divorce.* (1865–75).

*Law Reports. Probate Division.* (1875–90).
Recommended citation: (year of decision) volume number PD page number.
Published: 15 vols 1876–90. Covering: 1875–90. Notes: A division of the 2nd series of the *Law Reports*. Br & Ph 329.

*Law Reports. Probate Division.* [1891]–[1971]; see *Law Reports. Probate, Divorce and Admiralty Division.* [1891]–[1971].

*Law Reports. Probate, Divorce and Admiralty Division.* [1891]–[1971].
Recommended citation: [volume year] P page number.
Published: [1891]–[1971]. Notes: The subtitle for [1891]–[1941] was 'Probate Division'. The spine title for all vols may be 'Law Reports. Probate Division'. A division of the 3rd series of the *Law Reports.* Br & Ph 330.

*Law Reports. Queen's Bench Cases.* (1865–75); see *Law Reports. Court of Queen's Bench.* (1865–75).

*Law Reports. . . . Queen's Bench Division.* (1875–90).
Recommended citation: (year of decision) volume number QBD page number.
Published: 25 vols 1876–90. Covering: 1875–90. Notes: A division of the 2nd series of the *Law Reports.* Br & Ph 583.

*Law Reports. Queen's Bench Division.* [1891]–[1900] and [1952] 2– .
Recommended citation: [volume year] number if there is more than 1 vol. for the year QB page number.
Published: [1891]–[1900] and [1952] 2– . Notes: [1891]–[1900] 2 vols a year, [1952] vol. 2 only (vol. 1 is KB), [1953]–[1972] 2 vols a year, [1973]–[1989] 1 vol. a year, [1990] and [1991] 2 vols a year, [1992]–[1995] 1 vol. a year. If it is not known how many vols there will be for a year then the first is printed with 1 QB in the running head but if no further vols are published for the year then 1 is omitted from citations for that year. A division of the 3rd series of the *Law Reports.* See also *Law Reports. King's Bench Division.* Br & Ph 331.

*Law Reports. Scotch and Divorce Appeal Cases before the House of Lords.* (1866–75).
Recommended citation: (year of decision) LR volume number Sc & Div page number.
Published: 2 vols 1869–75. Covering: 1866–75. Notes: A division of the 1st series of the *Law Reports.* Br & Ph 534.

*Law Reports (Ireland).*
Recommended citation: (year of decision) volume number LR Ir page number.
Published: 32 vols 1879–93. Covering: 1878–93. Notes: Odd-numbered vols contain cases in the Chancery Division, Probate and Matrimonial Division, Bankruptcy Court and Admiralty Court; even-numbered vols contain cases in the common law divisions and the Land Commission together with registry appeals and Crown cases reserved. Sometimes regarded as the fourth series of the *Irish Reports.* Br & Ph 1326.

*Law Reports of the Commonwealth.*
Recommended citation: [volume year] volume number LRC page number.
Published: [1993]– . Notes: 4 vols a year.

*Law Reports of the Commonwealth. Commercial Law Reports.*
Recommended citation: [volume year] LRC (Comm) page number.
Published: [1980-4]–[1992]. Notes: All vols except [1980-4] were for a single year. Br & Ph 308.

*Law Reports of the Commonwealth. Constitutional Law Reports.*
Recommended citation: [volume year] LRC (Const) page number.
Published: [1985]–[1992]. Notes: Volumes for [1985]–[1990] titled *Law Reports of the Commonwealth. Constitutional and Administrative Law Reports* (same form of citation). Br & Ph 308.

*Law Reports of the Commonwealth. Constitutional and Administrative Law Reports*; see *Law Reports of the Commonwealth. Constitutional Law Reports.*

*Law Reports of the Commonwealth. Criminal Law Reports.*
Recommended citation: [volume year] LRC (Crim) page number.
Published: [1985]–[1992]. Br & Ph 308.

*Law Society's Gazette.*
Recommended citation: (year of decision or of publication of article) volume number LS Gaz page number.
Published: 90 vols 1903–93. Notes: Subsequent vols titled *Gazette* (q.v.).

*Law Teacher.*
Recommended citation: (year of publication of article) volume number Law Teach page number.
Published: 1971 (vol. 5)– . Notes: Volumes 1–4 titled *Journal of the Association of Law Teachers* (q.v.).

*Law Times.* 1843 to 1859.
Recommended citation: (year of decision or of publication of article) volume number LT OS page number.
Published: 34 vols 1843–59. Covering: 1843–59. Br & Ph 332.

*Law Times.* 1859 to 1965.
Recommended citation: (year of decision or of publication of article) volume number LT Jo page number.
Published: 236 vols 1859 to 1965. Covering: 1859–1965. Notes: Only short reports of cases. Full reports were published separately in the *Law Times Reports* (LT). Some cases reported in LT Jo are not in LT. In 1965 amalgamated with the *Law Journal* to form the *New Law Journal* (q.v.).

*Law Times Reports.*
Recommended citation: (year of decision) volume number LT page number.
Published: 177 vols 1860–1947. Covering: 1859–1947. Br & Ph 333.

Lawson, W., *Notes of Decisions under the Representation of the People Acts and the Registration Acts.*
Recommended citation: (year of decision) volume number Laws Reg Cas page number.
Published: 4 vols 1894–1914. Covering: 1885–1914. Br & Ph 1421.

Leach, Thomas, *Cases in Crown Law.*
Recommended citation: (year of decision) volume number Leach page number.
Published: 1 vol. 1789, 4th ed. in 2 vols 1815. Covering: 1730–1815. Notes: In 168 ER. Pagination is continuous, vol. 2 starting on p. 545. Br & Ph 728.

Lee, Sir George, *Reports . . . Arches and Prerogative Courts of Canterbury.*
Recommended citation: (year of decision) volume number Lee page number.
Published: 2 vols 1833–2. Covering: 1752–8. Notes: In 161 ER. Edited by Joseph Phillimore. Br & Ph 486.

*Legal Action.*
Recommended citation: (year of decision or of publication of article) month and year of issue without brackets Legal Action page number.
Published: January 1984– . Notes: Earlier issues titled *LAG Bulletin* (q.v.).

*Legal Action Group Circular*; see *LAG Bulletin.*

*Legal Decisions Affecting Bankers.*
Recommended citation: (year of decision) volume number LDB page number.
Published: 1900– . Br & Ph 831.

*Legal Reporter.*
Recommended citation: (year of decision) volume number Leg Rep page number.
Published: 3 vols 1840–3. Covering: 1840–3. Br & Ph 1327.

*Legal Studies.*
Recommended citation: (year of publication of article) volume number LS page number.
Published: 1981– . Notes: Successor to *Journal of the Society of Public Teachers of Law* (q.v.).
Leigh, E. Chandos, and Cave, Lewis W., *Crown Cases Reserved.*
Recommended citation: (year of decision) Le & Ca page number.
Published: 1 vol. 1866. Covering: 1861–5. Notes: In 169 ER. Br & Ph 729.
Leigh, Sir James; see Ley, Sir James.
Leonard, William, *Reports . . . Courts at Westminster.*
Recommended citation: (year of decision) volume number Leo page number.
Published: 4 vols 1658–75, 2nd ed. 1686–7. Covering: 1540–1615. Notes: 2nd ed. in 74 ER. Translated into English by William Hughes from a manuscript in law French. Br & Ph 584.
Levinz, Sir Creswell, *Reports.*
Recommended citation: (year of decision) volume number Lev page number.
Published: 3 vols in law French 1702, 2nd ed. with an English transl. by Salkeld 1722. 3rd ed. 1793–7 contains Salkeld's transl. and a transl. by Thomas Vickers of relevant pleadings originally published in Latin. Covering: 1660–97. Notes: 3rd ed. in 83 ER. Br & Ph 585.
Lewin, Sir Gregory A., *Report . . . Crown Side on the Northern Circuit.*
Recommended citation: (year of decision) volume number Lewin page number.
Published: 2 vols 1834–9. Covering: 1822–38. Notes: In 168 ER. Br & Ph 730.
Ley, Sir James, *Reports . . . Court of Wards [etc.].*
Recommended citation: (year of decision) Ley page number.
Published: 1 vol. 1659. Covering: 1608–29. Notes: In 80 ER. The author's name is sometimes spelt Leigh. Br & Ph 586.
Lilly, John, *Reports and Pleadings of Cases in Assise.*
Recommended citation: (year of decision) Lil page number.
Published: 1 vol. 1719. Covering: 1688–93. Notes: In 170 ER. Br & Ph 650.
*Litigation.*
Recommended citation: (year of publication of article) volume number Lit page number.
Published: 1981– .
Littleton, Edw., Baron de Mounslow, *Reports . . . Common Bank & Exchequer.*
Recommended citation: (year of decision) Litt page number.
Published: 1 vol. 1683. Covering: 1626–32. Notes: In 124 ER. In law French. Br & Ph 452.
*Liverpool Law Review.*
Recommended citation: (year of publication of article) volume number Liverpool L Rev page number.
Published: 1979– .
Lloyd, B.C., and Goold, F., *Reports . . . Chancery in Ireland, during the time of Lord Chancellor Sugden.*
Recommended citation: (year of decision) Ll & G t Sug page number.
Published: 1 vol. 1836. Covering: 1834–9. Br & Ph 1342.
Lloyd, B.C., and Goold, F., *Selection of Cases . . . Chancery in Ireland, during the time of Lord Chancellor Plunket.*
Recommended citation: (year of decision) Ll & G t Plunk page number.
Published: 1 vol. 1839. Covering: 1834–9. Br & Ph 1343.

Lloyd, J.H., and Welsby, W.N., *Mercantile Cases.*
Recommended citation: (year of decision) Ll & W page number.
Published: 1 vol. 1830. Covering: 1829–30. Br & Ph 832.
*Lloyd's Arbitration Reports.*
Recommended citation: [volume year] LAR page number.
Published: [1988]– .
*Lloyd's Law Reports.*
Recommended citation: [volume year] volume number Lloyd's Rep page number.
Published: [1951]– . Notes: 2 vols a year. Volumes for [1951] 1 to [1967] 2 titled
*Lloyd's List Law Reports* (same form of citation). For citation of earlier vols of
*Lloyd's List Law Reports* see the entry for that title. Br & Ph 833.
*Lloyd's List Law Reports.* 1919–51.
Recommended citation: (year of decision) volume number Ll L Rep page number.
Published: 84 vols 1919–51. Notes: For citation of later vols see *Lloyd's Law
Reports.* Br & Ph 833.
*Lloyd's Maritime and Commercial Law Quarterly.*
Recommended citation: [volume year] LMCLQ page number.
Published: [1974]– .
*Lloyd's Reinsurance Law Reports.*
Recommended citation: [volume year] LRLR page number.
Published: [1996]–.
*Lloyd's Reports of Prize Cases.*
Recommended citation: (year of decision) volume number Ll Pri Cas page number.
Published: 10 vols 1915–24. Covering: 1914–24. Br & Ph 813.
*Lloyd's Reports of Prize Cases,* 2nd Series.
Recommended citation: (year of decision) Ll Pri Cas NS page number.
Published: one volume 1957. Covering: 1939–53. Br & Ph 814.
*Local Government Reports*; see *Knight's Local Government Reports.*
*Local Government Review.*
Recommended citation: (year of decision or of publication of article) volume
number LG Rev page number.
Published: 1971 (vol. 136)– . Notes: Volume numbering continues from the
numbering of *Justice of the Peace and Local Government Review.*
*Locus Standi Reports.*
Recommended citation: [volume year] LSR page number.
Published: [1936-60] and [1961-83]. Notes: Volume for [1961-83] ed. H.M.
Barclay. Br & Ph 794.
Lofft, Capel, *Reports . . . King's Bench.*
Recommended citation: (year of decision) Lofft page number.
Published: 1 vol. 1776, 2nd ed. 1790. Covering: 1772–4. Notes: 2nd ed. in 98 ER.
Br & Ph 587.
Longfield, R., and Townsend, J.F., *Reports . . . Exchequer in Ireland.*
Recommended citation: (year of decision) Long & T page number.
Published: 1 vol. 1843. Covering: 1841-2. Br & Ph 1356.
Lowndes, J.J., and Maxwell, P.B., *Bail Court Cases.*
Recommended citation: (year of decision) Lownd & M page number.
Published: 1 vol. 1854. Covering: 1852-4. Br & Ph 364.
Lowndes, J.J., Maxwell, P.B., and Pollock, C.E., *Reports . . . Queen's Bench Practice
Court.*
Recommended citation: (year of decision) volume number Lownd M & P page
number.

Published: 2 vols 1851–2. Covering: 1850–1. Br & Ph 365.

Luders, A., *Reports . . . Controverted Elections.*
Recommended citation: (year of decision) volume number Lud El Cas page number.
Published: 3 vols 1788–90, [new ed.] of vol.1 1808. Covering: 1784–7. Br & Ph 859.

Lumley, W.G., *Abridgment of Cases upon Poor Law,* vols 1 and 2.
Recommended citation: (year of decision) volume number Lum PL Cas page number.
Published: 2 vols 1840–3. Covering: 1834–42. Notes: For vol. 3 see Archbold, J.F., for vol. 4 see Paterson, J. Br & Ph 925.

Lushington, Vernon, *Reports . . . Admiralty.*
Recommended citation: (year of decision) Lush page number.
Published: 1 vol. 1864. Covering: 1859–62. Notes: In 167 ER. Br & Ph 352.

Lutwyche, A.J.P., *Reports . . . Court of Common Pleas.* [Registration Cases.]
Recommended citation: (year of decision) volume number Lut Reg Cas page number.
Published: 2 vols 1847–54. Covering: 1843–53. Br & Ph 886.

Lutwyche, Sir Edward, *Un Livre des Entries . . . auxi . . . Report.*
Recommended citation: (year of decision) volume number Lut page number.
Published: 2 vols 1704. Covering: 1682–1704. Notes: In 125 ER. In law French and Latin. Br & Ph 453.

MacCarthy, J.H., *Leading Cases in Land Purchase Law.*
Recommended citation: (year of decision) MacCarthy page number.
Published: 1 vol. 1892. Covering: 1887–92. Br & Ph 1409.

MacDevitt, E.O., *Land Cases.* [Ireland.]
Recommended citation: (year of decision) MacDev page number.
Published: 1 vol. 1884. Covering: 1882–4. Br & Ph 1410.

Macfarlane, Robert, Lord Ormidale, *Reports . . . Court of Session.*
Recommended citation: (year of decision) Macf page number.
Published: 1 vol. 1841. Covering: 1838–9. Br & Ph 1638.

MacGillivray, E.J., *Copyright Cases.*
Recommended citation: (year of decision) volume number MacG page number.
Published: 2 vols 1905–51. Covering: 1901–49. Notes: Last part by E.J. MacGillivray and J.G. Le Quesne. Br & Ph 770.

MacLaurin, J., *Arguments and Decisions in Remarkable Cases before the High Court of Justiciary.*
Recommended citation: (year of decision) Macl Rem Cas page number.
Published: 1 vol. 1774. Covering: 1670–1773. Br & Ph 1602.

Maclean, Charles Hope, and Robinson, George, *Cases . . . House of Lords.*
Recommended citation: (year of decision) Macl & R page number.
Published: 1 vol. 1840. Covering: 1839. Notes: In 9 ER. Br & Ph 535, 1655.

Macnaghten, Steuart, and Gordon, Alexander, *Reports . . . Chancery.*
Recommended citation: (year of decision) volume number Mac & G page number.
Published: 3 vols 1850–2. Covering: 1849–51. Notes: In 41 ER (vol. 1) and 42 ER (vols 2 and 3). Br & Ph 401.

Macpherson, Norman, *Cases . . . Court of Session, Teind Court and House of Lords.* [Session Cases, 3rd series.]
Recommended citation: (year of decision) volume number M page number; (HL) page number for House of Lords cases.
Published: 11 vols 1863–73. Covering: 1862–73. Br & Ph 1640.

Macqueen, J.F., *Reports of Scotch Appeals ... House of Lords.*
Recommended citation: (year of decision) volume number Macq page number.
Published: 4 vols 1855–66. Covering: 1851–65. Br & Ph 1656.

Macrae, D.C., and Hertslet, C.J.B., *Reports ... Insolvency.*
Recommended citation: (year of decision) volume number Macr & H page number.
Published: 2 vols 1852–4. Covering: 1847–52. Br & Ph 703.

Macrory, E., *Reports of Cases Relating to Letters Patent for Inventions.*
Recommended citation: (year of decision) Macr Pat Cas page number.
Published: 1 vol. c. 1860. Covering: 1847–60. Br & Ph 771.

Maddock, Henry, *Reports ... Vice-Chancellor.*
Recommended citation: (year of decision) volume number Madd page number.
Published: 6 vols 1817–29. Covering: 1815–22. Notes: In 56 ER. Volume 6 is partly by Maddock and partly by T.C. Geldart. Br & Ph 678.

Manning, James, and Granger, T.C., *Cases ... Common Pleas.*
Recommended citation: (year of decision) volume number Man & G page number.
Published: 7 vols 1841–6. Covering: 1840–4. Notes: In 133 ER (vols 1–3), 134 ER (vols 4–6) and 135 ER (vol. 7). Br & Ph 454.

Manning, James, and Ryland, Archer, *Reports ... King's Bench.*
Recommended citation: (year of decision) volume number Man & Ry KB page number.
Published: 5 vols 1828–37. Covering: 1827–30. Br & Ph 631.

Manning, James, and Ryland, Archer, *Reports of Cases Relating to the Duty and Office of Magistrates.*
Recommended citation: (year of decision) volume number Man & Ry MC page number.
Published: 3 vols 1829–32. Covering: 1827–30. Br & Ph 804.

Manning, W.M., *Proceedings in Courts of Revision.*
Recommended citation: (year of decision) Man page number.
Published: 1 vol. 1836. Covering: 1832–5. Br & Ph 887.

Manson, E., *Reports ... Bankruptcy and Companies Winding-up.*
Recommended citation: (year of decision) volume number Mans page number.
Published: 21 vols 1894–1915. Covering: 1894–1914. Notes: Volumes 6–21 titled *Reports of Bankruptcy and Company Cases* (same form of citation). There were various co-editors. Br & Ph 704.

*Manx Law Bulletin.*
Recommended citation: (year of decision) volume number MLB page number.
Published: 1983?– .

*Manx Law Reports.*
Recommended citation: volume year without brackets MLR page number.
Published: 1961-71– . Notes: Volumes so far are for 1961-71, 1972-7, 1978-80, 1981-3, 1984-6, 1987-9, 1990-2, 1993-5.

March, John, *Reports: or, New Cases.*
Recommended citation: (year of decision) March NC page number.
Published: 1 vol. 1648, 2nd ed. 1675. Covering: 1639–42. Notes: 2nd ed. in 82 ER. Br & Ph 588.

Marrack, R., *European Assurance Arbitration before Lord Westbury.*
Recommended citation: (year of decision) Eur Ass Arb page number.
Published: 1 vol. 1875. Covering: 1872–4. Notes: Published with the *Law Times*. Br & Ph 834.

Marshall, C., *Reports . . . Common Pleas.*
　Recommended citation: (year of decision) volume number Marsh page number.
　Published: 2 vols 1815–17. Covering: 1813–16. Br & Ph 465.
Maule, George, and Selwyn, William, *Reports . . . King's Bench.*
　Recommended citation: (year of decision) volume number M & S page number.
　Published: 6 vols 1814–29. Covering: 1813–17. Notes: In 105 ER. Br & Ph 589.
Maxwell, T.H., *Irish Land Purchase Cases.*
　Recommended citation: (year of decision) Maxwell page number.
　Published: 1 vol. 1912. Covering: 1904–11. Br & Ph 1411.
M'Cleland, Thomas, *Reports . . . Exchequer.*
　Recommended citation: (year of decision) M'Cle page number.
　Published: 1 vol. 1825. Covering: 1824. Notes: In 148 ER. Br & Ph 506.
M'Cleland, Thomas, and Younge, Edward, *Reports . . . Exchequer.*
　Recommended citation: (year of decision) M'Cle & Y page number.
　Published: 1 vol. 1827. Covering: 1824–5. Notes: In 148 ER. Br & Ph 507.
*Medical Law Reports.*
　Recommended citation: (year of decision) volume number Med LR page number.
　Published: 1989– . Notes: The publisher's suggested form of citation includes a
　year in square brackets as well as the volume number but this is not
　recommended, as explained in section 2.4.2.6.
*Medicine Science and the Law.*
　Recommended citation: (year of publication of article) volume number Med Sci
　Law page number.
　Published: 1960– .
Meeson, R., and Welsby, W.N., *Reports . . . Exchequer.*
　Recommended citation: (year of decision) volume number M & W page number.
　Published: 16 vols 1837–49. Covering: 1836–47. Notes: In 150 ER (vols 1–4), 151
　ER (vols 5–8), 152 ER (vols 9–12) and 153 ER (vols 13–16). Vol. 16 is by R.P.
　Tyrwhitt and E.T. Hurlstone. Volume 17 is an index by Edward Wise. Br & Ph
　508.
Megone, William Bernard, *Reports of Cases under the Companies Acts.*
　Recommended citation: (year of decision) volume number Meg page number.
　Published: 2 vols 1890–1. Covering: 1888–90. Br & Ph 835.
Merivale, J.H., *Reports . . . Chancery.*
　Recommended citation: (year of decision) volume number Mer page number.
　Published: 3 vols 1817–19. Covering: 1815–17. Notes: In 35 ER (vols 1 and 2) and
　36 ER (vol. 3). Br & Ph 402.
Millin, S.S., *Digest . . . Decisions . . . Relating to Petty Sessions in Ireland.*
　Recommended citation: (year of decision) Millin page number.
　Published: 1 vol. 1898. Covering: 1875–98. Br & Ph 1383.
Milward, C.R., *Reports . . . Court of Prerogative in Ireland.*
　Recommended citation: (year of decision) Milw page number.
　Published: 1 vol. 1847. Covering: 1819–43. Br & Ph 1389.
Ministry of Pensions and National Insurance, *Reported Decisions of the Commis-
　sioner under the National Insurance Acts*; see Department of Health and Social
　Security, *Reported Decisions of the Commissioner under the National Insurance
　and Family Allowances Acts.*
Ministry of Pensions and National Insurance, *Reported Decisions of the Commis-
　sioner under the National Insurance (Industrial Injuries) Acts*; see Department
　of Health and Social Security, *Reported Decisions of the Commissioner under the
　Social Security and National Insurance (Industrial Injuries) Acts.*

*Modern Law Review.*
Recommended citation: (year of publication of article) volume number MLR page number.
Published: 1937– .

*Modern Reports.*
Recommended citation: (year of decision) volume number Mod page number.
Published: 12 vols 1682–1738, 5th ed. by Thomas Leach 1793–6. Covering: 1669–1732. Notes: In 86 ER (vols 1 and 2), 87 ER (vols 3–7) and 88 ER (vols 8–12). Volume 1 was by Anthony Colquitt. The 1st eds of vols 6–12 (1713–38) were not under the title *Modern Reports*: vols 6 and 7 were *Modern Cases* (vol. 7 by Thomas Farresley), vols 8 and 9 were *Modern Cases in Law and Equity*, vol. 10 was *Cases in Law and Equity, Chiefly during the Time the Earl of Macclesfield Presided in the Courts of King's Bench and Chancery* by Robert Lucas, vol. 11 reported cases during the reign of Queen Anne (cases from the reigns of George I and George II were added in Leach's ed.). Leach's ed. of vol. 7 includes cases reported by Luke Benne. Br & Ph 590–600.

Molloy, P., *Reports ... Chancery in Ireland.*
Recommended citation: (year of decision) volume number Mol page number.
Published: 3 vols 1832. Covering: 1827–31. Br & Ph 1344.

Montagu, B., *Reports ... Bankruptcy.*
Recommended citation: (year of decision) Mont page number.
Published: 1 vol. 1832. Covering: 1829–32. Br & Ph 705.

Montagu, B., and Ayrton, S., *Reports ... Bankruptcy.*
Recommended citation: (year of decision) volume number Mont & A page number.
Published: 3 vols 1834–8. Covering: 1833–8. Br & Ph 706.

Montagu, B., and Bligh, R., *Reports ... Bankruptcy.*
Recommended citation: (year of decision) Mont & B page number.
Published: 1 vol. 1835. Covering: 1832–3. Br & Ph 707.

Montagu, B., and Chitty, E., *Reports ... Bankruptcy.*
Recommended citation: (year of decision) Mont & Ch page number.
Published: 1 vol. 1840. Covering: 1838–40. Br & Ph 708.

Montagu, B., and MacArthur, J., *Reports ... Bankruptcy.*
Recommended citation: (year of decision) Mont & M page number.
Published: 1 vol. 1830. Covering: 1828–9. Br & Ph 710.

Montagu, B., Deacon, E.E., and De Gex, J., *Reports ... Bankruptcy.*
Recommended citation: (year of decision) volume number Mont D & De G Bcy page number.
Published: 3 vols 1842–5. Covering: 1840–4. Br & Ph 709.

Moody, William, *Crown Cases Reserved.*
Recommended citation: (year of decision) volume number Mood CC page number.
Published: 2 vols 1837–44. Covering: 1824–44. Notes: In 168 ER (vol. 1) and 169 ER (vol. 2). Br & Ph 731.

Moody, William, and Malkin, Benjamin Heath, *Reports ... Nisi Prius.*
Recommended citation: (year of decision) Mood & M page number.
Published: 1 vol. 1831. Covering: 1826–30. Notes: In 173 ER. Br & Ph 657.

Moody, William, and Robinson, Frederic, *Reports ... Nisi Prius.*
Recommended citation: (year of decision) volume number Mood & R page number.
Published: 2 vols 1837–44. Covering: 1830–44. Notes: In 174 ER. Br & Ph 658.

Moore, Edmund F., *Reports ... Privy Council.*
Recommended citation: (year of decision) volume number Moo PC page number.
Published: 15 vols 1840–67. Covering: 1836–62. Notes: In 12 ER (vols 1 and 2),
13 ER (vols 3–7), 14 ER (vols 8–12) and 15 ER (vols 13–15). See also Moore,
Edmund F., *Reports ... Privy Council.* [New Series.] Br & Ph 662.
Moore, Edmund F., *Reports ... Privy Council.* [New Series.]
Recommended citation: (year of decision) volume number Moo PC NS page
number.
Published: 9 vols 1862–73. Covering: 1862–73. Notes: In 15 ER (vols 1 and 2), 16
ER (vols 3–6) and 17 ER (vols 7–9). See also Moore, Edmund F., *Reports ... Privy
Council.* Br & Ph 663.
Moore, Edmund F., *Reports ... Privy Council, on Appeal from ... the East
Indies.*
Recommended citation: (year of decision) volume number Moo Ind App page
number.
Published: 14 vols. Covering: 1836–72. Notes: In 18 ER (vols 1–5), 19 ER (vols
6–10) and 20 ER (vols 11–14). Br & Ph 995.
Moore, Sir Francis, *Cases.*
Recommended citation: (year of decision) Moo KB page number.
Published: 1 vol. 1663, 3rd ed. (called 2nd on title-page) 1688. Covering:
1519–1621. Notes: 1688 ed. in 72 ER. In law French. Br & Ph 601.
Moore, J.B., *Reports ... Common Pleas.*
Recommended citation: (year of decision) volume number Moo page number.
Published: 12 vols 1818–31. Covering: 1818–27. Br & Ph 466.
Moore, J.B., and Payne, J., *Reports ... Common Pleas.*
Recommended citation: (year of decision) volume number Moo & P page number.
Published: 5 vols 1828–32. Covering: 1827–31. Br & Ph 467.
Moore, J.B., and Scott, J., *Cases ... Common Pleas.*
Recommended citation: (year of decision) volume number Moo & S page number.
Published: 4 vols 1833–4. Covering: 1831–4. Br & Ph 468.
Morison, W.M., *Decisions of the Court of Session ... in the Form of a
Dictionary.*
Recommended citation: (year of decision) Mor page number.
Published: 38 vols 1801–7 paginated continuously. Usually bound in 19 vols.
Appendix 1810. Supplemental volume 1815. Covering: 1540–1808. Notes: See
also Elchies, Lord (Patrick Grant), *Decisions of the Court of Session,* which is
sometimes regarded as app. 2 to Morison's *Dictionary,* and Morison, W.M.,
*Synopsis of ... Decisions of the Court of Session,* which is sometimes bound as
vols 23 and 24 of Morison's *Dictionary.* See also Brown, M.P., *Supplement to the
Dictionary of Decisions of the Court of Session.* Br & Ph 1652.
Morison, W.M., *Synopsis of ... Decisions of the Court of Session.*
Recommended citation: (year of decision) volume number Mor Syn page number.
Published: 2 vols 1814–? Covering: 1808–16. Notes: Sometimes bound as vols 23 and
24 of Morison, W.M., *Decisions of the Court of Session ... in the Form of a Dictionary.*
Morrell, C.F., *Reports of Cases under the Bankruptcy Act 1883.*
Recommended citation: (year of decision) volume number Morr page number.
Published: 10 vols 1885–94. Covering: 1884–93. Br & Ph 711.
Mosely, William, *Reports ... Chancery.*
Recommended citation: (year of decision) Mos page number.
Published: 1 vol. 1744, 2nd ed. 1793. Covering: 1726–31. Notes: 2nd ed. in 25 ER.
Br & Ph 403.

*Munitions Appeal Reports*; see *Appeals from Munitions Tribunals.*
*Munitions of War Acts 1915–1916. Scottish Appeal Reports.*
  Recommended citation: (year of decision) Mun App Sc page number.
  Published: 1 vol. 1920.
Murphy, F.S., and Hurlstone, E.T., *Reports ... Exchequer.*
  Recommended citation: (year of decision) Mur & H page number.
  Published: 1 vol. 1838. Covering: 1836–7. Br & Ph 520.
Murray, J., *Reports ... Jury Court.*
  Recommended citation: (year of decision) volume number Mur page number.
  Published: 5 vols 1818–31. Covering: 1815–30. Br & Ph 1676.
Mylne, J.W., and Craig, R.D., *Reports ... Chancery.*
  Recommended citation: (year of decision) volume number My & Cr page number.
  Published: 5 vols 1837–48. Covering: 1835–41. Notes: In 40 ER (vols 1–3) and 41
  ER (vols 4 and 5). Br & Ph 404.
Mylne, J.W., and Keen, Benjamin, *Reports ... Chancery.*
  Recommended citation: (year of decision) volume number My & K page number.
  Published: 3 vols 1834–7. Covering: 1832–5. Notes: In 39 ER (vols 1 and 2) and
  40 ER (vol. 3). Br & Ph 405.


Nelson, W., *Reports ... Chancery.*
  Recommended citation: (year of decision) Nels page number.
  Published: 1 vol. 1717. Covering: 1625–93. Notes: In 21 ER. Originally published
  in octavo format. There is also an 1872 ed. Br & Ph 406.
Nevile, S., and Manning, W.M., *Reports of Cases Argued and Determined in the
  Court of King's Bench.*
  Recommended citation: (year of decision) volume number Nev & M KB page
  number.
  Published: 6 vols 1834–9. Covering: 1832–6. Br & Ph 632.
Nevile, S., and Manning, W.M., *Reports of Cases Relating to the Duty and Office of
  Magistrates.*
  Recommended citation: (year of decision) volume number Nev & M MC page
  number.
  Published: 3 vols 1834–8. Covering: 1832–6. Br & Ph 805.
Nevile, S., and Perry, T.E., *Reports ... King's / Queen's Bench.*
  Recommended citation: (year of decision) volume number Nev & P KB/QB page
  number.
  Published: 3 vols 1837–8. Covering: 1836–8. Notes: KB up to vol. 2, p. 354, then
  QB. Br & Ph 633.
Nevile, S., and Perry, T.E., *Reports of Cases Relating to the Office of Magistrates.*
  Recommended citation: (year of decision) Nev & P MC page number.
  Published: 1 vol. 1837. Covering: 1836–7. Br & Ph 806.
*New Benloe*; see Benloe, William, *Reports.*
New Law Digest Service; see New Law Publishing.
*New Law Journal.*
  Recommended citation: (year of decision or of publication of article) volume
  number NLJ page number; Practitioner page number for Practitioner section in
  vol. 138.
  Published: 1965 (vol. 116)– . Notes: Volumes 1–115 titled *Law Journal* (q.v.): the
  title was changed on amalgamation with the *Law Times.* Volume 138 is the only
  volume in which the Practitioner section is separately paginated.
New Law Online Service; see New Law Publishing.

New Law Publishing.
Recommended citation: NLC case number.
Notes: The first digit of the number indicates the service (1 for Property, 2 for Commercial, 3 and 4 for Criminal), the second and third digits of the number are the last two of the calendar year, the fourth and fifth are the month (01 to 12), the sixth and seventh (or sixth, seventh and eighth) are the number of the communication, the last two are the number of the case within the communication. Published electronically, New Law Digest Service by fax, New Law Online Service by Internet.
*New Magistrates' Cases*; see *Reports of New Magistrates' Cases.*
*New Practice Cases.*
Recommended citation: (year of decision) volume number New Pr Cas page number.
Published: 3 vols 1847–8. Covering: 1844–8. Br & Ph 874.
*New Reports.*
Recommended citation: (year of decision) volume number New Rep page number.
Published: 6 vols 1863–5. Covering: 1862–5. Br & Ph 334.
*New Sessions Cases.*
Recommended citation: (year of decision) volume number New Sess Cas page number.
Published: 4 vols 1845–51. Covering: 1844–51. Notes: Reporters were J.M. Carrow, J. Hamerton and T. Allen (vols 1 and 2), Hamerton, Allen and C. Otter (vol. 3), G.C. Prideaux and H.T. Cole (vol. 4). Br & Ph 807.
Nisbet, Sir John; see Dirleton, Lord.
Nolan, M., *Reports of Cases Relating to the Duty and Office of a Justice of the Peace.*
Recommended citation: (year of decision) Nolan page number.
Published: 1 vol. 1793. Covering: 1791–2. Br & Ph 808.
*Northern Ireland Law Reports.*
Recommended citation: [volume year] NI page number.
Published: [1925]– . Br & Ph 1553.
*Northern Ireland Law Reports Bulletin of Judgments.*
Recommended citation: [volume year] issue number NIJB page number.
Published: [1970]– . Notes: Up to [1984] each case in an issue is paginated separately. Br & Ph 1552.
*Northern Ireland Legal Quarterly.*
Recommended citation: (year of publication of article) volume number NILQ page number.
Published: 1936– .
*Notes of Cases in the Ecclesiastical and Maritime Courts.*
Recommended citation: (year of decision) volume number Notes of Cas page number.
Published: 7 vols 1843–50. Covering: 1841–50. Notes: Edited by Thomas Thornton.
Noy, William, *Reports.*
Recommended citation: (year of decision) Noy page number.
Published: 1656, 2nd ed. 1669. Covering: 1559–1649. Notes: In 74 ER. Br & Ph 602.

*Occupational Pensions Law Reports.*
Recommended citation: [volume year] OPLR page number.
Published: [1992]– .

*Oil and Gas Law and Taxation Review.*
　　Recommended citation: [volume year] OGLTR page number; D-page number for News Section.
　　Published: [1982]– . Notes: The publisher's suggested form of citation gives the issue number after the [volume year] but this is superfluous.
*Old Bailey Sessions Papers.*
　　Recommended citation: (year of decision) OBSP.
　　Published: c. 100 vols 1714–1833 and other earlier vols now lost. Covering: 1714–1833. Br & Ph 732.
*Old Benloe*; see Benloe, William, *Reports*, and Dalison, Sir William, *Reports*.
*Old Faculty Reports*; see *Faculty Collection. Old Series.*
O'Malley, E.L., and Hardcastle, H., *Reports . . . Election Petitions.*
　　Recommended citation: (year of decision) volume number O'M & H page number.
　　Published: 7 vols 1870–1929. Covering: 1869–1929. Notes: Volume 4 by J.S. Sanders and A.P. Keep, vol. 5 by J.S. Sanders, vols 6 and 7 by H. Cohen. Br & Ph 860.
Ormidale, Lord; see Macfarlane, Robert.
Owen, Thomas, *Reports . . . King's Bench and Common Pleas.*
　　Recommended citation: (year of decision) Ow page number.
　　Published: 1 vol. 1656. Covering: 1556–1615. Notes: In 74 ER. In the *English Reports* the date of original publication is given as 1650 but this seems to be erroneous. Br & Ph 603.
*Oxford Journal of Legal Studies.*
　　Recommended citation: (year of publication of article) volume number Oxford J Legal Stud page number.
　　Published: 1981– .


Palmer, Sir Gefrey, *Reports.*
　　Recommended citation: (year of decision) Palm page number.
　　Published: 1 vol. 1678, later ed. 1721. Covering: 1619–29. Notes: 1721 ed. in 81 ER. In law French. Br & Ph 604.
*Palmer's Company Cases.*
　　Recommended citation: volume year without brackets PCC page number.
　　Published: 1985–1989.
Parker, Sir Thomas, *Reports . . . Exchequer.*
　　Recommended citation: (year of decision) Park page number.
　　Published: 1 vol. 1776, 2nd ed. 1791. Covering: 1743–67. Notes: 2nd ed. in 145 ER. Br & Ph 509.
Paterson, J., *Abridgment of Cases upon Poor Law*, vol. 4.
　　Recommended citation: (year of decision) Pat PL Cas page number.
　　Published: 1 vol. 1864. Covering: 1857–63. Notes: For vols 1 and 2 see Lumley, W.G.; for vol. 3 see Archbold, J.F. Br & Ph 926.
Paterson, J., *Reports of Scotch Appeals . . . House of Lords.*
　　Recommended citation: (year of decision) volume number Paters page number.
　　Published: 2 vols 1879–95. Covering: 1851–73. Br & Ph 1657.
Paton, Thomas S., *Reports . . . House of Lords . . . Scotland.*
　　Recommended citation: (year of decision) volume number Pat page number.
　　Published: 6 vols 1849–56. Covering: 1726–1821. Notes: Volume 1 sometimes known as 'Craigie, Stewart and Paton'. Br & Ph 1658.
Peake, Thomas, *Additional Cases . . . Nisi Prius.*
　　Recommended citation: (year of decision) Peake Add Cas page number.

Published: 1 vol. 1829. Covering: 1795–1812. Notes: In 170 ER. Br & Ph 651.

Peake, Thomas, *Cases Determined at Nisi Prius.*
Recommended citation: (year of decision) Peake page number.
Published: 1 vol. 1795, 3rd ed. 1820. Covering: 1790–4. Notes: 3rd ed. in 170 ER.
Br & Ph 652.

Peckwell, R.H., *Cases of Controverted Elections.*
Recommended citation: (year of decision) volume number Peck page number.
Published: 2 vols 1805–6. Covering: 1802–6. Br & Ph 861.

Peere Williams, William, *Reports . . . Chancery.*
Recommended citation: (year of decision) volume number P Wms page number.
Published: 2 vols 1740, 6th ed. in 3 vols by J.B. Munro, W.L. Lowndes and J.
Randall 1826. Covering: 1695–1735. Notes: 6th ed. in 24 ER. Br & Ph 407.

Perry, H.J., and Knapp, J.W., *Cases of Controverted Elections.*
Recommended citation: (year of decision) Per & K page number.
Published: 1 vol. 1833. Covering: 1833. Br & Ph 862.

Perry, T., *Reports . . . Court for the Relief of Insolvent Debtors.*
Recommended citation: (year of decision) Per Insolv page number.
Published: 1 vol. 1831. Covering: 1831. Br & Ph 712.

Perry, T.E., and Davison, H., *Reports . . . Queen's Bench.*
Recommended citation: (year of decision) volume number Per & Dav page number.
Published: 4 vols 1839–42. Covering: 1838–41. Br & Ph 634.

*Personal Injuries and Quantum Reports.*
Recommended citation: [volume year] PIQR Ppage number for Personal Injuries
section; Qpage number for Quantum section.
Published: [1992]– .

Philipps, John, *Election Cases.*
Recommended citation: (year of decision) Ph El Cas page number.
Published: 1 vol. 1782. Covering: 1780–1. Br & Ph 863.

Phillimore, Joseph, *Reports . . . Ecclesiastical Courts.*
Recommended citation: (year of decision) volume number Phil Ecc page number.
Published: 3 vols 1818–27. Covering: 1809–21. Notes: In 161 ER. Br & Ph 487.

Phillimore, Sir Robert, *Principal Ecclesiastical Judgments.*
Recommended citation: (year of decision) Phil Judg page number.
Published: 1 vol. 1876. Covering: 1867–75. Br & Ph 488.

Phillips, T.J., *Reports . . . Chancery.*
Recommended citation: (year of decision) volume number Ph page number.
Published: 2 vols 1847–9. Covering: 1841–9. Notes: In 41 ER. Br & Ph 408.

Pigott, G., and Rodwell, H., *Reports . . . Court of Common Pleas.* [Registration Cases.]
Recommended citation: (year of decision) Pig & R page number.
Published: 1 vol. 1846. Covering: 1843–5. Br & Ph 888.

Pitcairn, Robert, *Criminal Trials in Scotland.*
Recommended citation: (year of decision) volume number Pitc page number.
Published: 3 vols 1833. Covering: 1488–1624.

*Planning and Compensation Reports*; see *Property, Planning and Compensation
Reports.*

*Planning Appeal Decisions.*
Recommended citation: (year of decision) volume number PAD page number.
Published: 1986– .

*Planning Law Reports*; see *Estates Gazette Planning Law Reports.*

*Pleading and Practice Cases.*
Recommended citation: (year of decision) Pl & Pr Cas page number.

Published: 1 vol. c. 1840. Covering: 1837–8. Br & Ph 875.

Plowden, Edmund, *Commentaries, or Reports.*
Recommended citation: (year of decision) volume number Plow page number; App page number for appendix.
Published: 2 vols in law French 1571–9, in English 1761, new ed. (English) 1816. Covering: 1550–80. Notes: 1816 ed. in 75 ER. The pagination is continuous, vol. 2 beginning on p. 403. Br & Ph 605.

Pollexfen, Sir Henry, *Arguments and Reports ... in Some Special Cases.*
Recommended citation: (year of decision) Pollex page number.
Published: 1 vol. 1702. Covering: 1669–85. Notes: In 86 ER. Br & Ph 606.

Popham, Sir John, *Reports and Cases.*
Recommended citation: (year of decision) Pop page number.
Published: 1 vol. 1656, 2nd ed. 1682. Covering: 1592–1627. Notes: 1682 ed. in 79 ER. Br & Ph 607.

Power, D., Rodwell, H., and Dew, E.L., *Reports ... Controverted Elections.*
Recommended citation: (year of decision) volume number Pow R & D page number.
Published: 2 vols 1853–7. Covering: 1847–56. Br & Ph 864.

Pratt, John Tidd, *Laws Relating to the Poor, Being a Supplement to the Sixth Edition of Bott's Poor Laws*; see Bott, E., *Laws Relating to the Poor.*

*Precedents in Chancery.*
Recommended citation: (year of decision) Prec Ch page number.
Published: 1 vol. 1733, 2nd ed. by Thomas Finch 1786. Covering: 1689–1722. Notes: 2nd ed. in 24 ER. Br & Ph 409.

Price, George, *Notes of Points in Practice Rules.*
Recommended citation: (year of decision) Price Pr Cas page number.
Published: 1 vol. 1831. Covering: 1830–1. Br & Ph 510.

Price, George, *Reports ... Exchequer.*
Recommended citation: (year of decision) volume number Price page number.
Published: 13 vols 1816–28. Covering: 1814–24. Notes: In 145 ER (vol. 1), 146 ER (vols 2–8) and 147 ER (vols 9–13). Br & Ph 511.

*Private Client Business.*
Recommended citation: [volume year] PCB page number.
Published: [1993]– .

*Privy Council Appeals.* (1865–75); see *Law Reports. Privy Council Appeals.* (1865–75).

*Prize Cases ... during the Great War.*
Recommended citation: (year of decision) volume number Br & Col Pri Cas page number.
Published: 3 vols 1916–22. Covering: 1914–19. Notes: Also known as 'British and Colonial Prize Cases'. Edited by Trehern and Grant. Br & Ph 811.

*Probate and Divorce Cases.* (1865–75); see *Law Reports. Courts of Probate and Divorce.* (1865–75).

*Probate Division.* (1875–90); see *Law Reports. Probate Division.* (1875–90).

*Probate Division.* [1891]–[1971]; see *Law Reports. Probate, Divorce and Admiralty Division.* [1891]–[1971].

*Professional Negligence.*
Recommended citation: (year of publication of article) volume number PN page number.
Published: 1985– .

*Property and Compensation Reports*; see *Property, Planning and Compensation Reports*.
*Property, Planning and Compensation Reports*.
Recommended citation: (year of decision) volume number P & CR page number.
Published: 1951- . Notes: Volumes 1–18 titled *Planning and Compensation Reports* (same form of citation); vols 19–50 titled *Property and Compensation Reports* (same form of citation).
*Public Law*.
Recommended citation: [volume year] PL page number.
Published: [1956]– .
*Public Procurement Law Review*.
Recommended citation: (year of decision or of publication of article) volume number PPLR page number; CS page number for Current Survey section.
Published: 1992– .
*Publications of the European Court of Human Rights. Series A. Judgments and Decisions*.
Recommended citation: (year of decision) Eur Court HR Series A volume number. If there is more than one case in the volume the volume number is followed by a hyphen and the case letter.
Published: 1961– . Notes: If there is more than one case in a volume they are identified as A, B, C etc.
*Publications of the European Court of Human Rights. Series B. Pleadings, Oral Arguments and Documents*.
Recommended citation: (year of decision) Eur Court HR Series B volume number. If there is more than one case in the volume the volume number is followed by a hyphen and the case letter.
Published: 1961– . Notes: If there is more than one case in a volume they are identified as A, B, C etc.

*Queen's Bench Cases*. (1865–75); see *Law Reports. Court of Queen's Bench*. (1865–75).
*Queen's Bench Division*. (1875–90); see *Law Reports ... Queen's Bench Division*. (1875–90).
*Queen's Bench Division*. [1891]–[1900] and [1952] 2– ; see *Law Reports. Queen's Bench Division*. [1891]–[1900] and [1952] 2– .
*Queen's Bench Reports*.
Recommended citation: (year of decision) volume number QB page number.
Published: 18 vols 1843–56. Covering: 1841–52. Notes: In 113 ER (vol. 1), 114 ER (vols 2–5), 115 ER (vols 6–9), 116 ER (vols 10–13), 117 ER (vols 14–17) and 118 ER (vol. 18). The reporters were John Leycester Adolphus and Thomas Flower Ellis. See also Adolphus, John Leycester, and Ellis, Thomas Flower, *Reports ... King's / Queen's Bench* covering 1834–40. Br & Ph 608.

*Railway and Canal Cases*; see *Cases Relating to Railways and Canals*.
*Railway and Canal Traffic Cases*; see *Traffic Cases*.
*Railway, Canal and Road Traffic Cases*; see *Traffic Cases*.
Rastell, William, *A Collection of Entries*.
Recommended abbreviation: Rast.
Published: 1 vol. 1566, 4th ed. 1670.
*Rating and Income Tax*.
Recommended citation: (year of decision) volume number R & IT page number.

Published: 58 vols 1924–60. Covering: 1924–60. Br & Ph 906.

*Rating and Valuation Reporter.*

Recommended citation: [volume year] RVR page number.

Published: [1961]– . Br & Ph 907.

*Rating Appeals.*

Recommended citation: [volume year] RA page number.

Published: [1962]– . Br & Ph 908.

Raymond, Sir Robert, 1st Baron Raymond, *Reports . . . King's Bench and Common Pleas.*

Recommended citation: (year of decision) volume number Ld Raym page number.

Published: 1743, 4th ed. by John Bayley in 3 vols 1790. Covering: 1694–1732. Notes: 4th ed. in 91 ER (vol. 1) and 92 ER (vols 2 and 3). The pagination of vols 1 and 2 is continuous, vol. 2 beginning on p. 750. There is also a 5th ed. by C.J. Gale 1832. Br & Ph 609.

Raymond, Sir Thomas, *Reports.*

Recommended citation: (year of decision) T Raym page number.

Published: 1 vol. 1696, 3rd ed. 1793, 4th ed. 1803. Covering: 1660–84. Notes: 1803 ed. in 83 ER. Br & Ph 610.

Rayner, J., *Cases at Large Concerning Tithes.*

Recommended citation: (year of decision) volume number Rayn page number.

Published: 3 vols 1783. Covering: 1575–1782. Br & Ph 936.

*Real Property Cases*; see *Reports of Cases . . . Real Property and Conveyancing.*

Reilly, F.S., *Albert Life Assurance Company Arbitration Act 1871: Lord Cairns' Decisions.*

Recommended citation: (year of decision) volume number Cairns' Dec page number.

Published: 1 vol. 1875. Br & Ph 836.

*Reinsurance Law Reports.*

Recommended citation: (year of decision) volume number Re LR page number.

Published: 1992– . Notes: The publisher's suggested form of citation includes a year in square brackets as well as the volume number but this is not recommended, as explained in section 2.4.2.6.

*Reported Decisions of the Commissioner under the National Insurance Acts*; see Department of Health and Social Security, *Reported Decisions of the Commissioner under the National Insurance and Family Allowances Acts.*

*Reported Decisions of the Commissioner under the National Insurance and Family Allowances Acts*; see Department of Health and Social Security, *Reported Decisions of the Commissioner under the National Insurance and Family Allowances Acts.*

*Reported Decisions of the Commissioner under the National Insurance (Industrial Injuries) Acts*; see Department of Health and Social Security, *Reported Decisions of the Commissioner under the Social Security and National Insurance (Industrial Injuries) Acts.*

*Reported Decisions of the Commissioner under the Social Security and Child Benefit Acts*; see Department of Social Security, *Reported Decisions of the Social Security Commissioner.*

*Reported Decisions of the Commissioner under the Social Security and National Insurance (Industrial Injuries) Acts*; see Department of Health and Social Security, *Reported Decisions of the Commissioner under the Social Security and National Insurance (Industrial Injuries) Acts.*

*Reported Decisions of the Social Security Commissioner*; see Department of Social Security, *Reported Decisions of the Social Security Commissioner.*

*Reports, the.*
Recommended citation: (year of decision) volume number R page number.
Published: 15 vols 1894–6. Covering: 1893–5. Br & Ph 336.
*Reports, the*; see Coke, Sir Edward, *Reports.*
*Reports . . . Chancery during the Time Sir Heneage Finch . . . was Lord Chancellor.*
Recommended citation: (year of decision) Rep t Finch page number.
Published: 1 vol. 1725. Covering: 1673–81. Notes: In 23 ER. The reports were
edited by William Nelson and originally published in folio format. Br & Ph 411.
*Reports . . . Court of Exchequer, Scotland.*
Recommended citation: (year of decision) Exch Cas page number.
Published: 1 vol. 1853. Covering: 1840–53. Notes: Also known as 'Exchequer
Cases'. Br & Ph 1595.
*Reports in Chancery*; see *Reports of Cases . . . in the Court of Chancery.*
*Reports . . . Maritime Law.*
Recommended citation: (year of decision) volume number Crockford page number.
Published: 3 vols 1864–71. Covering: 1860–71. Notes: Crockford was the
publisher. Br & Ph 812.
*Reports of Bankruptcy and Companies Winding-up Cases.*
Recommended citation: [volume year] B & CR page number.
Published: [1918-19]–[1940-2]. Notes: The volume years are [1918-19], single
years [1920]–[1928], [1929-30], [1931-2], [1933], [1934-5], [1936-7], [1938-9] and
[1940-2]. Br & Ph 688.
*Reports of Bankruptcy and Company Cases*; see Manson, E., *Reports . . . Bank-
ruptcy and Companies Winding-up.*
*Reports of Cases Decided by Francis Bacon*, Prepared . . . by John Ritchie.
Recommended citation: (year of decision) Bac Rep page number.
Published: 1 vol. 1932. Covering: 1617–21. Br & Ph 372.
*Reports of Cases in Equity*; see Gilbert, J., *Reports of Cases in Equity.*
*Reports of Cases . . . in the Court of Chancery.*
Recommended citation: (year of decision) Rep Ch page number.
Published: 3 vols 1693–1716, 3rd ed. 1736. Covering: 1615–1710. Notes: In 21 ER.
Known as 'Reports in Chancery'. Includes a report of the *Earl of Oxford's Case*
which is separately paginated and was originally published with the 2nd ed. of
vol. 1. Br & Ph 410.
*Reports of Cases . . . on Six Circuits in Ireland.*
Recommended citation: (year of decision) Cas Six Cir page number.
Published: 1 vol. 1843. Covering: 1841–3. Br & Ph 1347.
*Reports of Cases . . . Real Property and Conveyancing.*
Recommended citation: (year of decision) volume number Real Prop Cas page
number.
Published: 2 vols 1846–8. Covering: 1843–8. Notes: Known as 'Real Property
Cases'. Br & Ph 781.
*Reports of Commercial Cases.*
Recommended citation: (year of decision) volume number Com Cas page number.
Published: 46 vols 1895–1941. Notes: Also known as 'Commercial Cases' and
'Times Reports of Commercial Cases'. Br & Ph 838.
*Reports of County Court Cases.*
Recommended citation: (year of decision) volume number Co Ct Rep page number.
Published: 34 vols 1861–1920. Covering: 1860–1920. Notes: Also known as
'County Court Reports', 'Cox's County Court Reports', 'Cox's County Courts
Equity and Bankruptcy Cases'. Br & Ph 473.

*Reports of New Magistrates' Cases.*
Recommended citation: (year of decision) volume number New Mag Cas page number.
Published: 5 vols 1846–51. Covering: 1844–51. Notes: Volumes 3 and 4 titled *Reports of New Magistrates' and Municipal Corporations Cases*, no title-page was issued for vol. 5. Volumes 3–5 were issued as supplements to vols 1–3 of *The Magistrate*. Volumes 1 and 2 were by Bittleston and Wise, vols 3 and 4 by Bittleston and Parnell. Br & Ph 641.

*Reports of Patent Cases*; see *Reports of Patent, Design and Trade Mark Cases.* 1884–1955.

*Reports of Patent, Design and Trade Mark Cases.* 1884–1955.
Recommended citation: (year of decision) volume number RPC page number.
Published: 72 vols 1884–1955. Notes: For citation of later vols see next entry. Volumes 1 and 2 titled *Reports of Patent Cases* (same form of citation). Br & Ph 772.

*Reports of Patent, Design and Trade Mark Cases.* [1956]– .
Recommended citation: [volume year] RPC page number.
Published: [1956]– . Notes: For citation of earlier vols see preceding entry. Br & Ph 772.

*Reports of Restrictive Practices Cases.*
Recommended citation: (year of decision) LR volume number RP page number.
Published: 7 vols 1959–73. Covering: 1957–72. Notes: After vol. 7 incorporated in *Industrial Court Reports* (which was titled *Industrial Cases Reports* after 1975). Br & Ph 758.

*Reports of State Trials, New Series.*
Recommended citation: (year of decision) volume number St Tr NS column number.
Published: 8 vols 1888–98. Covering: 1820–58. Notes: Volumes 1–3 ed. J. Macdonell, vols 4–8 ed. John E.P. Wallis. Within the work the columns (2 to a page) are referred to as 'pages'.

*Reports of Tax Cases.*
Recommended citation: (year of decision) volume number TC page number.
Published: 1875– . Notes: Also known as 'Tax Cases'. Cases are first published in leaflets, one case per leaflet, for which the recommended citation is: (year of decision) TC Leaflet No. number. Br & Ph 910.

*Reserved Cases*; see *Rules and Orders of the Common Law Judges and Reserved Cases.*

Rettie, M., *Cases ... Court of Session, Court of Justiciary and House of Lords.* [Session Cases, 4th series.]
Recommended citation: (year of decision) volume number R page number; (J) page number for Justiciary cases; (HL) page number for House of Lords cases.
Published: 25 vols 1874–98. Covering: 1873–98. Br & Ph 1641.

*Revised Reports.*
Recommended citation: (year of decision) volume number RR page number.
Published: 149 vols 1891–1917. Covering: 1785–1866. Notes: Contains edited versions of earlier published reports. There is also an Index-Digest (2 vols 1919) and a Table of Cases Reported (1 vol. 1920). See Robert G. Logan, 'The Revised Reports' (1982) 13 Law Libr 23.

Rickards, A.G., and Michael, M.J., *Cases ... Court of Referees.* [*Locus Standi.*]
Recommended citation: (year of decision) Rick & M page number.
Published: 1 vol. 1891. Covering: 1885–9. Br & Ph 796.

Rickards, A.G., and Saunders, R.C., *Cases... Court of Referees.* [*Locus Standi.*]
Recommended citation: (year of decision) Rick & S page number.
Published: 1 vol. 1895. Covering: 1890–4. Br & Ph 797.
Ridgeway, W., *Reports... High Court of Parliament in Ireland.*
Recommended citation: (year of decision) volume number Ridg Parl Rep page
number.
Published: 3 vols 1795–8. Covering: 1784–96. Notes: Also known as 'Ridgeway's
Appeal Cases'. Br & Ph 1331.
Ridgeway, W., *Reports... King's Bench and Chancery during the Time in which
Lord Hardwicke Presided.*
Recommended citation: (year of decision) Ridge t Hard page number.
Published: 1 vol. 1794. Covering: 1744–6. Notes: In 27 ER. Br & Ph 412.
Ridgeway, W., Lapp, W., and Schoales, J., *Irish Term Reports.*
Recommended citation: (year of decision) Ridg L & S page number.
Published: 1 vol. 1796. Covering: 1793–5. Br & Ph 1365.
*Ridgeway's Appeal Cases*; see Ridgeway, W., *Reports... High Court of Parliament
in Ireland.*
*Road Law.*
Recommended citation: [volume year] Road Law page number.
Published: [1985]– .
*Road Law Reports.*
Recommended citation: [volume year] RLR page number.
Published: [1985]– .
*Road Traffic Reports.*
Recommended citation: [volume year] RTR page number.
Published: [1970]– . Br & Ph 944.
Roberts, J., *Divorce Bills in the Imperial Parliament.*
Recommended citation: (year of decision) Roberts page number.
Published: 1 vol. 1906. Covering: 1816–1905. Br & Ph 1390.
Roberts, W.H., Leeming, H., and Wallis, J.E., *Reports... on the Law and Practice
of the New County Courts.*
Recommended citation: (year of decision) Rob L & W page number.
Published: 1 vol. 1850–1. Covering: 1849–51. Br & Ph 480.
Robertson, David, *Reports of Cases on Appeal from Scotland... House of Peers.*
Recommended citation: (year of decision) Robert page number.
Published: 1 vol. 1807. Covering: 1707–27. Br & Ph 1659.
Robertson. J.E.P., *Reports... Ecclesiastical Courts.*
Recommended citation: (year of decision) volume number Rob Ecc page number.
Published: 2 vols 1850–3. Covering: 1844–53. Notes: In 163 ER. Br & Ph 489.
Robinson, Chr., *Reports... Admiralty.*
Recommended citation: (year of decision) volume number C Rob page number;
App page number for appendices.
Published: 6 vols 1799–1808, 2nd ed. of vol. 3 1808. Covering: 1798–1808. Notes:
In 165 ER. Page numbers in the appendix to vol. 6 are roman numerals. Br & Ph
353.
Robinson, G., *Cases... House of Lords... Scotland.*
Recommended citation: (year of decision) volume number Robin page number.
Published: 2 vols 1840–2. Covering: 1840–1. Br & Ph 1660.
Robinson, William, *Reports... Admiralty.*
Recommended citation: (year of decision) volume number W Rob page number.
Published: 3 vols 1844–52. Covering: 1838–50. Notes: In 166 ER. Br & Ph 354.

Roche, C.R., Dillon, L., and Kehoe, D., *Reports ... Irish Land Commission.*
Recommended citation: (year of decision) Roche D & K page number.
Published: 1 vol. 1882. Covering: 1881–2. Br & Ph 1412.
Rolle, Henry, *Abridgment des Plusieurs Cases.*
Recommended abbreviation: Roll Abr.
Published: 2 vols 1668. Notes: In law French.
Rolle, Henry, *Reports ... Banke le Roy.*
Recommended citation: (year of decision) volume number Rolle page number.
Published: 2 vols 1675. Covering: 1614–25. Notes: In 81 ER. In law French. Br & Ph 611.
Romilly, Sir Samuel, *Notes of Cases.*
Recommended citation: (year of decision) Rom page number.
Published: 1 vol. 1872. Covering: 1767–87. Br & Ph 429.
Roscoe, E.S., *Reports of Prize Cases.*
Recommended citation: (year of decision) volume number Rosc Pri Cas page number.
Published: 2 vols 1905. Covering: 1745–1858. Br & Ph 816.
Rose, George, *Cases in Bankruptcy.*
Recommended citation: (year of decision) volume number Rose page number.
Published: 2 vols 1813–16, 2nd ed. 1821. Covering: 1810–16. Br & Ph 713.
Ross, George, *Leading Cases in the Commercial Law of England and Scotland.*
Recommended citation: (year of decision) volume number Ross LC Comm page number.
Published: 3 vols 1853–7. Covering: 1707–1855. Br & Ph 839.
Ross, George, *Leading Cases in the Law of Scotland ... Land Rights.*
Recommended citation: (year of decision) volume number Ross LC Land page number.
Published: 3 vols 1849–51. Covering: 1638–1849. Br & Ph 1684.
Rowe, R.R., *Reports of Interesting Cases.*
Recommended citation: (year of decision) Rowe page number.
Published: 1 vol. 1824. Covering: 1798–1823. Br & Ph 687.
*Rules and Orders of the Common Law Judges and Reserved Cases.*
Recommended citation: (year of decision) Reserv Cas page number.
Published: 1 vol. 1865. Covering: 1860–4. Notes: Also known as 'Reserved Cases'. Br & Ph 1349.
Russell, James, *Reports ... Chancery.*
Recommended citation: (year of decision) volume number Russ page number.
Published: 5 vols 1827–9. Covering: 1823–9. Notes: In 38 ER. Er & Ph 413.
Russell, James, and Mylne, J.W., *Reports ... Chancery.*
Recommended citation: (year of decision) volume number Russ & M page number.
Published: 2 vols 1832–7. Covering: 1829–31. Notes: In 39 ER. Br & Ph 414.
Russell, William Oldnall, and Ryan, Edward, *Crown Cases Reserved.*
Recommended citation: (year of decision) Russ & Ry page number.
Published: 1 vol. 1825. Covering: 1799–1823. Notes: In 168 ER. Br & Ph 733.
Ryan, Edward, and Moody, William, *Reports ... Nisi Prius.*
Recommended citation: (year of decision) Ry & M page number.
Published: 1 vol. 1827. Covering: 1823–6. Notes: In 171 ER. Br & Ph 659.
Ryde, E., and Ryde, A.L., *Reports ... Court of General Assessment.*
Recommended citation: (year of decision) volume number Ryde Rat App page number.

Published: 4th ed. by W.C. Ryde in 3 vols 1885–93. Covering: 1871–93. Notes: Earlier editions published under the title *Metropolitan Rating*. Br & Ph 913.

Ryde, W.C., and Konstam, E.M., *Reports of Rating Appeals*.
Recommended citation: (year of decision) Ryde & K Rat App page number.
Published: 1 vol. 1904. Covering: 1894–1904. Br & Ph 912.

*Ryde's Rating Cases*.
Recommended citation: (year of decision) volume number RRC page number.
Published: 21 vols 1957–79. Covering: 1956–79. Br & Ph 914.


Salkeld, William, *Reports . . . King's Bench*.
Recommended citation: (year of decision) volume number Salk page number.
Published: 3 vols 1717–24, 6th ed. by William David Evans 1795. Covering: 1689–1712. Notes: In 91 ER. The pagination of vols 1 and 2 is continuous, vol. 2 beginning on p. 411. Br & Ph 612.

Saunders, Sir Edmund, *Reports . . . King's Bench*.
Recommended citation: (year of decision) volume number Saund page number.
Published: 2 vols in law French and Latin 1686, 2nd ed. with English transl. 1722, 3rd ed. (English only) by John Williams 1799–1802, 6th ed. by Edward Vaughan Williams 1845. Covering: 1666–73. Notes: 6th ed. in 85 ER. Also known as 'Williams's Saunders' (for the editor of the 3rd ed.). There is also a 7th ed. 1871, substantially modernised and with different pagination. Br & Ph 613.

Saunders, R.C., and Austin, E., *Court of Referees. [Locus Standi.]*
Recommended citation: (year of decision) volume number Saund & A page number.
Published: 2 vols 1900–5. Covering: 1895–1904. Br & Ph 798.

Saunders, R.C., and Bidder, H.F., *Court of Referees. [Locus Standi.]*
Recommended citation: (year of decision) volume number Saund & B page number.
Published: 2 vols 1910–22. Covering: 1905–19. Br & Ph 799.

Saunders, T.W., and Cole, H.T., *Bail Court Reports*.
Recommended citation: (year of decision) volume number Saund & C page number.
Published: 2 vols 1847–9. Covering: 1846–8. Br & Ph 366.

Saunders, T.W., and Macrae, D.C., *County Court Cases*.
Recommended citation: (year of decision) volume number Saund & M page number.
Published: 2 vols (vols 2 & 3) 18??–58. Notes: For vol. 1 see Cox, E.W., Macrae, D.C., and Hertslet, C.J.B., *Reports of County Courts Cases*. Br & Ph 472.

Sausse, M.R., and Scully, V., *Reports . . . Rolls Court*. [Ireland.]
Recommended citation: (year of decision) Sau & S page number.
Published: 1 vol. 1841. Covering: 1837–40. Br & Ph 1373.

Savile, Sir John, *Les Reports . . . Common Bank*.
Recommended citation: (year of decision) Sav page number.
Published: 1 vol. 1675, 2nd ed. 1688. Covering: 1580–94. Notes: 2nd ed. in 123 ER. In law French. Br & Ph 456.

Sayer, Joseph, *Reports . . . King's Bench*.
Recommended citation: (year of decision) Say page number.
Published: 1 vol. 1775, 2nd ed. 1790. Covering: 1751–6. Notes: 2nd ed. in 96 ER. Br & Ph 614.

Schoales, J., and Lefroy, T., *Reports . . . Chancery in Ireland*.
Recommended citation: (year of decision) volume number Sch & L page number.

Published: 2 vols 1806–10. Covering: 1802–6. Br & Ph 1345.

*Scotch and Divorce Appeal Cases.* (1866–75); see *Law Reports. Scotch and Divorce Appeal Cases before the House of Lords.* (1866–75).

*Scots Law Times.* 1893–1908.

Recommended citation: (year of decision or of publication of article) volume number SLT page number.

Published: 16 vols 1893–1908. Notes: For citation of later vols see next entry. Br & Ph 1592.

*Scots Law Times.* 1909– .

Recommended citation: volume year without brackets number if there is more than 1 vol. for the year SLT abbreviation of section if necessary page number.

Published: 1909– . Notes: 1909–21 2 vols a year, 1922– 1 vol. a year. For citation of earlier vols see preceding entry. For the section called 'Reports' no abbreviation is added to SLT. The abbreviations for the other sections are: (Land Ct) (Reports of Cases Decided in the Scottish Land Court in vols for 1964–70, 1972–5 and 1977–81 and Scottish Land Court cases in vols for 1982– ), (Lands Tr) (Lands Tribunal for Scotland Reports in vols for 1971–81 and Lands Tribunal for Scotland cases in vols for 1982– ), (Lyon Ct) (Lyon Court Reports in vols for 1950, 1951, 1953, 1955, 1957, 1959, 1960, 1966, 1977, 1985–7, 1989, 1992, 1994), (News) (News in all vols), (Notes) (Notes of Recent Decisions in vols for 1946–80), (Sh Ct) (Sheriff Court Reports in vols for 1922– ), (PL) (Poor Law Reports in vols for 1932–41). In the vols for 1982–7 and 1991– the Scottish Land Court and Lands Tribunal for Scotland cases are in a section headed 'The Scottish Land Court and the Lands Tribunal for Scotland'; in the vols for 1988–90 this heading is preceded by 'Reports of Cases Decided in'. Br & Ph 1592.

*Scots Revised Reports.*

Recommended citation: (year of decision) volume number ScRR page number.

Published: 45 vols 1898–1909. Covering: 1707–1873. Br & Ph 1642.

Scott, J., *Cases . . . Common Pleas.*

Recommended citation: (year of decision) volume number Sc page number.

Published: 8 vols 1835–41. Covering: 1834–40. Br & Ph 469.

Scott, J., *New Reports . . . Common Pleas.*

Recommended citation: (year of decision) volume number Sc NR page number.

Published: 8 vols 1841–5. Covering: 1840–5. Br & Ph 470.

*Scottish Civil Law Reports.*

Recommended citation: volume year without brackets SCLR page number.

Published: 1987– .

*Scottish Criminal Case Reports.*

Recommended citation: volume year without brackets SCCR page number.

Published: 1981– . Br & Ph 1677.

*Scottish Criminal Case Reports Supplement (1950–80).*

Recommended citation: (year of decision) SCCR Supp page number.

Published: 1 vol. 1987.

*Scottish Current Law Year Book.*

Recommended citation: [volume year] CLY item number.

Published: [1948]–[1990]. Notes: Each volume consists of the *Current Law Year Book* for the same year plus a section devoted to Scottish law. The non-Scottish sections of the vols for [1948]–[1951] have been replaced by *Current Law Consolidation* which should be cited instead.

*Scottish Jurist.*

Recommended citation: (year of decision) volume number Sc Jur page number.

Published: 46 vols 1829–74. Br & Ph 1593.

*Scottish Land Court Reports.*
Recommended citation: (year of decision) volume number SLCR page number.
Published: 51 vols 1913–63. Covering: 1912–63. Notes: Published as a supplement to the *Scottish Law Review and Sheriff Court Reports*. Br & Ph 1685.

*Scottish Law Gazette.*
Recommended citation: (year of publication of article) volume number SLG page number.
Published: 1933– .

*Scottish Law Journal and Sheriff Court Record.*
Recommended citation: (year of decision) volume number SLJ page number.
Published: 3 vols 1859–61. Br & Ph 1670.

*Scottish Law Magazine and Sheriff Court Reporter.*
Recommended citation: (year of decision) volume number SLM page number.
Published: 6 vols 1862–7. Br & Ph 1671.

*Scottish Law Reporter.*
Recommended citation: (year of decision) volume number SLR page number.
Published: 61 vols 1866–1924. Br & Ph 1594.

*Scottish Law Review and Sheriff Court Reports.*
Recommended citation: (year of decision or of publication of article) volume number Scot L Rev for Review; Sh Ct Rep for Reports page number.
Published: 79 vols 1885–1963. Notes: For *Scottish Land Court Reports* see separate entry. Br & Ph 1672.

*Scottish Planning and Environmental Law.*
Recommended citation: (year of decision or of publication of article) SPEL issue number: page number.
Published: June 1993 (issue 39)– . Notes: Issues 1–38 titled *Scottish Planning Law and Practice* (q.v.).

*Scottish Planning Law and Practice.*
Recommended citation: (year of decision or of publication of article) SPLP issue number: page number.
Published: 38 issues September 1980–February 1993. Notes: From issue 39 titled *Scottish Planning and Environmental Law* (q.v.).

Searle, Richard, and Smith, James Charles, *Monthly Reports ... Court of Probate and in the Court for Divorce and Matrimonial Causes.*
Recommended citation: (year of decision) Sea & S page number.
Published: 1 vol. 1860. Covering: 1859–60. Br & Ph 338.

*Select Cases Argued and Adjudged ... before ... Lord Chancellor King.*
Recommended citation: (year of decision) Sel Cas t King page number.
Published: 1 vol. 1740, 2nd ed. by S. Macnaghten 1850. Covering: 1724–34. Notes: 2nd ed. in 25 ER. Br & Ph 415.

*Select Cases at Nisi Prius ... in Dublin.*
Recommended citation: (year of decision) Sel Cas NP page number.
Published: 1 vol. 1802. Covering: 1802. Br & Ph 1370.

*Select Cases in Chancery*; see *Cases Argued and Decreed in the High Court of Chancery*.

*Selected List of Lands Tribunal Rating Appeals.*
Recommended citation: (year of decision) volume number LTRA page number.
Published: 11 vols 1952–62. Covering: 1950–61. Notes: Also known as 'Lands Tribunal Rating Appeals'. Br & Ph 903.

*Session Cases, 1st series*; see Shaw, Patrick, *Cases ... Court of Session.*

*Session Cases, 2nd series*; see Dunlop, A., *Cases . . . Court of Session.*

*Session Cases, 3rd series*; see Macpherson, Norman, *Cases . . . Court of Session, Teind Court and House of Lords.*

*Session Cases, 4th series*; see Rettie, M., *Cases . . . Court of Session, Court of Justiciary and House of Lords.*

*Session Cases, 5th series*; see Fraser, H.J.E., *Cases . . . Court of Session, Court of Justiciary and House of Lords.*

*Session Cases. Cases Decided in the Court of Justiciary.* 1907–16.
   Recommended citation: volume year without brackets SC (J) page number.
   Published: 1907–16. Notes: Also known as 'Justiciary Cases'. Sometimes bound with *Session Cases. Cases Decided in the House of Lords,* and *Session Cases. Cases Decided in the Court of Session.* For citation of later vols see next entry. Br & Ph 1643.

*Session Cases. Cases Decided in the Court of Justiciary.* 1917– .
   Recommended citation: volume year without brackets JC page number.
   Published: 1917– . Notes: Also known as 'Justiciary Cases'. Sometimes bound with *Session Cases. Cases Decided in the House of Lords,* and *Session Cases. Cases Decided in the Court of Session.* For citation of earlier vols see preceding entry. Br & Ph 1601.

*Session Cases. Cases Decided in the Court of Session.*
   Recommended citation: volume year without brackets SC page number.
   Published: 1907– . Notes: Sometimes bound with *Session Cases. Cases Decided in the House of Lords,* and *Session Cases. Cases Decided in the Court of Justiciary.* Br & Ph 1643.

*Session Cases. Cases Decided in the House of Lords.*
   Recommended citation: volume year without brackets SC (HL) page number.
   Published: 1907– . Notes: Sometimes bound with *Session Cases. Cases Decided in the Court of Session,* and *Session Cases. Cases Decided in the Court of Justiciary.* Br & Ph 1643.

*Session Notes.*
   Recommended citation: volume year without brackets SN page number.
   Published: 1925–1948. Br & Ph 1644.

*Sessions Cases . . . Chiefly Touching Settlements.*
   Recommended citation: (year of decision) Sess Cas page number.
   Published: 2 vols 1750, 2nd ed. 1760. Covering: 1710–47. Notes: 2nd ed. in 93 ER. There is also an 1873 ed. Br & Ph 782.

Shaw, John, *Reports . . . High Court and Circuit Courts of Justiciary.*
   Recommended citation: (year of decision) J Shaw page number.
   Published: 1 vol. 1853. Covering: 1848–51. Br & Ph 1603.

Shaw, Patrick, *Cases . . . Court of Justiciary.*
   Recommended citation: (year of decision) Shaw Just page number.
   Published: 1 vol. 1831. Covering: 1819–31. Br & Ph 1604.

Shaw, Patrick, *Cases . . . Court of Session.* [Session Cases, 1st series.]
   Recommended citation: (year of decision) volume number S page number.
   Published: 16 vols 1822–38. 2nd ed. of vols 1–5 1834. Covering: 1821–38. Notes: The two editions of vols 1–5 have different pagination. Br & Ph 1645.

Shaw, Patrick, *Cases . . . House of Lords . . . Scotland.*
   Recommended citation: (year of decision) volume number Shaw App page number.
   Published: 2 vols 1826–8. Covering: 1821–6. Br & Ph 1661.

Shaw, Patrick, and Maclean, Charles Hope, *Cases . . . House of Lords . . . Scotland.*

Recommended citation: (year of decision) volume number Shaw & M page number.
Published: 3 vols 1836–9. Covering: 1835–8. Br & Ph 1662.
Shaw, Patrick, and others, *Cases . . . Court of Teinds.*
Recommended citation: (year of decision) Shaw Teind page number.
Published: 1 vol. 1831. Covering: 1821–31. Br & Ph 1673.
Sheppard, William, *Touchstone of Common Assurances.*
Recommended abbreviation: Shep Touch
Published: 1 vol. 1648, many later editions.
*Sheriff Court Reports*; see *Scottish Law Review and Sheriff Court Reports.*
Shillman, B., *Irish Workmen's Compensation Cases.*
Recommended citation: (year of decision) Shill WC page number.
Published: 1 vol. 1939. Covering: 1934–8. Br & Ph 1398.
Shower, Sir Bartholomew, *Cases in Parliament.*
Recommended citation: (year of decision) Show Parl Cas page number.
Published: 1 vol. 1698, 3rd ed. 1740. Covering: 1694–9. Notes: 3rd ed. in 1 ER.
There is a 4th ed. by R.L. Loveland 1876 with additional cases. Br & Ph 536.
Shower, Sir Bartholomew, *Reports . . . King's Bench.*
Recommended citation: (year of decision) volume number Show KB page
number.
Published: 2 vols 1708–20, 2nd ed. by Thomas Leach 1794. Covering: 1678–95.
Notes: 2nd ed. in 89 ER. There is also a 3rd ed., 1836, in 1 vol. by George Butts
re-edited from Shower's manuscripts. Br & Ph 615.
Siderfin, Thomas, *Reports . . . Bank le Roy.*
Recommended citation: (year of decision) volume number Sid page number.
Published: 2 vols 1683–4, 2nd ed. 1714. Covering: 1657–70. Notes: 2nd ed. in 82
ER. In law French. Br & Ph 616.
Simons, Nicholas, *Reports . . . Chancery.* [Vice-Chancellor.]
Recommended citation: (year of decision) volume number Sim page number.
Published: 17 vols 1829–54. Covering: 1826–52. Notes: In 57 ER (vols 1–3), 58 ER
(vols 4–7), 59 ER (vols 8–12) and 60 ER (vols 13–17). Volume 17 was completed
by C. Stewart Drury. Br & Ph 679.
Simons, Nicholas, *Reports . . . Chancery.* [Vice-Chancellor. New Series.]
Recommended citation: (year of decision) volume number Sim NS page
number.
Published: 2 vols 1851–2. Covering: 1850–2. Notes: In 61 ER. Volume 2 was
completed by C. Stewart Drury. Br & Ph 680.
Simons, Nicholas, and Stuart, John, *Reports . . . Chancery.* [Vice-Chancellor.]
Recommended citation: (year of decision) volume number Sim & St page number.
Published: 2 vols 1824–7. Covering: 1822–6. Notes: In 57 ER. Br & Ph 681.
*Simon's Tax Cases.*
Recommended citation: [volume year] STC page number.
Published: [1973]– . Br & Ph 915.
*Simon's Tax Cases Special Commissioners' Decisions.*
Recommended citation: [volume year] STC (SCD) page number.
Published: [1995]– .
*Simon's Tax Intelligence.*
Recommended citation: [volume year] STI page number.
Published: [1973]–[1994]. Notes: From [1995] titled *Simon's Weekly Tax Intelli-*
*gence* (q.v.).
*Simon's Weekly Tax Intelligence.*
Recommended citation: [volume year] SWTI page number.

Published: [1995]– . Notes: Earlier vols titled *Simon's Tax Intelligence* (q.v.).

Skinner, Robert, *Reports . . . King's Bench.*
　　Recommended citation: (year of decision) Skin page number.
　　Published: 1 vol. 1728. Covering: 1681–98. Notes: In 90 ER. Br & Ph 617.

Smale, John, and Giffard, J.W. de Longueville, *Reports . . . Chancery.* [Vice-Chancellor.]
　　Recommended citation: (year of decision) volume number Sm & G page number.
　　Published: 3 vols 1855–8. Covering: 1852–7. Notes: In 65 ER and 67 ER (appendix to vol. 1). Page numbers in the appendix are roman numerals. Br & Ph 682.

Smith, C.L., *Registration Cases.*
　　Recommended citation: (year of decision) volume number Smith Reg Cas page number.
　　Published: 3 vols 1906–15. Covering: 1895–1915. Br & Ph 889.

Smith, J.P., *Reports . . . King's Bench.*
　　Recommended citation: (year of decision) volume number Smith KB page number.
　　Published: 3 vols 1806–7. Covering: 1803–6. Br & Ph 635.

Smith, John William, *Selection of Leading Cases on Various Branches of the Law.*
　　Recommended citation: (year of decision) volume number Smith LC page number.
　　Published: 1837, 11th ed. by Thomas Willes Chitty, John Herbert Williams and Herbert Chitty 2 vols 1903.

Smith, T.B.C., and Batty, E., *Reports . . . King's Bench in Ireland.*
　　Recommended citation: (year of decision) Smith & B page number.
　　Published: 1 vol. 1830. Covering: 1824–5. Br & Ph 1366.

Smythe, H., *Reports . . . Common Pleas . . . in Ireland.*
　　Recommended citation: (year of decision) Smy page number.
　　Published: 1 vol. 1840. Covering: 1839–40. Br & Ph 1350.

Smythe, H., and Bourke, R., *The Queen v. Milles and the Queen v. Carroll.*
　　Recommended citation: (year of decision) Smy & B page number.
　　Published: 1 vol. 1842. Covering: 1842. Notes: Known as 'Smythe and Bourke's Irish Marriage Cases'. Br & Ph 1391.

*Society for Computers and Law Limited Newsletter*; see *Computers and Law.* 1974–89.

*Solicitors Journal.*
　　Recommended citation: (year of decision or of publication of article) volume number SJ page number; LBpage number for Lawbrief section.
　　Published: 1857– . Notes: Volumes 1–18 titled *Solicitors' Journal and Reporter* (same form of citation), vols 19–50 and 72–131, No. 18 (1 May 1987) titled *Solicitors' Journal* (same form of citation); vols 51–71 titled *Solicitors' Journal and Weekly Reporter* (same form of citation). The Lawbrief section started in vol. 135, No. 19 (17 May 1991).

*Solicitors' Journal and Reporter*; see *Solicitors Journal.*

*Solicitors' Journal and Weekly Reporter*; see *Solicitors Journal.*

Spinks, Thomas, *Ecclesiastical and Admiralty Reports.*
　　Recommended citation: (year of decision) volume number Sp Ecc & Ad page number; App page number for the appendix.
　　Published: 2 vols 1855. Covering: 1853–5. Notes: In 164 ER. Br & Ph 341.

Spinks, Thomas, *Reports . . . Admiralty Prize Court.*
　　Recommended citation: (year of decision) Sp Pri Cas page number.
　　Published: 1 vol. 1856. Covering: 1854–6. Notes: Extracts in 164 ER. Page numbers in the appendix are roman numerals. Br & Ph 818.

Stair, Lord (Sir James Dalrymple), *Decisions of the Lords of Council and Session.*
Recommended citation: (year of decision) volume number Stair page number.
Published: 2 vols 1683. Covering: 1661–81. Br & Ph 1646.

Starkie, Thomas, *Reports ... Nisi Prius.*
Recommended citation: (year of decision) volume number Stark page number.
Published: 3 vols 1817–23. Covering: 1815–23. Notes: In 171 ER. Br & Ph 653.

*State Trials*; see Cobbett, William, and Howell, T.B., *Complete Collection of State Trials*; *Reports of State Trials, New Series*; Townsend, William C., *Modern State Trials.*

*Statute Law Review.*
Recommended citation: [volume year] Stat LR page number.
Published: [1980]– .

Stillingfleet, E., *Ecclesiastical Cases.*
Recommended citation: (year of decision) volume number Stil page number.
Published: 2 vols 1702–4 (1st ed. of part 1 1698). Covering: 1698–1704. Br & Ph 741.

Stone, Arthur Paul, and Graham, W., *Courts of Referees. [Locus Standi.]*
Recommended citation: (year of decision) Sto & G page number.
Published: 1 vol. 1866. Covering: 1865. Br & Ph 800.

Strange, Sir John, *Reports.*
Recommended citation: (year of decision) volume number Str page number.
Published: 2 vols 1755, 3rd ed. by Michael Nolan 1795. Covering: 1716–49. Notes: 3rd ed. in 93 ER. Paginated continuously, vol. 2 beginning on p. 677. Br & Ph 618.

Stuart, R., Milne, J.S., and Peddie, W., *Reports ... Court of Session [etc.].*
Recommended citation: (year of decision) volume number Stu M & P page number.
Published: 2 vols 1852–3. Covering: 1851–3. Br & Ph 1653.

Style, William, *Narrationes Modernae, or Modern Reports.*
Recommended citation: (year of decision) Sty page number.
Published: 1 vol. 1658. Covering: 1646–55. Notes: In 82 ER. Br & Ph 619.

Swabey, M.C. Merttins, *Reports ... Admiralty.*
Recommended citation: (year of decision) Sw page number.
Published: 1 vol. 1860. Covering: 1855–9. Notes: In 166 ER. Page numbers in the appendix are roman numerals. Br & Ph 355.

Swabey, M.C. Merttins, and Tristram, Thomas Hutchinson, *Reports ... Probate ... Divorce and Matrimonial Causes.*
Recommended citation: (year of decision) volume number Sw & Tr page number.
Published: 4 vols 1860–71. Covering: 1858–65. Notes: In 164 ER. Br & Ph 342.

Swanston, Clement Tudway, *Reports ... Chancery.*
Recommended citation: (year of decision) volume number Swans page number.
Published: 3 vols 1821–7. Covering: 1818–19. Notes: In 36 ER. Br & Ph 416.

Swinton, Archibald, *Digest of Decisions in the Registration Appeal Court at Glasgow.*
Recommended citation: (year of decision) Swin Reg App page number.
Published: 1 vol. 1840, 2nd ed. 1844. Covering: 1835–43.

Swinton, Archibald, *Reports ... High Court and Circuit Courts of Justiciary.*
Recommended citation: (year of decision) volume number Swin page number.
Published: 2 vols 1838–42. Covering: 1835–41. Br & Ph 1605.

Syme, David, *Reports ... High Court of Justiciary.*
Recommended citation: (year of decision) Syme page number.
Published: 1 vol. 1829. Covering: 1826–9. Br & Ph 1606.

Talbot, Charles, 1st Baron Talbot of Hensol, *Cases in Equity*; see *Cases in Equity during the Time of the Late Lord Chancellor Talbot.*

Tamlyn, John, *Reports ... Chancery.* [Rolls Court.]
    Recommended citation: (year of decision) Taml page number.
    Published: 1 vol. 1831. Covering: 1829–30. Notes: In 48 ER. Br & Ph 666.

Taunton, William Pyle, *Reports ... Common Pleas.*
    Recommended citation: (year of decision) volume number Taunt page number.
    Published: 8 vols 1811–23. Covering: 1807–19. Notes: In 127 ER (vols 1 and 2), 128 ER (vols 3–6) and 129 ER (vols 7 and 8). Br & Ph 457.

*Tax Cases*; see *Reports of Tax Cases.*

*Taxation.*
    Recommended citation: (year of decision or of publication of article) volume number Tax page number.
    Published: 1927– .

*Taxation Reports.*
    Recommended citation: [volume year] TR page number.
    Published: [1939]–[1981]. Br & Ph 918.

Temple, L., and Mew, G., *Reports ... Court of Criminal Appeal.*
    Recommended citation: (year of decision) T & M page number.
    Published: 1 vol. 1852. Covering: 1848–51. Br & Ph 734.

*Term Reports.*
    Recommended citation: (year of decision) volume number TR page number.
    Published: 8 vols 1787–1800, new ed. 1817. Covering: 1785–1800. Notes: 1817 ed. in 99 ER (vol. 1), 100 ER (vols 2–4) and 101 ER (vols 5–8). The reporters were Charles Durnford and Edward Hyde East. Br & Ph 620.

*Times Law Reports.* 1885–1950.
    Recommended citation: (year of decision) volume number TLR page number.
    Published: 66 vols 1885–1950. Covering: 1884–1950. Notes: These are not the reports that appear in *The Times* newspaper. Volume 66 is in 2 separately paginated parts cited 66 (pt 1) and 66 (pt 2). For citation of later vols see next entry. Br & Ph 343.

*Times Law Reports.* 1951–2.
    Recommended citation: [volume year] volume number TLR page number.
    Published: [1951]–[1952]. Notes: 2 vols a year. These are not the reports that appear in *The Times* newspaper. From [1951] 2 titled *Times Law Reports and Commercial Cases.* For citation of earlier vols see preceding entry. Br & Ph 343.

*Times Reports of Commercial Cases*; see *Reports of Commercial Cases.*

Tothill, William, *Transactions ... Chancery.*
    Recommended citation: (year of decision) Toth page number.
    Published: 2 vols 1649, 3rd ed. 1820. Covering: 1559–1646. Notes: 1st ed. (but dated 1650) in 21 ER. There is also an 1872 ed. using the text of the 3rd ed. Br & Ph 417.

Townsend, William C., *Modern State Trials.*
    Recommended citation: (year of decision) Town St Tr page number.
    Published: 2 vols 1850.

*Trading Law.*
    Recommended citation: (year of publication of article) volume number TrL page number.
    Published: 1982– .

*Trading Law Reports.*
    Recommended citation: (year of decision) volume number TrLR page number.
    Published: 1983 (vol. 2)– . Notes: Published with *Trading Law.* Br & Ph 840.

*Traffic Cases.*
Recommended citation: (year of decision) volume number Traff Cas page number.
Published: 33 vols 1874–1976. Covering: 1855–1975. Notes: Spine title of vols 1–29 may be 'Railway and Canal Traffic Cases' or 'Railway, Canal and Road Traffic Cases'. Volume 1 titled *Collection of Cases Decided under the 2nd Sect. of the Railway and Canal Traffic Act 1854*; vols 2–6 titled *Reports of Cases Decided by the Railway Commissioners*; vols 7–19 titled *Reports of Cases Decided by the Railway and Canal Commissioners*; vols 20 and 21 titled *Reports of Cases Decided under the Railway and Canal Traffic Acts and the Railway Act*. Br & Ph 942, 945.

Tristram, T.H., *Principal Judgments ... Consistory Courts.*
Recommended citation: (year of decision) Tr Consist J page number.
Published: 1 vol. 1893. Covering: 1872–90. Br & Ph 490.

*Trust Law and Practice.*
Recommended citation: (year of decision or of publication of article) volume number Trust L & P page number.
Published: 4 vols 1986–90. Notes: From vol. 5 titled *Trust Law International* (q.v.).

*Trust Law International.*
Recommended citation: (year of decision or of publication of article) volume number TruLI page number.
Published: 1991 (vol. 5)–. Notes: Volumes 1–4 titled *Trust Law and Practice* (q.v.).

Turner, George, and Russell, James, *Reports ... Chancery.*
Recommended citation: (year of decision) Turn & R page number.
Published: 1 vol. 1832. Covering: 1822–4. Notes: In 37 ER. Br & Ph 418.

Tyrwhitt, R.P., *Reports ... Exchequer.*
Recommended citation: (year of decision) volume number Tyr page number.
Published: 5 vols 1832–7. Covering: 1830–5. Br & Ph 521.

Tyrwhitt, R.P., and Granger, T.C., *Reports ... Exchequer.*
Recommended citation: (year of decision) Tyr & G page number.
Published: 1 vol. 1837. Covering: 1835–6. Br & Ph 522.

*Utilities Law Review.*
Recommended citation: (year of publication of article) volume number Util LR page number.
Published: 1990–.

*Value Added Tax Tribunals Reports.*
Recommended citation: [volume year] VATTR page number.
Published: [1973]–. Br & Ph 919.

Vaughan, Sir John, *Reports.*
Recommended citation: (year of decision) Vaugh page number.
Published: 1 vol. 1677, 2nd ed. 1706. Covering: 1665–74. Notes: 1st ed. in 124 ER. Br & Ph 458.

Ventris, Sir Peyton, *Reports.*
Recommended citation: (year of decision) volume number Vent page number.
Published: 2 vols 1696, 4th ed. 1726. Covering: 1668–88. Notes: 4th ed. in 86 ER. Br & Ph 621.

Vernon, G.W., and Scriven, J.B., *Irish Reports.*
Recommended citation: (year of decision) Vern & S page number.
Published: 1 vol. 1790. Covering: 1786–8. Br & Ph 1367.

Vernon, Thomas, *Cases ... Chancery.*
Recommended citation: (year of decision) volume number Vern page number.
Published: 2 vols 1726–8, 3rd ed. by John Raithby 1828. Covering: 1681–1719.
Notes: 3rd ed. in 23 ER. Br & Ph 419.

Vesey, Francis, Junior, *Reports ... Chancery.*
Recommended citation: (year of decision) volume number Ves Jr page number.
Published: 19 vols 1793–1822, new ed. 1827. Covering: 1789–1817. Notes: 1827
ed. in 30 ER (vols 1–3), 31 ER (vols 4–6), 32 ER (vols 7–11), 33 ER (vols 12–16)
and 34 ER (vols 17–19). Volume 20 is an index. For the supplement see
Hovenden, John Eykyn, *A Supplement to Vesey Junior's Reports of Cases in
Chancery.* Br & Ph 421.

Vesey, Francis, Junior, and Beames, John, *Reports ... Chancery.*
Recommended citation: (year of decision) volume number Ves & B page number.
Published: 3 vols 1813–15, 2nd ed. 1818. Covering: 1812–14. Notes: 2nd ed. in 35
ER. Br & Ph 422.

Vesey, Francis, Senior, *Reports ... Chancery.*
Recommended citation: (year of decision) volume number Ves Sen page number.
Published: 2 vols 1771, 4th ed. by Robert Belt 1818. Covering: 1746–56. Notes:
4th ed. in 27 ER (vol. 1) and 28 ER (vol. 2). For the supplement (sometimes
referred to as vol. 3) see Belt, Robert, *Supplement to the Reports in Chancery of
Francis Vesey Senior.* Br & Ph 420.

Viner, Charles, *Abridgment of the Modern Determinations in the Courts ... being
a Supplement to Viner's Abridgment.*
Recommended abbreviation: Vin Supp.
Published: 6 vols 1799–1806. Notes: By J.E. Watson et al.

Viner, Charles, *A General Abridgment of Law and Equity.*
Recommended citation: Vin Abr title (sequence of letters and numbers ident-
ifying subheading) item number.
Published: 23 vols 1742–[56?], 2nd ed. 1791–5. Notes: Volume 24 is an index.


Wallis, J., *Reports ... Chancery in Ireland.*
Recommended citation: (year of decision) Wal Lyn page number.
Published: 1 vol. 1839. Covering: 1766–91. Notes: Edited by James Lyne. Br &
Ph 1346.

*Water Law.*
Recommended citation: [volume year] Water Law page number.
Published: [1990]– .

Webster, T., *Reports and Notes of Cases on Letters Patent for Inventions.*
Recommended citation: (year of decision) volume number Web Pat Cas page
number.
Published: 2 vols 1844–55. Covering: 1601–1855. Br & Ph 773.

*Weekly Law Reports.*
Recommended citation: [volume year] volume number WLR page number.
Published: [1953]– . Notes: 3 vols a year. Initially published in parts which contain
pages of both vol. 1 and either vol. 2 or vol. 3. Volumes 2 and 3 contain reports
which are subsequently republished, with reports of arguments, in *Law Reports.
Chancery Division, Law Reports. Family Division* (or, until 1971, *Law Reports.
Probate, Divorce and Admiralty Division), Law Reports. House of Lords,* or *Law
Reports. Queen's Bench Division.* A citation of 2 WLR or 3 WLR should be replaced
by a citation of the *Law Reports* when the case is republished. Occasionally cases
in 1 WLR are also republished in the *Law Reports.* Br & Ph 344.

*Weekly Notes.*
Recommended citation: [volume year] WN page number.
Published: [1866]–[1952]. Br & Ph 345.
*Weekly Reporter.*
Recommended citation: (year of decision) volume number WR page number.
Published: 54 vols 1853–1906. Br & Ph 346.
Welsh, T., *Registry Cases.*
Recommended citation: (year of decision) Welsh Reg Cas page number.
Published: 1 vol. 1845. Covering: 1832–40. Br & Ph 1422.
West, Martin John, *Cases ... House of Lords.*
Recommended citation: (year of decision) West HL page number.
Published: 1 vol. 1842. Covering: 1839–41. Notes: In 9 ER. Br & Ph 537.
West, Martin John, *Reports ... Chancery ... from the Original Manuscripts of Lord Chancellor Hardwicke.*
Recommended citation: (year of decision) West t Hard page number.
Published: 1 vol. 1827. Covering: 1736–9. Notes: In 25 ER. Br & Ph 423.
Western, T.G., *Cases Relating to Tithes of the City of London.*
Recommended citation: (year of decision) West Ti Cas page number.
Published: 1 vol. 1823. Covering: 1535–1822. Br & Ph 937.
White, James C., *Reports ... High Court and Circuit Courts of Justiciary.*
Recommended citation: (year of decision) volume number White page number.
Published: 3 vols 1888–93. Covering: 1885–93. Br & Ph 1607.
Wightwick, John, *Reports ... Exchequer.*
Recommended citation: (year of decision) Wight page number.
Published: 1 vol. 1819. Covering: 1810–11. Notes: In 145 ER. Br & Ph 512.
Willes, Sir John, *Reports ... Common Pleas.*
Recommended citation: (year of decision) Willes page number.
Published: 1 vol. 1799, 2nd ed. 1800. Covering: 1737–60. Notes: 2nd ed. in 125 ER. The reports were edited by Charles Durnford. Br & Ph 459.
*Williams's Saunders*; see Saunders, Sir Edmund, *Reports ... King's Bench.*
Willmore, G., Wollaston, F.L., and Davison, H., *Reports ... King's Bench ... and ... Bail Court.*
Recommended citation: (year of decision) Will Woll & D page number.
Published: 1 vol. 1839. Covering: 1837. Br & Ph 367.
Willmore, G., Wollaston, F.L., and Hodges, W., *Reports ... Queen's Bench ... and ... Bail Court.*
Recommended citation: (year of decision) volume number Will Woll & H page number.
Published: 2 vols 1839–41. Covering: 1838–9. Br & Ph 636.
Wilmot, Sir John Eardley, *Notes.*
Recommended citation: (year of decision) Wilm page number.
Published: 1 vol. 1802. Covering: 1757–70. Notes: In 97 ER. Br & Ph 622.
Wilson, George, *Reports ... Courts at Westminster.*
Recommended citation: (year of decision) volume number Wils KB page number.
Published: 1770–5, 3rd ed. in 3 vols 1799. Covering: 1742–74. Notes: In 95 ER. Br & Ph 623.
Wilson, James, and Shaw, Patrick, *Cases ... House of Lords ... Scotland.*
Recommended citation: (year of decision) volume number Wils & S page number.
Published: 7 vols 1829–39. Covering: 1825–35. Br & Ph 1663.
Wilson, John, *Reports ... Chancery.*
Recommended citation: (year of decision) volume number Wils Ch page number.

Published: 2 vols 1819. Covering: 1818–19. Notes: In 37 ER. Br & Ph 430.
Wilson, John, *Reports ... Exchequer in Equity.*
Recommended citation: (year of decision) Wils Ex page number.
Published: 1 vol. 1817. Covering: 1805–17. Notes: Extracts in 159 ER. Br & Ph 513.
Winch, Sir Humphry, *Reports.*
Recommended citation: (year of decision) Winch page number.
Published: 1 vol. 1657. Covering: 1621–5. Notes: In 124 ER. Br & Ph 460.
Wolferstan, F.S.P., and Bristowe, S.B., *Reports ... Election Committees.*
Recommended citation: (year of decision) Wolf & B page number.
Published: 1 vol. 1865. Covering: 1859–64. Br & Ph 866.
Wolferstan, F.S.P., and Dew, E.L., *Reports ... Controverted Elections.*
Recommended citation: (year of decision) Wolf & D page number.
Published: 1 vol. 1859. Covering: 1856–8. Br & Ph 867.
Wollaston, F.L., *Reports ... Bail Court.*
Recommended citation: (year of decision) Woll page number.
Published: 1 vol. 1841. Covering: 1840–1. Br & Ph 368.
Wood, H., *Collection of Decrees ... in Tithe-causes.*
Recommended citation: (year of decision) volume number Wood page number.
Published: 4 vols 1798–9. Covering: 1650–1798. Br & Ph 938.
*Workmen's Compensation Cases.*
Recommended citation: (year of decision) volume number WCC page number.
Published: 9 vols 1902–8. Covering: 1898–1907. Br & Ph 761.


*Yearbook of European Law.*
Recommended citation: volume number YEL volume year without brackets page number.
Published: 1982–.
*Yearbook of Law Computers and Technology.*
Recommended citation: (year of publication of article) volume number YLCT page number.
Published: 1984–.
Yelverton, Sir Henry, *Reports ... King's Bench.*
Recommended citation: (year of decision) Yel page number.
Published: 1 vol. in law French 1661, in English (called 3rd ed.) 1735, 4th ed. (English) 1792. Covering: 1603–13. Notes: 4th ed. in 80 ER. Br & Ph 624.
Younge, Edward, *Reports ... Exchequer in Equity.*
Recommended citation: (year of decision) Y page number.
Published: 1 vol. 1833. Covering: 1830–2. Notes: In 159 ER. Br & Ph 514.
Younge, Edward, and Collyer, John, *Reports ... Chancery.* [Vice-Chancellor.]
Recommended citation: (year of decision) volume number Y & C Ch page number.
Published: 2 vols 1843–4. Covering: 1841–3. Notes: In 62 ER (vol. 1) and 63 ER (vol. 2). Br & Ph 683.
Younge, Edward, and Collyer, John, *Reports ... Exchequer in Equity.*
Recommended citation: (year of decision) volume number Y & C Ex page number.
Published: 4 vols 1836–46. Covering: 1834–42. Notes: In 160 ER. Br & Ph 515.
Younge, Edward, and Jervis, John, *Reports ... Exchequer.*
Recommended citation: (year of decision) volume number Y & J page number.
Published: 3 vols 1828–30. Covering: 1826–30. Notes: In 148 ER. Br & Ph 516.

# GLOSSARY OF BIBLIOGRAPHICAL TERMS

*edition*. All the copies of a book printed from the same setting of the text, apart from minor alterations. If a different title-page with a new date is added to unused sheets of an edition previously put on sale, the edition is said to be 'reissued'. (Distinguishing between a reissue and a new edition of a seventeenth or eighteenth-century book requires careful examination of the volumes which has not been possible in preparing the list of recommended forms of citation in this book.) If the same setting is used for a new printing or if printing is from photographic images of a previously used setting there is said to be a 'reprint'. In the nineteenth and early twentieth centuries, 'reprint' was used to describe a new setting of a text without significant alteration, as in the *English Reports*, but the word is not used in that sense in this book.

*folio*. 1. A book made of sheets of paper, each of which is folded once with the folds forming the spine of the book. 2. A leaf of a book in which the numbering is by leaf rather than page.

*octavo*. A book made of sheets of paper, each of which is folded three times with the second fold at right angles to the first and the third at right angles to the second.

*quarto*. A book made of sheets of paper, each of which is folded twice with the second fold at right angles to the first.

*recto*. The side of a leaf of a book which faces the reader when the leaf is on the reader's right-hand side of the open book.

*roll*. A document written on many pieces of parchment joined together to form a long continuous strip intended to be rolled up for storage.

*serial*. A publication issued from time to time in volumes under the same title and intended to continue indefinitely.

*spine title*. The title on the spine of a book's binding or paper cover.

*title-page*. A page at the beginning of a book devoted to displaying the book's title and the name of its author and publisher and stating the year of publication

*verso*. The side of a leaf of a book which faces the reader when the leaf is on the reader's left-hand side of the open book.

# INDEX